AF757988

NIAAA Research Monograph No. 36

THE EPIDEMIOLOGY OF ALCOHOL PROBLEMS IN SMALL GEOGRAPHIC AREAS

Edited by:
Robert A. Wilson, Ph.D.
Mary C. Dufour, M.D., M.P.H.

U.S. DEPARTMENT OF HEALTH AND HUMAN SERVICES
Public Health Service
National Institutes of Health
National Institute on Alcohol Abuse and Alcoholism
6000 Executive Boulevard
Bethesda, MD 20892

About the Editors: Robert A. Wilson, Ph.D., is director of the Health Services Policy Research Group with the School of Urban Affairs and Public Policy at the University of Delaware. Mary C. Dufour, M.D., M.P.H., is deputy director of the National Institute on Alcohol Abuse and Alcoholism (NIAAA) and director of NIAAA's Division of Biometry and Epidemiology.

NIAAA has obtained permission from the copyright holders to reproduce figures and tables throughout this monograph. Further reproduction of these materials is prohibited without specific permission from the copyright holders. All other material contained in this monograph, except quoted passages from copyrighted sources, is in the public domain and may be reproduced without permission from NIAAA or the authors. Citation of the source is appreciated. The U.S. Government does not endorse or favor any specific commercial product (or commodity, service, or company). Trade or proprietary names (or company names) that appear in this publication are used only because they are considered essential in the context of the studies reported herein.

The opinions expressed herein are those of the authors and do not necessarily reflect the official position of NIAAA or any other part of the National Institutes of Health.

Key words are included in the beginning of each article. These descriptors are drawn from *The Alcohol and Other Drug Thesaurus: A Guide to Concepts and Terminology in Substance Abuse and Addiction, Second Edition, 1995* and may be used to retrieve this monograph in the Alcohol and Alcohol Problems Science Database (commonly referred to as ETOH).

NIH Publication No. 00–4357
Printed 2000

CONTENTS

FOREWORD

The study of small geographic areas is a relatively recent addition to alcohol epidemiological research. Over the years, epidemiology has given us a great deal of information about alcohol use problems nationally. However, the global understanding of alcohol problems from national studies does not always convey the information needed by local communities to understand the problems in their own backyard. Recognizing this need, the National Institute on Alcohol Abuse and Alcoholism convened a symposium to explore ways in which existing epidemiological research methods could be adapted or new methodologies developed to look at alcohol problems locally as well as nationally. This monograph, *The Epidemiology of Alcohol Problems in Small Geographic Areas,* derives from the work begun during this symposium. It is intended to inform alcohol researchers, policymakers, and public health personnel about the progress that has been made in this important research area. It also will help them understand how data from such studies can be used to reduce the burden of alcohol problems in their jurisdictions.

I am indebted to Dr. Mary C. Dufour for her efforts to establish the epidemiology of small geographic areas as a part of the alcohol research agenda and to her and Dr. Robert A. Wilson for their work in bringing this monograph to completion. My sincere thanks also to the many fine scientists who gave their time and their talent to this important endeavor.

Enoch Gordis, M.D.
Director
National Institute on Alcohol Abuse and Alcoholism

PREFACE

Large-scale population-based surveys have provided valuable information on alcohol and other drug (AOD) use nationwide. The collection of epidemiological data on the state, county, or local level requires a more specialized approach. For example, within a single community, rates of alcohol use between neighborhoods may range from 39 to 97 percent (see chapter 10 by Paul J. Gruenewald). Local variability in drinking patterns is influenced by the spatial distribution of demographic characteristics and environmental risk factors (e.g., the location of alcohol outlets) and, in turn, influences the local incidence and prevalence of alcohol-related problems. The results of research into small-area alcohol epidemiology can help state and local health administrators target prevention programs and allocate limited alcoholism treatment resources rationally.

This monograph reviews some of the progress made over the past decade in the study of alcohol consumption and problems in small geographic areas. The research reported here has three broad goals. One goal is to adapt the traditional techniques of epidemiological monitoring and surveillance to the local needs of AOD program management and planning. This function has played an important role in the development of highway safety initiatives and primary prevention programs for youth. A second research goal is to evaluate AOD treatment and prevention programs within small areas. Such studies (i.e., needs assessments) identify local deficiencies in funding, types of programs, and the number and capacity of outpatient and residential treatment sites. Finally, in support of the first two goals, researchers are developing new methods for measuring alcohol problems and analyzing the relationships between these problems and local demographics, service utilization, and environmental risk factors.

The projects described in this monograph range from simple descriptive studies of local survey results to complex multivariate analyses that examine the relationships between alcohol problems and their geographic correlates. Small areas are delineated on an administrative or demographic basis. The types of geographic areas represented include states, counties, metropolitan areas, ZIP Codes, census tracts, and census block groups, as well as study areas defined by clustering techniques based on the density of points representing the spatial locations of alcohol problems. As expected, this monograph features a large number of tables and illustrations. For clarity and ease of reading, these graphic elements have been placed at the end of each chapter, immediately following the reference section.

Progress in small-area alcohol epidemiology has been spurred by Federal block grant legislation that calls for assessing alcohol problems and corresponding treatment resources in planning areas within states. Through its extramural grant program, the National Institute on Alcohol Abuse and Alcoholism (NIAAA) has sponsored basic research that examines relevant issues, such as the effects of pricing and outlet density on geographic patterns of drinking-and-driving mortality. The advances described in this publication are derived in large part from this research.

The chapters of this monograph cover many similar issues, each from a different perspective. The text below presents brief chapter summaries organized along broad conceptual lines (i.e., measurement issues, data analysis, and examples of practical applications, followed by a summary chapter). This arrangement, adopted for convenience, emphasizes common themes but does not necessarily reflect the scope of individual chapters.

At least one-half of the chapters in this monograph focus on the development, use, and validation of techniques for measuring alcohol consumption and its consequences. Robert A. Wilson presents a social indicator methodology for estimating the prevalence of alcohol problems. A social indicator is a nonspecific, comparative measure of the well-being of a local population. Social indicators for alcohol problems include criminal court records, hospital discharge data, and alcoholism treatment statistics. Although they do not quantify the actual magnitude of alcohol problems, such indicators are valuable tools for surveillance and monitoring. For example, social indicators may pinpoint a local "hot spot" of alcohol problems or detect an increase in alcohol problems over time within a geographic area.

Robert A. Wilson and William E. McAuliffe discuss the use of synthetic estimators, combinations of survey and archival data that permit researchers to estimate problem rates within demographic and geographic subgroups. These authors stress the importance of local age-sex concentrations as predictors of risk for different types of AOD problems. The usefulness of this measure is reflected by the tendency of treatment programs to specialize in patients from a narrow range of the age-sex spectrum. Similarly, in another chapter, Laurie Ellis McLeod hypothesizes that age structure is a significant independent variable for differentiating between counties with high and low rates of alcohol-related morbidity and mortality.

In a comprehensive analysis, Laura A. Schmidt and Constance M. Weisner review the strengths and limitations of general population surveys, providers' estimates, and social indicators as methods for evaluating the size and distribution of problem-drinking populations using a northern California county as an example.

Severity is an important and often neglected factor in the assessment of public health problems. Harold F. Goldsmith and colleagues have developed a scale to rate the severity of psychiatric and AOD problems. These researchers conclude that severity measurement provides a more accurate estimate of the relative need for mental health and addiction services than measures based largely on the enumeration of disorders or symptoms. The relative advantages of severity-based indexes were more evident in metropolitan areas than in nonmetropolitan areas.

Two chapters focus on geographic information systems (GIS). GIS are computer-based systems that analyze spatial data, generating maps to facilitate visual interpretation. Using a GIS-based model, Richard Scribner analyzes the effects of alcohol outlet density at the census-tract level on individual drinking habits. In another chapter, William F. Wieczorek demonstrates how environmental risk factors can interact with individual differences in family history, personality, and expectancies to generate drinking "cultures" specific to counties or neighborhoods.

The concept of influencing alcohol consumption through controls on alcohol pricing and availability has long been of interest to public health agencies. Gruenewald and colleagues report that measures of physical access to alcohol may be used to index rates of abstention and the frequency of alcohol use in neighborhoods and communities. On a broader geographic level, McAuliffe and colleagues evaluate the Alcohol Problem Index (API) for measuring interstate variations in alcohol abuse problems. The API measures social indicators, such as alcoholism treatment utilization, deaths, and arrests, and may help policymakers evaluate the adequacy of state AOD prevention and treatment programs.

In a summary chapter, Gruenewald compares the performance of various synthetic estimation and social indicator models for estimating AOD service requirements within small census tracts. Gruenewald points out hidden pitfalls in small area analysis and suggests future areas for research.

The research summarized in this monograph represents the application of geostatistical methods to the fields of epidemiology, medicine, demography, geography, sociology, and psychology. Additional basic interdisciplinary research is needed to develop and refine additional tools for evaluating local alcohol problems and intervention needs.

Robert A. Wilson, Ph.D.
Director, Health Services Policy Research Group
School of Urban Affairs and Public Policy
University of Delaware

Mary C. Dufour, M.D., M.P.H.
Deputy Director, National Institute on Alcohol Abuse and Alcoholism
National Institutes of Health

ABBREVIATIONS AND ACRONYMS

AAF	alcohol-attributable fraction
ADBH	alcohol, drug, and other behavioral health
ADM	alcohol, drug abuse, and mental health
AIDS	acquired immunodeficiency syndrome
AOD	alcohol or other drugs
AODC	causes of AOD use, abuse, and dependence
AODD	AOD use disorder
AODE	effects of AOD use, abuse, and dependence
AODR	AOD related
AODU	AOD use, abuse, and dependence
API	Alcohol Problem Index
BAC	blood alcohol concentration
BRFSS	Behavioral Risk Factor Surveillance System
CDC	Centers for Disease Control and Prevention
CEL	Community Epidemiology Laboratory
CSAT	Center for Substance Abuse Treatment
DAWN	Drug Abuse Warning Network
DC*MADS	Washington DC Metropolitan Area Drug Study
DIS	Diagnostic Interview Schedule
DPI	Drug Problem Index
DSM	*Diagnostic and Statistical Manual of Mental Disorders*
DSM-III	*Diagnostic and Statistical Manual of Mental Disorders, Third Edition*
DSM-III-R	*Diagnostic and Statistical Manual of Mental Disorders, Third Edition, Revised*
DSM-IV	*Diagnostic and Statistical Manual of Mental Disorders, Fourth Edition*
DUI	driving under the influence *or* (more generally) drinking and driving
DWI	driving while intoxicated *or* (more generally) drinking and driving
ECA	Epidemiologic Catchment Area
FARS	Fatality Analysis Reporting System *or* Fatal Accident Reporting System
FBI	Federal Bureau of Investigation
GAD	generalized anxiety disorder
GAF	Global Assessment of Functioning [Scale]

GAO	General Accounting Office
GIS	geographic information systems
LAPNAD	Louisiana Alcohol Policy Needs Assessment Database
LSDV	least squares dummy variable
m	meter
MAST	Michigan Alcoholism Screening Test
MC	Moran coefficient
mL	milliliter
MTMM	multitrait-multimethod
NASADAD	National Association of State Alcohol and Drug Abuse Directors, Inc.
NCHS	National Center for Health Statistics
NCS	National Comorbidity Survey
NDATUS	National Drug and Alcoholism Treatment Unit Survey
NHDS	National Hospital Discharge Survey
NHSDA	National Household Survey on Drug Abuse
NHTSA	National Highway Traffic Safety Administration
NIAAA	National Institute on Alcohol Abuse and Alcoholism
NIDA	National Institute on Drug Abuse
NIMH	National Institute of Mental Health
OLS	ordinary least squares
PC	personal computer
PSE	Present State Examination
RDC	Research Diagnostic Criteria
RDD	random-digit dial
RFP	Request for Proposal
SAMHSA	Substance Abuse and Mental Health Services Administration
SAPT	Substance Abuse Prevention and Treatment
SE	standard error
SFDD	single-family, detached dwelling unit
TIGER	Topologically Integrated Geographic Encoding and Referencing
2SLS	two-stage least squares
UCR	Uniform Crime Reports
YPLL	years of potential life lost
YRBSS	Youth Risk Behavior Surveillance System

Chapter 1

A Social Indicator Methodology for Estimating the Prevalence of Alcohol Problems in Small Geographic Areas

Robert A. Wilson, Ph.D.

KEY WORDS: statistical estimation; prevalence; geographical area; problematic AOD use; validity (research methods); diagnostic criteria; AODR mortality; addiction care; needs assessment; age differences; gender differences; patient admission; patient discharge; justice system; Delaware; survey; literature review

The study described in this chapter explored the feasibility of employing social indicators to estimate the prevalence of alcohol abuse, alcoholism, and other alcohol problems in small geographic areas. A *social indicator* is a general measure of the well-being of the population within a specific geographic area. A parallel concept from medicine is the patient's temperature, which may signal an illness is present, but may not inform as to the specific illness or its cause. Examples of social indicators include the infant mortality rate, the literacy rate, and the poverty rate. The sources of small area social indicators used in this study are the U.S. census, death certificates, criminal court records, hospital discharge data, and information on the number of persons treated for alcoholism and alcohol abuse. In this study, "small areas" are geographic units that are smaller than a State.

A major issue in the field of alcohol treatment needs assessment is whether the *Diagnostic and Statistical Manual of Mental Disorders* (DSM) should be conceptualized as the "gold standard" to gauge the validity of other small area alcohol problem indicators. In public health, indicators of mortality and morbidity have long been used for surveillance of a variety of health

R.A. Wilson, Ph.D., is director of the Health Services Policy Research Group, School of Urban Affairs and Public Policy, University of Delaware, Newark, DE 19716.

problems. Indicators may pinpoint a "hot spot" in a small geographic area, reveal an increase in a statewide problem, or reveal an increase in a problem within a specific area or demographic group. Alcohol epidemiology has a tradition of using indirect indicators to estimate the prevalence of alcohol problems in small areas. The practice traces its roots to the work of Jellinek (1952), who devised a formula to estimate the number of living alcoholics in a geographic area, based on the number of persons dying of cirrhosis of the liver in a given year.

Recently, much of the attention to small geographic areas has been spurred by treatment planning initiatives emanating from the Federal Center for Substance Abuse Treatment (CSAT) (Becker 1991). The Federal block grant legislation calls for an assessment of the prevalence of alcohol problems in substate planning areas and the corresponding treatment resources that are available in each planning area (Substance Abuse and Mental Health Services Administration 1993). Most of the States have conducted (or are in the process of conducting) statewide treatment needs assessments to gauge the treatment needs within the smaller planning areas throughout the United States. Virtually all of these studies have employed statewide interview surveys incorporating the DSM-III-R criteria for alcohol abuse and dependence (American Psychiatric Association 1987; Robins 1981, 1989). Most of these State needs assessments have also included social indicator studies. Because the indicators are available on a recurring basis and at relatively low cost, they are a valuable tool for surveillance and monitoring. Indicators, in contrast to interview surveys, provide a relative measure or index of alcohol problem prevalence. Indicators may confirm that an alcohol problem is more severe in one population than in another, but they may not convey an estimate of the number of people who are alcoholics or alcohol dependent. McAuliffe (1993) raised another set of issues regarding the face validity of the most commonly employed small area indicators. He found that some of the indicators of alcohol problems for small areas actually were uncorrelated or even were negatively correlated with each other, calling into question their usefulness in representing a single alcohol problem dimension that underlies all of the indicators.

Most social indicator studies are conducted with a geographic area as the unit of analysis, rather than the individual. These social area analyses are vulnerable to the *ecological fallacy* (Robinson 1950). Simply stated, the ecological fallacy is the "error that occurs when the existence of a group association is used to imply, incorrectly, the existence of a relationship at the individual level" (Iverson et al. 1998, p. 546). In other words, one cannot (and should not) infer the behavior of individuals based on the characteristics of the geographic area in which they reside. An example of the fallacy in alcohol epidemiology is inferring that the residents of high-income areas who are alcoholics also have high incomes, from the finding that high-income geographic areas generally have the highest rates of alcohol sales per population unit. The ecological fallacy argument informs us that ecological descriptors may mask what we are supposedly interested in—the behavior of individuals. Yet we know that there are some group effects (contextual effects) that act upon individuals in a way that surpasses the effect of their individual characteristics (Diez-Roux 1998).

How do we approach the problem of validity of the area indicators, framed in terms of the ecological fallacy issues? One way is to decompose the indicators into individual cases (respondents, deaths, defendants, etc.) and then explore both area effects and individual effects upon individuals. From a methodological perspective, what does this mean? In this research it means creating two databases: one in which the ZIP Code areas of Delaware are the unit of analysis ($N = 53$) and one in which survey respondents are the unit of analysis ($N = 2,776$). How do we handle social area characteristics in the survey database? At this level of analysis, area characteristics become an attribute of individual respondents. Thus, respondent X may have codes confirming that he is 30 years old, that he resides in an area with a high alcohol-related crime rate, and that he resides in an area with a high rate of deaths from alcohol-related causes. The individual variables and area variables also include our candidate for the gold standard—alcohol abuse and dependence measured by interview items incorporating the DSM-III-R.

From this survey database we can address the following questions about the validity and utility of the indicators:

- Examining a number of alcohol problem indicators, both at the individual level and the ZIP Code area level, do the indicators confirm a single underlying alcohol problem dimension? If unidimensionality is present, the correlations between the indicators should all be positive. The indicators can then be said to display convergent validity.
- If the small area alcohol problem indicators have a single underlying dimension, can it be represented by alcohol abuse and dependence as measured with DSM-III-R?
- Or, absent a single underlying alcohol problem dimension, what dimensions appear to underlie each of the indicators?
- Is there an underlying concept or theory that could explain the relationships (correlations or lack thereof) among the indicators?

These issues are explored by examining the data from the Delaware Statewide Survey of Alcohol and Drug Abuse, conducted in 1993–94 by the University of Delaware's College of Urban Affairs and Public Policy for the State of Delaware, Health and Social Services, Division of Alcoholism, Drug Abuse, and Mental Health.

SCOPE AND METHODS

Residents of the State of Delaware, age 18 and older, were surveyed in this study. The telephone survey methodology was developed especially for small geographic treatment needs assessments in substate planning areas by CSAT (McAuliffe et al. 1994). The alcohol problem indicators used in this study were

- 18-month prevalence of alcohol abuse and alcoholism, from the 1994 statewide survey (the DSM-III-R items were from version 3 of the National Technical Center survey [McAuliffe et al. 1994]);
- alcohol-related mortality, extracted from Delaware death certificates 1988–92;
- alcohol-related hospital discharges 1993–94;
- alcohol-related criminal court cases 1988–92, generated from Superior Court records of the State of Delaware; and
- clients treated in State-supported alcohol treatment programs 1994–95.

For all of these indicators, the numerators are as shown (survey-based prevalence, alcohol-related mortality, etc.). The denominator in each case is population 18 and older. More detail on the data sources is provided in the Appendix to this chapter.

As of 1997, Delaware had a population of approximately 750,000 (Delaware Population Consortium 1997). Delaware has only three counties: New Castle County, in the north, which includes the State's largest city, Wilmington; Kent County, in the central part of the State, which includes the State capital, Dover; and Sussex County, in the south, which includes the Atlantic Ocean resort area. The State extends 90 miles north to south and averages 20 miles east to west. It has 53 ZIP Code areas and 129 census tracts. Figure 1 (see page 14) shows survey-based alcohol abuse and dependence by ZIP Code area for the State of Delaware.

This study uses the ZIP Code area as the geographic unit of analysis for practical reasons. Some of the small area indicators have as many as 80,000 observations, making it impractical to code the observations by census tract or block group. Figure 1 shows the 53 ZIP Code areas of Delaware with the estimated 18-month prevalence of DSM-III-R alcohol abuse and dependence based on a 1993–94 telephone survey (McAuliffe et al. 1994; Shreiner et al. 1996).

ANALYSIS

The correlations of Delaware alcohol problem indicators were calculated at both the respondent level and the ZIP Code area level. These correlations, which are summarized in table 1 (see page 12), allow us to address the questions listed earlier in this chapter about the validity and utility of the indicators.

We first ask whether the correlations between variables have a single underlying dimension and, if so, whether this dimension can be represented by the DSM-III-R alcohol abuse and dependence measure. As shown in table 1, the DSM-III-R measure is notable in its lack of correlation with other alcohol problem indicators at both the individual level and ZIP Code level—with the exception of criminal court cases and hospital discharges at the area level. If there is a common alcohol problem dimension underlying all of these indicators, it does not appear to be captured by the DSM-III-R measure.

All of the significant correlations between the small area indicators are positive. This suggests that there may be some common underlying characteristics of ZIP Code areas that are associated with some of the alcohol problem indicators. For example, at the individual level, alcohol-related mortality is significantly correlated with alcohol-related criminal court cases, alcohol-related hospital discharges, and alcohol treatment admissions. Stated another way, the survey respondent who lives in an area with a high rate of alcohol-related mortality is more likely to live in an area with a high rate of alcohol-related crime, a high rate of alcohol-related hospital discharges, and a high rate of admissions to alcohol treatment programs. Also, the survey respondent who lives in an area with a high level of treatment admissions is likely to live in an area that is high in alcohol-related mortality, crime, and hospital discharges.

There are several significant correlations with treatment admissions at the ZIP Code area level. An area that has a high rate of alcoholism treatment admissions is also more likely to have a high rate of alcohol-related crime and a high rate of alcohol-related mortality. Also at the area level, there are positive correlations for DSM-III-R abuse and dependence with criminal court cases and with hospital discharges, but not with treatment admissions. There are many more significant correlations at the respondent level than at the ZIP Code area level. However, there are many correlations between the indicators at both the individual and area levels that do not reach statistical significance.

If the survey-based DSM measure does not constitute a common underlying alcohol problem dimension, why is this so? One possible reason is that the DSM criteria were developed as a measure of alcohol problem severity wherein there was a consensus among mental health professionals that a patient with these symptoms was in need of treatment. The other indicators in this study capture a variety of alcohol problems in varying degrees of severity and transitional stages that are less strongly related to the all-inclusive DSM criteria. To understand what dimensions are represented by each of the indicators, a more encompassing paradigm, inclusive of alcohol problems not captured through the global DSM, is required. One strategy of exploring differences between social indicators is to disaggregate along the traditional demographic variables of age and sex.

Age- and Sex-Specific Alcohol Problem Indicator Rates

Figure 2 (see page 14) shows the survey-based 18-month prevalence of DSM-III-R alcohol abuse and dependence by age and sex. In the subsequent discussion, each of the social indicators is also analyzed by age and sex. The DSM-III-R measure is employed as a benchmark, hypothesizing that the DSM is the underlying alcohol problem dimension, even when age- and sex-specific rates are calculated. The DSM is treated here as a proportional hazard function (Smith 1992). Essentially, the age-specific 18-month prevalence rates are recomputed as a proportional prevalence (like proportional mortality), and these proportions are hypothesized to have roughly the same slopes as the DSM-III-R across age and sex groups. Validity is gauged by testing whether the population represented by a given small area social indicator (e.g., alcohol-related mortality) is distributed across the age-sex structure in the same proportions as the survey respondents manifesting alcohol abuse and dependence measured by the DSM-III-R. If a social indicator is a valid measure of the same underlying construct as the DSM, then the age-sex specific rates for the survey-based DSM and the age-sex specific rates for the indicator should parallel each other over the age spectrum. These comparisons are shown in figures 3–6. The source of the population base data for the rates shown in these figures is the 1990 census (U.S. Bureau of the Census 1990).

Figure 3 (see page 15) shows alcohol-related mortality over a 5-year period, by age and sex. Alcohol-related mortality peaks in the 60–69 age group for both men and women. The DSM proportional hazard function peaks at an earlier age than the mortality function, suggesting that the DSM function and alcohol-related mortality functions represent different segments of the Delaware population. For men, the DSM peak leads the mortality peak by about 40 years (spanning roughly the same period as the onset of heavy drinking until death from alcohol-related cirrhosis). For women, alcohol-related mortality follows a parallel trend. There is a 30-year gap between the age at which the DSM proportional hazard function reaches its peak and the age at which alcohol-related mortality registers its highest rate.

Alcohol-related hospital discharges reach a maximum at ages 70–79 for both men and women, as seen in figure 4 (see page 15). The DSM proportional hazard function shows several spikes for men, the first at ages 18–19 and a second, lower spike at ages 30–39. For women, the DSM proportional hazard function peaks at ages 30–39. This suggests that the DSM distribution and hospital discharge distribution represent different subpopulations.

Figure 5 (see page 16) shows criminal court cases with alcohol involvement register a sharp peak for men at ages 18–19 and drop off very rapidly as age increases. These cases include a large number of juvenile "status" offenses, such as alcohol beverages by minors, and it is expected that such cases will show a spike in the youngest age groups. Within the defendant population, alcohol abuse and dependence among men shows the familiar bimodal hazard function, with a spike at ages 18–19, followed by a shallow trough at 20–29, then another spike between 30 and 49 years of age. For women, alcohol-related court cases reach the highest level between the ages of 20 and 29. The DSM proportional hazard function rises gently to a peak at ages 30–39 and decreases evenly thereafter to its lowest level by age 70.

Is there any social indicator variable that mirrors the DSM-III-R with respect to its age and sex distribution? We have found one: clients treated in State-supported alcohol treatment programs. Treatment peaks at age 30–39 for both men and women, as seen in figure 6 (see page 16). For women, the peaks for the treatment indicator and the DSM proportional hazard function are identical. For men, after an initial spike at ages 18–19, the DSM proportional hazard function shows a second spike at 30–39 and decreases thereafter. It must be remembered that in this example the DSM age-sex distribution is superimposed on the treatment population, rather than the reverse. After age 39 the DSM proportional hazard function among the treatment population always surpasses the proportion of those actually undergoing treatment. It is not surprising, given the history of the development of the DSM, that the population proportions under treatment and the proportions manifesting the DSM are parallel throughout the age structure.

CONCLUSIONS

First, most social indicators appear to reflect different subpopulations than the survey-based DSM measure. There is not a single underlying alcohol problem dimension (at least in this cross-section) that is common to all of the indicators. The DSM represents a useful benchmark, but not an underlying construct for assessing the validity of small area alcohol problem indicators.

Second, the analysis using the individual (respondent) as the unit of analysis (rather than the ZIP Code area) appears to be more robust statistically. This procedure also obviates many of the criticisms rooted in the ecological fallacy, when the area is used as the unit of analysis.

Third, although each of the indicators represents an alcohol problem that may prompt a public policy response, the arena of response ranges widely—from the criminal justice system (captured in court cases) to the medical care system (captured in hospital discharges). As Gruenewald and colleagues (1997) suggested in their treatise on a systems approach to drug and alcohol problems, each indicator may represent a different kind of community system response to alcohol problems. Furthermore, the risk of encountering the government agency that is associated with a given indicator is affected by area demographics. Small area populations differ widely in terms of age-sex structure and other demographic variables.

If there is a unifying theoretical concept that underlies the indicators, it may be a developmental concept conveyed through an alcoholic lifetime (Creative Socio-Medics Corporation 1980):

> The concept of a flow or progression of alcohol abusers through various disposition states leads to consideration of the time required to reach each disposition. If the disposition is death, then the time required to reach it is referred to as the alcoholic lifetime; i.e., the time from onset of alcohol abuse until death [Creative Socio-Medics Corporation 1976].

Since the indicators peak at different stages of the human lifetime, they form a rough sequence of developmental benchmarks that begin with social drinking, progress to heavy drinking, and then manifest themselves through other age-graded markers, such as alcohol-related arrests, and culminate with alcohol-related hospital admissions and/or alcohol-related death.

A clue to these developmental stages is found in the median ages of those affected by alcohol problems, as reflected by indicators, as shown in table 2 (see page 12). Looking at the median age for each of the indicators employed in the study, the lowest median for men and women combined is 26 years, for alcohol-related criminal court cases. The median age reflected in the indicators next progresses to 33 for those in alcoholism treatment, to 34 for alcohol-related motor vehicle mortality, to 37 for survey-based alcohol abuse and dependence, to 46 for alcohol-related hospital discharges, to 56 for alcohol-related mortality where alcohol is a direct cause of death, and finally to 70 where alcohol is either a direct or an indirect cause of death.

The age structure of a geographic area alone appears to explain a significant amount of the risk of the different alcohol problems measured by these social indicators. There are, of course, a variety of other area risk factors, such as alcohol consumption levels. Some of the other social area factors may provide a more complete explanation of the alcohol problems that predominate in different geographic areas.

The analysis presented in this chapter suggests that developmental concepts, drawn from both biology and developmental psychology (Krohn et al. 1997; Schulenberg et al. 1996), have potential as a theoretical base for analyzing alcohol problems in small geographic areas. Both geographic areas and individuals may be characterized by life-cycle stages, each of which carries a different degree of risk for the alcohol problems reflected in social indicators.

ACKNOWLEDGMENTS

This chapter is based on a paper presented at the Annual Meeting of the Research Society on Alcoholism, San Francisco, July 22, 1997. The research is based on a drug and alcohol treatment needs assessment supported by the State of Delaware, Health and Social Services, Division of Alcoholism, Drug, Abuse and Mental Health. Federal funds were provided by the Center for Substance Abuse Treatment, through the State Needs Assessment Program.

REFERENCES

American Psychiatric Association. *Diagnostic and Statistical Manual of Mental Disorders.* 3d ed., rev. Washington, DC: the Association, 1987.

Becker, S. An overview of the State systems development program. Paper presented at the Resource Allocation Planning Conference [sponsored by Office of Treatment Improvement, Alcohol, Drug Abuse, and Mental Health Administration], Washington, DC, 1991.

Creative Socio-Medics Corporation. *Develop Improved Estimates of the Current Prevalence of Alcohol Abuse and Alcoholism: Interim Report.* National Institute on Alcohol Abuse and Alcoholism Contract No. ADM 281–756–0026. 1976.

Creative Socio-Medics Corporation. The Flow Model. [Paper describing an alcoholism prevalence estimation technique, based on the "Alcoholic Lifetime."] Vienna, VA: the Corporation, 1980.

Delaware Population Consortium. *Delaware Population Estimates, 1997.* Newark, DE: the Consortium, 1997.

Diez-Roux, A.V. Bringing context back into epidemiology: Variables and fallacies in multilevel analysis. *Am J Public Health* 88(2):216–226, 1998.

Gruenewald, P.; Treno, A.J.; Taff, G.; and Klitzner, M. *Measuring Community Indicators: A Systems Approach to Drug and Alcohol Problems.* Thousand Oaks, CA: Sage Publications, 1997.

Iverson, C.; Flanagin, A.; Fontanarosa, P.B.; Glass, R.M.; Glitman, P.; Lantz, J.C.; Meyer, H.S.; Smith, J.M.; Winker, M.A.; and Young, R.K., eds. *American Medical Association Manual of Style: A Guide for Authors and Editors.* 9th ed. Baltimore, MD: Williams & Wilkins, 1998.

Jellinek, E. The estimate of the number of alcoholics in the U.S.A. in light of the Sixth Revision of the International Lists of Causes of Death. *Q J Stud Alcohol* 13:255–260, 1952.

Krohn, M.; Lizotte, A.; and Perez, C. The interrelationship between substance use and precocious transitions to adult statuses. *J Health Soc Behav* March 1997.

McAuliffe, W. Approaches to using social indicators. Paper presented at Center for Substance Abuse Treatment Workshop on Social Indicator Models, Cambridge, MA, 1993.

McAuliffe, W.; LaBrie, R.A.; Mulvaney, N.; Shafer, H.J.; Geller, S.; Fournier, E.A.; Levine, E.B.; Wang, Q.; Wortman, S.M.; and Miller, K.A. *Assessment of Substance Abuse Treatment Needs: A Telephone Survey Manual and Questionnaire.* Cambridge, MA: National Technical Center for Substance Abuse Treatment Needs Assessment, 1994.

Robins, L.N. *NIMH Diagnostic Interview Schedule Version III: Instructions for Use.* Rockville, MD: National Institute of Mental Health, 1981.

Robins, L.N. Diagnostic grammar and assessment: Translating criteria into questions. In: Robins, L.N., and Barrett, J.E., eds. *The Validity of Psychiatric Diagnosis.* New York: Raven Press, 1989. pp. 263–278.

Robinson, W. Ecological correlations and the behavior of individuals. *Am Sociol Rev* 15:351–357, 1950.

Schulenberg, J.; O'Malley, P.; Bachman, J.; Wadsworth, K.; and Johnston, L. Getting drunk and growing up: Trajectories of frequent binge drinking during the transition to young adulthood. *J Stud Alcohol* 57(3):289-304, 1996.

Shreiner, J.; Mateja, W.; and Wilson, R. *Final Report: Delaware Alcohol and Drug Prevalence Surveys.* Newark: University of Delaware, 1996.

Smith, D. *Formal Demography.* New York: Plenum, 1992. pp.196–198.

Substance Abuse and Mental Health Services Administration (SAMSHA). *Application for FY 1994 Block Grant for Prevention and Treatment of Substance Abuse.* Rockville, MD: SAMHSA, 1993.

U.S. Bureau of the Census. *1990 Census of Population and Housing.* Summary Tapes 1A (STF1A), 1B (STF1B), and 3B (STF3B). Washington, DC: Bureau of the Census, 1990.

APPENDIX:

ADDITIONAL DETAIL ON DATA SOURCES

Alcohol-related mortality was extracted from Delaware death certificates 1988–92. Causes of death include the following ICD-9 codes:

Alcoholic Psychoses (291)

Alcohol Dependence Syndrome (303)

Alcohol Abuse (305.0)

Alcoholic Polyneuropathy (357.5)

Alcoholic Cardiomyopathy (425.5)

Alcoholic Gastritis (535.3)

Alcoholic Fatty Liver (571.0)

Acute Alcoholic Hepatitis (571.1)

Alcoholic Cirrhosis of Liver (571.2)

Alcoholic Liver Damage NOS (571.3)

Excessive Blood Level of Alcohol (790.3)

Accidental Poisoning by Alcohol NEC (E860)

Accidental Poisoning by Other and Unspecified Ethyl Alcohol and Its Products (E860.1)

Alcohol-related hospital discharges 1993–94 include the following alcohol-related diagnoses from hospital discharge records (by ICD code):

Alcohol Amnestic Syndrome (291.1)

Other Alcoholic Dementia (291.2)

Alcohol Withdrawal Hallucinosis (291.3)

Idiosyncratic Alcohol Intoxication (291.4)

Alcoholic Jealousy (291.5)

Other Specified Alcoholic Psychosis (291.8)

Alcoholic Psychosis NOS (291.9)

Alcohol Dependence Syndrome (303)

Acute Alcoholic Intoxication (303.0)

Acute Alcoholic Intoxication—Unspecified (303.00)

Acute Alcoholic Intoxication—Continuous (303.01)

Acute Alcoholic Intoxication—Episodic (303.02)

Acute Alcoholic Intoxication—in Remission (303.03)

Alcohol Dependence NEC/NOS (303.9)

Alcohol Dependence NEC/NOS—Unspecified (303.90)

Alcohol Dependence NEC/NOS—Continuous (303.91)

Alcohol Dependence NEC/NOS—Episodic (303.92)

Alcohol Dependence NEC/NOS—in Remission (303.93)

Alcohol Abuse (305.0)

Alcohol Abuse—Unspecified (305.00)

Alcohol Abuse—Continuous (305.01)

Alcohol Abuse—Episodic (305.02)

Alcohol Abuse—in Remission (305.03)

Acute and Subacute Necrosis of Liver (570)

Chronic Liver Disease and Cirrhosis (571)

Alcoholic Fatty Liver (571.0)

Acute Alcoholic Hepatitis (571.1)

Alcoholic Cirrhosis of Liver (571.2)

Alcoholic Liver Damage NOS (571.3)

Cirrhosis of Liver Without Mention of Alcohol (571.5)

Biliary Cirrhosis (571.6)

Other Chronic Nonalcoholic Liver Disease NEC (571.8)

Chronic Liver Disease Without Mention of Alcohol NOS (571.9)

Liver Abscess and Sequela of Chronic Liver Disease (572)

Toxic Effect of Alcohol (980)

Toxic Effect of Alcohol—Ethyl Alcohol (980.0)

Toxic Effect of Alcohol—Methyl Alcohol (980.1)

Toxic Effect of Alcohol—Isopropyl Alcohol (980.2)

Toxic Effect of Alcohol NEC (980.8)

Toxic Effect of Alcohol NOS (980.9)

Accidental Poisoning by Alcohol NEC (E860)

Accidental Poisoning by Alcohol Beverages (E860.0)

Accidental Poisoning—Other and Unspecified Ethyl Alcohol and Its Products (E860.1)

Accidental Poisoning—Methyl Alcohol (E860.2)

Accidental Poisoning—Isopropyl Alcohol (E860.3)

Accidental Poisoning—Other Specified Alcohols NEC (E860.8)

Accidental Poisoning NOS (E860.9)

Table 1. Significant Correlations of Delaware Alcohol Problem Indicators at the Respondent

	Mortality		Criminal Court Cases	
	Individual	**Area**	**Individual**	**Area**
Mortality			**	**
Criminal court cases	**	**		
Hospital discharges	**		**	*
Treatment admissions	**	**	**	**
DSM-III-R abuse and dependence				**

*Positive correlation; $p < 0.05$.
**Positive correlation; $p < 0.01$.
Source: Health Services Policy Research Group, University of Delaware, 1997.

Table 2. Median Age of Individuals Affected by Alcohol Problems, by Alcohol Problem

Cases
Alcohol-related criminal court cases
Clients treated in State-supported alcoholism treatment programs
Alcohol-related motor vehicle mortality
Survey-based alcohol abuse and dependence
Alcohol-related hospital discharges
Alcohol-related mortality
Nondependent alcohol deaths
Alcohol cirrhosis deaths
Alcoholism deaths
All alcohol-related mortality

Source: Health Services Policy Research Group, University of Delaware, 1997.

Level ($N = 2{,}831$) and the ZIP Code Level ($N = 52$).

Hospital Discharges		Treatment Admissions		DSM-III-R Abuse and Dependence	
Individual	**Area**	**Individual**	**Area**	**Individual**	**Area**
**		**	**		
**	*	**	**		**
		**			**
**					
	**				

Indicator, State of Delaware, 1988–95.

Total	Males	Females
26	25	28
33	34	33
34	34	34
37	35	33
46	46	46
56	55	59
40	39	63
54	52	58
58	58.5	54
70	64	77

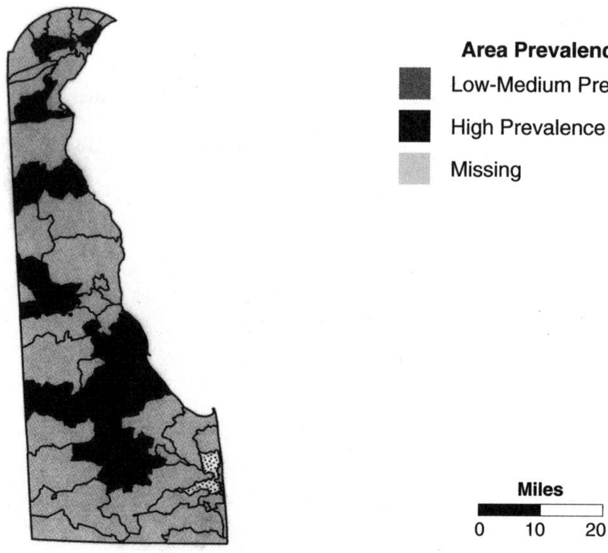

Figure 1. Survey-based prevalence of DSM-III-R alcohol abuse and dependence in the Delaware population age 18 and older, by ZIP Code area. See text for survey details.

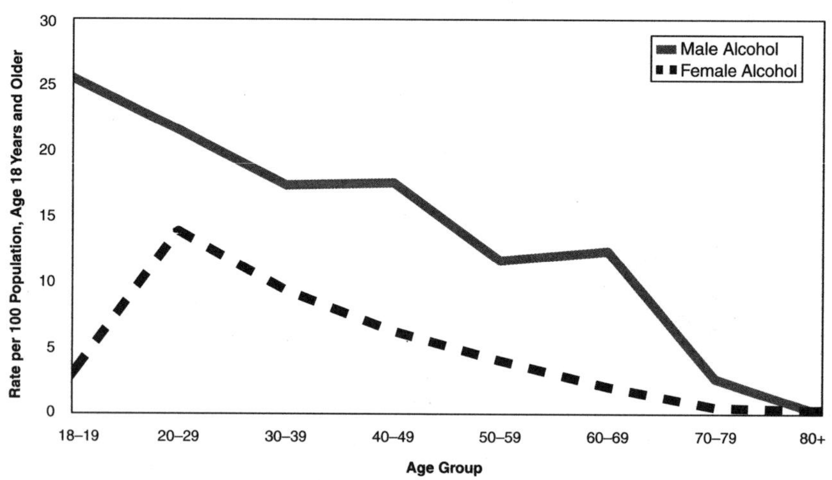

Figure 2. Survey-based 18-month prevalence of alcohol abuse and dependence by age and sex.

Source: Health Services Policy Research Group, University of Delaware, 1997.

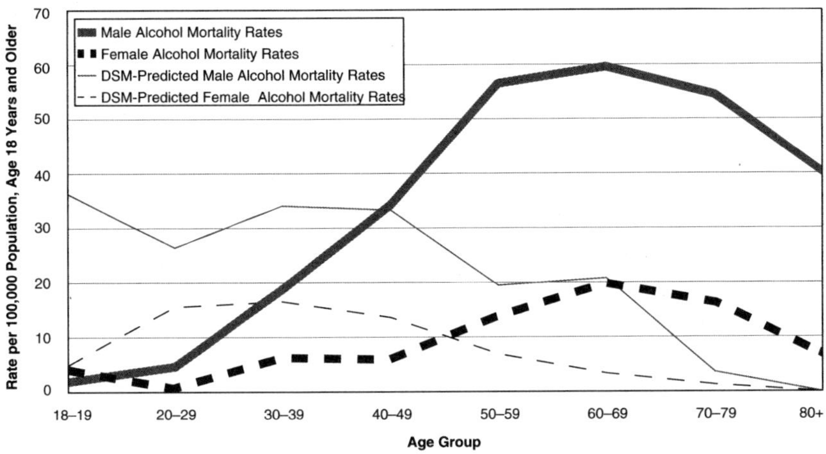

Figure 3. Alcohol-related mortality by age and sex, with DSM proportional hazard function superimposed.

Source: Health Services Policy Research Group, University of Delaware, 1997.

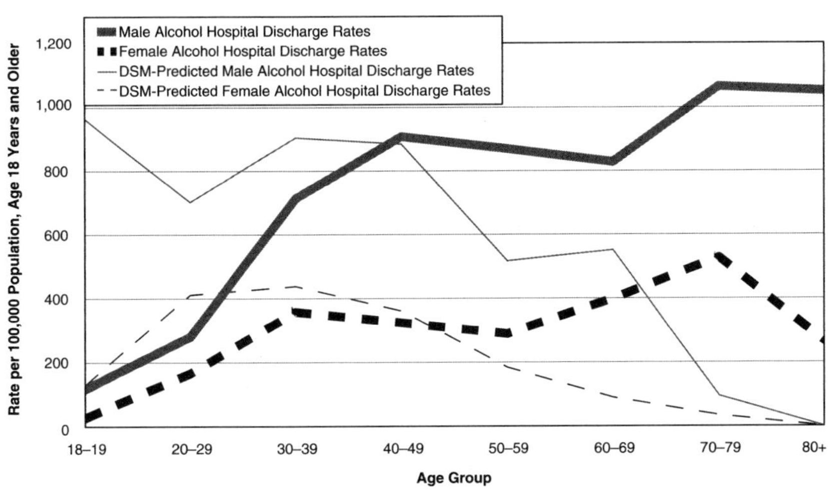

Figure 4. Alcohol-related hospital discharges by age and sex, with DSM proportional hazard function superimposed.

Source: Health Services Policy Research Group, University of Delaware, 1997.

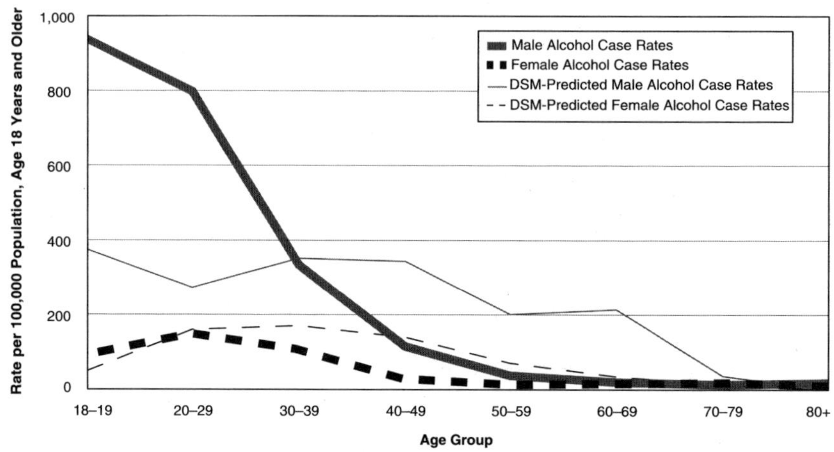

Figure 5. Alcohol-related criminal court cases by age and sex, with DSM proportional hazard function superimposed.

Source: Health Services Policy Research Group, University of Delaware, 1997.

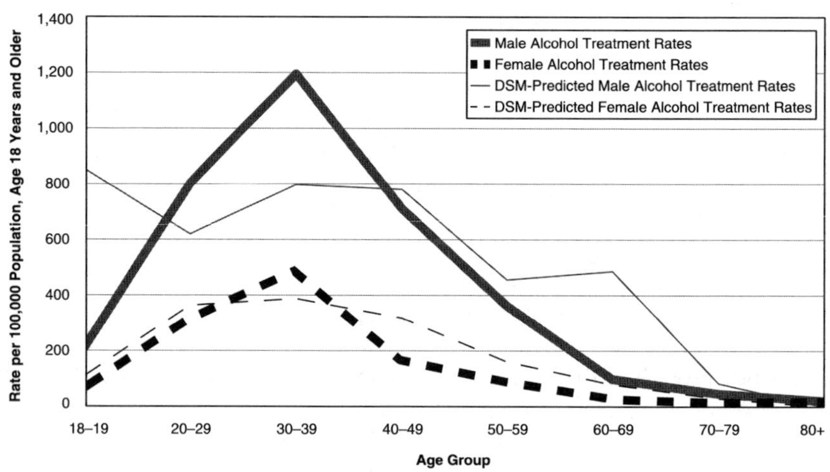

Figure 6. Clients treated in State-supported alcohol treatment programs by age and sex, with DSM proportional hazard function superimposed.

Source: Health Services Policy Research Group, University of Delaware, 1997.

Chapter 2

Synthetic Estimates of the Prevalence of DSM-III-R Alcohol Abuse and Dependence: Issues of Validity and Methodology

Robert A. Wilson, Ph.D., and William E. McAuliffe, Ph.D.

KEY WORDS: statistical estimation; prevalence; diagnostic criteria; AOD abuse; AOD dependence; geographical area; household survey; validity (research methods); reliability (research methods); addiction care; needs assessment; age differences; gender differences; questionnaire; Delaware; literature review

Accurate estimates of the prevalence of alcohol abuse and dependence are required for treatment needs assessment and resource allocation in small geographic areas. Small sample sizes, however, frequently preclude accurate estimates for substate planning areas. Small area prevalence can be estimated by a "synthetic" procedure that "allocates" statewide prevalence across geographic areas based on age-sex-race–specific rates from a statewide survey. This "synthetic" routine can generate estimates for areas as small as a census tract or city block.

In this chapter we explore several critical issues about the use of interview surveys (employing the DSM-III-R criteria [American Psychiatric Association 1987]) to estimate the prevalence of alcohol dependence and abuse in a household population (Kessler et al. 1994). Specifically, we discuss the efficiency, validity, and reliability of synthetic indicators derived from household surveys, applied to small geographic planning areas. The questionnaire for the Delaware study used as an example

---

R.A. Wilson, Ph.D., is director of the Health Services Policy Research Group, School of Urban Affairs and Public Policy, University of Delaware, Newark, DE 19716. W.E. McAuliffe, Ph.D., is an associate professor at Harvard Medical School and director of the National Technical Center for Substance Abuse Needs Assessment, North Charles Research and Planning Group, 875 Massachusetts Ave., 7th Floor, Cambridge, MA 02139.

later in this chapter was designed by the Harvard Medical School for States participating in treatment needs assessment projects funded by the Center for Substance Abuse Treatment (CSAT) (McAuliffe et al. 1994).

Treatment needs assessment projects, like the one for which this survey was designed, are intended to provide information on treatment needs that can be incorporated into the Federal Block Grant Plan, which is submitted by the 50 States and territories to support Federal funding for State alcohol and other drug programs.

Beginning in 1993, the Federal Block Grant regulations required the States to develop alcohol problem prevalence estimates for substate planning areas to be used as the basis for treatment needs estimation. At this writing, all States have been awarded needs assessment contracts by CSAT. All participating States are conducting statewide prevalence surveys using the DSM-III-R criteria.

All of the States conducting surveys have four or more geographic planning areas for which DSM-III-R prevalence estimates must be generated. A minimum survey sample size of 5,000 respondents is recommended for statewide surveys. This recommendation is based on the necessity to provide both a point estimate of DSM-III-R prevalence and a demographic profile of respondents who meet the DSM-III-R criteria for alcohol abuse and dependence.

Several States have fielded surveys with over 10,000 respondents. With survey costs sometimes exceeding $100 per interview, there is obviously a need to make estimates for some geographic areas that do not have an adequate sample. Too, there will be a demand for prevalence estimates during the time periods between surveys. Thus, some form of survey-based prevalence estimates, which do not necessarily meet the traditional sampling requirements, is called for. In this chapter we explore a type of prevalence estimation based on interview surveys that does not employ a traditional sampling frame. This procedure is commonly referred to as a *synthetic estimate*. This chapter focuses on six issues concerning survey-based synthetic prevalence estimates for small geographic areas:

1. How is DSM-III-R alcohol abuse and dependence measured in a survey?
2. What is a synthetic estimate?
3. Why are synthetic estimates important in treatment needs assessment?
4. How are synthetic estimates made?
5. Are synthetic estimates valid for small geographic areas?
6. What should be done to make synthetic estimates more useful?

HOW IS DSM-III-R ALCOHOL ABUSE AND DEPENDENCE MEASURED IN A SURVEY?

The criteria used to measure alcohol abuse and dependence in statewide prevalence surveys are shown in figure 1 (see p. 32). These criteria are based on the DSM-III-R criteria, and for the sake of simplicity they are referred to as the DSM-III-R criteria. In order to participate in the abuse and dependence section of the interview, respondents must "qualify" on a set of screening questions on drinking recency, frequency, quantity, variability, and treatment history. In the present analysis a 1-year prevalence window is employed. Keeping in mind that the DSM-III-R criteria yield a prevalence estimate that is typically somewhat lower than the traditional measures of heavy drinking or problem drinking, and remembering that the DSM-III-R prevalence estimates may be much lower, particularly in very small geographic areas, alcohol abuse and dependence are combined into a single category.

WHAT IS A SYNTHETIC ESTIMATE?

There are two types of synthetic estimates. The first type is the *true synthetic estimate*, which is an estimate of a population parameter for a geographic area that is based on a model generated from data from geographic areas that include the geographic area for which the estimate is being made and other areas. The estimate, therefore, includes some data from the area for which the estimate is being made and some data from the larger area of which the smaller target area is a part. This kind of estimate is also known as a *borrowed strength model.* The weaker estimate "borrows" some of the statistical power of a more robust indicator.

Synthetic projections are the second type of synthetic estimate, also commonly referred to as a "synthetic estimate." This type of estimate is based on a model that may not be generated from data from the area for which the estimate is being produced (Schaible 1979). The best known example of a synthetic projection is the *Marden method*, which applies age-sex specific prevalence rates derived from a national survey to small geographic areas that were not included in the sampling frame of the national survey (Marden 1974).

ISSUES WITH SURVEY-BASED SYNTHETIC ESTIMATES OF DSM-III-R PREVALENCE

There are two issues that we need to be concerned about in relation to survey-based synthetic estimates of DSM-III-R prevalence. The first issue is *precision.* Do either true synthetic estimates or synthetic projections produce estimates of DSM-III-R prevalence for small areas that are sufficiently close to those derived from sample surveys of the same geographic areas?

One position is that the required degree of accuracy of an estimate for treatment needs allocation depends on the decision that will be made on the basis of the estimate (the cost of being wrong). In epidemiology such errors are commonly defined in terms of "false positives" or "false negatives." A false positive, in small area planning, means that prevalence was incorrectly estimated to be higher than it really was. A false negative, in contrast, means that prevalence was incorrectly estimated to be lower than it really was. The consequence of these errors in this treatment planning scenario is an overallocation or an underallocation of treatment resources or, in the worst case, a total neglect of a major alcohol problem in a small area.

The second issue is *equity*, which is related to the possible consequences of errors in accuracy. That is, inaccurate synthetic estimates can lead to inequitable allocation of resources because these estimates of alcoholism prevalence are commonly used for resource allocation at the geographic service area level. The decisions made on the basis of the estimate will be translated into needed programs, beds, slots, and staff. If the utility of the estimate is to be gauged, it will be evaluated in terms of dollars gained or lost for programs in a substate planning area.

WHY ARE SYNTHETIC ESTIMATES IMPORTANT IN TREATMENT NEEDS ASSESSMENT?

Federal regulations require that State Block Grant Applications incorporate prevalence estimates from several substate planning areas. To produce survey-based estimates of DSM-III-R prevalence with adequate demographic detail typically requires a sample size of 5,000–6,000 respondents, a procedure which is prohibitively expensive if done on a frequent basis. Synthetic procedures, in contrast, are inexpensive and allow estimations for areas as small as a census tract or even a city block.

HOW ARE SYNTHETIC ESTIMATES MADE?

Following are some examples of synthetic estimates from the first wave (N = 907) of telephone surveys conducted in the State of Delaware (1993–94). Note that even in a small State like Delaware (population approximately 750,000), a sample of 907 is barely large enough to provide an accurate point prevalence estimate, using the standard sampling techniques shown in table 1 (see p. 34). The DSM-III-R estimate for one of the demographic groups (males ages 18–29), has an unacceptably large standard error. Another problem is that no females age 65 and over in the entire statewide sample meet the DSM-III-R criteria for alcohol abuse or dependence.

The limitations of small sample size become more critical in making estimates at the substate level. Moving to the county level (see table 2, p. 34), no 65-year-olds (male or female) in the county subsample (n = 226) meet the DSM-III-R criteria. Are we to assume that there is no one in the county age 65 and over who is an alcohol abuser? Also note that the standard error for males ages 30–44 grows to 25 percent, and the confidence band for males ages 18–29 is unacceptably wide.

At this point we have exhausted the standard inferential estimating techniques. To produce a semblance of order in the age-specific estimates, we must follow some of the rules of population forecasting. For example, when the population for which the forecast is to be made is so small that the forecast (normally framed in terms of a "high," "medium," and "low" estimate) becomes unstable, go to the next larger area estimate and "allocate" the forecast to the smaller area in terms of its share of the present population (Rives and Serow 1984).

Following this axiom, we use the prevalence rates from the statewide sample for the prevalence estimate for Sussex County (see table 3, p. 35). But even at the State level, we still have no females age 65+ in the sample. At this point we use the first synthetic projection, based on the 1988 Alcohol Supplement of the National Health Interview Survey (NHIS) (Grant et al. 1991). There is another complicating factor, however. Between 1988 and 1993 the prevalence of drinking declined by about 10 percent, based on findings from the National Household Survey on Drug Abuse (NHSDA) (Gfroefer and Wright 1993). Applying a correction factor of minus 10 percent to the 1988 NHIS rates for respondents over 65 years old produces the estimates shown in table 4 (see p. 35). These nationwide rates from the 1988 NHIS, adjusted for the overall decrease in drinking reported in the NHSDA, comprise our final synthetic estimate for 65-year-olds. These final rates are applied, in turn, to generate synthetic estimates for smaller areas, such as tracts (see figure 2, p. 33) or ZIP Code areas, for which the statewide survey sample is inadequate to produce accurate estimates.

ARE SYNTHETIC ESTIMATES VALID FOR SMALL GEOGRAPHIC AREAS?

Validity, in the most general usage, infers that a measurement has been corroborated by another measurement that is assumed to be "true." In the present study, we assume that a standard sample survey (with competent questionnaire design, good sampling, and professional administration) will yield a DSM-III-R prevalence estimate for a small geographic area that is relatively unbiased. The validity of a synthetic estimate for a small area may be gauged in two ways: (1) in comparison to a "true" sample survey of the same area (if the synthetic and the "real" survey produce similar prevalence estimates, the synthetic estimate is assumed to be valid); and (2) in comparison to an "independent" prevalence indicator that has been validated in the present survey or in another study.

There are a variety of social indicators that are associated with DSM-III-R prevalence, but few that have been validated against DSM-III-R measures in small geographic areas. One notable exception is a set of census-based indicators derived from the Health Demographic Profile developed by the National Institute of Mental Health (Goldsmith et al. 1984). In a study conducted by Ciarlo and colleagues (1992) in Colorado, DSM-III-R alcohol prevalence in the State's 48 catchment areas was found to be significantly correlated with eight ecological variables that were descriptive of the demographic context of the areas. These ecological indicators were hypothesized to be correlated with synthetic estimates of DSM-III-R prevalence for the 168 census tracts of Delaware (see table 5, p. 36; see also figure 2, p. 33). The tract estimates were generated by multiplying the statewide DSM-III-R prevalence rates, like those in table 1, by the 1990 census enumerations for the corresponding age/sex categories, summing the estimates, and dividing by the 1990 population (age 18 and over) of the tract (U.S. Bureau of the Census 1990).

The predictive power of the ecological indicators used in the Colorado study is supported in the Delaware study. The same eight Health Demographic Profile indicators for Delaware census tracts correlate significantly with the synthetic estimates for the same tracts in the hypothesized direction (table 5). In sum, the synthetically generated DSM-III-R prevalence rates are validated by correlations with the ecological indicators produced from the 1990 census. Essentially, this finding suggests that the ecological model that proved to be associated with varying DSM-III-R prevalence in Colorado operates in a parallel fashion with the demographic structure of tracts and synthetic estimates in Delaware. The synthetic estimates for Delaware are validated in the sense that the direction and strength of the correlations are identical with those reported in the Colorado study.

The tract map of Delaware (figure 2) portrays the synthetically estimated DSM-III-R prevalence by tract. Probably the most understandable interpretation of this mosaic is the relative risk of DSM-III-R given some of the salient population characteristics of a census tract.

The survey-based synthetic estimates of DSM-III-R are also correlated at the tract level with the alcohol-related mortality ratio (1988–92) for the tracts (table 5). Thus, the synthetic estimate is validated through a convergence with the same demographic variables found to correlate with a true survey-based estimate in the Colorado study and through a second independent estimator—alcohol-related mortality (Stinson et al. 1993). Although both the Colorado and Delaware studies suggest that the Health Demographic Profile indicators are valid predictors of DSM-III-R, the theoretical specification on the underlying process that operates to define risk through these demographic variables remains vague.

WHAT SHOULD BE DONE TO MAKE SYNTHETIC ESTIMATES MORE USEFUL?

Lest we be tempted to base small area estimates on synthetic estimates produced from national surveys, we need to reaffirm that demographic (census-based) indicators do not necessarily produce accurate prevalence estimates for small geographic areas. There may be enormous variations in prevalence across areas having the same demographics. A good case in point are "dry" counties of several States, which resemble "wet" areas demographically but which vary significantly in alcohol use and alcohol problems.

A synthetic model, then, offers an explanation (an abstraction) of what the prevalence of an area should look like, everything else being equal. Although a synthetic model may produce an estimate that is adequate to assess some risk factors, other factors may operate to bring about a pattern that is different than expected. Area factors may reflect local cultural patterns that affect alcohol abuse. Other factors relate to variables that should be incorporated into the synthetic model. Good candidates for variables that might be incorporated in a general synthetic model include age structure, urbanization, economic status, and other census variables that indicate different lifestyles.

While some of the ecological variables from the U.S. census appear to be strong predictors of small area prevalence, no comprehensive theory has evolved to explain variations in DSM-III-R across areas. One variable that is conspicuously absent from the Colorado study is age structure, which forms the very foundation of most epidemiologic research. Age structure, however, in social indicator studies is frequently age-adjusted away, despite the well-known fact that the prevalence of alcohol abuse and dependence is invariably highest within the younger age groups.

A good place to start in identifying candidate variables for synthetic estimation is within the statewide survey itself—identifying respondent demographics, including characteristics of the area of residence, that are associated with DSM-III-R prevalence. Translating these characteristics, in turn, into social area characteristics that are hypothesized to correlate with survey-based DSM-III-R prevalence provides a fertile area for testing epidemiologic models that have great relevance to small area planning for alcohol treatment planning.

If the treatment needs assessments are to contribute to a scientific body of knowledge about synthetic estimation, the methodology must progress beyond mere multiplication of age-sex–specific prevalence by local planning area population estimates. A set of robust prevalence indicators that are independent of interview surveys will be required to establish validity of the survey in each State. (By "validity" we mean convergent validity, verified through a multitrait, multimodality paradigm.)

Two sets of indicators offer excellent potential for validating survey-based estimates. First are the alcohol and drug mortality rates (or mortality ratios), which have excellent face validity. Second are the census-based demographic variables, which include those discussed in this chapter. Although both mortality and social area demographics have been tested to the point where a modicum of reliability has been established, what appears to be lacking is an explanation of the precise social processes that operate in small geographic areas. Another way of describing the current state of integration of social indicator and survey theory is to say that DSM-III-R prevalence is now beginning to be understood as a hazard function. The hazard function is conceptualized in terms of alcohol- and drug-related mortality and demographic variables such as poverty, family structure, and housing characteristics. What is lacking, however, is an integrated theory of area social structure and process that is conceptually integrated with DSM-III-R concepts.

One body of theory that appears to have potential for explaining the community process underlying substance abuse problems is developmental psychology. Different drinking and drug-use pathologies predominate in different parts of the age spectrum. The three social area variables that measure a community's developmental stage all relate to an area's age structure. These variables are the area's age-sex distribution (usually envisioned as a population pyramid), age-specific morbidity, and age-sex–specific mortality. Different age-sex concentrations, in themselves, place small geographic areas at risk for different alcohol and drug problems. For example, eating disorders are most common among young women, and alcohol-related liver disease is most common among older males. Treatment programs, too, usually specialize in patients from a narrow range of the age-sex spectrum. (Drinking and driving programs catering to young males and crack cocaine treatment programs directed at teenagers provide excellent examples.)

Where does this leave us in regard to synthetic estimates? Age-sex–based synthetic estimates are both a necessity and practical reality. However, synthetic estimates must be validated with a set of social indicators that have both reliability and validity. While reliability is readily tested in comparison with a growing number of studies that employ both surveys and social indicators, validity remains a problem—particularly in establishing causality and in providing a theory for substate treatment planning. The state of the science of needs assessment now hinges on explaining the relationship of individual behavior, as reflected through surveys, and underlying community structure, as reflected through social indicators. Although the standard age-sex–based synthetic estimation was originally developed because these variables had statistical power, age and sex also were components of a theoretical base in developmental theory and a practical application in age-sex–based program development. Elaborations of the development concept may readily be envisioned in terms of small area subcultures. These subcultures might include, for example, young adults, Native Americans, and African Americans. These and a variety of other subcultures and lifestyles may be the focus of CSAT needs assessment studies.

ACKNOWLEDGMENTS

This chapter is a revision of a paper prepared by Drs. Wilson and McAuliffe for the Annual Meeting of the Research Society on Alcoholism, June 1994. The research is based on a drug and alcohol treatment needs assessment supported by the State of Delaware, Health and Social Services, Division of Alcoholism, Drug Abuse and Mental Health. Federal funds were provided by the Center for Substance Abuse Treatment, through the State Needs Assessment Program. The authors thank Richard LaBrie, Laurie McLeod, and Walter Mateja for their assistance in preparing this chapter.

REFERENCES

American Psychiatric Association. *Diagnostic and Statistical Manual of Mental Disorders.* 3d ed., rev. Washington, DC: the Association, 1987.

Ciarlo, J.A., and Tweed, D.L. Implementing indirect needs-assessment models for planning state mental health and substance abuse services. *Evaluation and Program Planning* 15:195–210, 1992.

Ciarlo, J.A.; Tweed, D.L.; Shern, D.L.; Kirkpatrick, L.A.; and Sachs-Ericsson, N. Validation of indirect methods to estimate need for mental health services: Concepts, strategy, and general conclusions. *Evaluation and Program Planning* 15:115–131, 1992.

Gfroefer, J., and Wright, D. *Preliminary Estimates From the 1992 National Household Survey on Drug Abuse. Advance Report No. 3.* Rockville, MD: Substance Abuse and Mental Health Services Administration, Office of Applied Studies, June 1993.

Goldsmith, H.F.; Jackson, D.J.; Doenhoeffer, S.; Johnson, W.; Tweed, D.L.; Stiles, D.; Barbano, J.P.; and Warheit, G.J. *The Health Demographic Profile System's Inventory of Small Area Social Indicators.* National Institute of Mental Health Series BN No. 4. DHHS Pub. No. ADM 84–1354. Washington, DC: U.S. Government Printing Office, 1984.

Grant, B.F.; Harford, T.C.; Chou, P.; Pickering, R.; Dawson, D.A.; Stinson, F.S.; and Noble, J. Prevalence of DSM-III-R alcohol abuse and dependence, United States, 1988. *Alcohol Health Res World* 15(1):91–96, 1991.

Kessler, R.C.; McGonagle, K.A.; Zhao, S.; Nelson, C.; Hughes, M.; Eshleman, S.; Wittchen, H.; and Kendler, K. Lifetime and 12-month prevalence of DSM-III-R psychiatric disorders in the United States. *Arch Gen Psychiatry* 51:8–19, 1994.

Marden, P. *A Procedure for Estimating the Potential Number of Alcoholism Service Program Clientele.* Rockville, MD: National Institute on Alcohol Abuse and Alcoholism, 1974.

McAuliffe, W.; LaBrie, R.A.; Mulvaney, N.; Shafer, H.J.; Geller, S.; Fournier, E.A.; Levine, E.B.; Wang, Q.; Wortman, S.M.; and Miller, K.A. *Assessment of Substance Abuse Treatment Needs: A Telephone Survey Manual and Questionnaire.* Cambridge, MA: National Technical Center for Substance Abuse Treatment Needs Assessment, 1994.

Rives, N., and Serow, W. *Introduction to Applied Demography: Data Sources and Estimation Techniques.* Newbury Park, CA: Sage, 1984. pp. 66–67.

Schaible, W.L. *A Composite Estimator for Small Area Statistics.* National Institute on Drug Abuse Research Monograph Series, 24. February 1979. pp. 36–53.

Stinson, F., and DeBakey, S. Alcohol-related mortality in the United States, 1979–1988. *British Journal of Addictions* 5:777–783, 1992.

Stinson, F.S.; Dufour, M.C.; Steffens, R.A.; and DeBakey, S.F. Alcohol-related mortality in the United States, 1979–1989. *Alcohol Health Res World* 17(3):251–260, 1993.

U.S. Bureau of the Census. *1990 Census of Population and Housing.* Summary Tapes 1A (STF1A), 1B (STF1B), and 3B (STF3B). Washington, DC: Bureau of the Census, 1990.

APPENDIX:

SOCIAL INDICATOR GROUPS FOR ICD-9 MORTALITY CODES

The social indicator groups are as follows: 3 = directly attributable to alcohol; 4 = indirectly attributable to alcohol; 5 = alcohol-related underlying causes of death. Mortality classifications are based on Stinson and DeBakey 1992.

ICD-9 Code	Group	Definition
011	4	Pulmonary Tuberculosis
011.0	4	Tuberculosis of Lung, Infiltrative
011.1	4	Tuberculosis of Lung, Nodular
011.2	4	Tuberculosis of Lung w/Cavitation
011.3	4	Tuberculosis of Bronchus
011.4	4	Tuberculous Fibrosis of Lung
011.5	4	Tuberculous Bronchiectasis
011.6	4	Tuberculous Pneumonia
011.7	4	Tuberculous Pneumothorax
011.8	4	Other Specified Pulmonary Tuberculosis
011.9	4	Pulmonary Tuberculosis, Unspecified
012	4	Other Respiratory Tuberculosis
140	4	Malignant Neoplasm of Lip
141	4	Malignant Neoplasm of Tongue
142	4	Malignant Neoplasm of Major Salivary Glands
143	4	Malignant Neoplasm of Gum
144	4	Malignant Neoplasm of Floor of Mouth
145	4	Malignant Neoplasm of Other & Unspecified Parts of Mouth
146	4	Malignant Neoplasm of Oropharynx
147	4	Malignant Neoplasm of Nasopharynx
148	4	Malignant Neoplasm of Hypopharynx
149	4	Malignant Neoplasm of Other and Ill-Defined Sites Within the Lip, Oral Cavity, and Pharynx
150	4	Malignant Neoplasm of Esophagus
151	4	Malignant Neoplasm of Stomach
155	4	Malignant Neoplasm of Liver and Intrahepatic Bile Ducts
161	4	Malignant Neoplasm of Larynx
250	4	Diabetes Mellitus
291	3	Alcoholic Psychoses
303	3	Alcohol Dependence Syndrome
357.5	3	Alcoholic Polyneuropathy
401	4	Essential Hypertension
425.5	3	Alcoholic Cardiomyopathy
430	4	Subarachnoid Hemorrhage
432	4	Other & Unspecified Intracranial Hemorrhage

433	4	Occlusion & Stenosis of Precerebral Arteries
434	4	Occlusion of Cerebral Arteries
435	4	Transient Cerebral Ischemia
437	4	Other & Ill-Defined Cerebrovascular Disease
438	4	Late Effects of Cerebrovascular Disease
530	4	Diseases of Esophagus
531	4	Gastric Ulcer
531.0	4	Gastric Ulcer Acute w/Hemorrhage
531.1	4	Gastric Ulcer Acute w/Perforation
531.2	4	Gastric Ulcer Acute w/Hemorrhage & Perforation
531.3	4	Gastric Ulcer Acute w/o Mention of Hemorrhage or Perforation
531.4	4	Gastric Ulcer Chronic or Unspecified w/Hemorrhage
531.5	4	Gastric Ulcer Chronic or Unspecified w/Perforation
531.6	4	Gastric Ulcer Chronic or Unspecified w/Hemorrhage & Perforation
531.7	4	Gastric Ulcer Chronic w/o Mention of Hemorrhage or Perforation
531.9	4	Gastric Ulcer Unspecified as Acute or Chronic, w/o Mention of Hemorrhage or Perforation
532	4	Duodenal Ulcer
532.0	4	Duodenal Ulcer Acute w/Hemorrhage
532.1	4	Duodenal Ulcer Acute w/Perforation
532.2	4	Duodenal Ulcer Acute w/Hemorrhage & Perforation
532.3	4	Duodenal Ulcer Acute w/o Mention of Hemorrhage or Perforation
532.4	4	Duodenal Ulcer Chronic or Unspecified w/Hemorrhage
532.5	4	Duodenal Ulcer Chronic or Unspecified w/Perforation
532.6	4	Duodenal Ulcer Chronic or Unspecified w/Hemorrhage & Perforation
532.7	4	Duodenal Ulcer Chronic w/o Mention of Hemorrhage or Perforation
532.9	4	Duodenal Ulcer Unspecified as Acute or Chronic, w/o Mention of Hemorrhage or Perforation
533	4	Peptic Ulcer, Site Unspecified
533.0	4	Peptic Ulcer Acute w/Hemorrhage
533.1	4	Peptic Ulcer Acute w/Perforation
533.2	4	Peptic Ulcer Acute w/Hemorrhage & Perforation
533.3	4	Peptic Ulcer Acute w/o Mention of Hemorrhage and Perforation
533.4	4	Peptic Ulcer Chronic or Unspecified w/Hemorrhage
533.5	4	Peptic Ulcer Chronic or Unspecified w/Perforation

533.6	4	Peptic Ulcer Chronic or Unspecified w/Hemorrhage & Perforation
533.7	4	Peptic Ulcer Chronic w/o Mention of Hemorrhage or Perforation
533.9	4	Peptic Ulcer Unspecified as Acute or Chronic, w/o Mention of Hemorrhage or Perforation
534	4	Gastrojejunal Ulcer
534.0	4	Gastrojejunal Ulcer Acute w/Hemorrhage
534.1	4	Gastrojejunal Ulcer Acute w/Perforation
534.2	4	Gastrojejunal Ulcer Acute w/Hemorrhage & Perforation
534.3	4	Gastrojejunal Ulcer Acute w/o Mention of Hemorrhage or Perforation
534.4	4	Gastrojejunal Ulcer Chronic or Unspecified w/Hemorrhage
534.5	4	Gastrojejunal Ulcer Chronic or Unspecified w/Perforation
534.6	4	Gastrojejunal Ulcer Chronic or Unspecified w/Hemorrhage & Perforation
534.7	4	Gastrojejunal Ulcer Chronic w/o Mention of Hemorrhage or Perforation
534.9	4	Gastrojejunal Ulcer Unspecified as Acute or Chronic, w/o Mention of Hemorrhage or Perforation
535	4	Gastritis & Duodenitis
535.3	3	Alcoholic Gastritis
536	5	Disorders of Function of Stomach
536.0	5	Achlorhydria
536.1	5	Acute Dilatation of Stomach
536.2	5	Persistent Vomiting
536.8	5	Dyspepsia & Other Specified Disorders of Function of Stomach
536.9	5	Unspecified Functional Disorder of Stomach
537	5	Other Disorders of Stomach and Duodenum
571.0	3	Alcoholic Fatty Liver
571.1	3	Acute Alcoholic Hepatitis
571.2	3	Alcoholic Cirrhosis of Liver
571.3	3	Alcoholic Liver Damage, Unspecified
571.5	4	Cirrhosis of Liver w/o Mention of Alcohol
571.6	4	Biliary Cirrhosis
577.0	4	Acute Pancreatitis
577.1	4	Chronic Pancreatitis
790.3	3	Excessive Blood Level of Alcohol
E810	4	Motor Vehicle Traffic Accident Involving Collision w/Train
E811	4	Motor Vehicle Traffic Accident Involving Re-entrant Collision w/Another Motor Vehicle

E812	4	Other Motor Vehicle Traffic Accident Involving Collision w/Motor Vehicle
E813	4	Motor Vehicle Traffic Accident Involving Collision w/Other Vehicle
E814	4	Motor Vehicle Traffic Accident Involving Collision w/Pedestrian
E815	4	Other Motor Vehicle Traffic Accident Involving Collision on the Highway
E816	4	Motor Vehicle Traffic Accident Due to Loss of Control, w/o Collision on the Highway
E817	4	Noncollision Motor Vehicle Traffic Accident While Boarding or Alighting
E818	4	Other Noncollision Motor Vehicle Traffic Accident
E819	4	Motor Vehicle Traffic Accident of Unspecified Nature
E820	4	Nontraffic Accident Involving Motor-Driven Snow Vehicle
E821	4	Nontraffic Accident Involving Other Off-Road Motor Vehicle
E822	4	Other Motor Vehicle Nontraffic Accident Involving Collision w/Moving Object
E823	4	Other Motor Vehicle Nontraffic Accident Involving Collision w/Stationary Object
E824	4	Other Motor Vehicle Nontraffic Accident While Boarding or Alighting
E825	4	Other Motor Vehicle Nontraffic Accident of Other & Unspecified Nature
E826	5	Pedal Cycle Accident
E829	5	Other Road Vehicle Accidents
E830	5	Accident to Watercraft Causing Submersion
E831	5	Accident to Watercraft Causing Other Injury
E832	5	Other Accidental Submersion or Drowning in Water Transport Accident
E833	5	Fall on Stairs or Ladders in Water Transport
E834	5	Other Fall From One Level to Another in Water Transport
E835	5	Other & Unspecified Fall in Water Transport
E836	5	Machinery Accident in Water Transport
E837	5	Explosion, Fire, or Burning in Watercraft
E838	5	Other & Unspecified Water Transport Accident
E840	5	Accident to Powered Aircraft at Takeoff or Landing
E841	5	Accident to Powered Aircraft, Other & Unspecified
E842	5	Accident to Unpowered Aircraft
E843	5	Fall in, on, or From Aircraft
E844	4	Other Specified Air Transport Accidents
E845	5	Accident Involving Spacecraft
E860	3	Accidental Poisoning by Alcohol, Not Elsewhere Classified

E860.1	3	Other and Unspecified Ethyl Alcohol and Its Products
E880	5	Fall on or From Stairs or Steps
E880.0	5	Fall on Escalator
E880.9	5	Fall on Other Stairs or Steps
E881	5	Fall on or From Ladders or Scaffolding
E881.0	5	Fall From Ladder
E881.1	5	Fall From Scaffolding
E882	5	Fall From or out of Building or Other Structure
E883	5	Fall Into Hole or Other Opening in Surface
E883.0	5	Accident From Diving or Jumping Into Water [Swimming Pool]
E883.1	5	Accidental Fall Into Well
E883.2	5	Accidental Fall Into Storm Drain or Manhole
E883.9	5	Fall Into Other Hole or Other Opening in Surface
E884.0	5	Fall From Playground Equipment
E884.1	5	Fall From Cliff
E884.2	5	Fall From Chair or Bed
E884.9	5	Other Fall From One Level to Another
E885	5	Fall on Same Level From Slipping, Tripping, or Stumbling
E886	5	Fall on Same Level From Collision, Pushing, or Shoving, by or w/Other Person
E886.0	5	Fall on Same Level From Collision, Pushing, or Shoving, by or w/Other Person in Sports
E886.9	5	Fall on Same Level From Collision, Pushing, or Shoving, by or w/Other Person, Other & Unspecified
E887	5	Fracture, Cause Unspecified
E888	5	Other & Unspecified Fall
E890	5	Conflagration in Private Dwelling
E890.0	5	Explosion Caused by Conflagration
E890.1	5	Fumes From Combustion of Polyvinylchloride (PVC) & Similar Material in Conflagration
E890.2	5	Other Smoke & Fumes From Conflagration
E890.3	5	Burning Caused by Conflagration
E890.8	5	Other Accident Resulting From Conflagration
E890.9	5	Unspecified Accident Resulting From Conflagration in Private Dwelling
E891	5	Conflagration in Other & Unspecified Building or Structure
E891.0	5	Explosion Caused by Conflagration
E891.1	5	Fumes From Combustion of Polyvinylchloride (PVC) & Similar Material in Conflagration
E891.2	5	Other Smoke & Fumes From Conflagration
E891.3	5	Burning Caused by Conflagration
E891.8	5	Other Accident Resulting From Conflagration

E891.9	5	Unspecified Accident Resulting From Conflagration of Other & Unspecified Building or Structure
E892	5	Conflagration Not in Building or Structure
E893	5	Accident Caused by Ignition of Clothing
E893.0	5	Accident Caused by Ignition of Clothing From Controlled Fire in Private Dwelling
E893.1	5	Accident Caused by Ignition of Clothing From Controlled Fire in Other Building or Structure
E893.2	5	Accident Caused by Ignition of Clothing From Controlled Fire Not in Building or Structure
E893.8	5	Accident Caused by Ignition of Clothing From Other Specified Sources
E893.9	5	Accident Caused by Ignition of Clothing, Unspecified Source
E894	5	Ignition of Highly Inflammable Material
E895	5	Accident Caused by Controlled Fire in Private Dwelling
E896	5	Accident Caused by Controlled Fire in Other & Unspecified Building or Structure
E897	5	Accident Caused by Controlled Fire Not in Building or Structure
E898	5	Accident Caused by Other Specified Fire & Flames
E898.0	5	Accident Caused by Other Specified Fire & Flames, Burning Bedclothes
E898.1	5	Accident Caused by Other Specified Fire & Flames, Other
E899	5	Accident Caused by Unspecified Fire
E901	5	Excessive Cold
E910	5	Accidental Drowning & Submersion
E911	5	Inhalation & Ingestion of Food Causing Obstruction of Respiratory Tract or Suffocation
E917	5	Striking Against or Struck Accidentally by Objects or Persons
E918	5	Caught Accidentally in or Between Objects
E919	5	Accidents Caused by Machinery
E920	5	Accidents Caused by Cutting and Piercing Instruments or Objects
E922	5	Accident Caused by Firearm Missile
E980	5	Poisoning by Solid or Liquid Substances, Undetermined Whether Accidentally or Purposely Inflicted

Diagnostic Criteria for Alcohol Dependence

A. At least three of the following:

- Drinking in larger amounts or over a longer period than intended
- Persistent desire or one or more unsuccessful attempts to cut down
- Spending a great deal of time drinking or getting over the effects of drinking
- Frequent intoxication or withdrawal when expected to fulfill major role obligations, or when drinking is physically hazardous
- Important social, occupational, or recreational activities given up or reduced because of drinking
- Continuing to drink despite a persistent or recurrent social, psychological, or physical problem that is caused or exacerbated by drinking
- Tolerance
- Characteristic withdrawal state
- Drinking to relieve or avoid withdrawal symptoms

B. Some symptoms of the disturbance have persisted for at least 1 month, or have occurred over a longer period of time.

Diagnostic Criteria for Alcohol Abuse

A. A maladaptive pattern of drinking indicated by at least one of the following:

- Continuing to drink despite a persistent social, occupational, psychological, or physical problem that is caused or exacerbated by drinking
- Recurrent drinking in situations in which alcohol use is physically hazardous

B. Some symptoms of the disturbance have persisted for at least 1 month, or have occurred over a longer period of time.

C. Never met the criteria for alcohol dependence.

Figure 1. Diagnostic criteria for alcohol abuse and dependence commonly used in statewide prevalence surveys, based on DSM-III-R criteria.

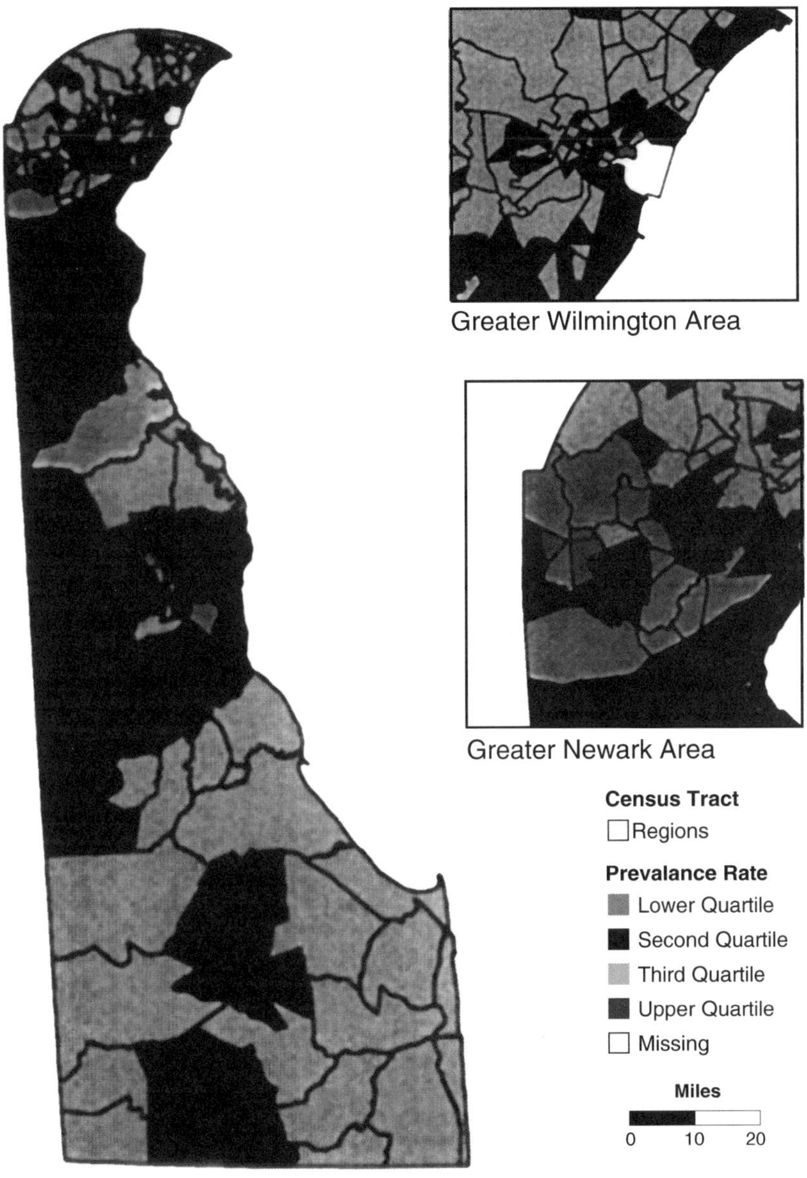

Figure 2. One-year DSM-III-R alcohol dependence and abuse rates by census tract, State of Delaware, 1993.

Table 1. Statewide 1-Year DSM-III-R Prevalence Rates for Alcohol Dependence and Abuse, State of Delaware, 1993.

Population Group	Dependence and Abuse (%)	Standard Error @ 0.05 (%)
Total males	8.54	3.08
18–29	20.29	9.49
30–44	5.45	4.24
45–64	6.33	4.71
65 and older	3.45	4.71
Total females	3.79	1.55
18–29	5.83	4.52
30–44	6.56	3.59
45–64	2.82	2.72
65 and older	?	?
Total	5.47	1.48
18–29	11.63	4.79
30–44	6.14	2.75
45–64	4.07	2.61
65 and older	0.0095	1.31

Note: Data are from the Delaware Statewide Survey of Alcohol and Drug Abuse, conducted by the University of Delaware (*N* = 907).

Table 2. 1-Year DSM-III-R Prevalence Rates for Alcohol Dependence and Abuse, Sussex County (DE), 1993.

Population Group	Dependence and Abuse (%)	Standard Error @ 0.05 (%)
Total males	10.25	6.73
18–29	35.71	25.09
30–44	7.69	10.24
45–64	5.55	10.57
65 and older	?	?
Total females	3.42	2.94
18–29	?	?
30–44	5.55	7.44
45–64	6.25	6.85
65 and older	?	?
Total	5.75	3.03
18–29	14.28	11.59
30–44	6.45	6.11
45–64	6.06	5.76
65 and older	?	?

Note: Data are from the Delaware Statewide Survey of Alcohol and Drug Abuse, conducted by the University of Delaware (*n* = 226).

Table 3. 1-Year DSM-III-R Prevalence Rates for Alcohol Dependence and Abuse (With Statewide Rates Added), Sussex County (DE), 1993.

Population Group	Dependence and Abuse (%)	Standard Error @ 0.05 (%)
Total males	10.25	6.73
18–29	20.29	9.49
30–44	7.69	10.24
45–64	5.55	10.57
65 and older	3.45	4.71
Total females	3.42	2.94
18–29	5.83	4.52
30–44	5.55	7.44
45–64	6.25	6.85
65 and older	?	?
Total	5.75	3.03
18–29	14.28	11.59
30–44	6.45	6.11
45–64	6.06	5.76
65 and older	0.0095	1.31

Note: Data are from the Delaware Statewide Survey of Alcohol and Drug Abuse, conducted by the University of Delaware ($n = 226$).

Table 4. 1-Year DSM-III-R Prevalence Rates for Alcohol Dependence and Abuse (With National Institute on Alcohol Abuse and Alcoholism [NIAAA] Rates Added), Sussex County (DE), 1993.

Population Group	Dependence and Abuse (%)	Standard Error @ 0.05 (%)
Total males	10.25	6.73
18–29	20.29	9.49
30–44	7.69	10.24
45–64	5.55	10.57
65 and older	2.77	0.34
Total females	3.42	2.94
18–29	10.10	0.45
30–44	5.55	7.44
45–64	6.25	6.85
65 and older	0.37	0.10
Total	5.75	3.03
18–29	14.28	11.59
30–44	6.45	6.11
45–64	6.06	5.76
65 and older	1.37	0.15

Note: Data are from the Delaware Statewide Survey of Alcohol and Drug Abuse, conducted by the University of Delaware ($n = 226$), and from an NIAAA study ($N = 42{,}809$) (Grant et al. 1991).

Table 5. Correlations Between Survey-Based DSM-III-R Estimates and Indicators From the Health Demographic Profile, and Between Survey-Based DSM-III-R Estimates and Alcohol-Related Mortality Ratio (1988–92), for 168 Census Tracts of Delaware.

Indicator	**Correlation Coefficient**
Socioeconomic status	
Unemployment rate	0.28*
Low occupational status rate	0.23*
Percentages of families in poverty	0.30*
Urbanization	
Overcrowded housing rate	0.35*
Percentage of detached-dwelling units	0.37*
Percentage of female-headed households	0.16*
Family functioning	
Percentage of divorced or separated males	0.14*
Percentage of divorced or separated females	0.08
Percentage of school-aged children not in school	0.23*
Alcohol-related mortality ratio	**0.20****

Note: Data are from the Delaware Statewide Survey of Alcohol and Drug Abuse, conducted by the University of Delaware, and from 1990 population census data (U.S. Bureau of the Census 1990) using the typology found in the Health Demographic Profile System (Goldsmith et al. 1984). The ICD-9 mortality codes used to compute the mortality ratios are shown in the appendix (Stinson and DeBakey 1992). A mortality ratio was computed for each census tract by dividing the number of deaths with one or more of the ICD-9 codes listed in the appendix by the total number of deaths in that census tract. The use of this unusually broad classification for alcohol-related deaths is essential in small geographic area estimations because of the small number of alcohol-related deaths registered at the tract level.

*$p < 0.01$; **$p < 0.05$.

Chapter 3

Small Area Analysis and GIS Technology: Incorporating Group Level Effects Into Explanatory Models

Richard Scribner, M.D., M.P.H.

KEY WORDS: geographical area; statistical estimation; information source; group as study subject; individual as study subject; theoretical study; location and density of AOD outlets; AOD availability; AOD use behavior; risk factors; neighborhood; epidemiology; suicide; Christianity; survey; literature review

If understanding and preventive efforts in alcohol research are to progress it is essential that we confront the empirical and theoretical challenges necessary to integrate group-level effects fully into our explanatory models.

—Bryan Johnstone (1994)

Group-level effects have long been considered outside the frame of explanation of alcohol research (Room 1988, p. 31). Yet interventions that target group-level factors have been demonstrated to be the most effective type of preventive intervention in the alcohol field (i.e., minimum drinking age laws and alcohol taxes) (Moskowitz 1989; Cook and Moore 1993; Wagenaar et. al. 1993). The explanation of this apparent paradox has been the

R. Scribner, M.D., M.P.H., is an associate professor at the School of Medicine, Louisiana State University Medical Center, 1600 Canal St., New Orleans, LA 70112.

inability of current alcohol research methods to integrate group-level risk into our explanatory models. This inability is due to a number of factors, including the absence of the appropriate data to characterize certain types of group-level variables and the lack of a suitable approach for conducting multilevel analyses of group-level effects. As a result, theories to explain group-level effects in terms of either their individual- or group-level components are limited.

The merger of small areas statistics and geographic information systems (GIS) mapping technology as well as recent progress in multilevel data analysis are two developments that suggest overcoming the challenge of integrating group-level effects may soon be possible. GIS-enabled small area statistics represents a paradigm platform in which the occurrence of disease outcomes can be explained in terms of both individual-level risk and group-level risk. This chapter is designed to characterize this capability.

The chapter is organized in four sections. In the first section, the empirical and theoretical challenges associated with incorporating the group-level risk factor alcohol outlet density are characterized. In the second section, varying perspectives on group-level effects from sociology and epidemiology are contrasted to clarify some of the confusion surrounding the nature of a group-level effect. In the third section, a conceptual model for characterizing group-level effects in statistical terms is provided. The final section provides an example of the concepts discussed using data from a multilevel analysis of the effect of alcohol outlet density at the census tract level on alcohol-related norms at the individual level.

THE CHALLENGES POSED BY GROUP-LEVEL EFFECTS

The first obstacle posed by group-level effects is in understanding what is meant by the term. For this discussion, *group-level effect* refers to a statistical relation between a group-level variable and an individual-level outcome. However a group-level effect has both an individual-level component and a group-level component, and either or both of these could account for a group-level effect. For example, the observed group-level effect of the variable "percent African American" on rates of assaultive violence in community-level studies has both an individual- and group-level component, each estimating separate constructs (Roberts 1997). At the individual level, percent African American represents the aggregate of acquired or inborn factors peculiar to African Americans that might account for the relatively high rate of violence in predominantly African American neighborhoods. At the neighborhood level, percent African American estimates the type of neighborhood African Americans tend to reside in, which may have an independent effect on violent behavior over and above the individual effects of race/ethnicity. For example, predominantly African American neighborhoods have higher densities of alcohol outlets. A group-level study using percent African American as a variable does not differentiate between these possibilities.

Differentiating between the individual- and group-level components is problematic because the fundamental unit of analysis for studying all disease outcomes is the individual (Von Korff et al. 1992). Therefore, the incorporation of group-level effects into our explanatory models requires a multilevel perspective. This fact is at the center of the challenge of integrating group-level effects into our explanatory models. A multilevel perspective requires both multilevel methods and multilevel theory, neither of which has been developed in alcohol prevention research, in particular, and behavioral research in general (Susser and Susser 1996; Sampson et al. 1997).

The Empirical Challenge

From the perspective of a researcher attempting to characterize the effect associated with the density of alcohol outlets, there are a number of empirical challenges associated with the development of a multilevel approach to study design. The first challenge involves the development of statistical models that permit multilevel analyses of group-level effects. The second challenge involves the identification of the unit of analysis that is most appropriate for modeling the effects of a variable like alcohol outlet density. The final challenge involves characterizing the individual- and group-level components of a variable like alcohol outlet density that is defined only at the group level.

Multilevel Models

The statistical methods that could permit testing of multilevel models by partitioning a group-level effect into its individual- and group-level components have only recently been developed. According to Bryk and Raudenbush (1992), it was not until the early 1980's that a conceptually feasible and broadly applicable approach to multilevel analysis was described and only in the past few years that computing programs became available. Prior to multilevel models, there were three types of analysis of multilevel data (Sirotnik 1980). First, there were analyses at the individual level that simply ignored group membership. Second, there were individual-level analyses that were conducted within groups and then averaged across group. Third, there were group-level analyses that used only the aggregated scores for groups and analyzed across groups. None of these methods of analysis is appropriate for characterizing group-level effects.

What a multilevel model does is decompose the multilevel relationships between the variables into their within-group and between-group components by partitioning the variance and covariance structures at the individual and group level (Raudenbush et al. 1991). This allows the formulation and testing of hypotheses about how variables at one level affect relations at another level.

Unit of Analysis

Identifying a unit of analysis that is appropriate for a hypothesized group-level effect is not an issue for a researcher with an individual-level perspective. From an individual-level perspective, any grouping of the data ideally represents the aggregate of the individual-level effects. The choice of a unit of analysis is more an issue of data availability than conscious selection. From a multilevel perspective, the choice of a unit of analysis becomes an important issue because it cannot be assumed that the individual-level component alone is responsible for a group-level relation. For example, if the group-level relation between alcohol outlet density and outcomes is due to the group-level component—i.e., aggregate demand for alcohol driven by neighborhood norms—that group-level component is defined at a particular unit of analysis (i.e., the neighborhood). The ideal unit of analysis for describing such an effect would be the neighborhood rather than the State. Consequently, a multilevel perspective demands that the choice of a unit of analysis be driven by the hypothesis being tested.

In fact, initial studies of the group-level effects of alcohol outlet density used data aggregated at the State or county level, and the results of these studies were equivocal (Smart 1977). It was only after studies of alcohol outlet density were conducted at more local units of analysis (e.g., city) that the strong relations between alcohol outlet density and alcohol-related outcomes were made (Watts and Rabow 1983; Scribner et. al. 1994, 1995; Gruenewald 1996*b*). Now, the georeferencing capabilities of GIS mapping programs not only permit analysis at even smaller units of analysis (e.g., census tract and block group) where the relationships continue to be strong (Scribner et al. 1999), but georeferenced data at the address level can be aggregated to any unit of analysis the hypothesis dictates.

The unit of analysis issue is compounded by the fact that spatial autocorrelation increases as the unit of analysis gets smaller (Chou 1991). Spatial autocorrelation refers to the degree to which entities with similar values cluster in space. Rather than viewing this as a problem, statistics measuring the degree of spatial autocorrelation (e.g., Moran's coefficient) may also prove useful in identifying the most appropriate unit for analysis. While the effect of spatial autocorrelation on the variance structure in small area analysis of alcohol outlet density is only beginning to be described (Gruenewald et al. 1996*a*), the use of spatial statistics as a research tool cannot be far off. Since spatial autocorrelation increases as map resolution increases, an approach that identifies the ideal level of analysis might involve a method of maximizing the size of the effect while at the same time minimizing spatial autocorrelation, much like adjusting the lens of a microscope to bring the image into focus.

Integral Variables Versus Contextual Variables

The final issue with regard to the empirical challenges of incorporating group-level effects into explanatory models has to do with the fact that many variables responsible for group-level effects are defined at the group level. Instead of being aggregated from individual-level data they are defined by the unit of analysis. This type of group-level variable is known as an *integral variable* because it is an "integral" component of the environment defined by the unit of analysis (Firebaugh 1979). In contrast, a group-level variable composed by aggregating an individual-level attribute to the group level is known as either a *nonintegral variable* or a *contextual variable* (Susser 1994).

Alcohol outlet density is a variable that is defined by the unit of analysis, therefore it is an integral variable. Alcohol outlets are a material part of the physical environments in which people reside. An individual does not have an alcohol outlet density apart from the unit of analysis the researcher selects. Consequently, an individual's alcohol outlet density is an integral aspect of living in a particular environment. In contrast, most of the variables that have been used in community-level research are contextual variables, variables aggregated to the level of the group (e.g., percent Hispanic, mean income, percent college educated). Contextual variables tend to describe the attributes of the people living in an environment rather than the environment itself.

Integral variables like alcohol outlet density pose a special problem for multilevel analysis. How do you know whether the effect of outlet density is due to the effect of individual proximity to alcohol outlets (i.e., high outlet density equates with closer average proximity) or due to the effect that the overall density of outlets has on the neighborhood environment? Either of these two constructs could account for the group-level effect observed for alcohol outlet density, one at the individual level and the other at the group level.

One way to address this problem is to transform an integral variable like alcohol outlet density into a contextual variable in order to partition its possible effects into individual- and group-level components. For alcohol outlet density this can be accomplished by collecting individual-level data on individual exposure to alcohol outlets from residents within a number of geographic areas. The individual scores can then be aggregated to obtain a mean score for each area. The individual scores would estimate the individual-level component, while the mean scores would estimate the group-level component. The degree to which mean exposure to alcohol outlets estimates the same group-level construct as alcohol outlet density can be estimated by the degree of correlation between the contextualized group-level variable, mean exposure to alcohol outlets, and the integral variable, alcohol outlet density.

The Theoretical Challenge

Separate theoretical models are needed to characterize the constructs estimated by the individual- and group-level components of a group-level effect for alcohol outlet density. In fact, alcohol outlet density is a variable that may have separate causal effects at both the individual level and group level. At the individual level, alcohol outlet density is likely to estimate the effect of proximity to alcohol outlets. The closer an individual resides to an alcohol outlet, the easier it is to obtain alcohol. Therefore, high alcohol outlet density indicates a higher availability of alcohol resulting in increased alcohol consumption and concomitant increase in alcohol-related outcomes (MacDonald and Whithead 1983) (see figure 1, p. 53).

At the group level, a causal effect for alcohol outlet density could be explained in terms of a dynamic relation between the concentration of alcohol outlets and community norms. As the normative pattern of drinking in a neighborhood becomes "wetter," outlet density responds. The increase in outlet density then results in even "wetter" drinking norms. This type of ratcheting process is characteristic of dynamic relations. Gruenewald and colleagues (1993) demonstrated reciprocal effects of this type for the relation between alcohol outlets and consumption in a time series analysis of State-level data.

However, the theoretical challenge is not as simple as describing competing group- and individual-level causal mechanisms. There is a fundamental difference between the mechanisms described. The mechanism described at the individual level represents a linear relationship between predictor and outcome (figure 1). An individual is exposed to an outlet, and that exposure results in an alcohol-related outcome. As shown in figure 1, the group-level variables in this model are merely indirect estimates of the causal relation at the individual level.

On the other hand, a causal effect for the group-level component of alcohol outlet density represents a nonlinear relationship (see figure 2, p. 53). The causal arrows go back and forth between the individual behavior and the behavioral norms to signify nonlinearity or a dynamic relation. This type of mechanism is peculiar to relations in which a group-level factor is responsible for the occurrence of an individual-level outcome (Koopman and Longini 1994). It is also the type of relation one would expect if alcohol norms represented a collectivity of drinking behavior. Skog (1985) described a collectivity as a population in which one individual's attitudes toward alcohol are dependent on the attitudes of all other individuals within the population.

Interestingly, this type of mechanism has been described in the infectious disease literature and is known as contagion (Susser 1994). The term *contagion* is unfortunate because it implies an infectious disease process. However, the concept merely implies a dynamic process in which one individual's outcome increases the risk of a subsequent outcome in the unaffected population. In other words, behavioral outcomes are not independent events; instead, the occurrence of a certain behavior (e.g., drinking in public) increases the chance that someone else in the community will perform the same behavior. For a contagious disease this is called a dependent happening, in which incidence depends on prevalence of disease currently existing in the population (Halloran and Struchiner 1991). The distinction between dependent and independent happenings was described over 80 years ago by Sir Ronald Ross (1916). For behavioral outcomes the same mechanism may apply. In certain circumstances the incidence of a behavior is dependent on the prevalence of the behavior currently within a group.

Using the contagion model, alcohol outlets can be viewed as a vector for transmission of alcohol-related behaviors in the neighborhood environment. Transmission of alcohol-related behaviors is promoted by the fact that on average more alcohol-related behaviors will be observed in neighborhoods where alcohol outlet density is higher (i.e., the perceived prevalence increases). Assuming the prevalence of the behavior has reached a level of saliency required to affect a change in perceived norms, the behavioral norms of the neighborhood will adapt as incidence increases. Once the norms of the neighborhood have been affected, even the behavior of "unexposed" individuals will be affected as they align their own behavior with the perceived norms of their community.

CONCEPTUAL DIFFERENCES IN CHARACTERIZING GROUP-LEVEL EFFECTS

In the absence of a multilevel approach in alcohol research, we must go outside the alcohol field for a discussion of group-level effects. Such a discussion is needed to address the misconceptions associated with the nature of group-level effects. The most important misconceptions are those associated with the term *ecological fallacy* (or *ecologic fallacy*). The literature on group-level effects tends to be divided between sociologists who acknowledge a role for group-level factors (Firebaugh 1978) and epidemiologists who tend to view group-level effects primarily in terms of ecological fallacy; that is, confounding and bias (Piantadosi et al. 1988; Greenland and Morgenstern 1989).

Sociologists like Firebaugh (1978) argue that group-level variables can and do have effects over and beyond those attributes of individual group members. In many cases sociologists label these effects as "structural" to acknowledge the role of external constraints in influencing individual behavior (Blau 1960). Sociologists trace the origins of this perspective to Emil Durkheim (Firebaugh 1978). Durkheim's treatise on suicide was the first to describe a group-level effect. Durkheim postulated that the "regulative action of society" affects individuals living in different regions with "unequal force," resulting in a "social suicide-rate" (Durkheim 1951, p. 241).

Epidemiology views group-level effects differently. Susser and Susser (1996) have described this view as the chronic disease epidemiology perspective. Chronic disease epidemiologists, faced with the task of identifying causes for chronic diseases of completely unknown origin, rely on understanding the complexities of design and causal inference in interpreting group-level data. Susser and Susser refer to this as a "black box" methodology, since what goes into the box are typically group-level data and what comes out is the most proximal risk factor (i.e., individual-level risk factor). The box is black because the processes going on inside the box, the place where theory is typically used to guide scientific inquiry, are hidden from view or absent in this case. In the place of theory is the assumption that a risk factor's statistical proximity to the biological outcome is synonymous with likelihood of causality. Consequently, when a chronic disease epidemiologist detects a group-level effect in an ecological association, it is assumed to be confounding or biasing the relation of interest between the proximal cause and the outcome. The possibility that the group-level effect could represent anything other than confounding or bias is not even a consideration. The unfortunate association of group-level effects with ecological fallacy has created a validity problem for researchers interested in a multilevel perspective. Schwartz (1994) has noted:

> Examining the issue from a different perspective—as a general validity problem—will show that the ecological fallacy, as often used, encourages three interrelated fallacious notions: 1) that individual-level models are more perfectly specified than ecological-level models, 2) that ecological correlations are always substitutes for individual-level correlations, and 3) that group-level factors do not cause disease. (p. 819)

In 1982 Morgenstern used Durkheim's analysis of the higher rates of suicide in Protestant countries compared with Catholic countries to demonstrate the danger of using ecological data for investigation of individual-level risk. Morgenstern's criticism of Durkheim's ecological analysis provides an ideal example of how the chronic disease perspective fails to acknowledge a role for group-level factors. In explaining ecological fallacy Morgenstern presented the following argument:

> The central problem, known as ecological fallacy, results from making a causal inference about individual phenomena on the basis of observations of groups. In Durkheim's data . . . it may have been the Catholics (not Protestants) who were committing suicide in predominantly Protestant provinces. Indeed it is quite plausible that members of a certain religious minority might have been more likely to take their own lives than were members of the majority . . . . In fact, Durkheim actually compared suicide rates for Protestants, Catholics and Jews living in Prussia . . . . The rate was about twice as great among Protestants as among other religious groups, suggesting a substantial difference between the results obtained at the ecological level (RR = 7.57) and those obtained at the individual level (RR = 2). Yet Durkheim failed to notice this quantitative difference because he did not actually estimate the magnitude of the effect in either analysis. (p. 1339)

Morgenstern's critique has two parts. First, he offers a hypothetical argument that has become famous among students of ecological analysis. It may in fact have been oppressed Catholics in predominantly Protestant countries who were committing suicide, not the Protestants, an effect that cannot be detected by group-level analysis alone. In the second part he abandons the oppressed Catholic argument and acknowledges that Durkheim's data do in fact show higher rates of suicide among the Protestants than the Catholics. Morgenstern goes on to point out Durkheim's "real" error, which is that he failed to notice that the relative risk measured at the individual level (RR = 2) was much smaller than the relative risk at the group level (RR = 7.57). It is clear that Morgenstern believes that by not distinguishing between the relative risk at the group level and the relative risk at the individual level, Durkheim missed out on the only meaningful aspect of the relationship, namely the relationship at the individual level. The point Morgenstern fails to acknowledge, as do most chronic disease epidemiologists, is that the percent Protestant variable measures different constructs at the individual and the group levels. Ironically, the primary reason Durkheim's treatise on suicide is remembered today is because he did go on to identify a group-level factor that accounts for the inflated relative risk at the ecological level (Durkheim 1951).

At the individual level Durkheim argued that the percent Protestant variable is a measure of the protective effect of religious integration typical of individuals of the Catholic and Jewish faiths compared with Protestants. This effect Durkheim acknowledged as a within-group or individual-level cause of suicide that he termed "egoistic suicide" (Durkheim 1951). At the group level Durkheim coined the term *anomy*, a state of social and individual deregulation, to account for the group-level effect of the percent Protestant variable. He argued that a major factor contributing to anomy is divorce, which is highly correlated with suicide: "when one is no longer checked (in marriage), one becomes unable to check one's self" (p. 271). He therefore reasoned that laws liberalizing divorce were responsible for the higher rates of suicide in predominantly Protestant countries, where the liberal divorce laws were more common due to the liberal nature of Protestant society compared with Catholic society. Protestants as well as Catholics and Jews living in predominantly Protestant countries would have higher rates of divorce and subsequent suicide independent of the individual-level effect of religious identification due to the group-level effect of liberal divorce laws. Consequently, the variable percent Protestant measures an entirely different construct at the group level compared with the individual level.

Today the between-group effects are described with many different terms. Sociologists call it a structural effect (Blau 1960), statisticians in school-based research call it a compositional or contextual effect (Bryk and Raudenbush 1992), and some epidemiologists call it a group-level effect. Unfortunately, the chronic disease perspective within epidemiology continues to use the term *aggregation bias.* To suggest that only the individual-level component of an ecological association is valid has more to do with the limitations of the perspective of chronic disease epidemiologists than with the validity of group-level effects.

A CONCEPTUAL MODEL FOR DESCRIBING THE GROUP-LEVEL COMPONENT OF A GROUP-LEVEL EFFECT

Whether a group-level effect estimates an individual-level or a group-level construct can be analyzed by partitioning the effect into its group- and individual-level components. The group- and individual-level components of a group-level relation can be demonstrated graphically using regression coefficients to describe the component effects. The slopes of three regression coefficients are needed to describe these components: (1) β_g is the group-level or ecological coefficient that describes the relation between groups usually measured as the group mean, (2) β_i is the overall or total individual-level coefficient that describes the relation among all individuals across all groups, and (3) β_a is the average of the individual-level coefficients within each group—weighted by the sum of the squares for the group—that describes the individual-level effect across all groups without the effects of grouping. It is widely acknowledged that in most research applications the coefficient of interest in estimating individual-level effects is β_a rather than β_i, because β_a removes the effect of the grouping (i.e., the group-level component) (Firebaugh 1978; Piantadosi et al. 1988; Bryk and Raudenbush 1992, p. 119).

To further aid the conceptualization of multilevel data, the distribution of individual data points for each group can be represented as an ellipse—four groups, four ellipses (see figure 3, p. 54). The boundary of the ellipse represents the boundary of an imaginary scatter plot for all individuals within group. A point at the center of each ellipse represents the plot of the mean values for the predictor and the outcome variable for each group. A line down the long axis of each ellipse would represent the individual-level regression coefficient for each group. The average of these coefficients could then be generated to provide the average within-group, individual-level coefficient, β_a.

From the individual-level perspective, the ideal situation occurs when the group-level relation is the same as the individual-level relation. In other words, the group-level regression coefficient equals the individual-level regression coefficients $\beta_i=\beta_a=\beta_g$. In this situation there is only the individual-level component of the group-level effect to account for the relation. This relation is pictured in figure 3. In this graph the group-level coefficient β_g is represented by the regression line approximating the relation between the means of each group (i.e., the points located in the center of the ellipses). The average for all the individual-level coefficients within groups, β_a, is represented by a line parallel to the long axis of the four ellipses. The overall individual-level coefficient β_i is represented by the line drawn through the long axis of the large ellipse, which approximates the boundaries of a scatter plot drawn around the plots of all individuals across all groups. As shown in the diagram, these coefficients are all equal with the same intercept. This example indicates a situation when the individual-level component of the group-level effect accounts for all of the effect that would be observed in group-level analysis.

The case in which the group-level component accounts for all the effect is shown in figure 4 (see p. 54). In this case the group-level coefficient, β_g, again estimates the group-level effect and is represented by the same line as in figure 3, that is, the line approximating the relation between the means for each group.

What is different in this graph is that the four ellipses demonstrating the relation between the predictor and the outcome at the individual level within each group are horizontal, indicating $\beta_a = 0$. However, the coefficient for the group-level relation remains strongly positive. The overall individual-level coefficient, β_i, is represented by the large ellipse surrounding all groups. It can be seen that β_i is affected by both the individual-level and group-level components of the relation. The slope of β_i always lies somewhere between β_a and β_g when the two are different (Piantadosi et al. 1988). Figure 4 demonstrates the partitioning of the group- and individual-level components of the group-level effect. When the effect is partitioned it can be shown that the group-level predictor, the group means of the variable *X*, estimates a different construct that the individual-level predictor, the individual value for the variable *X*. The fact that the group-level construct accounts for the overall relation indicates that some property of the group itself causes the occurrence of the outcome.

THE EFFECT OF ALCOHOL OUTLET DENSITY AT THE GROUP AND INDIVIDUAL LEVELS

An example of the concepts discussed thus far is provided by the Louisiana Alcohol Policy Needs Assessment Database (LAPNAD). The LAPNAD was developed to validate the use of alcohol outlet density as an indicator of policy need using small area analyses of GIS-enabled data. Studies using LAPNAD data have successfully demonstrated group-level relations between alcohol outlet density and various related outcomes (e.g., homicide rates) (Scribner et. al. in press). The validity of alcohol outlet density as an indicator of policy need depends on whether the observed group-level effects are due to an individual-level component or a group-level component. Therefore, validation requires multilevel analysis to partition the effects into their group and individual components.

In the interest of simplicity the analysis presented here is analogous to the conceptual model presented above. Regression coefficients from group-level analysis β_g (i.e., census tracts), individual-level analysis ignoring group β_i, and individual-level analysis averaging across groups β_a are presented for the relation between exposure to alcohol outlets and a 15-item index of alcohol norms. The analysis also involves a number of methodological issues relevant to small area analysis, including (1) the development of a sampling methodology for conducting telephone surveys at the census tract level using GIS georeferencing capabilities, (2) the contextualization of alcohol outlet density for analysis at the group and individual level, and (3) the use of group-level and individual-level regression models for distinguishing between group- and individual-level effects. A complete description of the study is published elsewhere (Scribner et al. 2000).

GIS-TARGETED TELEPHONE SURVEY

One of the problems facing small area analysis, if it is to emerge as a separate discipline within epidemiology, is the need to validate the group-level associations with individual-level data. This is problematic because the individual-level data must be geographically nested at a relevant unit of analysis. Given the large number of individual surveys required to enable comparisons both within groups and between groups, face-to-face interviews are impractical for a number of reasons. On the other hand, telephone surveys using random-digit dial (RDD) methodologies are practical, but they do not have the geographic specificity to target the small geographic areas of interest. GIS mapping technology offers a practical solution. By geocoding automated telephone registries to address and then aggregating the geocoded telephone households using GIS boundary files, telephone sampling frames can be generated for any unit of analysis desired. The drawback for this methodology compared with traditional RDD surveys is the exclusion of unlisted telephone numbers from the sample.

Such a methodology was used in the LAPNAD. A registry-based telephone survey of georeferenced telephone households was conducted at the census tract level in 24 census tracts of New Orleans (N = 2,608). The 24 census tracts were selected from the universe of urban residential census tracts in New Orleans with populations greater than 1,000 (N = 145). Study census tracts were selected by dividing eligible census tracts into quartiles based on the percentage of households in poverty and selecting three pairs of census tracts with the highest and lowest alcohol outlet density from each quartile.

Sampling frames were generated from georeferenced lists of all residential telephone households within each census tract. Sampling frames consisted of approximately seven randomly chosen telephone households per frame. Once the sampling frames were generated, the procedure was the same as for any RDD survey.

Contextualization of Alcohol Outlet Density

The notion of contextualizing an integral variable like alcohol outlet density represents a conceptual linchpin for linking an abstract concept like alcohol outlet density to a material factor in the environment. Historically, the demonstration of structural effects has been limited to contextual variables derived by aggregating individual-level data. Consequently, the aggregated variable represents an abstract concept (e.g., percent unemployed, percent households in poverty, mean level of education) rather than the material feature of the environment (e.g., alcohol outlet density, density of vacant housing).

To assess the effect of alcohol outlets at the group and individual level, the integral variable (alcohol outlet density) had to be contextualized. This was accomplished by using a survey item to assess individual proximity to the closest alcohol outlet where alcohol could be purchased for off-site, retail consumption. The individual scores were then aggregated for each of the 24 census tracts to obtain a mean proximity to alcohol outlets for each census tract. The aggregated mean for proximity to alcohol outlets for study census tracts was strongly correlated (r = 0.75) with alcohol outlet density, indicating that it is a reliable surrogate for alcohol outlet density. The result of this procedure is an individual- and group-level measure of alcohol outlet density assessing the group- and individual-level components of the group-level effect.

Individual- and Group-Level Regression Models

For this example three types of regression coefficients are presented to demonstrate how the effect of proximity to alcohol outlets can be partitioned in its individual- and group-level components. The outcome variable for the analysis was a 15-item index of alcohol norms. The regression coefficient for the individual-level effect of individual proximity to alcohol outlets on alcohol norms for all individuals (N = 2,608) across all census tracts is represented by β_i. The regression coefficient for the average individual-level effect of individual proximity to alcohol outlets within each census tract is represented by β_a. Finally, the group-level effect of mean proximity to alcohol outlets (i.e., the contextualized surrogate for alcohol outlet density) on alcohol norms between census tracts (N = 24) is represented by β_g.

Proximity to alcohol outlets was scaled from 0 (a mile or more away from the closest outlet) to 10 (next door to the closest outlet), and individual scores were centered on the grand mean for the total sample. Positive values mean closer proximity to alcohol outlets. Alcohol norms were estimated using 15 survey items assessing the respondents' attitudes toward drinking. The resulting index was scaled from 1 to 10, with 1 representing the most conservative attitudes and 10 representing the most liberal attitudes.

The results indicate that after controlling for the effect of age, race, and sex, the magnitude of the effect for proximity to alcohol outlets on alcohol norms at the individual level is extremely small. The coefficient for the average effect across all census tracts at the individual level is virtually nonexistent (β_a = 0.0026), indicating no relationship. On the other hand, the effect of mean proximity to alcohol outlets at the census tract level was an order of magnitude larger (β_g = 0.132). The coefficient for the individual-level effect across all census tracts was also positive but small (β_i = 0.012), indicating the biasing effect of β_g on β_i. These relations can be graphed to demonstrate the results in terms of the conceptual model presented earlier (see figure 5, p. 55). The results suggest that the group-level component of the group-level relation between alcohol outlet density and various alcohol-related outcomes accounts for the relation. This means that individuals with similar attitudes toward alcohol are grouped together in neighborhoods and that grouping is predicted by alcohol outlet density.

The implications of these results are significant. Whether or not alcohol outlet density drives alcohol-related behavior in a neighborhood or merely reflects the aggregate demand, differences in alcohol norms do exist at the neighborhood level and those differences can be predicted by alcohol outlet density. Combined with research indicating that the relation between outlet density and consumption represents a reciprocal relation (Gruenewald et al. 1993), these results are consistent with a causal model in which individual alcohol consumption is both reflected and driven by the density of alcohol outlets in a neighborhood (see figure 2). If these results can be validated with longitudinal data, it would represent a paradigmatically distinct approach to explaining the occurrence of alcohol-related problems.

SUMMARY

Small area analysis is the study of group-level effects. Incorporating these group-level effects into explanatory models has always posed empirical and theoretical challenges for alcohol prevention research. The merging of small area statistics with GIS mapping technology and the availability of multilevel models indicate that these challenges may no longer represent an obstacle. The empirical challenges involve three issues: (1) statistical methods for partitioning group-level effects into their group- and individual-level components, (2) identifying the appropriate unit of analysis for analysis purposes, and (3) differentiating between the effects of various types of group-level variables (i.e., integral vs. contextual variables). The theoretical challenge revolves around widely held misconceptions regarding the potential for group-level factors to cause behavioral outcomes. Incorporating group-level effects into our explanatory models requires a multilevel perspective. Within this perspective both group- and individual-level factors are viewed as potential sources for a causal relation.

The group-level relation between alcohol outlet density and numerous alcohol-related outcomes provides an example where a multilevel perspective is useful. Using small area analysis techniques enabled by GIS mapping technology, the group-level effect associated with alcohol outlet density at the neighborhood level can be partitioned into its group- and individual-level components. Once partitioned it can be shown that the group-level component is responsible for the overall relation. Mean exposure to alcohol outlets, the contextualized surrogate for alcohol outlet density, predicts neighborhood alcohol norms, and those differences are reflected in individual attitudes toward alcohol. This relation is consistent with explanatory models that are paradigmatically distinct from current models used in alcohol prevention research.

REFERENCES

Blau, P.M. Structural effects. *Am Sociol Rev* 25:178–193, 1960.

Bryk, A.S., and Raudenbush, S.W. *Hierarchical Linear Models.* Newbury Park, CA: Sage Publications, 1992.

Chou, Y.H. Map resolution and spatial autocorrelation. *Geographical Analysis* 23:229–245, 1991.

Cook, P.J., and Moore, M.J. Taxation of alcoholic beverages. In: Hilton, M.E., and Bloss, G., eds. *Economics and the Prevention of Alcohol-Related Problems.* NIAAA Research Monograph No. 25. NIH Pub No. 95–3513. Rockville, MD: National Institute on Alcohol Abuse and Alcoholism, 1993. pp. 33–58.

Durkheim, E. *Suicide.* New York: Knickerbocker Press, 1951.

Firebaugh, G. A rule for inferring individual-level relationships from aggregate data. *Am Sociol Rev* 43:557–572, 1978.

Firebaugh, G. Assessing group effects: A comparison of two methods. *Sociological Methods Research* 7:384–395, 1979.

Greenland, S., and Morgenstern, H. Ecological bias, confounding, and effect modification. *Int J Epidemiol* 18:269–274, 1989.

Gruenewald, P.J.; Ponicki, W.R.; and Holder, H.D. The relationship of outlet densities to alcohol consumption: A time series cross sectional analysis. *Alcohol Clin Exp Res* 17:38–47, 1993.

Gruenewald, P.J.; Millar, A.B.; and Roeper, P. Access to alcohol: Geography and prevention for local communities. *Alcohol Health Res World* 20(4):244–251, 1996*a*.

Gruenewald, P.J.; Millar, A.B.; Treno, A.J.; Ponicki, W.R.; Yang, Z.; and Roeper, P. The geography of availability and driving after drinking. *Addiction* 91:967–983, 1996*b*.

Halloran, M.E., and Struchiner, C.J. Study designs for dependent happenings. *Epidemiology* 2:331–338, 1991.

Johnstone, B.M. Sociodemographic, environmental, and cultural influences on adolescent drinking behavior. In: Zucker, R.; Boyd, G.; and Howard, J. eds. *The Development of Alcohol Problems: Exploring the Biopsychosocial Matrix of Risk.* NIAAA Research Monograph No. 26. NIH Pub. No. 94–3495. Rockville, MD: National Institute on Alcohol Abuse and Alcoholism, 1994. pp. 169–203.

Koopman, J.S, and Longini, I.M. The ecological effects of individual exposures and nonlinear disease dynamics in populations. *Am J Public Health* 84:836–842, 1994.

Morgenstern, H. Uses of ecologic analysis in epidemiologic research. *Am J Public Health* 72:1336–1344, 1982.

Moskowitz, J. The primary prevention of alcohol problems: A critical review of the research literature. *J Stud Alcohol* 50:54–88, 1989.

Piantadosi, S.; Byar, D.P.; and Green, S.B. The ecologic fallacy. *Am J Epidemiol* 127:893–903, 1988.

Raudenbush, S.W.; Rowan, B.; and Kang, S.J. A multilevel, multivariate model for studying school climate with estimation via the EM algorithm and application to US high school data. *Journal of Educational Statistics* 16:295–330, 1991.

Roberts, E.M. Neighborhood social environment and the distribution of low birthweight in Chicago. *Am J Public Health* 87:597–603, 1997.

Room, R. Cross-cultural research in alcohol studies: Research traditions and analytical issues. In: Towle, L.H., and Harford, T.C. eds. *Cultural Influences and Drinking Patterns: A Focus on Hispanic and Japanese Populations.* NIAAA Research Monograph No. 19. NIH Pub No. 88–1563. Washington, DC: U.S. Government Printing Office, 1988. pp. 9–40.

Ross, R. An application of the theory of probabilities to the study of a priori pathometry. Part 1. *Proc R Soc A* 92:204–230, 1916.

Sampson, R.J.; Raudenbush, S.W.; and Earls, F. Neighborhoods and violent crime: A multilevel study of collective efficacy. *Science* 277:918–924, 1997.

Scribner, R.A.; MacKinnon, D.P.; and Dwyer, J.H. Alcohol outlet density and motor vehicle crashes in Los Angeles County cities. *J Stud Alcohol* 55:447–453, 1994.

Scribner, R.A.; MacKinnon, D.P.; and Dwyer, J.H. The risk of assaultive violence and alcohol availability in Los Angeles County. *Am J Public Health* 85:335–340, 1995.

Scribner, R.A.; Cohen, D.; Kaplan, S.; and Allen, S.H. Alcohol availability and homicide in New Orleans: Conceptual considerations for small area analysis of the effect of alcohol outlet density. *J Stud Alcohol*, 60:310–316, 1999.

Scribner, R.A.; Cohen, D.A.; and Fisher, W. Evidence of a structural effect for alcohol outlet density: A multilevel analysis. *Alcohol Clin Exp Res* 24:188–195, 2000.

Schwartz, S. The fallacy of the ecological fallacy: The potential misuse of a concept and the consequences. *Am J Public Health* 84:819–824, 1994.

Sirotnik, K.A. Psychometric implication of the unit-of-analysis problem (with examples from the measurement of organizational climate). *Journal of Educational Measurement* 17:245–281, 1980.

Skog, O. The collectivity of drinking cultures: A theory of the distribution of alcohol consumption. *Br J Addict* 80:83–99, 1985.

Smart, R.G. The relationship of availability of alcoholic beverages to per capita consumption and alcoholism rates. *J Stud Alcohol* 38:891–896, 1977.

Susser, M. The logic in ecological: I. The logic of analysis. *Am J Public Health* 84:825–829, 1994.

Susser, M., and Susser, E. Choosing a future for epidemiology: I. Eras and paradigms. *Am J Public Health* 86:668–673, 1996.

Von Korff, M.; Loepsell, T.; Curry, S.; and Diehr, P. Multi-level analysis in epidemiologic research on health behaviors and outcomes. *Am J Epidemiol* 135:1077–1082, 1992.

Wagenaar, A.C. Minimum drinking age and alcohol availability to youth: Issues and research needs. In: Hilton, M.E., and Bloss, G., eds. *Economics and the Prevention of Alcohol-Related Problems.* NIAAA Research Monograph No. 25. NIH Pub. No. 95–3513. Rockville, MD: National Institute on Alcohol Abuse and Alcoholism, 1993. pp. 175–200.

Watts, R.K., and Rabow, J. Alcohol availability and alcohol-related problems in 213 California cities. *Alcohol Clin Exp Res* 7(1):47–57, 1983.

Whitehead, P.C., and Macdonald, S. Availability of outlets and consumption of alcoholic beverages. *J Drug Issues* 13(4):477–486, 1983.

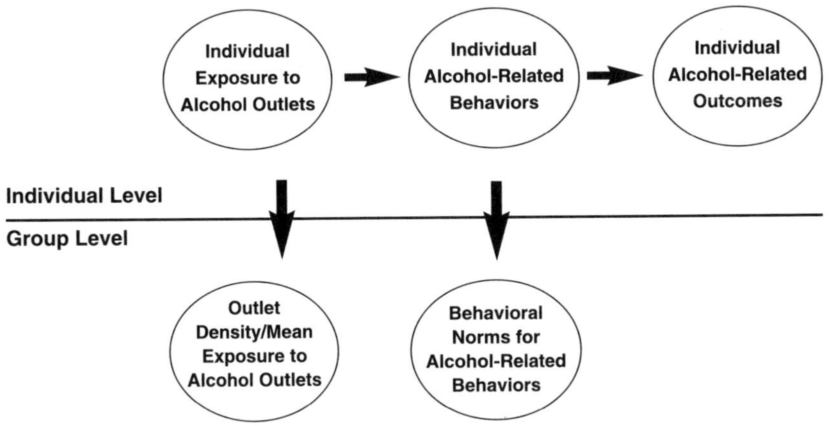

Figure 1. Individual-level perspective of the effect of alcohol outlet density on alcohol-related norms. Norms are viewed as indirect measures of causal factors at the individual level.

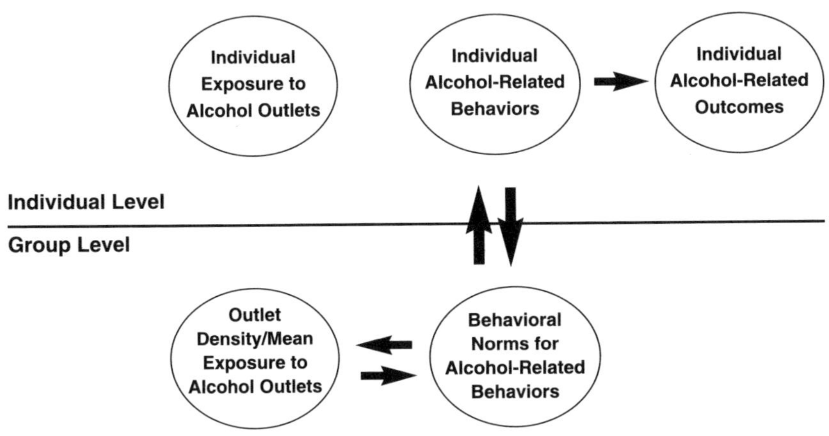

Figure 2. Group-level perspective of the effect of alcohol outlet density on alcohol-related norms. The mechanism involves a dynamic model.

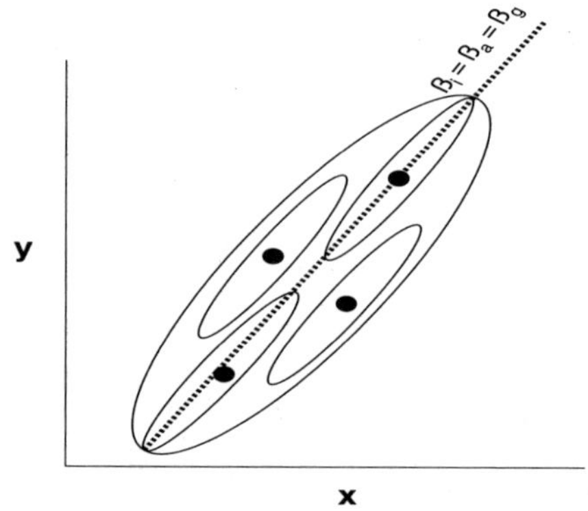

Figure 3. Group-level effect due to the individual-level component of the relation. The small ellipses represent the distribution of individuals within groups; the large ellipse represents the distribution of all individuals across groups. The points represent the within-group means.

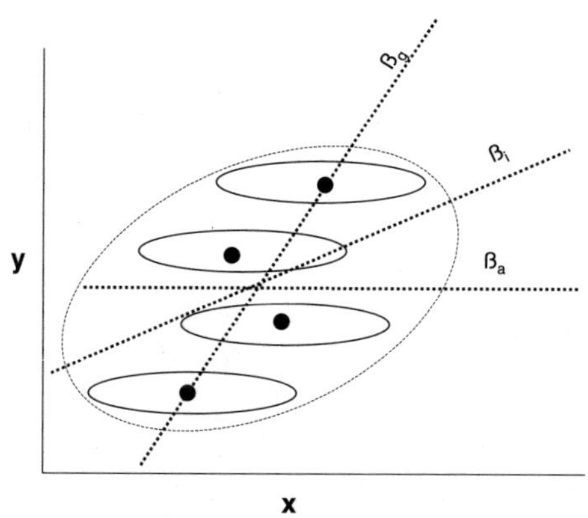

Figure 4. Group-level effect due to the group-level component of the relation. The small ellipses represent the distribution of individuals within groups; the large ellipse represents the distribution of all individuals across groups. The points represent the within-group means.

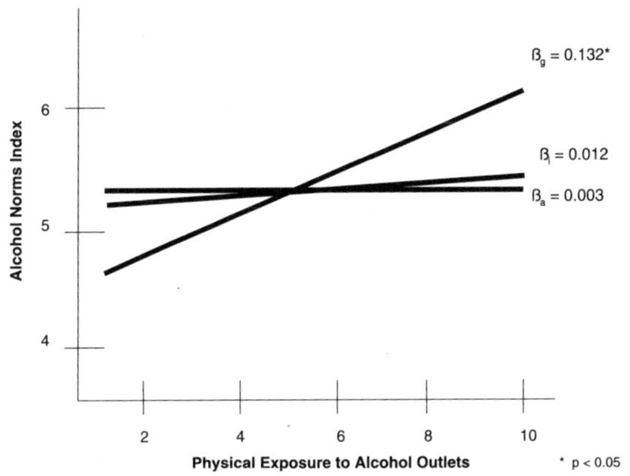

Figure 5. Three estimates of the relationship between exposure to alcohol outlets and the alcohol norms index using the same data. The census tract or group-level coefficient is represented by β_g; the individual-level coefficient is represented by β_i; and the average, individual-level, within-group coefficient is represented by β_a.
**p*<0.005.

Chapter 4

Estimating Alcohol Problems in Small Areas: Contrasting Data Sources, Definitions, and Measures

Laura A. Schmidt, Ph.D., and Constance M. Weisner, Dr.P.H.

KEY WORDS: statistical estimation; geographical area; information source; disorder definition; demographic characteristics; survey; evaluation; California; problematic AOD use; health care delivery; patient admission; patient discharge; DWI arrest; public drunkenness; traffic accident; AOD availability; AODR mortality; data collection; literature review

Alcohol problems can be defined in a variety of different ways, and depending on the data available and on the purposes to which they are being put, there are a number of acceptable approaches for operationalization and measurement. The differences between competing definitions of the alcohol problems—alcohol dependence, problem drinking, abuse, harm, and separate indicators of alcohol-related problems—may seem rather abstract and technical. However, decisions about how to define alcohol problems and what data to use to measure them have important consequences for the practical planning situations that communities and their decision-makers find themselves in. Different definitions of alcohol problems reflect fundamentally different disciplinary frames, ranging from medical to "social problems" perspectives on the problem (Room 1980; Institute of Medicine 1990). But they also reflect differing views on how serious an alcohol problem needs to be before intervention is called for, and on which authorities in the community should rightly claim "ownership of

L.A. Schmidt, Ph.D., is a scientist with the Alcohol Research Group, Public Health Institute, 2000 Hearst Ave., Suite 300, Berkeley, CA 94709, and is also affiliated with the Department of Sociology, University of California at Berkeley. C.M. Weisner, Dr.P.H., wrote this chapter while employed as a senior scientist with the Alcohol Research Group, Public Health Institute. She is currently a professor at the Department of Psychiatry, University of California, San Francisco.

the problem" (Gusfield 1981). Ultimately, alternative conceptions of drinking problems lead communities to draw different boundaries around the population in need of services and to sponsor different kinds of interventions. While studies of dependence say something about the need for intensive medical services, data on problem drinking and abuse say more about what kinds of screening, referral, and early intervention programs are needed. Separate indicators of alcohol-related problems may speak to the need for particular harm reduction and prevention approaches, such as drinking and driving programs, community-level interventions, and educational campaigns.

In practical situations of planning for treatment and prevention services at the local level, decisionmakers are likely to use whatever data are on hand. Typically, they will be choosing from among three different sources of data and, in the process, will be making commitments to one or more abstract definitions of alcohol problems. One approach, which is increasingly being adopted in the United States, is to conduct a survey of the region's household population that incorporates standardized instruments for measuring alcohol problems. While this is often viewed as the most rigorous, reliable, and flexible approach, it has its drawbacks besides the obviously high costs of implementation. General population surveys have, for example, come under recent public scrutiny. They can produce biased estimates due to the underreporting of drug use and the exclusion of nonhousehold populations in which problems of substance abuse are overrepresented (nonhousehold populations are those people living in nonconventional housing units and institutions such as homes for the elderly, jails, welfare hotels, and residential treatment programs) (General Accounting Office 1993). Two far less costly alternatives, which are often taken by State and regional authorities for substance abuse, are to compile prevalence estimates from institutional records or from the reports of service providers about their caseloads. These strategies have other limitations involving serious constraints on how alcohol problems can be measured, problems with maintaining comparability across the measures that are available, institutional reporting bias, and difficulties with obtaining an unduplicated count of problem drinkers from a range of institutional settings, given that some individuals use multiple services.

The purpose of this chapter is to evaluate the different kinds of data and measures that are available for studying alcohol problems in small areas, and to consider the different vantage points that these sources of information provide on the size and demographic profile of populations in need of alcohol services. We will review some of the strengths and limitations of general population surveys, providers' estimates, and social indicators as methods for evaluating the size and distribution of problem-drinking populations. For each approach, we will also compare and contrast some results on drinking problems, by comparing these three sources of data in a single northern

California county (for methodological background on each data source, see the appendix to this chapter). We have chosen to focus on a single county because it is at this level of government that the organizing and planning of public services goes on in most States. A county also provides a contained geographic region that facilitates collecting and comparing the different types of data that are typically used to analyze drinking practices and problems.

While certainly unique, the county we chose to study encompasses much of the ethnic and socioeconomic diversity that is characteristic of the larger U.S. population. The county is located southeast of San Francisco, it is ethnically diverse, and the most recent estimates (based on the U.S. census projections for 1993) put its population at 855,109 people. The population is relatively affluent, with a median housing value for owner-occupied units of $219,400 and an average monthly rent contract of $613. But there are also some inner-city areas that meet Federal criteria as poverty zones, and some rural areas occupied by low-income enclaves of seasonal farm workers. The county includes 18 cities in which about 70 percent of the population resides, including several self-contained industrial cities where steel production is the major industry, and several middle-class bedroom communities.

GENERAL POPULATION SURVEYS OF DRINKING PRACTICES

Although epidemiologic surveys of the general population have the most potential for providing accurate information on the magnitude of alcohol problems in communities, high costs and other logistical constraints may prohibit their extensive use by local planners and decisionmakers. General population studies are hardly immune from methodological problems, and their precision can be easily overestimated by public and political consumers of statistical information (see, for example, discussions of false precision in the political uses of research on substance use during pregnancy: Koren et al. 1989; Knupfer 1991; Kaskutas 1995).

One of the perennial problems with general population surveys involves the tendency of survey participants to underreport their use of alcohol and other drugs, particularly where the use is illicit. All respondents may underreport their drinking or, even more problematically, reporting bias may be unevenly distributed across groups of respondents whose drinking is subject to different degrees of stigmatization. Methodological studies have confirmed what seems intuitively plausible—that surveys are more susceptible to this form of bias when questions about substance use cover long periods of time, when the behavior in question is highly stigmatized, and when respondents fear for their anonymity (Collins et al. 1985; for reviews, see Harrell 1985 and Midanik 1988). Some studies have found variations in self-report bias for surveys conducted by phone as opposed to in-person interviews and variations by particular qualities of the interviewer. For example, in a classic set of studies, Mulford and Miller (1959, 1960,

1964) found that interviewers who themselves drank were able to elicit reports of more drinking from respondents than interviewers who abstained. The careful wording of questions, efforts to match interviewers and respondents on demographic characteristics, and the collateral interviewing of family members and friends about the respondent's drinking are common methods for reducing self-report bias (National Institute on Drug Abuse [NIDA] 1985). Indirect survey-based estimation is another method for obtaining estimates of substance use that are less subject to reporting bias. The national surveys on drug use conducted by NIDA, for example, have used a "nominative estimation technique" that projects estimates for groups based on asking respondents to report on a close friend's illicit drug use rather than on their own use (Miller 1985).

General population surveys of alcohol and drug use have also come under fire for excluding substantial segments of nonhousehold populations (Smart 1985; NIDA 1991; General Accounting Office 1993). The exclusion of nonhousehold populations can introduce systematic bias into survey-based estimates of substance abuse in small areas. In our own analyses of drinking in the study county selected for this chapter, we have turned up evidence that drinking problems are overrepresented in the kinds of institutional populations that general population surveys typically exclude (Weisner et al. 1995). We measured drinking problems in the county's household population using the standard protocol of sampling blocks, listing dwellings on selected blocks, and then sampling individuals within selected dwellings. But we also measured drinking problems among clients throughout the county's health and welfare system populations, as people were being admitted to services. We found that 17 percent of the people entering alcohol, drug, mental health, welfare, and criminal justice agencies in the county did not live in housing units that would have been included in our general population survey's sampling frame. The prevalence of problem drinking within this group was 43.8 percent, compared with 11.3 percent in the household population. This suggests that by excluding nonhousehold populations from general population studies, we are likely to come up with downwardly biased estimates of alcohol problems. Statistics on the county's population size further suggested that the combined size of the nonhousehold populations left out of the general population survey was large enough to introduce meaningful bias into estimates based solely on the household survey. Some researchers have argued that in national samples, the size of excluded nonhousehold populations may not be large enough to seriously bias overall prevalence estimates (Kessler et al. 1997). But it could still influence estimates of prevalence within particular ethnic or socioeconomic groups.

One solution to this problem is to include household and nonhousehold populations within the same sampling frame, although obtaining complete coverage of a region can be a significant challenge. The National Institute of Mental Health's Epidemiologic Catchment Area (ECA) studies examined the distribution of mental illnesses in five selected metropolitan areas of the United States. They not only sampled households, but also certain types of institutions located within the areas sampled, including nursing homes, long-term mental hospitals, and penal institutions (Helzer and Pryzbeck 1988; Robins and Regier 1991). While this may be possible for regional surveys, it would be quite difficult to do in the context of a national survey that was attempting to make estimates for the U.S. population as a whole. And it was not possible in the ECA studies to completely control for the duplication of respondents across institutional and household settings, although the researchers collected some information on respondents' service use (Narrow et al. 1993). A slightly different approach was taken in the Washington DC Metropolitan Area Drug Study (DC*MADS) sponsored by NIDA, which separately sampled institutional and homeless populations at the same time as conducting a household population survey in the same metropolitan area (NIDA 1992*b*).

One of the main advantages of general population surveys is that they allow researchers to include a broad range of measures of alcohol problems. The most common measures represent a range of degrees of severity and operationalization. Alcohol dependence suggests that a person would likely need considerable help to stop drinking because of serious physical and psychological symptoms. Alcohol abuse, harm, and problem drinking are defined by much lower thresholds of severity, and suggest that while social functioning or health may be impaired, physical and psychological compulsions are not yet a major aspect of the problem. Disaggregated indicators of alcohol problems—including specific health, psychological, and social consequences related to drinking, such as liver cirrhosis, drunken driving, and alcohol-related crimes—suggest a social problems perspective. With this perspective, one need make no assumptions about an underlying condition or disease entity such as alcoholism or addiction; rather, the various manifestations of heavy drinking are simply taken at face value (for discussions, see Cahalan et al. 1969 and Room 1977).

It is precisely, however, because of the flexibility in measurement that general population surveys afford that there are often inconsistencies in how different measures of alcohol problems are operationalized across studies and in off-the-shelf instruments designed for general population research, such as the *Composite International Diagnostic Interview* and the *Diagnostic Interview Schedule* (Robins et al. 1989; Robins and Regier 1991). Despite their seeming precision, estimates of alcohol problems based on general population research can vary quite a lot depending on what measures are used and how those measures are operationalized (for related discussions, see Edwards

1973 and Room 1980). Measures of problem drinking tend to be less consistently conceptualized across studies than psychiatric diagnoses for abuse and dependence (see, for example, minor differences in measures used by Weisner and Schmidt 1992 and Wilsnack et al. 1991). Meanwhile, symptoms comprising the diagnoses for alcohol dependence and abuse have changed across different editions of the American Psychiatric Association's *Diagnostic and Statistical Manual of Mental Disorders*—from DSM-III (American Psychiatric Association 1980) to DSM-III-R (American Psychiatric Association 1987) to the most recent version, DSM-IV (American Psychiatric Association 1994). Even slight differences in levels of severity and in the timeframes covered by questions can produce sizable differences in results on the magnitude of alcohol problems in a given population. For example, according to the 1990 National Alcohol Survey, 3.9 percent of the U.S. adult population met the criteria for a 12-month alcohol dependence diagnosis, as defined by DSM-IV (Caetano and Room 1994). In contrast, the national projection of DSM-IV alcohol dependence based on the ECA studies—which used a 6-month timeframe—was 2.8 percent (Regier et al. 1993). One likely reason these estimates vary is because of the different timeframes of the measures.

In table 1 (see p. 80), we compare some alternative ways of measuring the prevalence of alcohol problems based on a 1989 general population survey in the study county (for details on the survey's methodology, see the appendix). We not only consider differences in the apparent magnitude of drinking problems resulting from each measure, but we also look at variation in the demographics of the different problem-drinking populations captured by these measures. The measures of alcohol problems range from disaggregated indicators of alcohol-related health problems and social consequences to measures of problem drinking and alcohol dependence used in clinical practice. Depending on what measure is used, levels of the apparent need for services may vary radically within the same community, with estimates of prevalence ranging from 0.4 to 34.3 percent. Alcohol dependence, a condition that implies a high level of severity, yields the lowest estimates of any clinical measure, but some disaggregated indicators of alcohol problems produce comparably low prevalences, such as alcohol-related hallucinations, delirium tremens, and rates of specific types of alcohol-related arrests. In contrast, heavy- and problem-drinking measures yield much higher estimates, as do some specific health indicators, such as alcohol-related heart disease.

The demographic distribution of the population with alcohol problems can look quite different depending on what measure is used. Alcohol-related health problems, such as heart disease, liver problems, delirium tremens, and hallucinations, capture an older population than alcohol-related social problems, such as crimes, arrests, and accidents. Women and African

Americans are more predominant in populations experiencing some alcohol-related health problems, such as serious heart conditions, including heart failure, heart attacks, and chest pains. If the measure involves alcohol-related arrests, African Americans and Hispanics are overrepresented relative to whites. Different clinical measures of alcohol problems also suggest different demographic profiles of the population with problems. While there is about a 4:1 ratio of male to female problem drinkers and heavy drinkers, for the higher threshold condition of dependence, there are six men with a drinking problem for every one woman. However, when we ask respondents to evaluate whether their own drinking is problematic, the gender gap narrows considerably: approximately 1.5 men to every 1 woman reported that they have a problem with their drinking. Overall, only about half as many individuals who could be defined as problem drinkers by a composite measure of heavy drinking, dependence symptoms, and social consequences were willing to label themselves as such (11.3 percent vs. 5.4 percent). This suggests a high potential for underreporting when questioning about alcohol problems is done in a very direct way.

Some of the most interesting variation across these different measures of alcohol problems involves the differences between self-reported criminal behaviors involving drinking, as opposed to alcohol-related arrests. Discrepancies between self-reported criminal behaviors and actual arrests illustrate some of the problems with reporting bias in official statistics, a topic that we will return to later, when we discuss social indicators of alcohol problems. When individuals in the general population survey were asked whether they had ever in their lifetimes committed certain alcohol-related crimes—whether or not they were caught by authorities—rates of criminal behavior were 3 times higher than when we based the question on lifetime arrests—that is, alcohol-related crimes (DUI, public drunkenness, and other alcohol-related arrests) that definitely came to the attention of the authorities (34.3 percent versus 11.6 percent). Notably, the discrepancies between self-reported criminal behaviors and actual arrests varied considerably by gender and ethnic status. Women and whites were much more likely to report that they had committed crimes for which they could have been arrested than they were to report actually getting arrested. Approximately 5.5 times as many women reported having committed criminal behaviors than reported being arrested in their lifetimes (23.9 percent vs. 4.3 percent). Meanwhile, approximately 2.4 times as many men reported criminal behaviors than reported actual arrests (47.4 percent vs. 20.1 percent). There were similar discrepancies among ethnic groups, where the gap between reports of committing criminal acts and getting caught by the police was narrower for members of ethnic minority groups. For example, whereas approximately 3.5 times as many whites reported criminal behaviors than reported arrests (37.8 percent vs. 10.9 percent), only 1.3 times as many African Americans reported criminal behaviors than arrests (25.2 percent vs. 19.7 percent).

SERVICE PROVIDER REPORTS OF PROBLEM-DRINKING CASELOADS

A second way to make estimates of the prevalence of alcohol problems in communities is to compile data from reports by staff in human service agencies who regularly come into contact with problem drinkers, through their work in either specialty alcohol treatment agencies or other health and human service systems (for examples, see Zax et al. 1967; Dorsch et al. 1969; Cook and Holder 1973; Biegel and Ghertner 1977; Shaw et al. 1978; Blaxter 1984). Unlike estimates based on general population surveys, estimates of problem drinking based on provider reports reflect the demand for services rather than the need for services. Unfortunately, decision-makers and planners are usually interested in knowing the size of populations that are potentially in need of help, whereas provider reports only shed light on populations that have already made their way to services. Further, there are many ambiguities that can make it difficult to use data on demand to approximate the extent of need in a population.

Clearly, not all individuals who might be considered in need of alcohol services by clinicians actually obtain help, but it is also probably the case that at least some people engaged in treatment have symptoms below clinical thresholds. And, of course, the economist's concept of "demand" has a special meaning when applied to services for alcohol problems. Entry into alcohol treatment usually involves some degree of external coercion, through encounters with the criminal justice system, employer or welfare system requirements, or social pressuring from family and community (Stitzer and McCaul 1987; Gerstein and Ewin 1990; Weisner 1990; Schmidt et al. 1998). In comparison with populations treated for other kinds of health-related problems, the populations in substance abuse treatment may include a larger percentage of clients for whom the need for services has been defined by the treatment community itself (see Beniger 1983). The demand for alcohol services can also change over time, along with shifting norms about the seriousness of alcohol problems (Room et al. 1991), changing provider conceptions about what the problem is (Institute of Medicine 1990), changes in treatment capacity (Schmidt and Weisner 1993), and any other factors that influence the propensity to use services.

One way to improve estimates of alcohol problems based on provider reports is to combine estimates from providers working in a broad spectrum of health and human service systems (Edwards et al. 1973; Blaxter 1984; Institute of Medicine 1990). In most communities, the burden of alcohol-related problems is distributed across a variety of different health and welfare agencies, and, therefore, studies focusing only on specialty alcohol treatment programs are likely to produce underestimates of even the proportion of problem drinkers who have obtained help (Glaser et al. 1978; Rush and Timney 1983; Moore et al. 1989). For example, in our analyses of representative samples of the caseloads of public service systems in the study county, rates of problem drinking varied considerably—from a low of 15 percent in the county's primary health clinics, to 19 percent in its emergency rooms, 24 percent in the welfare system, 26 percent in the mental health system, 54 percent in the criminal justice system, and finally to a high of 73 percent in the alcohol and drug treatment system (Weisner and Schmidt 1993; see also table 2, p.81). Estimates confined to specialty alcohol treatment programs can also provide a rather skewed demographic picture of problem-drinking populations. For example, although female problem drinkers are likely to be underrepresented relative to males in alcohol treatment programs, they are likely to be overrepresented in psychiatric and mental health programs (Weisner and Schmidt 1992).

However, one problem with combining provider reports across a broad spectrum of human services is obtaining an unduplicated count of problem-drinking clients, given the fact that some individuals are consumers of multiple types of services (Newman 1964; Zax et al. 1967; Biegel and Ghertner 1977). In most cases, data on clients' service records are logistically difficult to obtain, and concerns for client confidentiality can be a barrier to obtaining this information as well. Our research on different institutional populations in the study county suggests that the inability to control for duplicated cases can lead to upwardly biased estimates of alcohol-related problems, because people who rely on a variety of public services have an increased risk of alcohol problems (Weisner et al. 1995; Tam et al. 1996). Descriptions of the "multiproblem client" and "public agency client" also support the notion that public service systems in U.S. communities usually serve a core group of consumers who use many different public agencies, and among whom alcohol problems are overrepresented (Geismar and LaSorte 1964; Wiseman 1970). Finally, the literature on case management describes not only the fragmentation among U.S. health and social service systems that makes the monitoring of duplication in cases so difficult, but also the extensive overlap between populations in the substance abuse treatment, welfare, and criminal justice systems (Weil and Karls 1985; Stitzer and McCaul 1987; Gerstein and Ewin 1990).

Provider-based estimates of alcohol problems are also susceptible to reporting bias, where the different kinds of providers being surveyed use alternative measures and definitions of alcohol problems and possess different attitudes toward their problem-drinking clients. Variation in professionals' definitions of the "typical" alcoholic, in their attitudes toward alcoholism, in their tendencies to view these problems as salient, and in organizational incentives and disincentives to notice alcohol problems may influence providers' estimates of drinking problems among their clientele (Scheff 1966; Edwards 1973; Cartwright 1980; Blaxter 1984). Numerous studies of medical professionals, especially of general practitioners, have suggested that physicians tend to be biased against recognizing drinking problems because they either view substance abuse interventions as outside their professional role or see such interventions as disruptive of their relationships with patients (Lisansky 1975; Strong 1980; Ritson and Roumanie 1984; Thom and Tellez 1986; Roche et al. 1991; Rush et al. 1995; McCrady et al. 1996). On the other hand, studies of other professionals suggest that alcoholics tend to stand out as undesirable, as having poor prospects for rehabilitation, as "system abusers" or multi-problem clients (MacDonald and Patel 1975; Udell and Hornstra 1975; Lang 1981; Moodley-Kunnie 1988; Schmidt 1991). Providers' assumptions about alcoholics may reflect their personal attitudes and professional roles toward alcoholism, but they may also stem from organizational or systemwide policies regarding the management of alcohol problems. For example, prior to welfare reform, eligibility workers in U.S. welfare systems were often trained to avoid addressing alcohol problems directly with their clients and to avoid documenting suspected cases of substance abuse in their case records. This reflected the liberal spirit of welfare policy that tried to avoid discriminating against clients in income maintenance programs on the basis of their personal tastes, habits, and problems (Schmidt 1990).

We can begin to get a grasp on how much service providers' estimates of problem drinking in their caseloads vary by looking at 1993 survey data, based on representative samples of service providers working in agencies and in private practices in our study county's substance abuse, mental health, criminal justice, welfare, and health systems (see the appendix for a description of the methodology). In table 2, we make some very broad comparisons between providers' estimates of the prevalence of problem drinkers in their caseloads and the actual prevalence of problem drinking in the client population of each county agency system, based on epidemiologic studies. The proportion of providers in each system who gave an estimate that was consistent with the actual prevalence is shown in bold typeface.

Table 2 shows that providers working in different health and human service systems vary in their tendencies to over- or underestimate drinking problems among their clienteles. Groups of providers working in service systems with a clear mandate to serve problem drinkers, such as the substance abuse and mental health systems, seem more likely to provide exaggerated estimates of problem drinking within their caseloads. Thus provider estimates may be partly influenced by assumptions about which public services in the community should claim ownership of the problem. For example, providers in the county's mental health system had a tendency to overestimate the prevalence of problem drinking in their caseloads; more than 50 percent of the mental health providers reported prevalences that were higher than the actual rates of problem drinking we found in epidemiologic studies of the mental health caseload. On the other hand, professionals in the criminal justice system—whose caseload had nearly twice the prevalence of problem drinkers than the mental health caseload—had a tendency to underestimate alcohol problems in the criminal justice population. More than half of the sample of criminal justice providers, which was mainly comprised of patrol and probation officers, gave an estimate that was lower than the rate of problem drinking found in our epidemiologic survey, and only 14 percent overestimated the rate. Welfare and emergency room providers appeared to have a slight tendency toward overestimation, while primary health providers had roughly equal tendencies to over- and underestimate alcohol problems.

SOCIAL INDICATORS OF ALCOHOL PROBLEMS

A final option for evaluating alcohol problems in communities is to draw on the official monitoring statistics of public agencies, which may include admission and discharge rates reported by treatment programs and hospitals, drinking and driving arrests, liquor law violations, public drunkenness arrests, fatal automobile crashes, nighttime crashes, alcohol availability, and mortality rates due to alcohol use (for examples, see National Institute on Alcohol Abuse and Alcoholism [NIAAA] 1991 and Horgan in press). Social indicators are easily obtained through public agencies, and may be the preferred choice for evaluating alcohol problems that are amenable to prevention, where target populations tend to be narrowly defined around particular problems such as underage drinking, and where rates of clinically significant alcohol problems in the population are low. In some cases, social indicators may provide information not merely about the demand for services but also about the need for services, for example, where rates of drinking and driving arrests are used to evaluate the need for DUI programs. Moreover, in some of the more well-established parts of the public sector, such as the health and criminal justice systems, there is likely to be a high degree of consistency in the kinds of social indicators reported by local authorities around the country, which can facilitate geographic comparisons at the local and State levels.

Social indicators data, however, are only as good as the record-keeping systems on which they are based. The degree of public funding and monitoring of reporting procedures can clearly influence the consistency and accuracy of the data produced. Some institutions and service providers may be subject to particular incentives that give rise to deliberate reporting errors. For example, mental health programs may inaccurately register their clients under one diagnostic category or another in order to maximize their third-party reimbursements (Surber et al. 1987). It is probably more common that the problems are due to inadequate surveillance and consistency of reporting. For example, one study found gross underreporting of cocaine-related trauma cases in institutions participating in the Federal Drug Abuse Warning Network (DAWN)—even where institutions were in full compliance with Federal requirements for reporting (Brookoff et al. 1993). In the region studied, the DAWN system reported only 48 hospital visits involving cocaine, while the group of independent researchers was able to document 82 cases by merely looking at partial records that included toxicological data—data that were readily available to the DAWN system, but were not required by the reporting protocol. It is perhaps even more alarming that while NIDA's national surveys have shown overall declines in drug use over recent years, DAWN reports from those same years have reported that deaths related to the use of certain drugs, such as cocaine, have as much as tripled (Schnoll and Karan 1990; Harrison 1992; NIDA 1992*a*). The discrepancy could be due to the problems in one or both methods of collecting data: while the DAWN system has its problems, the NIDA household survey's exclusion of nonhousehold populations may mean that it misses populations that are at risk for cocaine-related fatalities, namely, those being captured by DAWN.

Social indicators are also influenced by the degree to which people interact with public agencies. For instance, the official "unemployment rate" is limited to people who are registered with the government as unemployed for tax reasons, rather than including the entire group of people who are actually looking for work. Meanwhile, poverty rates are based on the national census, which provides far-from-perfect coverage of low-income segments of the population (Krieger 1992*a*). U.S. reporting systems are particularly weak when it comes to monitoring the linkages between low socioeconomic status and health outcomes, including social indicators of alcohol problems. Limitations in the data usually mean that researchers are left using partial or indirect measures of social class, such as the respondent's education level (Krieger 1992*b;* Krieger and Fee 1993).

The accuracy of social indicators is subject to the degree of active surveillance of alcohol problems in the community, or to "rate-producing processes" that are influenced by citizens' and public authorities' degrees of commitment to dealing with alcohol problems in the community (Kitsuse and Cicourel 1963). Arrest statistics are particularly notorious for being subject to the level of enforcement in a community, but certainly detoxification rates, rates of drinking and driving program admissions, and assessments of alcohol-related mortality and crashes are influenced by surveillance levels as well. In a classic demonstration of precisely these issues, William Chambliss (1973) followed the activities and police encounters of two gangs of juvenile delinquents, one living in a middle-class community, the other in a working-class community. While authorities tended to view the lower class boys as dangerous and deviant, they frequently wrote off comparably delinquent acts by the middle-class boys as childish pranks. The social handling of the lower class boys by the police turned out to be much more punitive and led to more frequent incarceration.

In table 3 (see p. 82), we illustrate some of the different vantage points that social indicators provide by comparing data on 1989 admissions to county-operated and -contracted alcohol treatment agencies, admissions to drinking and driving (DUI) programs, and alcohol-related State hospital admissions from our study county, which are available through the California Management Information System. These statistics are clearly influenced by the amount of treatment capacity available and by policies influencing selection into treatment. In this county, it appears that the vast majority of individuals receiving public alcohol treatment services receive them in detoxification programs, and that most clients were between 25 and 44 years old, male, and white. We get a different vantage point on the population with alcohol problems by looking at admissions to DUI programs and State psychiatric hospitals for an alcohol-related diagnosis. For one thing, the population "in need" looks much larger from the perspective of the DUI programs that draw from a large population base throughout the county. Women are not as well represented in the DUI population, and the DUI and State hospital populations are slightly younger than the alcohol treatment population.

It is notable that the gender and age profiles of people in alcohol treatment programs are roughly consistent with what we found in the 1989 general population survey for those classified as alcohol dependent, although the age distribution is slightly older in treatment programs (shown in table 1). As in the treatment programs, people in the general population with alcohol dependence are primarily male and younger adults. However, while rates of dependence are low among African Americans in the general population, this group is overrepresented in alcohol treatment programs in the county. And while rates of dependence are relatively high among Hispanics in the general population study, their representation in most treatment programs is rather minimal. It is, however, notable that Hispanics are overrepresented in the county's DUI programs, despite low reports of DUI arrests in the general population survey. These discrepancies suggest that there may be some client selection or sorting process based on ethnicity going on within the county's alcohol treatment system.

Alcohol problems in the community look somewhat different when viewed through the lens of alcohol-related arrest and motor vehicle accident statistics, available through the California Bureau of Criminal Statistics (see table 4, p. 83). Women are underrepresented in the populations with public drunkenness and drinking and driving arrests relative to their representation in the county's alcohol treatment system (as was shown in table 3). Social indicators of alcohol-related arrests also capture a younger population than treatment admission statistics. There are again rather interesting ethnic differences if one compares treatment admissions with criminal justice statistics. While only 14.5 percent of people arrested for DUI in 1989 were Hispanic, 33 percent of the population in DUI treatment programs were Hispanic. Meanwhile, it appears that whites were overrepresented in DUI arrests relative to their proportions in DUI programs throughout the county.

Table 4 also shows the rates of alcohol-related motor vehicle accidents for 1989. It is noteworthy that alcohol-related fatalities make up 59.6 percent of motor vehicle fatalities, while alcohol-related injuries only make up 17.8 percent of motor vehicle injuries. One interpretation of these radically different rates of alcohol involvement in traffic accidents is that drinking leads to more serious accidents. However, an alternative interpretation is that these differences are due to differences in the reporting of alcohol-related accident data. In cases of fatalities, alcohol's role in the incident is likely to be determined through a coroner's report based on autopsy information. In cases where the accident leads to only an injury, the assessment of alcohol's role is usually based upon police observations—a much less thorough and consistent way of assessing alcohol involvement. Therefore, rates of alcohol-related fatalities and injuries could be influenced by differences in reporting rather than actual differences in how drinking enters into motor vehicle accidents.

Table 5 (see p. 84) illustrates a final type of widely available social indicator, alcohol-related mortality, which is available at the county level throughout the United States for eight alcohol-related causes of death: liver cirrhosis, alcohol dependence syndrome, nondependent abuse of alcohol, alcoholic psychosis, alcohol poisoning, motor vehicle accidents, suicide, and homicide (NIAAA 1991). We have combined data from 1979, 1980, and 1983–85 to achieve stable estimates of mortality per 100,000 population in the study county, which are shown for both underlying causes of death for individuals ages 15–74, and age-adjusted underlying and multiple causes. Although mortality data have the advantage of being consistently available at the county level, estimates can be unstable for smaller communities and will, for most indicators, reflect a significant time lag between the early manifestations of a drinking problem and the serious health consequences that can lead to death. Like rates of dependence in general populations, and like alcohol treatment admissions statistics, mortality data capture an extreme segment of the problem-drinking population and produce extremely low prevalences. As table 5 shows, even the maximum estimated alcohol-involved mortality rate (age adjusted) due to all causes and measured over 5 years is only 36.1 per 100,000 population.

Other than a general population survey, mortality data provide the most choices among different measures of alcohol-related problems. However, it is notable that the prevalences obtained from mortality data provide almost the mirror opposite of the prevalences that one is likely to find in a general population survey. In the mortality data, rates of less severe conditions, such as alcohol abuse, figure much less prominently than rates of higher severity conditions like dependence, whereas the opposite is the case in the survey of the county's general population (see table 1). The pattern is the same for separate indicators of alcohol-related problems. Motor vehicle accidents are the largest episodic cause of alcohol-related mortality, and cirrhosis is the largest indicator of chronic use in the mortality data. In contrast, alcohol-related accidents and cirrhosis had some of the lowest prevalences in the general population survey.

THE HAZARDS OF ESTIMATING RATES OF ALCOHOL PROBLEMS

Different methods of gathering statistics about alcohol problems can leave us with quite different images of the magnitude of the problem and of who the people are that need services. Ultimately, they may lead us to make different assumptions about the causes and cures of alcohol problems in the community. Although general population studies have the best reputation for precision and flexibility with regard to choosing measures of alcohol problems, in actual practice even minor variations in the severity and timeframe of measures used in general population research can lead to large differences in prevalence estimates. In the county we studied, depending on the measure, the overall size of the problem-drinking population could range from 0.4 percent of the county's population to 34.3 percent. General population estimates are also subject to reporting bias, which may not be evenly spread across gender and ethnic groups. We found, for example, that if we directly asked people about whether they had a drinking problem during the prior year, we obtained a prevalence rate that was about half the size of the rate for a composite measure of problem drinking that combined questions on heavy drinking, dependence symptoms, and social consequences. Relative to their rates of problem drinking, women were more likely to answer positively to direct questions about having an alcohol problem than men were. We also found that discrepancies between self-reported criminal behaviors and actual arrests varied considerably by gender and ethnicity.

Prevalence estimates based on service provider reports and social indicators offer easier and less costly alternatives to general population surveys. But they also come with a variety of problems, including constraints on measurement choices, institutional reporting bias, and difficulties with obtaining an unduplicated count of problem drinkers from a range of institutional settings. We found indications that rates based on service providers' estimates about problem drinking in their caseloads may vary in accuracy across different kinds of health and human services. Providers working in service systems with a relatively strong mandate to treat alcoholics had a tendency to exaggerate estimates of alcohol problems in their caseloads. For example, over half of the mental health providers we interviewed overestimated the rate of problem drinking in their caseload; criminal justice providers had the opposite tendency to underestimate drinking problems among the people they encountered in their daily work. Finally, although social indicators data are probably the most commonly used source of data on drinking problems, they can often lead to a rather skewed picture of who the problem drinkers are in a community. Data on alcohol treatment admissions and mortality capture an extreme segment of the problem-drinking population and, correspondingly, result in extremely low prevalence rates; analyses of DUI program admissions and arrests clearly cast a wider net. In the study county, statistics on alcohol treatment admissions captured a largely white, middle-aged male population, while data on alcohol-related arrests and DUI admissions captured a younger, more ethnically diverse population. Our comparisons across different social indicators also suggested that in this particular community, there was probably some selection and sorting of clients across institutions on the basis of their ethnicity.

The different vantage points afforded by social indicators, provider estimates, and general population surveys remind us that, fundamentally, the meanings of alcohol problems and alcoholism are still open to debate. Despite their seeming objectivity and technical precision, statistical measures in a contested terrain like alcoholism policy and research are never totally value free. One can easily see that there is an ebb and flow in the use of particular statistics on alcohol problems, just as there is variability over time in public concerns about the intersections between alcohol problems and crime, as opposed to mental illness, traffic crashes, poverty, and so on. Choices about whether to use arrest statistics, mental hospital admissions, statistics on alcohol-related traffic fatalities, or welfare statistics may very well reflect the various pressures on authorities to take action on particular social problems or efforts to justify choices that have already been made about where to commit resources. Since producing the most technically sound estimates of alcohol problems is usually not the main priority in planning for local areas, decision-makers and their communities may do well to simply be cautious consumers of statistical data on alcohol problems. This means knowing the limitations of particular approaches to estimating alcohol problems. It means understanding that choices of data sources and measurement usually mean making a commitment to one underlying conception of the problem or another.

ACKNOWLEDGMENTS

This work was supported by a National Alcohol Research Center Grant (AA–05595) from the National Institute on Alcohol Abuse and Alcoholism. Diana Prufer and Maria Dinis provided assistance with data gathering for this chapter.

APPENDIX: DATA SOURCES

In this chapter, we compare three different sources of data from a large northern California county to estimate the prevalence and nature of alcohol problems: data from epidemiologic surveys of household and clinical populations, survey data collected from providers of health and human services, and social indicators data that are compiled by public agencies for monitoring purposes.

General Population Survey

The epidemiologic data compared in the chapter are drawn from the Alcohol Research Group's Community Epidemiology Laboratory (CEL), a multisample project sponsored by NIAAA. We use data from the CEL's household survey to examine the prevalences of problem drinking, alcohol dependence, and various alcohol-related problem measures, and the demographic distributions of individuals who meet our definition of problem drinking. The 1989 general population survey involved a two-stage area probability sample of the entire county, with census blocks and households used as selection strata. Within each household, one adult was randomly selected and participated in face-to-face interviews using a structured survey instrument that focused on evaluating drinking patterns and problems. The sample included 3,069 people and had a response rate of 68 percent. In analyses, data are weighted to adjust for household composition in the county. A fuller description of the CEL and methodological considerations can be found in a published introduction to the CEL project (Weisner and Schmidt 1995).

The interview encompassed a variety of measures of alcohol-related social problems and clinical conditions. These included alcohol-related health problems (e.g., cirrhosis, delirium tremens, hallucinations, heart conditions), individuals' identifications of themselves as problem drinkers, alcohol-related criminal behaviors (e.g., motor vehicle thefts, public drunkenness, driving with a suspended license, burglary, prostitution), alcohol-related arrests (e.g., drunk driving, public drunkenness, other arrests), and alcohol-related traffic accidents. Alcohol dependence was measured using nine items, which covered eight of the nine indicators from DSM-III-R (American Psychiatric Association 1987). The indicator not covered is "a great deal of time spent in activities necessary to get the substance, taking the substance or recovering from its effects." Problem drinking was operationalized as meeting two of the following three criteria during the previous year: (1) drinking five or more drinks on any occasion at least once a month; (2) a positive response on at least one of nine dependence symptoms; and (3) a positive response to at least one of eight social consequence items.

Service Provider Reports

Additional survey data in this chapter were based on a probability sample of health and human services providers in the study county that served as the site of the CEL. The survey was conducted in 1993 using a two-stage probability sampling approach, stratified by service sector, including the county's substance abuse treatment, criminal justice, welfare, mental health treatment, and health care systems (in the final two systems, we included both organization-based providers and providers working in solo practices throughout the county).

To draw the sample, we developed a comprehensive listing of individuals and organizations using telephone listings, snowballing, and followup telephone screening interviews with each provider in the county. From a listing of 1,006 eligible organizations, we drew a stratified random sample of 118 separate facilities; at the same time, we drew a simple random sample of solo practitioners (including physicians and psychotherapists) from separate listings. We gained permission to interview providers working in each of the 118 organizations and gathered a complete listing of all professionals who worked at least part-time (thus excluding office staff, janitors, technicians, etc.). Individual providers were sampled proportionate to organization size, and those selected participated in on-site, in-person interviews; solo practitioners were interviewed using an identical protocol. Interviews included information on providers' conceptions of alcohol problems and their perceptions about prevalence of substance abuse problems in their caseloads. A total of 457 service providers were interviewed, achieving a response rate of 73 percent, which takes into account nonresponse occurring at both the organizational and individual levels. Our analysis in this chapter uses statistical weights that adjust for design effects and nonresponse, so that each sample of providers in a service system represents the true proportions of different kinds of providers working there.

In our analysis (see table 2), for each service system we compared providers' estimates of the prevalence of problem drinking in their caseloads with epidemiologic data on the rates of problem drinking in their client populations at the agency system level. Data on the clients seen in each system are taken from the CEL's agency-based studies, which include probability samples of individuals entering the study county's alcohol treatment programs (N = 381) and drug treatment programs (N = 307) which are combined for purposes of this analysis, as well as mental health facilities (N = 406), emergency rooms (N = 2,626), primary health clinics (N = 394), welfare programs (N = 621), and people being booked through the county jail (N = 1,147). The client surveys are representative of admissions to the countywide systems of care. The studies were conducted between 1987 and 1989. Each client survey included all agencies within the public sector system except those targeted to individuals under age 18 or over 65, and those that carried no caseloads (e.g. information and referral agencies). In two cases (the drug and mental health samples), one or more eligible agencies in the county had caseloads too small to feasibly cover, or did not consent to participate in the project. Response rates varied across CEL client population samples from 66 to 88 percent. We used statistical weights to adjust for differences in sampling ratios, field time, and nonresponse across studies (for details on weighting procedures, see Tam 1993). We used consistent fieldwork, in-person interview procedures, and questionnaires across the client surveys. The measure of problem drinking used in this analysis is detailed above in the discussion of the general population survey.

Social Indicators Data

Social indicators data included in this chapter were gathered from the study county's public services, in most cases for the year 1989, which was the year of the CEL's general population survey and a number of the client surveys. Social indicators include published and unpublished statistics that are collected for monitoring and planning purposes by national, State, and county-level public agencies. Treatment admissions statistics were obtained from the State of California's Management Information System, which gathers data from county-level systems throughout the State; arrest statistics were located through California's Bureau of Criminal Statistics; and mortality data were obtained through the U.S. Alcohol Epidemiologic Data System sponsored by NIAAA.

REFERENCES

American Psychiatric Association. *Diagnostic and Statistical Manual of Mental Disorders.* 3d ed. Washington, DC: the Association, 1980.

American Psychiatric Association. *Diagnostic and Statistical Manual of Mental Disorders.* 3d ed., rev. Washington, DC: the Association, 1987.

American Psychiatric Association. *Diagnostic and Statistical Manual of Mental Disorders.* 4th ed. Washington, DC: American Psychiatric Press, 1994.

Beniger, J.R. *Trafficking in Drug Users: Professional Exchange Networks in the Control of Deviance.* Cambridge, England: Cambridge University Press, 1983.

Biegel, A., and Ghertner, S. Toward a social model: An assessment of social factors which influence problem drinking and its treatment. In: Kissin, B., and Begleiter, H., eds. *The Biology of Alcoholism.* New York: Plenum Press, 1977. pp. 197–233.

Blaxter, M. Research into sociomedical problems: An example in the field of alcohol abuse. In: Holland, W.A., ed. *Oxford Textbook of Public Health.* New York: Oxford University Press, 1984.

Brookoff, D.; Campbell, E.A.; and Shaw, L.M. The underreporting of cocaine-related trauma: Drug Abuse Warning Network reports vs. hospital toxicology tests. *Am J Public Health* 83(3):369–371, 1993.

Caetano, R., and Room, R. Alcohol dependence in the 1990 U.S. National Alcohol Survey: Operationalizing and comparing two nosological systems. *Drug and Alcohol Review* 13:257–267, 1994.

Cahalan, D.; Cisin, I.H.; and Crossley, H.M. *American Drinking Practices: A National Study of Drinking Behavior and Attitudes.* New Brunswick, NJ: Rutgers Center of Alcohol Studies, 1969.

Cartwright, A.K.J. The attitudes of helping agents towards the alcoholic client: The influence of experience, support, training and self-esteem. *British Journal of Addiction* 75:413–431, 1980.

Chambliss, W. The saints and the roughnecks. *Society* Nov./Dec. 1973, pp. 24–31.

Collins, L.M.; Graham, J.W.; Hansen, W.B.; and Johnson, C.A. Agreement between retrospective accounts of substance abuse and earlier reported substance use. *Applied Psychological Measurement* 9(3):301–309, 1985.

Cook, I., and Holder, H.D. *Alcoholism in Wake County: A Base Line Study With Initial Planning.* Raleigh, NC: Institute of Human Ecology, 1973.

Dorsch, G.; Talley, R.; and Bynder, H. Response to alcoholics by the helping professions and community agencies in Denver. *Q J Stud Alcohol* 30:905–920, 1969.

Edwards, G. Epidemiology applied to alcoholism. *Q J Stud Alcohol* 34:28–56, 1973.

Edwards, G.; Hawker, A.; and Hensman, C. Alcoholics known or unknown to agencies: Epidemiological studies in a London suburb. *Br J Psychiatry* 123:169–183, 1973.

Geismar, L.L., and LaSorte, M.A. *Understanding the Multi-Problem Family.* New York: Association Press, 1964.

General Accounting Office (GAO). *Drug Use Measurement: Strengths, Limitations, and Recommendations for Improvement.* Washington, DC: GAO, 1993.

Gerstein, D.R., and Ewin, L.S. Treating drug problems. *N Engl J Med* 323(12):844–848, 1990.

Glaser, F.B.; Greenberg, S.W.; and Barrett, M. *A Systems Approach to Alcohol Treatment.* Toronto: Addiction Research Foundation, 1978.

Gusfield, J. *The Culture of Public Problems: Drinking-Driving and the Symbolic Order.* Chicago: University of Chicago Press, 1981.

Harrell, A.V. Validation of self-report: The research record. In: Rouse, B.A.; Kozel, N.J.; and Richards, L.G., eds. *Self-Report Methods of Estimating Drug Use: Meeting Current Challenges to Validity.* Rockville, MD: National Institute on Drug Abuse, 1985. pp. 12–21.

Harrison, L.D. Trends in illicit drug use in the United States: Conflicting results from national surveys. *International Journal of the Addictions* 27(7):817–847, 1992.

Helzer, J.E., and Pryzbeck, T.R. The co-occurrence of alcoholism with other psychiatric disorders in the general population and its impact on treatment. *J Stud Alcohol* 49:219–224, 1988.

Horgan, C. *Chartbook of Social Indicators for Substance Abuse.* Princeton, NJ: Robert Wood Johnson Foundation, in press.

Institute of Medicine. *Broadening the Base of Treatment for Alcohol Problems* [chapter 1]. Washington, DC: National Academy Press, 1990.

Kaskutas, L.A. Interpretations of risk: The use of scientific information in the development of the alcohol warning label policy. *International Journal of the Addictions* 30(12):1519–1548, 1995.

Kessler, R.C.; Frank, R.G.; Edlund, M.; Katz, S.J.; Lin, E.; and Leaf, P. Differences in the use of psychiatric outpatient services between the United States and Ontario. *N Engl J Med* 336(8):551–557, 1997.

Kitsuse, J.I., and Cicourel, A.V. A note on the uses of official statistics. *Social Problems* 11(2):131–139, 1963.

Knupfer, G. Abstaining for foetal health: The fiction that even light drinking is dangerous. *British Journal of Addiction* 86:1063–1073, 1991.

Koren, G.; Graham, K.; Shear, H.; and Einarson, T. Bias against the null hypothesis: The reproductive hazards of cocaine. *Lancet* 2:1440–1442, 1989.

Krieger, N. The making of public health data: Paradigms, politics, and policy. *J Public Health Policy* 13:412–427, 1992*a*.

Krieger, N. Overcoming the absence of socioeconomic data in medical records: Validation and application of a census-based methodology. *Am J Public Health* 82(5):703–710, 1992*b*.

Krieger, N., and Fee, E. What's class got to do with it? The state of health data in the United States today. *Socialist Review* 23:59–82, 1993.

Lang, C.L. Good cases, bad cases: Client selection and professional prerogative in a community mental health center. *Urban Life* 10:289–309, 1981.

Lisansky, E.T. Why physicians avoid early diagnosis of alcoholism. *NY State J Med* 75(10):1788–1792, 1975.

MacDonald, E.B., and Patel, A.B. Attitudes towards alcoholism. *Br Med J* 2:430–431, 1975.

McCrady, B.S.; Richter, S.S.; Morgan, T.J.; Slade, J.; and Pfeifer, C. Involving health care workers in screening for alcohol problems. *J Addict Dis* 15(3):45–58, 1996.

Midanik, L.T. Validity of self-reported alcohol use: A literature review and assessment. *British Journal of Addiction* 83:1019–1029, 1988.

Miller, J.D. The nominative technique: A new method of estimating heroin prevalence. In: Rouse, B.A.; Kozel, N.J.; and Richards, L.G., eds. *Self-Report Methods of Estimating Drug Use: Meeting Current Challenges to Validity.* Rockville, MD: National Institute on Drug Abuse, 1985. pp. 104–124.

Moodley-Kunnie, T. Attitudes and perceptions of health professionals toward substance use disorders and substance-dependent individuals. *International Journal of the Addictions* 23:469–475, 1988.

Moore, D.R.; Bone, L.R.; Geller, G.; Mamon, J.; Stokes, E.; and Levine, D. Prevalence, detection, and treatment of alcoholism in hospitalized patients. *JAMA* 261:403–407, 1989.

Mulford, H.E., and Miller, D.E. Drinking in Iowa: I. Socio-cultural distribution of drinkers. *Q J Stud Alcohol* 20:704–726, 1959.

Mulford, H.E., and Miller, D.E. Drinking in Iowa: II. The extent of drinking and selected sociocultural categories. *Q J Stud Alcohol* 21:26–39, 1960.

Mulford, H., and Miller, D. Drinking and deviant drinking, U.S.A., 1963. *Q J Stud Alcohol* 25:634–650, 1964.

Narrow, W.E.; Regier, D.A.; Rae, D.S.; Manderscheid, R.W.; and Locke, B.Z. Use of services by persons with mental and addictive disorders: Findings from the National Institute of Mental Health Epidemiologic Catchment Area program. *Arch Gen Psychiatry* 50:95–107, Feb 1993.

National Institute on Alcohol Abuse and Alcoholism (NIAAA). *U.S. Alcohol Epidemio-*

logic Data Reference Manual, Vol. 3: County Alcohol Problem Indicators, 1979–1985. Washington, DC: NIAAA, 1991.

National Institute on Drug Abuse (NIDA). *Self-Report Methods of Estimating Drug Use: Meeting Current Challenges to Validity.* Rockville, MD: NIDA, 1985.

National Institute on Drug Abuse (NIDA). *National Household Survey on Drug Abuse: Main Findings 1990.* U.S. Department of Health and Human Services, 1991.

National Institute on Drug Abuse (NIDA). *Epidemiologic Trends in Drug Abuse.* Washington, DC: NIDA, 1992*a*.

National Institute on Drug Abuse (NIDA). *The Washington DC Metropolitan Area Drug Study: Prevalence of Drug Use in the DC Metropolitan Area Household Population: 1990.* Rockville, MD: NIDA, Division of Epidemiology and Prevention Research, 1992*b*.

Newman, A.F. Frontenac County survey: The alcohol population. Toronto: Addiction Research Foundation, 1964.

Regier, D.A.; Narrow, W.E.; Rae, D.S.; Manderscheid, R.W.; Locke, B.Z.; and Goodwin, F.K. The de facto US mental and addictive disorders service system: Epidemiologic Catchment Area prospective 1-year prevalence rates of disorders and services. *Arch Gen Psychiatry* 50:85–94, Feb 1993.

Ritson, B., and Roumanie, M.D. Community attitudes and responses to alcohol problems. In: Krasner N.; Madden; J.S.; and Walker, R.J., eds. *Alcohol-Related Problems.* New York: John Wiley & Sons, 1984. pp. 267–277.

Robins, L.N., and Regier, D.A., eds. *Psychiatric Disorders in America: The Epidemiological Catchment Area Study.* New York: Free Press, 1991.

Robins, L.N.; Wing, J.K.; Wittchen, H.-U.; et al. The Composite International Diagnostic Interview: An epidemiological instrument suitable for use in conjunction with different diagnostic systems and in different countries. *Arch Gen Psychiatry* 45:1069–1077, 1989.

Roche, A.M.; Guray, C.; and Saunders, J.B. General practitioners' experiences of patients with drug and alcohol problems. *British Journal of Addiction* 86:263–275, 1991.

Room, R. Measurement and distribution of drinking patterns and problems in general populations. In: Edwards, G.; Gross, M.M.; Keller, M.; Moser, J.; and Room, R., eds. *Alcohol-Related Disabilities.* Geneva, Switzerland: World Health Organization, 1977.

Room, R. Treatment-seeking populations and larger realities. In: Edwards, G., and Grant, M., eds. *Alcoholism Treatment in Transition.* London: Croom Helm, 1980. pp. 205–224.

Room, R.; Greenfield, T.; and Weisner, C. People who might have liked you to drink less: Changing responses to drinking by U.S. family members and friends, 1979–1990. *Contemporary Drug Problems* 18(4):573–595, 1991.

Rush, B., and Timney, C. The detection and assessment of alcohol-related problems in health and social service agencies. *Can J Public Health* 74:270–275, 1983.

Rush, B.R.; Powell, L.Y.; Crowe, T.G.; and Ellis, K. Early intervention for alcohol use: Family physicians' motivations and perceived barriers. *CMAJ* 152(6):863–869, 1995.

Scheff, T.J. Typifications in the diagnostic practices of rehabilitation agencies. In: Sussman, M.B., ed. *Sociology and Rehabilitation.* Cleveland, OH: American Sociological Association, 1966. pp. 139–144.

Schmidt, L.A. Problem drinkers and the welfare bureaucracy. *Social Service Review* 61(4):390–406, 1990.

Schmidt, L.A. Specialization in alcoholism and mental health treatment: The "dual diagnosis" problem. *Journal of Drug Issues* 21(4):859–874, 1991.

Schmidt, L.A., and Weisner, C.M. Developments in alcohol treatment systems: A ten-year review. *Recent Dev Alcohol* 11:368–396, 1993.

Schmidt, L.; Weisner, C.; and Wiley, J. Substance abuse and the course of welfare dependency. *Am J Public Health* 88(11):1616–1622, 1998.

Schnoll, S.H., and Karan, L.D. Substance abuse. *JAMA* 263:2682–2683, 1990.

Shaw, S.; Cartwright, A.; Spratley, T.; and Harwin, J. *Responding to Drinking Problems.* Baltimore, MD: University Park Press, 1978.

Smart, R.G. Sampling and coverage difficulties in Canadian drug use surveys and efforts to avoid them. In: Rouse, B.A.; Kozel, N.J.; and Richards, L.G., eds. *Self-Report Methods of Estimating Drug Use: Meeting Current Challenges to Validity.* Rockville, MD: National Institute on Drug Abuse, 1985. pp. 55–62.

Stitzer, M.L., and McCaul, M.E. Criminal justice interventions with drug and alcohol abusers: The role of compulsory treatment. In: Morris, E.K., and Braukmann, C.J., eds. *Behavioral Approaches to Crime and Delinquency.* New York: Plenum Press, 1987. pp. 331–360.

Strong, P.M. Doctors and dirty work—the case of alcoholism. *Sociology of Health and Illness* 2(1):24–47, 1980.

Surber, R.W.; Winkler, E.L.; and Monteleone, M. Characteristics of high users of acute psychiatric inpatient services. *Hospital and Community Psychiatry* 38:1112–1114, 1987.

Tam, T.; Schmidt, L.A.; and Weisner, C.M. Patterns in the institutional encounters of problem drinkers in a community human service network. *Addiction* 91(5):657–669, 1996.

Tam, T.W. *Technical Report: Community Epidemiology Laboratory: Within- and Across-Study Weights.* Berkeley, CA: Alcohol Research Group, 1993.

Thom, B., and Tellez, C. A difficult business: Detecting and managing alcohol problems in general practice. *British Journal of Addiction* 81:405–418, 1986.

Udell, B., and Hornstra, R.K. Good Patients and Bad: Therapeutic Assets and Liabilities. *Arch Gen Psychiatry* 32:1533–1537, 1975.

Weil, M., and Karls, J.M. *Case Management in Human Service Practice.* San Francisco: Jossey-Bass, 1985.

Weisner, C. Coercion in alcohol treatment. In: Institute of Medicine, ed. *Broadening the Base of Treatment for Alcohol Problems, Report of a Study by a Committee of the Institute of Medicine.* Washington, DC: National Academy of Sciences Press, 1990. pp. 579–609.

Table 1. General Population Prevalence (Percent) of Alcohol-Related Disorders and Social

	Heart Disease	Alcohol-Related Liver Problems	Delirium Tremens	Hallucinations	Criminal Behaviors 12 mo.	Criminal Behaviors Lifetime
Unweighted *N*	(2,101)	(2,102)	(2,102)	(2,102)	(3,069)	(3,069)
Total sample	8.1	0.4	0.4	0.2	8.9	34.3
Gender						
Male	7.7	0.8	0.8	0.3	14.4	47.4
Female	8.5	0.0	0.0	0.1	4.2	23.9
Age						
18–24	2.5	0.0		0.0	25.8	38.2
25–34	4.7	0.4	0.9	0.3	16.0	48.5
35–44	5.0	0.4	0.4	0.2	6.2	38.6
45–54	11.4	0.8	0.3	0.3	2.8	31.8
55+	15.0	0.3	0.1	0.2	0.6	17.0
Ethnicity						
White		0.3	0.3	0.2	9.4	37.8
African American	15.8	0.9	0.9	0.9	7.6	25.2
Hispanic	4.5	1.1	1.1	0.0	9.4	26.5
Other	6.0	0.0	0.0	0.0	5.6	12.1

Note: Data are based on a survey of the household population in the study county. For details on methodology, see the covers 12 months prior to interview unless otherwise specified.

Weisner, C.M., and Schmidt, L.A. Gender disparities in treatment for alcohol problems. *JAMA* 268(14):1872–1876, 1992.

Weisner, C.M., and Schmidt, L.A. Alcohol and drug problems among diverse health and social service populations. *Am J Public Health* 83(6):824–829, 1993.

Weisner, C.M., and Schmidt, L.A. The Community Epidemiology Laboratory: Studying alcohol problems in community and agency-based populations. *Addiction* 90:329–342, 1995.

Weisner, C.M.; Schmidt, L.A.; and Tam, T. Assessing bias in community-based prevalence estimates: Toward an unduplicated count of problem drinkers and drug users. *Addiction* 90:391–406, 1995.

Wilsnack, S.C.; Klassen, A.D.; Schur, B.E.; and Wilsnack, R.W. Predicting onset and chronicity of women's problem drinking: A five-year longitudinal analysis. *Am J Public Health* 81(3):305–318, 1991.

Wiseman, J. *Stations of the Lost: The Treatment of Skid Row Alcoholics.* Englewood Cliffs, NJ: Prentice-Hall, 1970.

Zax, M.; Gardner, E.A.; and Hart, W.T. A survey of the prevalence of alcohol in Monroe County, NY, 1961. *Q J Stud Alcohol* 28:316–327, 1967.

Problems, 1989.

Lifetime Arrests	DUI Arrests	Public Drunkenness Arrests	Alcohol-Related Traffic Accidents	Self-Label Alcoholic or Problem Drinker	Heavy Drinker	Problem Drinker	Alcohol Dependent
(3,069)	(3,069)	(3,069)	(3,069)	(2,494)	(3,069)	(2,494)	(3,069)
11.6	1.3	0.5	0.4	5.4	13.8	11.3	2.3
20.1	2.4	0.7	0.4	6.5	23.6	18.8	4.2
4.3	0.4	0.2	0.4	4.3	5.4	4.8	0.7
14.5	1.0	1.0	0.7	7.3	24.6	21.6	4.0
15.9	3.7	1.1	0.3	7.1	20.3	16.8	4.5
10.0	1.2	0.2	0.8	5.8	13.5	11.1	2.1
11.8	0.1	0.0	0.2	5.2	9.2	7.6	0.7
7.6	0.1	0.0	0.0	2.5	5.8	3.8	0.8
10.9	1.3	0.5	0.3	5.7	14.4	11.6	2.6
19.7	2.8	0.0	0.7	2.9	11.3	10.2	0.8
15.3	2.0	0.3	0.5	7.7	18.9	15.8	3.1
6.4	0.0	0.3	0.0	2.0	7.0	5.9	0.6

appendix. Data are weighted by number of adults residing in household. Timeframe for alcohol problems indicators

Table 2. Actual Prevalence of Problem Drinking in County Health and Human Service System Caseloads as Compared With Provider Estimates.

	Actual % Problem Drinkers in	Provider Estimates of % Problem Drinkers[2]						
		Prevalence of Problem Drinkers in Caseload is . . .						
System	Caseloads[1]	100%	75–99%	50–74%	25–49%	10–24%	<10%	None
Substance abuse system	73	13	37	**17**	12	9	9	3
Mental health system	26	6	22	27	**12**	25	4	4
Criminal justice system	54	0	14	**32**	28	19	7	0
Welfare system	24	0	12	12	19	**18**	12	14
Primary health system	15	0	3	8	22	**35**	32	0
Emergency rooms	19	0	3	9	33	**33**	21	0

[1]Data are from Weisner and Schmidt 1993, based on epidemiologic studies of representative samples of systemwide caseloads. For details on methodology, see the appendix.
[2]Data are based on representative samples of service providers in each system. For details on methodology, see the appendix. The percentages of providers estimating correctly are shown in bold typeface.

Table 3. County Alcohol Treatment Statistics, 1989.

	Admissions to Alcohol Treatment Programs	**Admissions to DUI Programs[1]**	**Alcohol-Related Admissions to State Psychiatric Hospitals[2]**
Admissions per 100,000	0.06	0.68	0.02
Number of admissions	5,695	67,850	1,648
Detox	78.2%		
Recovery homes	7.8%		
Residential treatment	0.8%		
Outpatient	13.1%		
Gender			
Male	76.4%	86.9%	78.5%
Female	23.5%	13.1%	21.5%
Age			
18–24	7.3%	21.2%	17.7%
25–34	37.6%	36.0%	46.5%
35–44	34.6%	25.3%	24.4%
45+	18.8%	17.1%	10.4%
Ethnicity			
White	59.6%	55.8%	32.5%
African-American	34.0%	6.4%	18.7%
Hispanic	4.7%	33.2%	46.7%
Other	1.7%	4.5%	2.2%

Note: Data are from the California Management Information System, operated by the State Department of Alcohol and Drug Programs.

[1]Includes first offender and multiple offender programs.

[2]Any alcohol-related admission from the study county to a State psychiatric hospital.

Table 4. County-Level Arrests for Alcohol-Related Offenses and Motor Vehicle Accident Fatalities and Injuries, 1989.

	Public Drunkenness	Drinking and Driving
Arrests per 100,000	0.04	0.08
Number of arrests	3,523	7,534
Gender		
Male	87.0%	84.6%
Female	13.0%	15.4%
Age		
18–24	21.0%	24.3%
25–29	17.5%	21.9%
30–39	37.1%	28.6%
40–49	17.3%	15.5%
50–59	5.3%	7.0%
60+	1.8%	2.7%
Ethnicity		
White	59.6%	74.5%
African American	17.1%	8.3%
Hispanic	21.3%	14.5%
Other	2.0%	2.7%

Motor Vehicle Accidents

Fatalities		Injuries	
Number of fatalities due to alcohol-related accidents	52	Number of injuries due to alcohol-related accidents	853
Number of individual fatalities	56	Number of individuals injured	1,310
Percentage of fatalities that were alcohol-related	59.6	Percentage of injuries that were alcohol-related	17.8

Note: Data are from the State of California Office of the Attorney General, Criminal Identification and Information, Bureau of Criminal Statistics.

Table 5. Countywide Mortality From Selected Alcohol-Related Causes for Ages 15–74, Rates per 100,000 Averaged for 1979, 1980, and 1983–85.

	Underlying Cause of Death	Average Age-Adjusted Mortality (Underlying Cause)[1]	Average Age-Adjusted Mortality (Multiple Causes)[2]
Cirrhosis	20.2	14.3	20.6
Alcohol dependence syndrome	2.4	1.8	0.5
Nondependent abuse	0.2	0.1	0.7
Alcohol psychosis	0.2	0.1	0.2
Alcohol poisoning	0.5	0.4	1.9
Motor vehicle accident	21.5	18.3	NA
Alcohol-related suicide	17.3	13.3	NA
Alcohol-related homicide	10.6	8.6	NA
Any alcohol-related	NA	NA	27.0
Minimum estimated alcohol-involved mortality rate	29.1	NA	22.7
Maximum estimated alcohol-involved mortality rate	47.1	NA	36.1

Note: Data are from NIAAA 1991, pp. 31, 204, 205. NA = not available.

[1]Disease or injury leading to death (only one disease identified). Codes for causes of death are based on the *International Classification of Diseases, 9th Revision.*

[2]Underlying cause plus two sets of conditions listed as causes of death.

Chapter 5

Analysis of Alcohol-Related Mortality in U.S. Counties

Laurie Ellis McLeod, M.A.

KEY WORDS: AODR mortality; United States; geographical area; demographic characteristics; urban area; injury; age differences; hypothesis testing; regression analysis; causal model

Alcohol abuse and alcoholism have significant effects on many aspects of U.S. society, including the economy and the health care system. The economic costs of alcohol-related problems in 1995 were estimated at $185 billion (Harwood 2000). In addition to lost productivity, the economic costs are accrued directly from alcohol-related illness as well as from secondary or non-health effects of illness (e.g., crime, motor vehicle crashes, destruction of property, and social welfare). Approximately one-fourth of persons admitted to hospitals either have alcohol problems or are being treated for ailments or conditions that resulted from drinking alcohol (National Institute on Alcohol Abuse and Alcoholism [NIAAA] 1994*b*). Moderate to heavy consumption of alcohol is a major risk factor in the fourth leading cause of death in the United States, injury and trauma (NIAAA 1994*b*).

Despite an overall decline in per capita alcohol consumption during the 1980's through 1996 (Williams et al. 1998), about a third of traffic crash fatalities continue to involve alcohol (Yi et al. 1998), with young drivers overrepresented in drinking driver deaths. In addition to the alco-

L.E. McLeod, M.A., is a Ph.D. candidate in the Department of Individual and Family Studies, College of Human Resources, Education and Public Policy, University of Delaware, 121 Alison Hall West, Newark, DE 19716.

hol-related injury deaths, alcohol contributes to numerous chronic disease deaths. Thus each year over 100,000 deaths or about 5 percent of all deaths in the United States are alcohol-related.

In 1992, there were 107,440 alcohol-related deaths in the United States. Of this total, 18 percent were directly attributable to alcohol, 39 percent were from diseases indirectly attributable to alcohol, and 43 percent were from injuries indirectly attributable to alcohol (Stinson et al. 1996). Deaths where alcohol is mentioned on the death certificate are considered to be directly attributable to alcohol for research purposes. By contrast, deaths where alcohol is known to have been involved but is not noted on the death certificate for various reasons are considered to be alcohol-related or indirectly attributable to alcohol (see table 1, p. 100). This alcohol-related fraction (ARF) of involvement in injury or disease mortality is calculated based on known causes for various diseases and injuries. For research purposes, the ARF is added to the directly attributable rate of mortality for injury or disease in order to arrive at a more complete estimation of the total alcohol involvement in mortality (Dufour et al. 1993).

Figures 1 and 2 (p. 97) provide a visual representation of alcohol-related disease mortality compared with alcohol-related injury mortality, showing the prevalence of these types of mortality by county in the United States for the years 1988–92. Most striking is the fact that these levels (quartiles) of mortality represent only those deaths where alcohol was not explicitly mentioned on the death certificate.

This study analyzes the relationship of different types of alcohol-related mortality and population characteristics within a given geographic area. The *county* is the unit of analysis. Counties are analyzed using variables beyond the traditional social area measures of social status, urbanization, and ethnicity (Shevky and Bell 1955). The age structure of a given geographic area serves as one distinguishing characteristic of an area. Using the county unit of analysis, the relationship between the demographic characteristics of a geographic area and the risk of alcohol-related death and injury mortality is assessed. County age structure is significant in differentiating between counties with high and low alcohol-related injury fatality rates, and high and low alcohol-related disease mortality rates.

Alcohol-related mortality is defined as pertaining to "only to those patients diagnosed as having diseases directly caused by alcohol use, such as alcoholic cirrhosis of the liver" (NIAAA 1994*b*, p. 11), and mortality of this type is regularly reported in the National Hospital Discharge Survey (NHDS). There is another category of alcohol-related mortality that is not captured in the NHDS; this category includes all diseases or injuries *indirectly* attributable to alcohol (see table 1). The entire effect of alcohol on hospitalization is usually underestimated because the indirect connection with alcohol abuse is not included (NIAAA 1994*b*).

This study focuses on differences in alcohol-related mortality across counties. Mortality is analyzed by county age structures and other census-based variables. This model is tested for all 3,141 U.S.

counties. The result is the identification of a path model of counties having varying probability of alcohol-related deaths. The model produces an analysis of mortality risk through a social area typology. One of the major advantages of using the county as a unit of analysis is that the county is the typical geographic unit used by State government for assessing treatment needs and allocating funds. In one study conducted by McAuliffe and colleagues (1991), results of a statewide survey and social indicators indicated the need to increase the treatment services twofold within several of the smaller planning areas of the State of Rhode Island. Ford and Schmittdiel (1983) analyzed alcoholism treatment needs for small geographic areas. Several variables, particularly total population, deaths, and arrests, are predictive of alcoholism service levels by State, as reflected in the National Drug and Alcoholism Treatment Unit Survey.

THE USE OF SOCIAL AREA ANALYSIS IN SMALL GEOGRAPHIC AREAS

Social area analysis has proved to be effective for alcohol problem surveillance (NIAAA 1994*b*). Social indicators are especially effective for small geographic areas. Examples of such indicators include NIAAA's County Alcohol Problem Indicators (mortality rates) and the National Institute of Mental Health (NIMH) Mental Health Demographic Profile System (census data). When indicators, such as mortality, are analyzed by age, the analysis is especially useful for targeting prevention programs or other modalities sensitive to age (NIAAA 1994*b*). Cirrhosis mortality rates have been traditionally viewed as an indicator of alcohol problems. Cirrhosis mortality varies considerably by gender, race, and urbanization. Individuals who develop alcoholic cirrhosis show a higher likelihood of a prolonged history of drinking, usually 10–20 years (Grant et al. 1988; Parrish et al. 1991).

The findings that cirrhosis deaths are connected to alcohol consumption and that rates of all cirrhosis mortality (not just those coded alcohol-related) vary with alcohol consumption in the same time periods lead many researchers to treat cirrhosis mortality as an indicator of alcohol-related mortality (Dufour et al. 1993). Although cirrhosis may result from a variety of other causes (including hepatitis, exposure to toxic chemicals, use or abuse of various drugs, and viral or other infectious diseases), alcohol accounts for a large majority of cirrhosis deaths in the United States. The alcohol connection with cirrhosis, however, may be underestimated for two important reasons. First, the alcohol connection may go unspecified on death certificates. There are several reasons for this underreporting: (1) the physician may lack knowledge of the patient's drinking history, (2) the physician may desire to protect the decedent's family from the stigma of an alcoholic death (Van Natta and Aitken 1985), and (3) the relationship of the diagnoses to alcohol on the hospital discharge record is frequently disregarded or not specific enough to label a diagnosis alcohol-related. The second reason that the alcohol connection with cirrhosis might be underestimated is that alcohol may serve as a trigger to other cirrhosis risk factors such as drug abuse and AIDS.

A second type of mortality investigated in this study is alcohol-related injuries. Research findings document that alcoholics are at least five times more likely than nonalcoholics to die in motor vehicle crashes (Eckardt et al. 1988). At macro levels, fatal traffic crashes have been linked to per capita alcohol consumption in the same way that cirrhosis has been associated with drinking. Lowenfels and Wynn (1992) examined 19 countries around the world that have more than 200 vehicles per 1,000 population. They found that per capita alcohol consumption accounted for almost 70 percent of the variance in the death rates from vehicular accidents per 100 million vehicle-kilometers (Lowenfels and Wynn 1992). Further, their study revealed a direct association between alcohol consumption and vehicular deaths, both of which were reduced by the same amount during the period being studied (NIAAA 1994*b*).

Alcohol consumption impairs those skills needed to safely operate motor vehicles (Hindmarch et al. 1991). Still, the relationship between motor vehicle safety and drinking is more complex and involves a variety of other factors less well understood. Research strongly indicates that the effects of alcohol on traffic safety vary by age and gender (NIAAA 1994*b*). Thus, the age structure of the geographic area of analysis such as the county or planning area becomes an important variable when looking at relationships between motor vehicle fatalities and alcohol problems at the macro level.

OTHER GEOGRAPHIC FACTORS ASSOCIATED WITH ALCOHOL-RELATED MORTALITY

The relationship between alcohol abuse and urbanization creates a confounding problem in trying to establish a cause of mortality (Donnelly 1977). Household composition has an effect on alcohol consumption patterns (NIAAA 1994*b*). Moreover, studies on treated alcoholic patients show that a disproportionate number are products of homes in which parents had separated or divorced (Robins and Guze 1970). With the effect of household structure in mind, it was hypothesized that the percentage of single-family, detached dwelling units (SFDDs) would be negatively associated with alcohol-related disease mortality. The Shevky-Bell index of urbanization includes the proportion of SFDDs as an indicator that is inversely related to the composite index; for example, the lower the proportion of SFDDs, the higher the level of urbanization (Shevky and Bell 1955). The percentage of SFDDs has been found to be negatively related to cirrhosis deaths (Donnelly 1977). It was also expected that the percentage of families with income levels below the poverty level would be positively related to alcohol-related disease mortality. Areas with higher proportions of families with incomes below the poverty level tend to have less access to health care or no health care insurance, leaving them more at risk to develop health problems (NIAAA 1994*b*).

Alcohol-related chronic disease and injury mortality vary across geographic areas in a manner that reflects variables other than total population size. Shevky and Bell (1955) hypothesized that persons living in a particular type of social area differ systematically with respect to characteristic attitudes and behaviors from persons living in another type of social area (see also Holzer et al. 1989). In this study, the county is compared with other social areas using variables beyond the traditional social area measures (social status, urbanization, and ethnicity). From an epidemiologic perspective, the age structure of a geographic area may serve as a distinguishing characteristic of that area defining a population at risk. The county age structure is an important independent variable because it provides great explanatory power and has frequently been disregarded in social area analysis. Rather than being used as an independent variable, age is all too often standardized, adjusted to control for other variables of interest. Furthermore, age is rarely used to its full advantage in exploring treatment needs or planning programs.

In this study, age structure was expected to have a significant effect on the interaction between the dependent variables (unadjusted rate of *disease mortality* without alcohol mention, and unadjusted rate of *injury mortality* without alcohol mention) and to have considerable explanatory and statistical power (see table 1 for ICD-9 codes). Beyond the standard age strata effect, the indirect path model tests the intervening effect of urbanization and poverty as explanatory variables. Urbanization was found to be important in Donnelly's work (Donnelly 1977, 1978), and poverty was found to be important by Ciarlo and colleagues (1992).

Although it is known that geographic areas with older populations tend to have higher cirrhosis rates (NIAAA 1994*b*) and that States having a higher concentration of younger populations are typified by a higher motor vehicle fatality rate, this ecology has rarely been explored at the county level. The risk factors for accidents increase by the presence of more young people in an area. Similarly, it is well documented that drinking and driving fatalities are more prevalent in certain age groups, specifically the 16–24 and 25–44 groups (Donnelly 1977; Aitken and Zoebeck 1985; NIAAA 1997). The effects of some dimensions of social areas, such as urbanization and social rank (Goldsmith et al. 1984), have rarely been tested as explanatory variables in alcohol epidemiology (Donnelly 1977; Holzer et al. 1989). By integrating three explanatory concepts—age structure, socioeconomic status, and urbanization—within a single path model, both the main effects (direct paths) and interaction effects (indirect paths) of these independent variables on alcohol-related mortality are tested.

STATISTICAL METHOD

The method used in the analysis for this study is rooted in a research approach developed in sociology called causal network analysis (Davis 1994). The most well known application of this approach is path analysis (Duncan 1966), which was used in the development and analysis of the models in this study. According to Davis (1994), "when the data are construed as a network of linear relationships, it is possible to analyze variable means and pair relationships into exact components that can be tied to plausible causal structures" (p. 191).

Two path models were developed, a direct path model and an indirect path model. The models represent the interaction and possible paths between the independent variables—age structure of the population by county and intervening variables such as urbanization and poverty—and the dependent variables related to the prevalence of alcohol problems like disease mortality and injury mortality figures of different areas.

Independent Variables

The age structure variables were developed from the *1990 Census of Population and Housing Summary Tape File 3C* (U.S. Bureau of the Census 1990). There were eight separate age groups used for this study. Using the county unit of analysis, the raw population figures in each age group were divided by the total population for a given county in order to determine the *percentage* of population 15–19 years of age, for example. The other seven age groups included the percentage of population 20–24, 25–29, 30–39, 40–49, 50–59, 60–69, and 70 or more years of age.

The urbanization variables were also developed from the 1990 census summary tape file. These variables were the percentage of population in urban areas, the percentage of SFDDs, and the percentage of trailer-dwellings. The first of these three variables, percentage urban, included (as defined by the U.S. census) those persons identified as residing inside an urbanized area divided by the total population (urban and rural) within a given county. The second urbanization variable included the total number of SFDDs divided by the total number of all housing units in a given county. The last urbanization variable included the total number of trailer-dwellings divided by the total number of housing units in a given county.

The percentage of families with income below the poverty level by county was the last of the independent variables in the indirect path model. This variable was calculated from the total number of families identified as having income below the poverty level in 1989 divided by the total number of all families with income above and below the poverty level in 1989 (U.S. Bureau of the Census 1990).

Dependent Variables

Two dependent variables—alcohol-related disease mortality and alcohol-related injury mortality—were analyzed as part of both the direct and indirect path models in the study. The two variables were computed as the unadjusted rate of disease mortality without alcohol mention and the unadjusted rate of injury mortality without alcohol mention. These rates were derived from the NIAAA 1986–90 mortality data provided by the National Center for Health Statistics and the 1990 population census data. The mortality data consisted of death certificate information reported for the 48 continental States by county for the years 1986–90. The denominator was the average population age 15 and above, extracted from Census Bureau summary tapes. The mortality rate was calculated per hundred thousand population age 15 and above to determine the unadjusted age rate.

Direct Path Model

The hypothesis for the direct path model was that the relationship between age structure (middle to older age groups) and the unadjusted rate of alcohol-related disease mortality would be positive. That is, mortality would be highest in counties having a concentration of population in older age groups. This hypothesis did not hold in the direct path model (figure 3, p. 98). However, as will be seen, other intervening variables (indirect relationships) play a part in the relationship between age and the rate of disease mortality in the indirect path model. For example, the percentage of SFDDs revealed a 0.06 regression coefficient at $p < 0.001$ with disease mortality, and the 25–29 age group was 0.08 at $p < 0.05$ (figure 4, p. 99). Thus, age structure interacts with housing characteristics to affect alcohol-related disease mortality.

Injury mortality was hypothesized to be highest in counties having population concentrations in the younger age groups. This was true of two age groups in particular in the direct path model, those 20–24 and 30–39 (figure 3). These regression coefficients were both significant at the $p < 0.001$ level, −0.11 and −0.17, respectively (table 2, p. 101). Three other age groups—25–29, 40–49, and 60–69—were positively associated with the unadjusted rate of injury mortality in the direct path model. However, it should not be concluded that because a county might have a higher proportion of a certain age group that this is the particular group contributing to a higher incidence of alcohol-related disease or injury mortality. The relationship may be far more complex or include other intervening factors that lead to higher levels of mortality, for instance. These relationships should be examined closely for external or additional factors that might be indicative of high-risk populations existing in a given county or small area.

Indirect Path Model

The hypothesis for the indirect path model was that age would be positively associated with the unadjusted rate of disease mortality. For the 25–29 age group the regression coefficient was positive (0.08) and significant at the $p < 0.05$ level. The proportion of those ages 25–29 (relative to other age groups) was positively associated with alcohol-related disease mortality. The indirect path model included four intervening (control) urbanization variables: percentage of the population residing in urban areas, percentage of SFDDs, percentage of trailer-dwellings, and percentage of families with income below the poverty level.

The indirect path model tested two assumptions: (1) that age was negatively related to the unadjusted rate of alcohol-related injury mortality (the greater the concentration in younger age groups, the greater the injury mortality rates) and (2) that age would be positively associated with disease mortality. Neither assumption was borne out. The multiple regression analysis revealed three positive relationships in the indirect path model relating mortality to age. Concentrations of population in the 25–29, 40–49, and 70 and over age groups were found to be positively associated with the unadjusted rate of injury mortality in this model (figure 4). The regression coefficients were 0.21 at $p < 0.001$, 0.15 at $p < 0.001$, and 0.11 at $p < 0.05$, respectively. Nor was increasing age related to higher rates of disease mortality. The path analysis intervening variables (urbanization factors and the poverty) play a role in these relationships that had not been anticipated in this study.

In the indirect path model where all of the intervening variables are included, it was expected that the percentage of families living in trailer-dwellings would be positively associated with the unadjusted rate of injury mortality. This hypothesis was supported in the path analysis. The regression coefficient was 0.11 with $p < 0.001$.

The degree of urbanization was expected to be negatively correlated with alcohol-related injury mortality. Accordingly, it was expected that the percentage of SFDDs would be negatively associated with the rate of alcohol-related disease mortality. This did not prove to be the case, as is shown in figure 4; instead, the relationship was in the opposite direction. The percentage of SFDDs was positively related to the unadjusted rate of disease mortality with a modest coefficient of 0.06, $p < 0.05$.

It was also expected that the percentage of families in a county with income below the poverty level would be positively associated with the unadjusted rate of disease mortality. However, the association between poverty and disease mortality in the indirect path model was not significant and was eliminated from the final model for variables that would predict the rate of disease mortality (figure 4).

The percentage of families with income below the poverty level was positively significantly correlated with the unadjusted rate of alcohol-related injury mortality in a county. The regression analysis revealed a coefficient of 0.13, $p < 0.001$. The indirect path model revealed a positive relationship between families with income below the poverty level and the rate of injury mortality when other urbanization variables as well as age structure were included in the model. These intervening variables included the percentage of population in urban areas, the percentage of SFDDs, the percentage of trailer-dwellings, and the unadjusted age structure variables. The rate of injury was the dependent variable.

CONCLUSIONS

The salience of county age structure in explaining alcohol-related mortality in United States counties was confirmed. High rates of alcohol-related *disease mortality* were found disproportionately in counties having age distributions that are skewed toward either younger or older ages. High rates of alcohol-related *injury mortality*, in contrast, were found disproportionately in counties with concentrations of population in the 25–49 age range. The relative concentration of county population segments within certain age groups provides valuable information about the overall context of mortality risk. Age concentrations provide information beyond the age-specific mortality rates.

The urbanization variables also contribute to this model by showing that there is an interaction between age structure and urbanization that contributes to the understanding of alcohol-related mortality beyond the effect of age structure or urbanization alone. Urbanization mediates injury mortality in a different way than it mediates disease mortality. One might say that alcohol-related injury mortality appears to be related to a rural poverty culture. This pattern is also signified by the association of alcohol-related injury mortality with counties having large concentrations of trailers and low-income households. Alcohol-related disease mortality, on the other hand, tends to be more generally distributed across counties irrespective of their urbanization levels.

This study examined how summary measures of geographic areas provide valuable clues for identifying factors relating to the risk of different alcohol-related causes of death. Age structure was hypothesized to have a significant effect on the interaction between the dependent variables, and to have considerable explanatory and statistical power. This hypothesis was supported for demographic concentrations of several age groups that were correlated with alcohol-related mortality rates. The proportion of the county population 25–29 years of age was positively associated with the rate of disease mortality. This same relationship was also generally true of older populations in a given geographic area. The reasons for the findings in this path model are not entirely evident from this study. However, one explanation might be that the 25–29 age group, like its older counterparts, is also at risk for alcohol-related diseases when looking at the entire U.S. population. Generally, older people have a higher rate of illness and disease relative to their younger counterparts, whether alcohol-related or not (NIAAA 1994*b*).

The indirect path model did not reveal a higher rate of mortality associated with older age groups. There were no significant relationships between the proportions of persons in the various age groups and the rate of disease mortality in the direct path model (with no intervening urbanization or poverty variables). This suggests the likelihood that other factors are at work in the case of alcohol-related disease mortality. The indirect path model (including intervening variables) showed evidence of additional factor involvement in the 25–29 age group as well as with the percentage of SFDDs in a county.

Generally, the higher the age of a county population, the lower was the rate of alcohol-related injury mortality. Counties having a high proportion of the population in the 20–24 and 30–39 age groups were negatively related to the rate of injury mortality in the direct path model. This finding was consistent with previous research compiled by Zoebeck and colleagues (1993), who found that 33 percent of the alcohol-related traffic fatalities involved persons ages 16–24 years in 1991. More recently, in 1993, this age group accounted for 28 percent of all alcohol-impaired driver deaths (NIAAA 1997).

In contrast, the counties with high proportions of the population in the 25–29, 40–49, and 60–69 age groups showed concentrations of the rate of injury mortality (predominantly automobile fatalities). The reason for the difference in age groups remains unknown. A high proportion of the counties with older age groups such as those 40–49 and 70 and over also revealed a positive relationship to the rate of alcohol-related injury mortality. Most notably, a concentration in the 25–29 age group showed a positive association with both disease mortality and injury mortality (figure 4). This age group tends to have some overlap with the 25–44 age group, which is commonly associated with the highest levels of drinking and driving.

The percentage of trailer-dwellings in a county was found to be correlated with alcohol-related injury mortality. This hypothesis was supported in the indirect path model where the path coefficient was 0.11 with $p < 0.001$, signifying an existing relationship with one or more of the urbanization and poverty variables. The percentage of trailer-dwellings in counties was positively associated with the rate of injury mortality. Also, counties having persons residing in places of less than 2,500 outside of urbanized areas exhibit a higher rate of injury and have a negative relationship with cirrhosis mortality (Donnelly 1977, 1978).

There was no significant relationship between the percentage of trailer-dwellings and the rate of alcohol-related disease mortality in the indirect path model where the intervening variables included the percentage of families with income below the poverty level. Areas with concentrations of trailers may prove to be more prone to register high rates of alcohol-related deaths in particular regions of the country (Wilson et al. 1994*b*), but this could not be generalized to the U.S. counties.

Social area models are useful in identifying a typology of geographic areas having variable risks for alcohol-related mortality. Social area analysis is clearly less useful in identifying individuals having alcohol problems. For example, social indicators will identify geographic areas with high rates of alcohol problems but will not predict whether people needing treatment will actually avail themselves of the services. Age structure was significantly associated with different patterns of alcohol-related mortality. Urbanization was clearly identified as a critical intervening variable. The percentage of SFDDs was positively associated with alcohol-related disease mortality.

There also appear to be other unidentified factors contributing to the overall relationship in the indirect path model used in this study. Further exploratory analysis would be necessary to confirm these possibilities. Again, exploration of the direct relationships between the three urbanization variables might reveal some linkages that were not detected in this model. The poverty variable should probably be included in this type of exploration as well.

In summary, census-based variables appear to hold promise as synthetic indicators, or indirect estimators, of the prevalence of alcohol abuse and other alcohol-related disorders. This study supports the potential utility of models incorporating area demographic characteristics in prevalence estimation at the census tract level (Goldsmith et al. 1984; Ciarlo et al. 1992).

REFERENCES

Aitken, S.S., and Zoebeck, T. Epidemiologic Bulletin No. 8: Trends in alcohol-related fatal motor vehicle accidents for 1983. *Alcohol Health Res World* 9(4):60–62, 1985.

Ciarlo, J.A., and Tweed, D.L. VI. Implementing indirect needs-assessment models for planning state mental health and substance abuse services. *Evaluation and Program Planning* 15:195–210, 1992.

Ciarlo, J.A.; Tweed, D.L.; Shern, D.L.; Kirkpatrick, L.A.; and Sachs-Ericsson, N. Validation of indirect methods to estimate need for mental health services. *Evaluation and Program Planning* 15:115–131, 1992.

Davis, J.A. What's wrong with sociology? *Sociological Forum* 9(2):179–197, 1994.

Donnelly, P.G. An ecological analysis of problem drinking. Master's thesis, University of Delaware, 1977.

Donnelly, P.G. Alcohol problems and sales in the counties of Pennsylvania. *J Stud Alcohol* Vol. 39(5), 1978.

Dufour, M.C.; Stinson, F.S.; and Fe Caces, M. Trends in cirrhosis morbidity and mortality: United States, 1979–1988. *Semin Liver Dis* 13(2):109–125, 1993.

Duncan, O.D. Path analysis: Sociological examples. *Am J Sociol* 72:1–16, 1966.

Eckardt, M.J.; Rawlings, R.R.; Graubard, B.I.; Faden, V.; Marin, P.R.; and Gottschalk, L.A. Neuropsychological performance and treatment outcome in male alcoholics. *Alcohol Clin Exp Res* 12(1):88–93, 1988.

Ford, W.E., and Schmittdiel, C.J. Predicting alcoholism service needs from a national treatment utilization survey. *International Journal of the Addictions* 18(8):1073–1084, 1983.

Goldsmith, H.F.; Jackson, D.J.; Doenhoeffer, S.; Johnson, W.; Tweed, D.L.; Stiles, D.; Barbano, J.P.; and Warheit, G.J. *The Health Demographic Profile System's Inventory of Small Area Social Indicators.* National Institute of Mental Health Series BN No. 4. DHHS Pub. No. ADM 84–1354. Washington, DC: U.S. Government Printing Office, 1984.

Grant, B.F.; Dufour, M.C.; and Harford, T.C. Epidemiology of alcoholic liver disease. *Semin Liver Dis* 8(1):12–25, 1988.

Harwood, H. *Updating Estimates of the Economic Costs of Alcohol Abuse in the United States: Estimates, Update Methods and Data.* Report prepared by the Lewin Group for the National Institute on Alcohol Abuse and Alcoholism (NIAAA). Bethesda, MD: NIAAA, 2000.

Hindmarch, I.; Kerr, J.S.; and Sherwood, N. The effects of alcohol and other drugs on psychomotor performance and cognitive function. *Alcohol* 26(1):71–79, 1991.

Holzer, C.E., III; Swanson, J.W.; Ganju, J.K.; Goldsmith, H.F.; and Jackson, D.J. Estimates of need for mental health services in Texas counties. In: Bojean, C.M.; Coleman, M.T.; and Iscoe, I., eds. *Community Care of the Chronically Mentally Ill.* Austin: Hogg Foundation for Mental Health, Univer-sity of Texas, 1989.

Lowenfels, A.B., and Wynn, P.S. One less for the road: International trends in alcohol consumption and vehicular fatalities. *Ann Epidemiol* 2(3):249–256, 1992.

McAuliffe, W.E.; Breer, P.; Ahmadifar, N.W.; and Spino, C. Assessment of drug abuser treatment needs in Rhode Island. *Am J Public Health* 81(3):365–371, 1991.

Morse, R.M., and Flavin, D.K. Special communication: The definition of alcoholism. *JAMA* 268:1012–1014, 1992.

National Institute on Alcohol Abuse and Alcoholism (NIAAA). *County Alcohol Problem Indicators 1986–1990.* Rockville, MD: NIAAA, 1994*a*.

National Institute on Alcohol Abuse and Alcoholism (NIAAA). *Eighth Special Report to the U.S. Congress on Alcohol and Health.* NIH Pub. No. 94–3699. Bethesda, MD: National Institutes of Health, 1994*b*.

National Institute on Alcohol Abuse and Alcoholism (NIAAA). *Ninth Special Report to the U.S. Congress on Alcohol and Health.* NIH Pub. No. 97–4017. Bethesda, MD: National Institutes of Health, 1997.

Parrish, K.M.; Higuchi, S.; and Dufour, M.C. Alcoholic consumption and the risk for developing cirrhosis: Implications for future research. *J Subst Abuse* 3(3):325–335, 1991.

Robins, L., and Guze, S. Drinking practices and problems in urban ghetto populations. Presented at Recent Advances in Studies of Alcoholism. Washington, D.C.: National Institute of Mental Health, 1970.

Shevky, E., and Bell, W. *Social Area Analysis.* Stanford, CA: Stanford University Press, 1955.

Shultz, J.M.; Rice, D.P.; and Parker, D.L. Alcohol-related mortality and years of potential life lost—United States, 1987. *MMWR Morb Mortal Wkly Rep* 39(11): 173–178, 1990.

Stinson, F.S.; Nephew, T.M.; Dufour, M.C.; and Grant, B.F. *State Trends in Alcohol-Related Mortality, 1979-92.* U.S. Alcohol Epidemiologic Data Reference Manual, Vol. 5, First Edition. Bethesda, MD: National Institute on Alcohol Abuse and Alcoholism, 1996.

U.S. Bureau of the Census. *1990 Census of Population and Housing Summary Tape File 3C.* Disk No. CD90–3C–1. Washington, DC: Bureau of the Census, Data User Services Division, 1990. Reissued May 1993.

Van Natta, P., and Aitken, S.S. Epidemiologic Bulletin No. 7: Chronic liver disease and cirrhosis as alcohol-related diagnoses. *Alcohol Health Res World* 9(4):56–63, Summer 1985.

Williams, G.D.; Stinson, F.S.; Sanchez, L.L.; and Dufour, M.C. *Surveillance Report No. 47: Apparent Per Capita Alcohol Consumption: National, State and Regional Trends, 1977–96.* Bethesda, MD: National Institute on Alcohol Abuse and Alcoholism, 1998.

Wilson, R.A.; McLeod, L.E.; and Dufour, M.C. County demographic structure and alcohol-related mortality: An exploratory model of alcohol-related mortality where alcohol is not mentioned on the death certificate. Paper presented at the Eastern Sociological Society Conference, Baltimore, MD, March 1994*b*.

Yi, H.; Stinson, F.S.; Williams, G.D.; and Bertolucci, D. *Surveillance Report No. 465: Trends in Alcohol-Related Fatal Traffic Crashes, United States, 1977–96.* Bethesda, MD: National Institute on Alcohol Abuse and Alcoholism, 1998.

Zoebeck, T.S.; Stinson, F.S.; Grant, B.F.; and Bertolucci, D. *Surveillance Report No. 26: Trends in Alcohol-Related Fatal Traffic Crashes, United States: 1979–1991.* Bethesda, MD: National Institute on Alcohol Abuse and Alcoholism, November 1993.

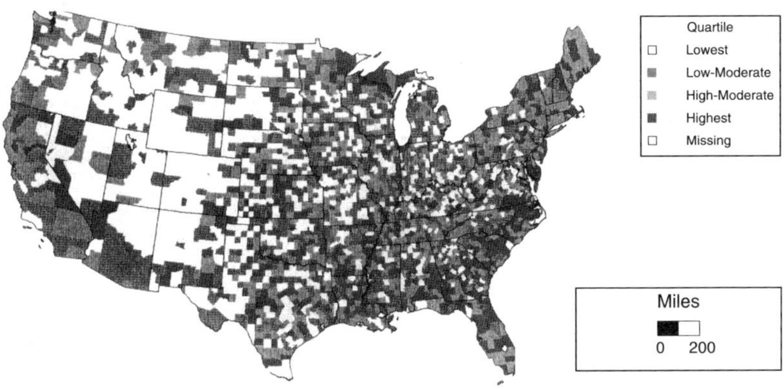

Figure 1. Alcohol-related disease mortality without mention of alcohol on the death certificate: U.S. counties. Data from U.S. Bureau of the Census 1990 and from NIAAA 1994*a*.

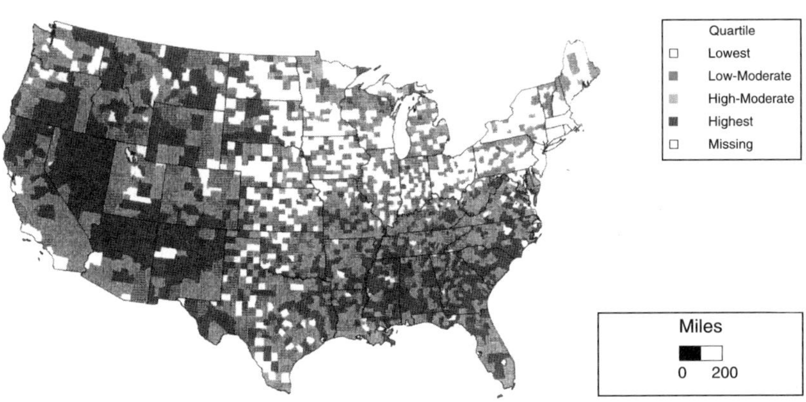

Figure 2. Alcohol-related injury mortality without mention of alcohol on the death certificate: U.S. counties. Data from U.S. Bureau of the Census 1990 and from NIAAA 1994*a*.

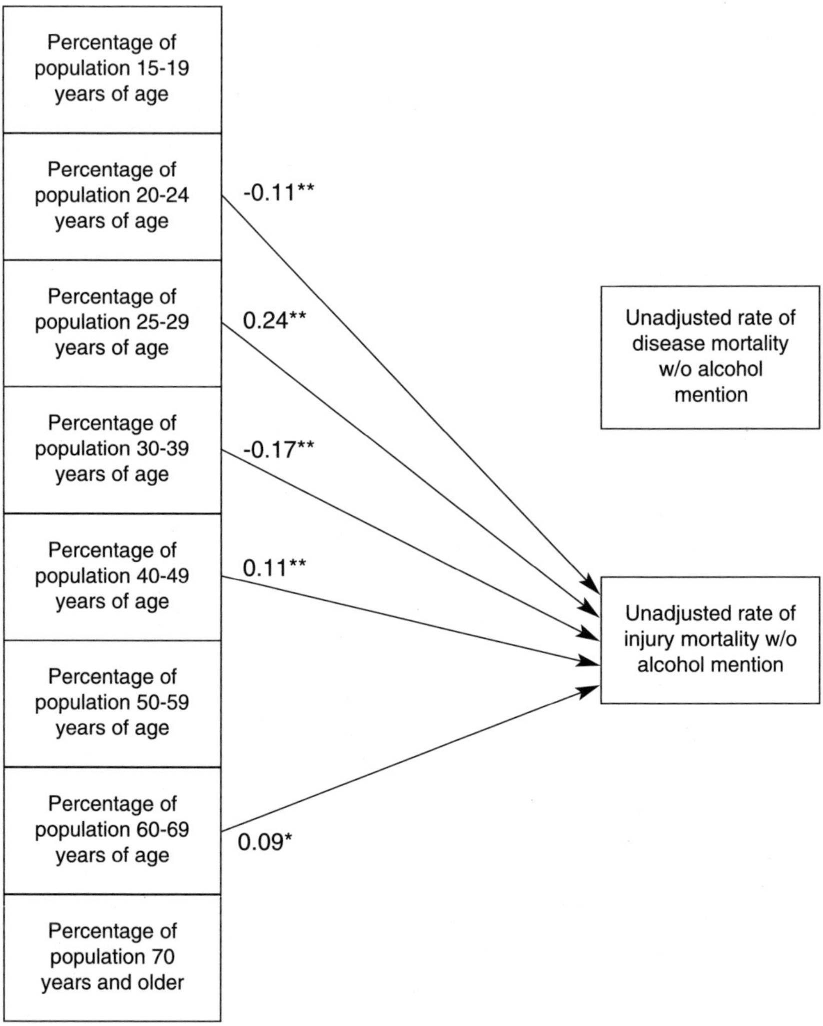

Figure 3. Direct path model between age structure and the unadjusted rate of disease mortality without alcohol mention and the unadjusted rate of injury mortality without alcohol mention. $*p < 0.05$; $**p < 0.001$.

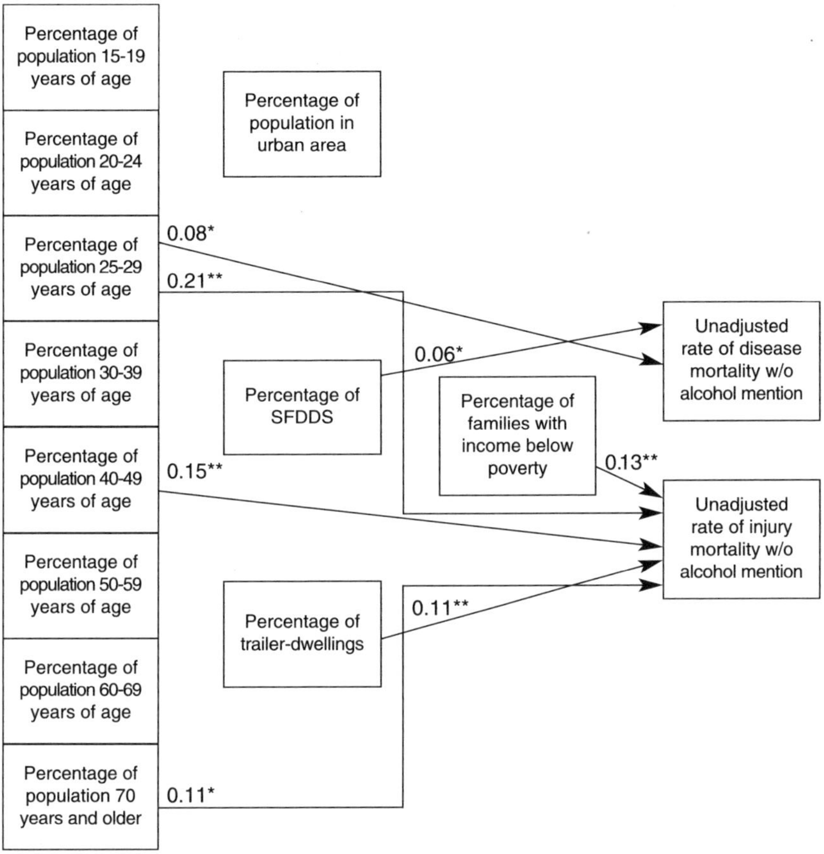

Figure 4. Indirect path model between age structure and the unadjusted rate of disease mortality without alcohol mention and the unadjusted rate of injury mortality without alcohol mention. SFDDs = single-family, detached dwelling units.
$^{*}p < 0.05$; $^{**}p < 0.001$.

Table 1. Classification of Alcohol-Related Causes of Death, Alcohol-Attributable Fractions (AAFs), and Ages for Which Fractions Are Used.

Classification and Diagnosis (ICD-9 Code)	AAF	Age
Diseases indirectly attributable to alcohol		
Pulmonary and other respiratory tuberculosis (011,012)	0.25	≥ 35
Malignant neoplasm of lip, oral cavity and pharynx (140-149)	0.50*	≥ 35
Malignant neoplasm of esophagus (150)	0.75	≥ 35
Malignant neoplasm of stomach (151)	0.20	≥ 35
Malignant neoplasm of liver and intrahepatic bile ducts (155)	0.15	≥ 35
Malignant neoplasm of larynx (161)	0.50*	≥ 35
Diabetes mellitus (250)	0.05	≥ 35
Essential hypertension (401)	0.076	≥ 35
Cerebrovascular disease (430-438)	0.065	≥ 35
Pneumonia and influenza (480-487)	0.05	≥ 35
Diseases of esophagus, stomach and duodenum (530-537, ex 535.3)	0.10	≥ 35
Cirrhosis of liver without mention of alcohol (571.5)	0.50	≥ 35
Biliary cirrhosis (571.6)	0.50	≥ 35
Acute pancreatitis (577.0)	0.42	≥ 35
Chronic pancreatitis (577.1)	0.60	≥ 35
Injuries and adverse effects indirectly attributable to alcohol		
Motor vehicle traffic and nontraffic accidents (E810-E825)	0.42	> 0
Pedal cycle and other road vehicle accidents (E826,E829)	0.20	> 0
Water transport accidents (E830-E838)	0.20	> 0
Air and space transport accidents (E840-E845)	0.16	> 0
Accidental falls (E880-E888)	0.35	≥ 15
Accidents caused by fire and flames (E890-E899)	0.45	> 0
Accidental drowning and submersion (E910)	0.38	> 0
Suicide and self-inflicted injury (E950-E959)	0.28	≥ 15
Homicide and injury purposely inflicted by other persons (E960-E969)	0.46	≥ 15
Other injuries and adverse effects	0.25	≥ 15
Excessive cold (E901)		
Inhalation or ingestion of food causing obstruction of respiratory tract or suffocation (E911)		
Striking against or struck accidentally by objects or persons (E917)		
Caught accidentally in or between objects (E918)		
Accidents caused by machinery (E919)		
Accidents caused by cutting and piercing instruments or objects (E920)		
Accident caused by firearm missile (E922)		
Poisoning by solid or liquid substances, undetermined whether accidentally or purposely inflicted (E980)		

Note: ICD-9 = International Classification of Diseases, Ninth Revision.
*AAF is 0.40 for females.
Source: Adapted from National Institute on Alcohol Abuse and Alcoholism. *Eighth Special Report to the U.S. Congress on Alcohol and Health.* NIH Pub. No. 94–3699. Bethesda, MD: National Institutes of Health, 1994.

Table 2. Significant Slopes: Alcohol-Related Injury Mortality and Selected Variables.

Age Structure	**Direct**	**Indirect**
% of population:		
15–19		
20–24	-0.11***	
25–29	0.24***	0.21***
30–39	-0.17***	
40–49	0.11***	0.15***
50–59		
60–69	-0.09*	
70+		0.11*
Urbanization		
Living in urban areas		
Single-family, detached dwelling units		
Trailer-dwellings		0.11***
Families with income below poverty level		0.13***

Note: There are no intervening variables in the direct path model. The indirect path model includes all intervening urbanization variables.
*$p < 0.05$; **$p < 0.0001$.

Chapter 6

Severity of Alcohol and Other Drug Abuse/Dependency and Other Behavioral Health Problems in Metropolitan and Nonmetropolitan Areas

Harold F. Goldsmith, Ph.D., Charles Holzer III, Ph.D., and Ronald W. Manderscheid, Ph.D.

Key Words: disease severity; needs assessment; psychological assessment; addiction care; psychiatric care; health care delivery; health care utilization; comorbidity; violence; behavioral and mental disorder; psychodiagnostic interview; diagnostic criteria; survey; validity (research methods); urban area; rural area; literature review

Administrators of alcohol, drug, and other behavioral health (ADBH) services are responsible for the rational allocation of limited staff and financial resources. To facilitate the planning process for these allocations, administrators promote and use needs assessment research. This research enables administrators to make practical choices about what kind of services should be provided and when, where, and how frequently these services should be provided to clients in their service areas (Goldsmith et al. 1988; Ciarlo et al. 1992). Appropriate estimation of need for ADBH services is a prerequisite for realizing these policy objectives. This chapter takes a step in

H.F. Goldsmith, Ph.D., is a consultant in applied demography, 5006 Russett Rd., Rockville, MD 20853. C. Holzer III, Ph.D., is a professor in the Department of Psychiatry and Behavioral Science Psychiatric Epidemiology at the University of Texas Medical Branch at Galveston, 1.213 Graves Bldg., 301 University Blvd., Galveston, TX 77555–0429. R.W. Manderscheid, Ph.D., is chief of the Survey and Analysis Branch at the Center for Mental Health Services, Substance Abuse and Mental Health Services Administration, Parklawn Bldg. 15C04, 5600 Fishers Lane, Rockville, MD 20857.

that direction by providing a working model of an important needs assessment tool: a severity-based measure of the need for ADBH services.

The chapter focuses upon the development of an ADBH severity scale rather than a direct measure of need for ADBH services because severity is more amenable to measurement than need, and the two are clearly related (Horn et al. 1983*a*, 1983*b*, 1984; Horn and Horn 1986; Holzer et al. 1988; Mezzich and Sharfstein 1985; Regier et al. 1984*b*; Taube et al. 1984; Ware et al. 1984; Horn et al., "Psychiatric severity of illness: A case mix study," Center for Hospital Finance and Management, Department of Health Policy and Management, School of Hygiene and Public Health, Johns Hopkins University, unpublished paper 1985.). The scale is developed using the core data from Wave I (1981–85) of the five-site Epidemiologic Catchment Area (ECA) survey sponsored by the National Institute of Mental Health (NIMH), the largest and most comprehensive survey of ADBH problems among community residents (Regier et al. 1984*a*). The reasonableness of using this scale in needs assessments is evaluated by examining the relationships between severity of ADBH problems and ADBH service utilization, impairment of routine role behavior, and comorbidity of ADBH problems.

THE ECA STUDY

The five ECA sites were in the vicinity of New Haven, CT (5,034 respondents); Baltimore, MD (3,481 respondents); St. Louis, MO (3,003 respondents); Durham, NC (3,921 respondents); and Los Angeles, CA (3,131 respondents). The goals and scope of the project have been presented by Regier and colleagues (1984*a*). The ECA study represents the first large-scale application of DSM-III (American Psychiatric Association 1980) diagnostic criteria in a community survey (see Robins 1986). Details of the sampling design have been reported by Eaton and colleagues (1984) and by Holzer and colleagues (1985).

All five ECA sites employed a nearly uniform interview protocol, the Diagnostic Interview Schedule (DIS), to gather information about psychiatric disorder's, utilization of health and mental health services, and sociodemographic characteristics (Robins 1986). In addition to core items collected by all five sites, each site designed unique sections dealing with possible risk factors for disorder and disability. The Wave I DIS is a structured instrument designed to be administered by lay interviewers to elicit the elements of 12 DSM-III diagnoses: alcohol abuse/dependence, anorexia, antisocial personality, bipolar depressive disorder, drug abuse/dependence, dysthymia, major depression, obsessive-compulsive disorder, panic, phobias, schizophrenia/schizophreniform disorder, and somatization. (For a discussion of the validity and reliability of the DIS, see Robins et al. 1982; Anthony et al. 1985; Helzer et al. 1985; Escobar et al. 1986; Helzer et al. 1987; Helzer and Robins 1988; Klerman 1989; Mirowsky and Ross 1989; Tweed and George 1989.)

The disorder with the highest prevalence rate not included in Wave I of the ECA survey was generalized anxiety disorder (GAD). Ignoring the diagnostic hierarchy, an estimated 3.8 percent of the population of the United States had such a disorder (Blazer et al. 1991, 1987*b*). If persons with both GAD and other disorders are excluded, the percentage of persons with GAD is reduced to only 1.7. The more recent National Comorbidity Survey (NCS) also found high levels of comorbidity for persons with GAD. Kessler (1994; see also R.C. Kessler, "Estimates of the prevalence of serious emotional disorder [SED]," Institute for Social Research/Survey Research Center, University of Michigan, unpublished statistical note 1994) reported that 90 percent of the NCS respondents with a lifetime diagnosis of GAD had another disorder. Accordingly, given the high comorbidity observed for persons with GAD, the effect on a severity scale of not having information on GAD in Wave I of the ECA survey should be negligible.

All Wave I interviews were conducted in the field between 1980 and 1984 by trained laypersons. Typically, interviews were completed in 60–90 minutes. The completion rates at each site ranged from 77 to 80 percent, with refusals accounting for a high proportion of nonresponses (Holzer et al. 1985).

The survey data were weighted to compensate for unequal probabilities of selection in the community's samples of each site. Design weights were implemented as the inverse of the probability of selection and were consequently different at each site (Kessler et al. 1985). Additional inequality of selection was introduced by nonresponse. To adjust for nonresponse and any remaining lack of fit to the population distributions of the specific sites, a set of poststratification weights was generated by taking into account the age, gender, and race (black vs. nonblack) characteristics of the survey areas after applying preliminary weights (Holzer et al. 1985; Kessler et al. 1985). An additional down weight developed by Max Woodbury was introduced to make the sample approximate the size of "a simple random sample with same variance" (Leaf et al. 1991, p. 28). Leaf and colleagues noted that using the Woodbury weighting procedure "produces results that tend to overcompensate rather than undercompensate for artifacts produced by stratification . . . . Because the correction is a constant applied to each respondent's weighted values, it has no effect on estimates of prevalence or their relationships" but does have an effect on tests of statistical significance. All percentages in the severity scale by risk factors presented in this analysis have been weighted as described.

Properly weighted, five-site data can be merged to form one large "sample" of approximately 18,000 cases. In this analysis, the data for metropolitan and nonmetropolitan portions of ECA sites were considered separately. This was done to provide better control over socioenvironmental factors. Metropolitan areas (generally counties socially and economically integrated with large cities on a daily basis) and nonmetropolitan areas (counties not socially and economically integrated with large cities) are expected to have different distributions of ADBH problems (Goldsmith et al. in press). Unlike earlier studies that evaluated the difference in prevalence of ADBH disorders or problems between metropolitan and nonmetropolitan ECA respondents (Blazer et al. 1985, 1987*a*), this study classifies Franklin County, NC, as a metropolitan rather than a nonmetropolitan county. This is because in 1983, when the ECA data were being collected, Franklin County was reclassified by the Bureau of the Census from a nonmetropolitan to a metropolitan county (U.S. Bureau of the Census 1984).

Some inherent limitations exist in constructing measures of the severity of ADBH problems from the multisite database. Sites vary somewhat in the variables they include and in probes for symptom recency and onset. However, data from the sites are sufficiently similar that common measures can be constructed (Boyd et al. 1984; Robins 1986). Usually, a single probe following a whole diagnostic section must be used to define the recency of ADBH problems, as well as age of onset for a specific symptom of interest.

SEVERITY OF ADBH PROBLEMS

In the remainder of this chapter, a severity of ADBH problems scale (hereafter, severity scale) will be operationally specified and evaluated. Consistent with the literature, any symptoms or signs that cause or are associated with ADBH problems that involve distress (impairments resulting in pain), dysfunction (including disabilities), or dangerousness, or the threat of these conditions, represent ADBH problems of clinical significance (see American Psychiatric Association 1980; Goldsmith et al. 1988).[1] The development of a severity scale thus represents an ordering of persons with clinically significant ADBH problems with respect to their extent of distress, dysfunction, and dangerousness (Endicott et al. 1976; Leff 1982; Regier et al. 1984*b;* Leff et al. 1985; Holzer and Swanson 1986; Goldsmith et al. 1988).

In this chapter, ADBH problems rather than ADBH disorders are being considered. This is because such problems are a more inclusive domain than disorders and are more directly related to service utilization and need for services (Brenner 1985; Shapiro et al. 1985; Tischler et. al. 1988*b*). Stated simply, persons who have severe ADBH problems do need services whether or not they meet the formal criteria for a particular psychiatric disorder. In fact, persons with problems and no diagnosable disorder are frequently major recipients of treatment (Wing 1986; Goldsmith et al. 1988; Tischler et al. 1988*b*).

Ideally, the severity scale that is being developed should rank persons along a continuum from good ADBH (no symptoms) to poor ADBH (severely distressed, incapacitated, and/or dangerous) and should be based upon separate measures of three conceptually independent domains of severity (distress, dysfunction, and dangerousness). However, the core ECA data do not have the items necessary to adequately specify recent distress, dysfunction, or dangerousness independent of measures of disorder. Using core ECA data, the best that can be done is to develop a set of categories, comparatively homogeneous with respect to severity of ADBH problems, which are approximately ordered along the dimensions of severity.

In developing such a scale, one could base the categories on the number of symptoms, as done in ADBH severity scales developed after World War II (Weissman and Klerman 1978; Murphy 1981; Weissman et al. 1986; Tischler et al. 1988*a*), or one could develop categories based on a hierarchical arrangement of symptom patterns. The latter approach is taken in this chapter. It is assumed that categories based on symptom patterns approximate a clinician's approach to severity of ADBH problems and thereby provide a better scale than one based simply on the number of symptoms. This position is influenced by the diagnostic hierarchy presented in DSM-III, wherein some disorders and clinically significant symptom patterns (problems) take precedence over others when only one diagnosis per patient is required (see Boyd et al. 1984), as well as by the logic of the Present State Examination (PSE) developed by Wing and others, which incorporates the hierarchical ordering of ADBH problems (Ingham 1981; Wing et al. 1981). Thus, we suggest that if only one diagnosis or clinically significant problem is assigned to a patient, it is reasonable to expect that the most severe diagnosis with respect to disease course and treatment will be assigned. Moreover, these ADBH problems can be ordered with respect to severity. Wing and colleagues (Wing et al. 1981; Wing 1986) suggested that persons with nonspecific symptoms are less severely ill than persons with specific symptoms, who in turn are less severely ill than persons with borderline disorders, who in turn are less severely ill than persons with other ADBH disorders (see also Ingham 1981).

Following the general order provided by Wing and colleagues but also taking account of distress, dysfunction, and dangerousness, our measurement of severity of recent problems begins with the definition of four categories (anchor points) judgmentally ordered by level of severity identifiable from core ECA data (Endicott et al. 1976). The four categories of severity are

1. recent ADBH disorder and threat of dangerousness,
2. recent *major* ADBH disorder and no threat of dangerousness
3. recent *minor* ADBH disorder and no threat of dangerousness, and
4. no recent ADBH disorder.

The fourth category is further subdivided into six subcategories: recent major ADBH subcriterion psychiatric symptom pattern, recent minor ADBH subcriterion symptom pattern, past major ADBH disorder, past minor ADBH disorder, three or more symptoms (no past disorder), and less than three symptoms (no past disorder). Specific rationales and operational procedures are described below.

Disorder and the Threat of Dangerousness

The first category of the severity scale consists of persons with a recent

ADBH disorder accompanied by indications of the threat of dangerousness to themselves or others. The reason that this category is the highest level of severity is that a consensus exists among mental health professionals that if a person with a ADBH problem has a life-threatening condition (i.e., is clearly dangerous to self or others), an immediate need exists for ADBH services (Regier et al. 1984*b;* also see Leff 1982; Leff et al. 1985; Holzer et al. 1989). Moreover, such persons are likely to require intensive care, at least initially (Endicott et al. 1976; Leff 1982; Leff et al. 1985).

Operationally, respondents are defined as having a recent ADBH condition with the threat of dangerousness if they satisfy two criteria: (1) they had a recent (past year) Wave I ADBH DIS/DSM-III diagnosis other than cognitive impairment and (2) they manifest recent (past year) dangerous tendencies.[2] First, the presence of a recent ADBH DIS/DSM-III disorder is considered sufficient evidence of clinically significant levels of distress and dysfunction (see American Psychiatric Association 1980). Persons with such disorders are presumed to be more distressed and dysfunctional as a result of an ADBH problem than other people. Summarizing the logic of the DIS probes, Robins and colleagues (1981) noted that such disorders were "sufficiently severe to lead to seeing a physician, taking medication more than once, or interfering significantly with a person's life . . . and [were] not explainable by physical exertion, a life-threatening situation, or a physical disorder" (p. 382). Second, DIS/DSM-III diagnoses are assumed to be exacerbated by the possibility of concurrent life-threatening behaviors.

The core ECA data set contains several symptoms that we can use to indicate the threat of dangerousness. Before indicating the symptoms, it should be noted that the label "threat of dangerousness" is used because actual dangerousness cannot be distinguished from potential dangerousness. Dangerousness to self is most obviously indicated by suicidal thoughts or actual attempts, and dangerousness to others can be indexed by symptoms relating to overt violence and abuse of others: history of fighting, hitting a spouse or child, neglecting a child, getting in fights while drinking, or using weapons in a fight (Holzer and Swanson 1986).[3] A respondent was coded positive if he or she reported such symptoms and also responded having some disorder-specific symptoms during the past year. The disorder-specific symptoms were based on responses to the "summary recency of symptoms probe" following a whole diagnostic section. This permitted the coding of dangerousness to be the same in all sites. This means that while the recency of symptoms could be determined precisely for three sites, such information was not utilized because its use would not have permitted dangerousness to be coded in the same manner in each site. Persons without a recent disorder (category 4) were considered not to have an ADBH problem that is directly related to the threat of dangerousness.

Major and Minor Disorders, Not Dangerous

After the category of persons with recent disorders with the threat of dangerousness, the next two categories include persons with recent major ADBH disorders and persons with recent minor ADBH disorders who are not dangerous. The distinction between major and minor ADBH disorders is based upon the diagnostic hierarchy presented in DSM-III. When only one diagnosis per respondent is required, the most severe disorder takes precedence over others and is the primary diagnosis assigned to a person. Accordingly, for the DIS/DSM-III disorders, we include as major disorders alcohol and drug abuse or dependence (other than cannabis), "major" schizophrenia (including schizophreniform), and major affective disorders (excluding dysthymia); these disorders take precedence over the remaining diagnoses when the diagnostic hierarchy is invoked. A similar designation of ADBH disorders that are severe, persistent, and disabling was made by NIMH in their 1991 publication *Caring for People With Severe Mental Disorders.*

"Minor disorders," then, is a residual category including antisocial behavior, phobias, panic disorders, somatization, dysthymia, obsessive-compulsive disorders, cannabis abuse, and anorexia (American Psychiatric Association 1980).[4] Persons with the diagnosis of cognitive impairment were excluded from consideration because their responses to the DIS were not considered sufficiently valid or reliable to be evaluated with respect to severity (Holzer et al. 1984, 1989).

Persons Without Recent Disorder

At this point we are left with the problem of determining a reasonable way to categorize persons with no recent Wave I ADBH DIS/DSM-III disorders. One way is to separate persons with any present or past psychiatric symptom patterns from persons without such symptoms. Following Wing and colleagues (Wing et al. 1981; Wing 1986), persons with no present or past symptoms can be considered to be at the lowest level of severity. Accordingly, these persons should constitute the lowest category of our severity scale. Unfortunately, it is not possible to accurately identify persons with no DIS/DSM-III symptoms using the existing core ECA data, because "symptom patterns may vary between sites because of difference in the skip pattern of the . . . questionnaires [used by the sites]" (Epidemiologic Catchment Area Code Book, Center for Epidemiologic Studies, NIMH, unpublished document May 15, 1985). Thus, the lowest severity category is arbitrarily set as persons with fewer than three symptoms. This provides some control over the skip patterns and clearly separates persons with very few symptoms from those with more symptoms.

For the remaining respondents, persons with recent or past Wave I ADBH DIS/DSM-III symptoms, we suggest that the anchor points provided by Wing and colleagues (Wing et al. 1981; Wing 1986) in the PSE be used to develop severity categories for ECA respondents with recent or past symptoms. Operationally, we approximate the more severe PSE categories, persons with recent symptoms (in the past year) but no disorders, by making use of *disorder-level* recency items in the DIS. Persons who have sufficient symptomatology to be asked a recency probe for a specific disorder and who respond positively to the probe of symptoms in the past year, but who do not meet diagnostic criteria, are considered to have recent subcriterion ADBH symptomatology (i.e., subcriterion ADBH symptom patterns). This category is likely to include persons with recent borderline ADBH disorders, as well as persons with specific ADBH symptoms as identified in the PSE.[5]

Clearly, the approach being taken is not ideal. It depends upon the skip rules of the DIS, rather than on consistency of severity levels as determined from symptom patterns or symptom counts. An alternative version of this approach would be to use the *item-level* recency probes to construct an index of current symptomatology. However, adopting this approach would eliminate the possibility of having index values for two sites, New Haven and St. Louis, where such information was not available. In order to maintain a structure similar to that of disorders, the recent ADBH subcriterion symptom patterns are subdivided into major types (alcohol abuse or dependency, other drug abuse or dependency [excludes marijuana, tobacco, and caffeine], and major affective or schizophrenia [including schizophreniform] subcriterion symptom patterns) and minor types (all other subcriterion symptom patterns). (Throughout this chapter, the term "other drug" will be used to refer to drugs including those such as cocaine or heroin but excluding marijuana, tobacco, or caffeine.)

For the remaining respondents, persons with some past or recent (past year) symptoms, but no recent subcriterion symptom patterns, it is not possible to determine if their reported lifetime symptoms are past or recent for all ECA sites. Consequently, we cannot separate persons with some recent symptoms from those with only past symptoms. The best that we can do is to separate the remaining persons with past ADBH disorder (i.e., sufficient symptoms to have had a disorder more than a year ago) from those with at least three past or present symptoms, but no subcriterion symptom patterns or past disorders. Persons having a past disorder but no recent disorder or subcriterion problem (hereafter, persons with past disorders) are considered to have more severe ADBH problems then persons with at least three symptoms but no past or recent disorder or problems (hereafter, persons with at least three symptoms).

The reasonableness of this classification rests on the assumption that persons with past ADBH disorders are more likely to have current ADBH symptoms that are distressful or result in dysfunctioning than are persons who have never had a past DIS/DSM-III disorder (i.e., the remaining persons with some or few symptoms). This assumption is made in the absence of better information. Again, for the sake of symmetry, persons with past disorders are divided into two groups: those with past major ADBH disorders and those with past minor ADBH disorders.

Alternative Designations of Severe Mental Illness and Subcriterion Problems

Several designations of severe ADBH illness have appeared in the recent psychiatric literature that are different from the designations in the severity scale presented in this chapter. Most often referenced is the severity designation suggested by the National Advisory Mental Health Council (1993). (See also Special Report 1993; Kessler unpublished statistical note 1994; Kessler et al. 1994.) The Council includes in its designation of severe mental illness (1) persons with recent (1 year) schizophrenia, schizoaffective disorder, bipolar mood disorder type I, or autism; (2) persons with lifetime schizophrenia, schizoaffective disorder, bipolar mood disorder type I, or autism "who did not reach diagnostic criteria during the past year" (p. 37) but who manifested recent severity (received psychiatric treatment, used antipsychotic medication, had psychotic symptomatology or a Global Assessment of Functioning (GAF) Scale rating of 50 or less during the past year); and (3) persons with recent major depression, panic disorder, or obsessive-compulsive disorder or lifetime bipolar disorder type II if there was evidence of recent severity (inpatient hospitalization, psychotic symptomatology, use of antipsychotic medication, or GAF rating of 50 or less).

Operationally, Kessler simplified the Council's designation of recent severe disorder to include "(1) 12-month mania or nonaffective psychosis (NAP), (2) lifetime mania or NAP with 12-month treatment or role impairment, or (3) 12-month depression or panic disorder with severe impairment (hospitalization or use of antipsychotic medication)" (Kessler et al. 1994, p. 9). Obsessive-compulsive disorder was not used by Kessler because it was not collected as part of the NCS. Kessler also suggested several alternative designations of serious mental disorders (unpublished statistical note 1994). Each of these designations includes a disorder plus one or more of the following criteria: (1) suicide attempt or planned suicide, (2) lack of a productive role (operationally, persons who are unemployed or employed part-time and not a student or primary caregiver of preschool children or with a work physical disability, or who had incomes at or below the poverty level or had incomes that were 50 percent of the income expected on the basis of a respondent's education or their parents' education), (3) role impairment (operationally, missed 1 full day of work per month attributable to a mental health problem), and (4) interpersonal impairment (operationally, not in a marital-type relationship, or relationships are devoid of intimacy or social support). Also, Kessler indicated that severe mental illness can be indexed by comorbidity. Specifically, he noted that there is a clear tendency for persons with multiple mental disorders to have severe and chronic illness courses and to use professional help (Kessler 1994, 1995). The least complicated designation was provided by Norquist and Wells (1991*a*, 1991*b*). They "categorized schizophrenia disorders, all affective disorders, alcohol and substance abuse, obsessive-compulsive disorder and panic disorder as serious and treatable disorders" (Norquist and Wells 1991*b*, p. 476).

An alternative attempt to identify subcriterion scale categories also exists in the psychiatric literature. Regier and colleagues (1993, p. 87) defined subthreshold clinical conditions using selected lifetime symptoms. For example, they designated two or more lifetime depressive symptoms associated with morbidity, or two or more mania symptoms associated with a patient's worst episode, as subthreshold clinical conditions or—in the terminology of this chapter—subcriterion ADBH problems.

For the severity scale presented in this chapter, we did not consider utilizing the severity criteria presented in the National Advisory Mental Health Council's designation of persons with the most severe ADBH disorders or Kessler's simplification of these criteria for several reasons. First, lifetime symptoms were not used to identify persons with severe ADBH disorders. This is because it was felt that underenumeration of past ADBH symptoms occurred as a result of the inability of respondents to accurately report past ADBH problems, particularly those from the distant past. It is noteworthy that this criterion was relaxed when the designation of persons with milder ADBH problems was considered (i.e., persons with past disorders or a few symptoms). Second, while treatment modalities are associated with the severity of a mental disorder, they were not incorporated into the scale because service use is linked to the availability and accessibility of services and because ECA treatment information is only available for the 6-month period preceding an interview with a respondent (Goldsmith et al. 1987). The former condition is particularly important for the ECA survey data because much of the ECA data utilized in this study are from the metropolitan areas that have large amounts and wide ranges of mental health services compared with other areas of the country (Wagenfeld et al. 1988; Goldsmith et al. 1994).

The suggestion of Norquist and Wells (1991*a*, 1991*b*) to include both panic disorders and obsessive-compulsive disorder as severe mental disorders (i.e., either category 8 or category 9 of the severity scale) was not incorporated because of the decision to base the severity scale on the general order of the PSE.

Taking up Kessler's (1994) alternative suggestions to identify severe mental disorders, it should be noted that his designation of severe disorder as a disorder with suicidal tendencies has been included in category 9 of the severity scale, a category that includes violent behavior toward others as well as self. We did not include disorder with role impairment or comorbidity in the scale because adequate impairment information was not available for respondents. Rather, recognizing these associations with the severity of an ADBH disorder, where reasonable they are used to validate the scale. Kessler's remaining alternative severity indicators, disorder and lack of a productive role or interpersonal impairment, were not considered for inclusion in scale criteria or scale validation because consistent measures of these dimensions are not available for all ECA sites.

Relative to subcriterion ADBH problems, for respondents that had a sufficient number of symptoms to have been asked the summary DIS recency of symptoms question and responded that they had symptoms in the past year, the Regier subcriteria designations (Regier et al. 1993, p. 87) were incorporated into the severity scale. Remaining ECA respondents classifiable as having a subthreshold clinical condition by Regier criteria would not have been identified as having a subcriterion ADBH problem using the designated severity scale criteria.

VALIDITY OF SEVERITY SCALE

Using core ECA data, a number of ways exist in which we can demonstrate the validity of the proposed severity scale. The association can be examined between (1) severity and utilization of mental health services, (2) severity and impairment of routine role behavior, and (3) severity and comorbidity. Operational procedures for measuring utilization, impairment of routine role behavior, and comorbidity are presented in this section.

Utilization of Mental Health Services

A number of studies have concluded that the more severe an ADBH problem, the more likely an individual is to use ADBH services (Mechanic 1982; Shapiro et al. 1985; Goldsmith et al. 1988; Tischler et al. 1988*b*). Accordingly, all other things being equal, a positive association should exist between severity scale categories and use of ADBH services. Following Tischler and colleagues (1988*b*), on average, the more severe the condition, the more likely an individual is not only to use some ADBH services, but also to use specialized ADBH services. Three measures of service utilization are employed to evaluate the expected relationship: (1) the percentage of respondents in a severity category who have received any ADBH services or counseling (except from friends) in the past 6 months for ADBH problems, (2) the percentage of respondents who have used the general medical system (physician or hospital emergency service) for ADBH problems in the past 6 months, and (3) the percentage of respondents who have used specialty ADBH services in the past 6 months.

Impairment of Routine Role Behavior

ECA variables that can be used to index impairment of routine role behavior are "whether or not a person has been employed during the past 6 months" and/or "whether or not the person is financially dependent upon public or private agencies for support." These variables were not utilized in the construction of the severity scale because it was not possible to determine if they were a direct consequence of an ADBH problem. However, it is suggested that if a person has an ADBH condition, these variables ought to index impairment (dysfunction with respect to routine role behavior associated with an ADBH problem) and, consequently, the relative severity of that condition. Thus, it is contended that a direct relationship should exist between severity of ADBH problems and impairment of routine role behavior, as indexed by financial dependency and employment status (Goldsmith and Greenspan 1977; Goldsmith et al. 1988).

Operationally, given the available ECA questions that relate to financial dependency and employment status, it is not possible to construct an impairment scale that applies equally to all ECA respondents. First, not being employed for at least a 6-month period prior to the interview is most likely to represent an impairment of routine role behavior for male respondents of labor force age (18–59) but not necessarily for women or other men. For men ages 18–59, employment is generally assumed to be an obligatory part of their adult role obligations (Goldsmith and Greenspan 1977), and failure to be employed would represent a failure to adequately perform standard adult role obligations. Thus, for men ages 18–59 with an ADBH problem, not working for an extended period of time is likely to represent an impairment in routine role behavior. A similar statement cannot be made for women or older men. For adult women, being a housewife is still an alternative to being in the paid labor force; and for older men, not being in the labor force (i.e., being retired) can be consistent with routine role behavior (Goldsmith and Greenspan 1977). For young adults, being in school can be considered equivalent to employment. However, being in school will not be directly controlled in this study. Rather, the relationship between severity and impairment for men least likely to be in school—that is, men ages 25–59—will be evaluated.

Second, with respect to financial dependency, it is assumed that for adults of labor force age socially expected role behavior requires that they earn their own living, or at least not be dependent upon public or private agencies for support. This means that if a person is dependent upon public or private agencies for support, they are deviating from routine role expectations and can expect some negative sanctions. Since people are most likely to engage in these behaviors when they are sick or disabled, it is assumed that persons with an ADBH problem who are financially dependent (operationally, persons receiving disability payments [benefits] from Social Security, Veterans Administration, State or other sources; welfare payments; or unemployment compensation) are likely to have a more severe condition than persons who are not financially dependent.

In using financial dependency to validate the severity index, it is expected that as severity increases, the proportion of persons ages 18–59 with financial dependency will also increase. Because of the differences in role expectations, this relationship is considered separately for men and women. To reduce the number of measures that require evaluation, we have merged male employment status and male financial dependency into a single male impairment scale. For women, only financial dependency is used to index impairment of routine role behavior.

Multiple ADBH Disorders and Problems

It is expected that persons with recent symptoms of more than one ADBH disorder or subcriterion symptom pattern will have more severe ADBH problems than persons with only one recent disorder or subcriterion symptom pattern. Our rationale is that since disorders involve some distress and/or dysfunction, and many involve potential dangerousness, a person with multiple disorders will have multiple sources of distress, dysfunction, and possibly threats of dangerousness.[6] Consequently, persons with multiple disorders can reasonably be expected to have a more severe ADBH condition than persons with only one disorder (Kessler 1994; Wittchen et al. 1994). We extend this position to include not only disorders but also subcriterion symptom patterns (Shapiro et al. 1985; Goldsmith et al. 1987; Tischler et al. 1988*b*).

RESULTS

Severity of ADBH Problems in Metropolitan and Nonmetropolitan Areas

Table 1 (see p. 127) presents the distribution of Wave 1 metropolitan and nonmetropolitan ECA respondents by the severity scale categories. Examination of this table shows that Wave 1 respondents with recent ADBH problems that are most likely to be of clinical significance (scale categories 5–9) constitute about 33.4 percent of all ECA respondents (33.8 percent of respondents residing in metropolitan areas and 29.0 percent of those in nonmetropolitan areas). The corresponding figures for respondents with alcohol abuse and dependency problems (hereafter alcohol use problems) are 9.3, 9.4, and 6.6. These figures exceed those for major affective or schizophrenia problems (6.8, 7.0, and 4.0, respectively) and other drug problems (1.4, 1.5, and 0.7, respectively).[7] Among all respondents, and metropolitan and nonmetropolitan respondents with clinically significant ADBH problems, approximately 18.0 percent, 18.3 percent, and 13.4 percent, respectively, are in category 9, the most severe scale category (respondents with a recent disorder who are dangerous), and an additional 14.4 percent, 14.5 percent, and 12.4 percent, respectively, are in category 8 (respondents with recent major disorders who are not dangerous). The corresponding percentages for alcohol use are 34.4, 34.0, and 36.4 for category 9 and 26.9, 26.6, and 34.8 for category 8.[8]

Persons who have had an ADBH disorder more than a year ago (past disorder) but who have no recent ADBH problems (scale categories 3 and 4) constitute an additional 7.4 percent of all ECA respondents, 7.2 percent of metropolitan respondents, and 7.0 percent of nonmetropolitan respondents. The corresponding figures for past alcohol use, past other drug use, and past major affective disorders or schizophrenia (category 4 only) are as follows: for all respondents, 3.4, 3.4, and 2.8; for metropolitan respondents, 0.4, 0.4, and 0.3; and for nonmetropolitan respondents 1.0, 1.0, and 0.3. Overall as well as for alcohol and behavioral health problems but not other drug problems, the differences between metropolitan and nonmetropolitan areas are statistically significant.

Validity of Severity Scale

We identified three dimensions—service utilization, impairment of routine role behavior among respondents with ADBH problems, and comorbidity of ADBH problems—in the core ECA data that would permit us to evaluate the validity of the severity scale. An examination of the data for utilization of services (table 2, p. 130), impairment of routine role behavior (table 3, p. 132), and comorbidity of ADBH problems (tables 4 and 5, pp. 134-135) shows that the findings are generally consistent with expectations, particularly for metropolitan areas. Based on these relationships, we conclude that the constructed severity scale is reasonable—that is, it has criterion validity. The specific relationships between the severity scale and utilization, role behavior impairment, and comorbidity are described below. Because over 90 percent of ECA respondents reside in metropolitan areas, the distributions for all respondents and metropolitan respondents should be very similar; consequently, only metropolitan and nonmetropolitan respondents will be evaluated.

Service Utilization

Service utilization for ECA respondents residing in metropolitan and nonmetropolitan counties is presented in table 2. Among ECA respondents who are residents of metropolitan areas, the expected pattern with no errors is observed for all scale categories, and for major affective or schizophrenia problems for any ADBH service, for alcohol use for general medical services, and for major affective or schizophrenia problems for specialty mental health services. Illustratively, as one goes from category 9 (most severe) to category 1 (least severe), utilization of any ADBH services decreases from 26.3 percent to 2.0 percent. Except for other drugs for any ADBH services and specialty ADBH services, for the remaining possible comparisons among severity categories, the deviations from the expected pattern tend to be small. For example, with respect to any service use for alcohol use, category 4 is slightly greater than category 6: 7.6 percent compared with 7.4 percent of ECA metropolitan respondents.

Deviations from the expected pattern—service utilization declining from more severe scale categories to less severe scale categories—are much more likely to occur among residents of nonmetropolitan areas than metropolitan areas. Excluding an analysis of other drugs because the number of cases in severity categories is small (always less than three respondents), the expected pattern with no errors is only observed for major affective or schizophrenia problems for specialty ADBH services. Further, unlike the metropolitan comparisons, the nonmetropolitan comparisons often have more than one deviation from the expected pattern. For example, for residents of nonmetropolitan areas, for any services and for general medical services, while the level of utilization generally declines from category 9 to category 1, category 8 exceeds category 9 (25.9 percent compared with 22.4 percent and 15.3 percent compared with 6.8 percent, respectively) and category 2 exceeds category 3 (3.8 percent compared with 0.0 percent and 3.1 compared with 0.0 percent, respectively).

Not only is the use of any services, general medical services, and specialty mental health services generally greater in metropolitan areas than in nonmetropolitan areas, but also, except for other drugs, the relationships are statistically significant when all scale categories are considered as well as when alcohol use and major mental health problems are considered.

Role Impairment

The relationship between the severity scale and role impairment is presented in table 3. Examination of this table reveals a pattern similar to that observed for service utilization. For persons ages 18–59, as one goes from category 9 to category 3 (the categories for which an examination of impairment as operationalized in this study is considered appropriate), the percentage of respondents who are impaired generally declines for male respondents residing in metropolitan areas for all scale categories as well as alcohol use, other drugs, and major affective or schizophrenia problems. However, only for alcohol use is there no deviation from the expected pattern; male role impairment for metropolitan respondents declines from 23.9 percent in category 9 to 18.8 percent in category 4. It is noteworthy that similar patterns occur when school-aged men (18–25) are excluded from the analysis.

For male respondents who are residents of nonmetropolitan areas, only for all categories and alcohol use is the number of respondents in severity category cells sufficiently large to permit reliable comparisons among scale categories. For these groups, the observed patterns are not consistent with expectations. For example, category 9 for alcohol use is less than category 8 (24.6 vs. 26.6). For men, the category differences between metropolitan and nonmetropolitan areas are statistically significant only for all scale categories. The difference for alcohol use is nearly significant.

Although there are more deviations from the expected pattern for women than for men, the observed patterns for metropolitan residents for all scale categories, other drugs, and major affective or schizophrenia problems, but not for alcohol use, tend to be reasonably consistent with expectations. For example, for all scale categories, female role impairment declines from 23.3 percent in category 9 to 14.0 percent in category 3. For female residents of nonmetropolitan areas, other drug use and alcohol use must be excluded from the analysis because the number of cases in scale categories does not permit reliable comparisons. For both all scale categories and major affective or schizophrenia problems, the levels of impairment within scale categories tend to be greater in metropolitan areas than nonmetropolitan areas. Only the difference for all scale categories is statistically significant.

Comorbidity

Tables 4 and 5 present patterns of comorbidity of ADBH problems for categories 5–9 of the severity scale. As expected, the more severe a category the more likely persons in the category are to have multiple ADBH problems. This holds for all scale categories, as well as severity of alcohol use, other drug use, and major affective or schizophrenia problems for metropolitan areas and generally for nonmetropolitan areas as well. Thus, 80.2 percent of the metropolitan respondents and 87.5 percent of the nonmetropolitan respondents in category 9 have multiple ADBH disorders or subcriterion problems compared with 9.3 percent and 11.8 percent of the respondents in category 5. For alcohol use, the corresponding percentages are 69.8 and 81.1 for category 9 and 16.2 and 32.3 for category 6.

Generally, the level of comorbidity in nonmetropolitan areas is slightly greater than that in metropolitan areas when all severity scale categories are considered as well as when severity of alcohol use, other drug use, and major affective or schizophrenia problems are considered. These differences are statistically significant for alcohol use and major affective or schizophrenia problems but not for other drug use. The number of empty cells for all scale categories precluded doing a statistical comparison using all categories. However, a statistical analysis limited to disorders is not significant.

CONCLUSION

In this study, Wave 1 ECA data were used to develop a categorical severity scale that orders persons from those with the most severe ADBH problems and, consequently, most in need of ADBH services, to those with the least severe problems and, thus, least in need of ADBH services. Separate analyses were made for severity of alcohol use, drug use, and major affective or schizophrenia problems by metropolitan and nonmetropolitan residence of respondents. The validity of the scale was tested using indicators of ADBH utilization, impairment of routine role behavior, and comorbidity of ADBH problems. These measures supported the criterion validity of the scale not only when all ADBH problems were aggregated, but also generally when alcohol, other drugs, and major mental health problems were considered separately. The relationships for metropolitan areas tended to be more consistent with expectations than those for nonmetropolitan areas. Thus, it appears that the severity scale provides a useful and simple way of ordering ADBH problems with respect to severity, taking into account not only ADBH disorders but subcriterion ADBH problems and consequently the need for ADBH services. The scale represents a significant improvement in the measurement of recent severity of ADBH problems over scales that consider only disorders or symptom counts.

The severity scale produced some interesting results. Nearly one-third of all Wave I ECA respondents and metropolitan respondents had recent ADBH problems that were likely to be considered of clinical significance (i.e., they had at least a subcriterion ADBH symptom pattern). Slightly over 9 percent of all respondents and metropolitan respondents had an alcohol problem, approximately 6.9 percent had a major affective or schizophrenia problem, and 1.4 percent had a problem with other drugs. Consistently, the percentages were slightly lower for nonmetropolitan areas. Moreover, except for other drug problems, the differences were statistically significant. Respondents with the most severe recent symptom patterns (those with recent disorders who are dangerous and respondents with recent major disorders who are not dangerous), respondents most likely to have multiple recent ADBH symptoms patterns and presumed to need immediate and perhaps intensive services, constituted approximately 11 percent of all respondents and metropolitan respondents. Corresponding percentages for alcohol use, major affective or schizophrenia, and other drug problems were 5.7, 4.6, and 1.0, respectively. Again, similar percentages for nonmetropolitan respondents were slightly lower.

Given that it is generally accepted that severity of ADBH problems and the need for ADBH services are closely associated, we conclude that the severity scale presented in this chapter is a better way to estimate the relative need for mental health services of the populations studied than simply using disorders or number of symptoms. Moreover, since the results in this study are based on a large-scale sample primarily from metropolitan areas of the United States, the scale provides useful clues about the distributions of severity in metropolitan populations and consequently their relative need for mental health services. For the nonmetropolitan areas this is not the case. The nonmetropolitan ECA sample is comparatively small and most likely not representative of other nonmetropolitan regions of the United States. Thus, the scale should be used cautiously for nonmetropolitan areas.

While we feel that the severity scale is a significant improvement over earlier procedures, it is by no means the final product required for needs assessment. First, the severity scale does not directly measure the components of severity—namely, distress, dysfunction, and dangerousness—and, second, the scale should be expanded to specifically include estimates of the number of persons in each scale category that can be expected to require different kinds of services in specified time periods (see Bell et al. 1988). The severity scale presented in this chapter represents a step in this direction.

NOTES

1. The broader definition of problems used in this analysis is consistent with physicians' view of disease. Goodwin and Guze (1984) stated that "any condition associated with discomfort, pain, disability, death or an increased liability of these states, regarded by physicians and the

public as properly the responsibility of the medical profession, may be considered a disease" (p. 266). The difference between the definition provided in this chapter and that of Goodwin and Guze is that, in this chapter, explicit recognition of the responsibility of the medical profession for treatment is left out. The position taken here emphasizes the wider domain of problems on the assumption that anyone with psychiatric symptoms "associated with discomfort, pain, disability [and] death" may be considered as needing mental health services.

2. The time period "past year" was selected because a year represents the time period for which mental health organizations are most likely to require severity information for program planning and evaluation.

3. At some of the sites, the section for assessing antisocial personality disorder (the disorder from which all but one of the items on violent behavior are derived) included a "skip out" for respondents who reported no misconduct during childhood or adolescence. As a result, except for getting in fights while drinking, no information about adult violent behavior is available for those respondents who skipped out of the interview by reporting none of the childhood (antisocial personality disorder) items such as playing hooky from school, telling lies, getting in fights at school, and running away from home overnight (Swanson et al. 1990).

4. The one exception to this in our list is anorexia, which would normally be considered a major disorder because when diagnosed clinically it is physically very serious and debilitating and has a high mortality. However, there are a very small number of lifetime cases of anorexia reported in the ECA data ($N = 8$), and none is reported as current. Further, these cases do not follow the typical demographic pattern expected for anorexia nervosa; that is, they are not primarily young females.

5. As an example, the basic differences between a DIS/DSM-III major depressive episode and subcriterion depressive episode are as follows: "For a recent DIS/DSM-III major depressive episode to exist, a person must have experienced (a) dysphoric mood for at least two weeks, (b) at least four of the following severe symptoms that contributed to dysfunctioning: poor appetite, insomnia/hypersomnia, slowness/restlessness, loss of interest, worthlessness, trouble thinking, and death thoughts, and (c) dysphoric mood and some of the symptoms must have occurred together in the past year. Further, the symptoms must have been sufficiently severe to lead to seeing a physician, taking medication more than once, or interfering significantly with a person's life (Feighner, RDC) and (d) it was not explainable by physical exertion, a life-threatening situation, or a physical disorder" (Robins et al. 1981, p. 382; see also American Psychiatric Association 1980, p. 150). A subcriterion depressive episode differs from a DIS/DSM major depressive episode in that only three severe symptoms are necessary (American Psychiatric Association 1980).

6. If hospital-based observations for physical disorders generalize to include psychiatric comorbidities in the general population, then some evidence exists to support the stated position. Essock-Vitale (1987, p. 268) pointed out that in at least one hospital setting "psychiatric patients with

medical comorbidities are significantly more expensive to treat [i.e., are more severely disabled] than those without such comorbidities." (See also Ware et al. 1984 and Young 1984.) Further indicating the reasonableness of this position, Horn and colleagues (unpublished paper 1985) were willing to include psychiatric diagnoses in the comorbidity segment of their severity of illness scale for use in a hospital environment.

7. "Major affective or schizophrenia problems" include (1) major affective disorders or schizophrenia and (2) major affective or schizophrenia subcriterion patterns.

8. It should be noted that including obsessive-compulsive and panic disorders with scale category 8, as suggested by Norquist and Wells (1991*a*, 1991*b*), rather than with category 7, would have very little effect on the distribution of respondents by the severity scale. Only 1.1 percent of the metropolitan ECA respondents would be shifted from category 7 to category 8. This is because 51.8 percent of the 362 respondents with a recent obsessive-compulsive or panic disorder were already classified as severity categories 8 and 9.

REFERENCES

American Psychiatric Association. *Diagnostic and Statistical Manual of Mental Disorder.* 3d ed. Washington, DC: the Association, 1980.

Anthony, J.C.; Folstein, M.; Romanski, A.J.; Von Korff, M.R.; Chahal, R.; Merchant, A.; Brown, H.; Shapiro, S.; Kramer, M.; and Gruenberg, E.M. Comparison of the lay diagnostic interview schedule and a standardized psychiatric diagnosis. *Arch Gen Psychiatry* 42:667–675, 1985.

Bell, R.A.; Goldsmith, H.F.; and Lin, E. A clinician's perspective on the measurement of need for mental health services: Complete or incomplete, right or wrong. In: Goldsmith, H.F.; Lin, E.; Bell, R.A.; and Jackson, D.J., eds. *Needs Assessment: Its Future.* Series BN: Needs Assessment and Evaluation. Washington, DC: U.S. Government Printing Office, 1988. pp. 17–21.

Blazer, D.; George, L.K.; Landerman, R.; Pennybacker, M.; Melville, M.L.; Woodbury, M.; and Manton, K.G. Psychiatric disorders: A rural/urban comparison. *Arch Gen Psychiatry* 42:651–656, July 1985.

Blazer, D.; Crowell, B.A., Jr.; and George, L.K. Alcohol abuse and dependence in the rural South. *Arch Gen Psychiatry* 44:736–740, August 1987*a*.

Blazer, D.; Hughes, D.; and George, L.K. Stressful life events and the onset of a generalized anxiety syndrome. *Am J Psychiatry* 144(9):1178–1183, 1987*b*.

Blazer, D.G.; Hughes, D.; George, L.K.; Swartz, M.; and Boyer, R. Generalized anxiety disorder. In: Robins, L.N., and Regier, D.A., eds. *Psychiatric Disorders in America.* New York: Free Press, 1991. pp. 180–203.

Boyd, J.H.; Burke, J.D.; Gruenberg, E.; Holzer, C.E.; Rae, D.S.; George, L.K.; Karno, M.; Stoltzman, R.; McEvoy, L.; and Nestadt, G. Exclusion criteria of DSM-III, a study of co-occurrence of hierarchy-free syndromes. *Arch Gen Psychiatry* 41:983–989, 1984.

Brenner, B. Social problems as affliction and social problems as hazard. *Clinical Sociology Review* 3:109–115, 1985.

Ciarlo, J.A.; Tweed, D.L.; Shern, D.L.; Kirkpatric, L.A.; and Sachs-Ericsson, N. Validation of indirect methods to estimate need for mental health services: Concepts, strategies, and general conclusions. In: Ciarlo, J.A., ed. Indirect Needs Assessment for Mental Health Services Planning. [Special Issue.] *Evaluation and Program Planning* 15(2):115–131, 1992.

Eaton, W.W.; Holzer, C.E., III; Von Korff, M.; Anthony, J.C.; Helzer, J.E.; George, L.; Burnam, M.A.; Boyd, J.H.; Kessler, L.G.; and Locke, B.Z. The design of the Epidemiologic Catchment Area surveys. *Arch Gen Psychiatry* 41:942–948, 1984.

Endicott, J.; Spitzer, R.L.; Fleiss, J.L.; and Cohen, J. The Global Assessment Scale: A procedure for measuring overall severity of psychiatric disturbances. *Arch Gen Psychiatry* 33(6):766–771, 1976.

Escobar, J.I.; Randolph, E.T.; Asaman, J.; and Karno, M. The NIMH-DIS in the assessment of DSM-III schizophrenia disorder. *Schizophr Bull* 11(2):187, 1986.

Essock-Vitale, S. Patient characteristics predictive of treatment costs on inpatient psychiatric wards. *Hospital and Community Psychiatry* 38:263–269, 1987.

Goldsmith, H.F., and Greenspan, S. Social change and the post-war generation. Paper presented at the VI World Congress of Psychiatry of the World Psychiatric Association, Honolulu, HI, 1977.

Goldsmith, H.F.; Holzer, C.E., III; Jackson, D.J.; Swanson, J.; Stiles, D.; and Manderscheid, R.W. Severity of psychopathological problems and mental health utilization in five metropolitan areas. Paper presented at the annual meeting of the American Public Health Association, New Orleans, LA, 1987.

Goldsmith, H.F.; Lin, E.; Jackson, D.J.; Bell, R.A.; and Manderscheid, R.M. The future of mental health needs assessment. In: Goldsmith, H.F.; Lin, E.; Bell, R.A.; and Jackson, D.J., eds. *Needs Assessment: Its Future.* Series BN: Needs Assessment and Evaluation. Washington, DC: U.S. Government Printing Office, 1988. pp. 79–93.

Goldsmith, H.F.; Wagenfeld, M.O.; Manderscheid, R.W.; Stiles, D.J.; Windel, C.; and Witkin, M.J. The ecology of mental health facilities in metropolitan and nonmetropolitan counties. In: Manderscheid, R.W., and Sonnenchein, M.A., eds. *Mental Health United States 1994.* Pub. No. (SMA)94–3000. Washington, DC: U.S. Government Printing Office, 1994.

Goldsmith, H.F.; Holzer, C.E., III; and Manderscheid, R.W. Depression in metropolitan and nonmetropolitan neighborhoods. In: Manderscheid, R.W., ed. *Mental Health United States: 1998.* Washington, DC: U.S. Government Printing Office, in press.

Goodwin, D.W., and Guze, S.G. *Psychiatric Diagnosis.* New York: Oxford University Press, 1984.

Helzer, J.E., and Robins, L.N. The Diagnostic Interview Schedule: Its development, evaluation and use. *Soc Psychiatry Psychiatr Epidemiol* 23:6–16, 1988.

Helzer, J.E.; Robins, L.N.; McEvoy, L.T.; Spitznagel, E.L.; Stoltzman, R.K.;

Farmer, A.; and Brockington, I.F. A comparison of clinical and Diagnostic Interview Schedule diagnoses. *Arch Gen Psychiatry* 42:657–666, 1985.

Helzer, J.E.; Spitznagel, E.L.; and McEvoy, L. The predictive validity of lay Diagnostic Interview Schedule diagnoses in the general population. *Arch Gen Psychiatry* 44:1069–1077, 1987.

Holzer, C.E., III, and Swanson, J.W. *Development of a Need-for-Service Dimension: Application of Data From the Epidemiologic Catchment Area Study.* Final Report, Contract No. 86M026 7687010. Texas Department of Mental Health and Mental Retardation, 1986.

Holzer, C.E., III; Tischler, G.L.; Leaf, P.J.; and Myers, J.K. An epidemiologic assessment of cognitive impairment in a community population. In: Greenley, J., ed. *Research in Community and Mental Health.* Greenwich, CT: JAI Press, 1984.

Holzer, C.E., III; Spitznagel, E.; Jordan, K.B.; Timbers, D.M.; Kessler, L.G.; and Anthony, J.C. Sampling the household population. In: Eaton, W.W., and Kessler, L.G., eds. *Epidemiologic Field Methods in Psychiatry.* New York: Academic Press, 1985.

Holzer, C.E., III; Goldsmith, H.F.; Jackson, D.J.; and Swanson, J.W. Indirect indicators of need for mental health services. In: Goldsmith, H.G.; Lin, E.; Bell, R.A.; and Jackson, D.J., eds. *Needs Assessment: Its Future.* Series BN: Needs Assessment and Evaluation. Washington, DC: U.S. Government Printing Office, 1988.

Holzer, C.E., III; Swanson, J.; Ganju, V.K.; Goldsmith, H.F.; and Jackson, D.J. Estimates of need for mental health services in Texas counties. In: Bojean, C.M.; Colman, M.T.; and Iscoe, I., eds. *Community Care of the Chronically Mentally Ill.* Austin: Hogg Foundation for Mental Health, University of Texas, 1989.

Horn, S.D., and Horn, R.A. Reliability and validity of the severity of illness index. *Med Care* 21:159–168, 1986.

Horn, S.D.; Chechich, B.; and Clopton, C. Measuring severity of illness: A reliability study. *Med Care* 21:705–714, 1983*a*.

Horn, S.D.; Sharkey, P.; and Bertram, D.A. Measuring severity of illness: Homogeneous case mix groups. *Med Care* 21:14–30, 1983*b*.

Horn, S.D.; Horn, R.A.; and Sharkey, P.O. The severity of illness index as a severity adjustment to diagnosis-related groups. *Health Care Finance Review: Annual Supplement* 1984, pp. 33–45.

Ingham, J. Neurosis: Disease or distress. In: Wing, J.K. Bebbington, P.; and Robins, L.N., eds. *What Is a Case? The Problem of Definition in Psychiatric Community Surveys.* London: Grant McIntyre, 1981.

Kessler, L.G.; Folsom, R.R.; Forsythe, A.; McEvoy, L.; Holzer, C.; Rae, D.; Woodbury, M. Parameter and variance estimation. In: Eaton, W.W., and Kessler, L.G., eds. *Epidemiologic Methods in Psychiatry: The NIMH Epidemiologic Catchment Area Program.* Orlando, FL: Academic Press, 1985. pp. 327–350.

Kessler, R.C. The National Comorbidity Survey: Preliminary results and future directions. *Int J Methods Psychiatr Res* 4:114.1–114.13, 1994.

Kessler R.C. Epidemiology of psychiatric comorbidity. In: Tsaung, M.; Tohen, M.; and Zahner, G., eds. *Textbook of Psychiatric Epidemiology.* New York: John Wiley and Sons, 1995. pp. 179–197.

Kessler, R.C.; McGonagle, K.A.; Zhao, S.; Nelson, C.B.; Hughes, M.; Eshleman, S.; Wittchen H.; and Kendler, K.S. Lifetime and 12-month prevalence of DSM-III-R psychiatric disorders in the United States. *Arch Gen Psychiatry* 51:6–19, 1994.

Klerman, G.L. Comment on psychiatric diagnosis as reified measurement. *J Health Soc Behav* 30:26–32, 1989.

Leaf, P.J.; Myers, J.K.; and Evoy, E.M. Procedures used in the Epidemiologic Catchment Area Study. In: Robins, L.N., and Regier, D.A., eds. *Psychiatric Disorders in America.* New York: The Free Press, 1991. pp. 11–32.

Leff, H.S. *A Computer Model for Community Support Systems.* Final Progress Report, Grant No. 1R01 MH 33581–02. National Institute of Mental Health, 1982.

Leff, H.S.; Graves, S.C.; Natkins, J.; and Bryan, J. A system for allocating mental health resources. *Administration in Mental Health* 13(1):43–67, 1985.

Mechanic, D. The epidemiology of illness behavior and its relationship to physical and psychological distress. In: Mechanic, D., ed. *Vol. 3: Symptoms, Illness Behavior, and Help-Seeking.* Monographs in Psychosocial Epidemiology. New Brunswick, NJ: Rutgers University Press, 1982.

Mezzich, J.E., and Sharfstein, S.S. Severity of illness and diagnosis formulation: Classifying patients for prospective payment systems. *Hospital and Community Psychiatry* 36:770–772, 1985.

Mirowsky J., and Ross, C.E. Psychiatric diagnosis as a reified measurement. *J Health Soc Behav* 30:11–25, 1989.

Murphy, J.M. *Psychiatric Instrument Development for Primary Care Research: Patient Self Report Questionnaire.* NIMH Contract No. 80M0142801010. Rockville, MD: Division of Biometry and Epidemiology, National Institute of Mental Health, 1981.

National Institute of Mental Health. *Caring for People With Severe Mental Disorders: A National Plan of Research To Improve Services.* DHHS Pub. No. (ADM)91–1762. Washington, DC: U.S. Government Printing Office, 1991.

National Advisory Mental Health Council. *Health Care Reform for Americans With Severe Mental Illnesses: Report of the National Advisory Mental Health Council.* Washington, DC: U.S. Department of Health and Human Services, March 3, 1993.

Norquist, G.S., and Wells, K.B. How do HMOs reduce outpatient mental health care costs? *Am J Psychiatry* 148(1):96–101, 1991*a*.

Norquist, G.S., and Wells, K.B. Mental health needs of the uninsured. *Arch Gen Psychiatry* 48:475–478, 1991*b*.

Regier, D.A.; Myers, J.K.; Kramer, M.; Robins, L.N.; Blazer, D.G.; Hough, R.L.; Eaton, W.W.; and Locke, B.Z. The NIMH Epidemiologic Catchment Area program. *Arch Gen Psychiatry* 41:934–941, 1984*a*.

Regier, D.A.; Shapiro, S.; Kessler, L.G.; and Taube, C.A. Epidemiology and health service resource allocation policy for alcohol, drug abuse, and mental disorders. *Public Health Rep* 99:483–492, 1984*b*.

Regier, D.A.; Narrow, W.; Rae, D.; Manderscheid, R.W.; Locke, B.Z.; and Goodwin, F.K. The de facto US mental and addictive disorder service system. *Arch Gen Psychiatry* 50:85–94, 1993.

Robins, L.N. The development and characteristics of the NIMH Diagnostic Interview Schedule. In: Weissman, M.W.; Myer, J.K.; and Ross, C.E., eds. *Community Surveys of Psychiatric Disorder.* New Brunswick, NJ: Rutgers University Press, 1986. pp. 403–427.

Robins, L.N.; Helzer, J.E.; Croughan, J.; and Ratcliff, K.S. National Institute of Mental Health Diagnostic Interview Schedule: Its history, characteristics and validity. *Arch Gen Psychiatry* 38:381–386, 1981.

Robins, L.N.; Helzer, J.E.; Ratcliff, K.S.; and Seyfried, W. Validity of the Diagnostic Interview Schedule, Version II: DSM III diagnosis. *Psychol Med* 12:855–870, 1982.

Shapiro, S.; Skinner, E.A.; Kramer, M.; Steinwachs, D.M.; Regier, D.A.; and Kessler, L.G. Measuring need for mental health services in a general population. *Med Care* 23:1033–1043, 1985.

Special Report: Health care reform for Americans with severe mental illnesses: Report of the National Advisory Mental Health Council. *Am J Psychiatry* 150(10): 1447–1464, 1993.

Swanson, J.; Holzer, C.E., III; Ganju, V.K.; and Jono, R.T. Violence and psychiatric disorder in the community: Evidence from the Epidemiologic Catchment Area surveys. *Hospital and Community Psychiatry* 41(7):761–770, 1990.

Taube, C.; Lee, E.S.; and Forthofer, R.N. Diagnoses-related groups for mental disorders, alcoholism, and drug abuse: Evaluation and alternatives. *Hospital and Community Psychiatry* 35:452–455, 1984.

Tischler, G.L.; Leaf, P.J.; and Holzer, C.E., III. The direct measurement of need: A clinician's perspective. In: Goldsmith, H.F.; Lin, E.; Bell, R.A.; and Jackson, D.J., eds. *Needs Assessment: Its Future.* Series BN: Needs Assessment and Evaluation. Washington, DC: U.S. Government Printing Office, 1988*a*. pp. 13–16.

Tischler, G.L.; Leaf, P.J.; and Holzer, C.E., III. The relationship between the need for mental health services and utilization of services. In: Goldsmith, H.F.; Lin, E.; Bell, R.A.; and Jackson, D.J., eds. *Needs Assessment: Its Future.* Series BN: Needs Assessment and Evaluation. Washington, DC: U.S. Government Printing Office, 1988*b*. pp. 65–71.

Tweed, D.L., and George, L.K. Comment on psychiatric diagnosis as reified measurement. *J Health Soc Behav* 30:35–37, 1989.

U.S. Bureau of the Census. *1980 Census of Population, Detailed Characteristics, United States Summary: Section A.* Washington, DC: U.S. Government Printing Office, 1984.

Wagenfeld, M.O.; Goldsmith, H.F.; Stiles, D.; and Manderscheid, R.W. Inpatient mental health services in metropolitan and nonmetropolitan counties. In:

Wagenfeld, M.O., ed. Mental Health and the Crisis of Rural America. [Special Issue.] *Journal of Rural Community Psychology* 9(2):13–28, 1988.

Ware, J.E., Jr.; Manning, W.G., Jr.; Dwan, N.; Wells, K.B.; and Newhouse, J.B. Health status and the use of mental health services. *Am Psychol* 39: 1090–1100, 1984.

Weissman, M.M., and Klerman, G.L. Epidemiology of mental disorders. *Arch Gen Psychiatry* 35:705–712, 1978.

Weissman, M.M.; Myers, J.K.; and Ross, C.E. Community studies in psychiatric epidemiology: An introduction. In: Weissman, M.W.; Myer, J.K.; and Ross, C.E., eds. *Community Surveys of Psychiatric Disorder.* New Brunswick, NJ: Rutgers University Press, 1986. pp. 1–20.

Wing, J.K.; Bebbington, P.; Harry, J.; and Tennant, C. The prevalence in the general population of disorders familiar to psychiatrists in hospital practice. In: Wing, J.K.; Bebbington, P.; and Robins, L.N., eds. *What Is a Case?* London: Grant McIntyre, 1981. pp. 48–61.

Wing, J.K. Describing and classifying psychiatric symptoms: The PSE-CATEGO System. In: Weissman, M.W.; Myer, J.K.; and Ross, C.E., eds. *Community Surveys of Psychiatric Disorder.* New Brunswick, NJ: Rutgers University Press, 1986. pp. 429–448.

Wittchen, H.; Zhao, S.; Kessler, R.C.; and Eaton, W. DSM-III-R generalized anxiety disorder in the National Comorbidity Survey. *Arch Gen Psychiatry* 51:355–364, 1994.

Young, W.A. Incorporating severity of illness and comorbidity in case-mix measurement. *Health Care Financing Review: Annual Supplement* 1984, pp. 23–31.

Table 1. Percentage Distribution of Wave I Epidemiologic Catchment Area (ECA) Respondents by Recent (Past-Year) Severity of Alcohol, Drug, and Other Behavioral Health (ADBH) Problems and Metropolitan or Nonmetropolitan Residence.

% Distribution Excluding Cognitive Impairments (Unweighted Number of Respondents)

Severity Category/ Severity of ADBH Problems[1]	All ECA Respondents	Metropolitan Respondents	Nonmetropolitan Respondents
9: Recent disorders and threat of dangerousness	6.0 (961)	6.2 (920)	3.9 (41)
Alcohol abuse or dependency	3.2 (453)	3.2 (429)	2.4 (24)
Other drug abuse or dependency	0.5 (79)	0.5 (79)	0.5 (3)
Major affective or schizophrenia	2.2 (397)	2.3 (383)	1.3 (14)
8: Recent major disorders and no threat of dangerousness	4.8 (829)	4.9 (791)	3.6 (38)
Alcohol abuse or dependency	2.5 (391)	2.5 (369)	2.3 (22)
Other drug abuse or dependency	0.3 (68)	0.4 (66)	0.1 (2)
Major affective or schizophrenia	2.3 (416)	2.3 (401)	1.4 (15)
7: Recent minor disorders and no threat of dangerousness	10.2 (1,922)	10.3 (1,761)	9.0 (161)
6: Recent major subcriterion symptom patterns	6.2 (1,003)	6.4 (953)	3.4 (50)
Alcohol abuse or dependency	3.6 (554)	3.7 (531)	1.9 (23)
Other drug abuse or dependency	0.6 (73)	0.6 (72)	0.1 (1)

Continued

Table 1. *Continued*

Severity Category/ Severity of ADBH Problems[1]	All ECA Respondents	Metropolitan Respondents	Nonmetropolitan Respondents
% Distribution Excluding Cognitive Impairments (Unweighted Number of Respondents)			
Major affective or schizophrenia	2.3 (425)	2.4 (399)	1.3 (26)
5: Recent minor subcriterion symptom patterns	6.2 (1,177)	6.0 (1,041)	9.1 (136)
4: Past major disorders	4.5 (767)	4.6 (718)	3.2 (49)
Alcohol abuse or dependency	3.4 (581)	3.4 (537)	2.8 (44)
Other drug abuse or dependency	0.4 (64)	0.4 (61)	0.3 (3)
Major affective or schizophrenia	1.0 (162)	1.0 (158)	0.3 (4)
3: Past minor disorders	2.9 (550)	2.6 (491)	3.8 (59)
2: Some symptoms (at least 3)	37.6 (7,307)	37.5 (6,680)	39.0 (627)
1: Few symptoms (less than 3)	21.6 (3,571)	21.3 (3,229)	25.0 (342)
Total	100.0 (18,087)	100.0 (16,584)	100.0 (1,503)

Note: Percentages are weighted for sample design. Chi-square for severity scale categories by metropolitan or nonmetropolitan residence: ≤ 0.001. Chi-square for alcohol abuse or dependency problems within severity scale categories by metropolitan or nonmetropolitan residence: ≤ 0.008. Chi-square for other drug abuse or dependency problems within severity scale categories by metropolitan or nonmetropolitan residence: ≤ 0.236. Chi-square for major affective or schizophrenia problems within severity scale categories by metropolitan or nonmetropolitan residence: ≤ 0.004.

[1]Other drug abuse or dependency problems category excludes caffeine, tobacco, and cannabis. Major affective or schizophrenia category includes schizophreniform.

Table 2. Percentages of Wave I ECA Respondents Utilizing Mental Health Services in the

	All ECA Respondents			Metropolitan
Severity Category/ Major Problems[1]	**Any Services (Except Friends)**	**General Medical Services**	**Specialty Services**	**Any Services (Except Friends)**
9	26.1	9.5	14.2	26.3
Alcohol	18.5	5.7	10.9	19.0
Other drug	28.8	9.1	14.2	31.2
Major affective	43.1	17.7	25.3	42.1
8	25.3	11.6	12.9	25.3
Alcohol	13.5	6.3	7.8	13.3
Other drug	24.6	7.5	15.3	25.3
Major affective	37.3	17.7	17.6	37.3
7	14.7	8.3	5.4	14.9
6	12.9	6.9	3.7	12.6
Alcohol	7.3	4.1	1.5	7.4
Other drug	9.9	5.9	2.9	8.8
Major affective	22.4	11.6	7.7	21.7
5	10.9	6.4	3.9	11.1
4	8.9	3.2	3.5	9.0
Alcohol	7.7	2.9	2.1	7.6
Other drug	21.1	8.2	8.1	20.4
Major affective	10.7	3.8	6.1	10.2
3	7.2	1.8	3.3	8.0
2	4.8	2.3	1.5	4.8
1	2.0	0.9	0.7	2.0
All respondents	8.6	4.0	3.4	8.8

Note: Percentages are weighted for sample design. See table 1 for unweighted numbers. Cochran-Mantel-Haenszel friends), general medical services, and specialty services, respectively: for severity scale categories, 0.001, 0.001, and 0.249; for major affective or schizophrenia problems, 0.010, 0.003, and 0.009.

[1]See table 1 for names of categories. Alcohol = alcohol abuse or dependency. Other drugs = other drug abuse or schizophreniform).

Past 6 Months by Severity of ADBH Problems and Metropolitan or Nonmetropolitan Residence.

Respondents		Nonmetropolitan Respondents		
General Medical Services	Specialty Services	Any Services (Except Friends)	General Medical Services	Specialty Services
9.6	14.5	22.4	6.8	9.8
6.1	11.0	10.0	0.0	10.0
9.9	15.4	0.0	0.0	0.0
17.5	25.2	68.6	20.2	25.4
11.4	13.1	25.9	15.3	10.6
5.5	8.4	16.3	16.3	0.0
7.8	15.7	0.0	0.0	0.0
18.0	17.1	38.8	12.3	26.5
8.3	5.5	12.4	9.0	3.6
6.8	3.7	19.7	9.0	3.6
4.2	1.6	4.5	0.0	0.0
5.9	2.9	100.0	0.0	0.0
11.0	7.6	36.6	22.6	9.0
6.3	3.7	9.9	7.3	5.1
3.1	3.5	7.6	4.5	2.3
2.8	2.1	8.8	4.3	2.7
6.8	8.6	33.4	33.4	0.0
3.1	6.2	30.5	30.5	0.0
2.0	3.7	0.0	0.0	0.0
2.2	1.6	3.8	3.1	0.9
0.8	0.7	2.1	1.8	0.5
4.0	3.6	6.7	4.4	2.2

general association chi-squares for metropolitan areas compared with nonmetropolitan areas, for any services (except 0.001; for alcohol abuse or dependency, 0.023, 0.020, and 0.022; for other drug abuse or dependency, 0.252, 0.234, and

dependency (excludes caffeine, tobacco, and cannabis). Major affective = major affective or schizophrenia (includes

Table 3. Percentages of Wave I ECA Respondents Ages 18–59 With Role Impairments by

	All ECA Respondents (Unweighted Number)			
Severity Category/Major Problems[1]	**Males**		**Females**	
9	24.6	(483)	22.4	(397)
Alcohol	23.9	(340)	25.2	(.89)
Other drug	22.7	(55)	21.4	(24)
Major affective	33.6	(98)	21.2	(261)
8	23.7	(318)	20.8	(330)
Alcohol	21.4	(229)	17.7	(81)
Other drug	21.2	(32)	19.5	(35)
Major affective	32.2	(79)	22.2	(231)
7	23.7	(346)	14.9	(977)
6	21.3	(450)	14.8	(327)
Alcohol	18.7	(344)	21.1	(112)
Other drug	27.1	(36)	11.0	(34)
Major affective	32.1	(99)	12.1	(198)
5	27.6	(260)	17.8	(569)
4	19.9	(362)	15.4	(165)
Alcohol	19.3	(318)	30.2	(55)
Other drug	16.7	(30)	18.5	(30)
Major affective	24.3	(41)	5.7	(88)
3	14.0	(128)	14.2	(235)
2	16.7	(1,535)	10.4	(2,339)
1	12.2	(973)	6.4	(1,163)
All respondents	18.5	(4,855)	12.5	(6,502)

Note: Percentages are weighted for sample design. Cochran-Mantel-Haenszel general association chi-squares for
for alcohol abuse or dependency, 0.053 for men, 0.633 for women; for other drugs abuse or dependency, 0.632 for men,
[1]See table 1 for names of categories. Alcohol = alcohol abuse or dependency. Other drug = other drug abuse or
(includes schizophreniform).

Gender, Metropolitan or Nonmetropolitan Residence, and Severity of ADBH Problems.

Metropolitan Respondents (Unweighted Number)		Nonmetropolitan Respondents (Unweighted Number)	
Males	Females	Males	Females
24.7 (459)	23.3 (385)	24.1 (24)	6.3 (12)
23.9 (320)	26.9 (86)	24.6 (20)	0.0 (3)
23.7 (52)	21.0 (24)	13.7 (3)	— (0)
33.6 (96)	21.9 (252)	33.7 (2)	9.1 (9)
23.8 (299)	21.2 (320)	21.4 (19)	11.1 (10)
21.0 (215)	18.1 (79)	26.6 (14)	0.0 (2)
22.0 (31)	19.9 (34)	0.0 (1)	0.0 (1)
35.2 (74)	22.6 (224)	0.0 (5)	13.7 (7)
23.6 (325)	15.2 (912)	27.4 (21)	13.3 (65)
21.8 (431)	15.5 (309)	27.4 (19)	2.1 (18)
19.2 (329)	22.9 (106)	7.3 (15)	0.0 (6)
27.7 (35)	11.0 (34)	0.0 (1)	— (0
33.2 (96)	12.5 (186)	0.0 (3)	4.0 (12)
24.8 (239)	17.2 (512)	48.8 (21)	22.3 (57)
19.7 (343)	15.9 (160)	24.4 (19)	0.0 (5)
18.8 (301)	32.0 (53)	26.6 (17)	0.0 (2)
17.6 (29)	19.9 (28)	0.0 (1)	0.0 (2)
24.5 (40)	5.9 (85)	0.0 (1)	0.0 (3)
16.2 (114)	14.0 (218)	0.0 (14)	11.4 (17)
16.2 (1,418)	10.2 (2,172)	22.4 (117)	13.4 (167)
12.7 (885)	6.7 (1,055)	6.5 (88)	2.8 (108)
18.5 (4,513)	12.6 (6,043)	18.8 (342)	10.8 (459)

metropolitan areas compared with nonmetropolitan areas: for severity scale categories, 0.001 for men, 0.030 for women;
0.437 for women; for major affective disorder or schizophrenia, 0.115 for men, 0.137 for women.
dependency (excludes caffeine, tobacco, and cannabis). Major affective = major affective disorder or schizophrenia

Table 4. Percentages of Wave 1 ECA Respondents With Comorbidity of ADBH Problems by Severity of Recent ADBH Problems.

Severity Category/ Severity of Major Problems[1]	Two or More Disorders	One Disorder and At Least One Subcriterion Problem	One Disorder Only	Two or More Subcriterion Problems	One Subcriterion Problem
9	57.8	22.8	19.4	—	—
Alcohol	49.1	21.3	29.6	—	—
Other drug	89.8	10.2	0.0	—	—
Major affective	95.8	3.5	0.7	—	—
8	46.2	18.1	35.7	—	—
Alcohol	22.1	17.5	60.4	—	—
Other drug	46.9	34.3	18.8	—	—
Major affective	79.8	14.2	6.2	—	—
7	10.3	33.3	56.4	—	—
6	—	—	—	39.1	60.9
Alcohol	—	—	—	16.9	83.1
Other drug	—	—	—	86.4	13.6
Major affective	—	—	—	68.9	31.1
5	—	—	—	9.5	90.5

Note: Percentages are weighted for sample design. See table 1 for unweighted numbers.
[1]See table 1 for names of categories. Alcohol = alcohol abuse or dependency. Other drug = other drug abuse or dependency (excludes caffeine, tobacco, and cannabis). Major affective = major affective or schizophrenia (includes schizophreniform).

Table 5. Percentages of Wave 1 ECA Respondents With Comorbidity of ADBH Problems by Severity of Recent ADBH Problems and Metropolitan/Nonmetropolitan Residence.

Severity Category/ Severity of Major Problems[1]	Two or More Disorders	One Disorder and At Least One Subcriterion Problem	One Disorder Only	Two or More Subcriterion Problems	One Subcriterion Problem
9	57.2/68.3	23.0/19.2	19.8/12.6	—	—
Alcohol	48.1/65.7	21.7/15.4	30.3/18.8	—	—
Other drug	89.0/100.0	11.0/0.0	0.0/0.0	—	—
Major affective	95.6/100.0	3.7/0.0	0.7/0.0	—	—
8	46.4/43.2	18.7/8.4	34.9/48.3	—	—
Alcohol	22.1/22.6	18.3/7.3	59.7/70.4	—	—
Other drug	48.3/0.0	35.3/0.0	16.4/100.0	—	—
Major affective	79.0/90.1	14.5/9.9	6.7/0.0	—	—
7	10.2/11.9	33.3/32.8	56.5/55.3	—	—
6	—	—	—	38.4/55.2	61.6/44.8
Alcohol	—	—	—	16.2/32.3	83.8/67.7
Other drug	—	—	—	86.2/100.0	13.7/0.0
Major affective	—	—	—	68.1/85.7	31.9/14.3
5	—	—	—	9.3/11.8	90.8/88.3

Note: Percentages are weighted for sample design. See table 1 for unweighted numbers. Cochran-Mantel-Haenszel general association chi-squares for metropolitan areas compared with nonmetropolitan areas: for severity scale categories, not run (too many cells with zeroes) for all categories, 0.232 for only disorders; for alcohol abuse or dependency, 0.010 for all categories, 0.453 for only disorders; for other drug abuse or dependency, 0.216 for all categories, 0.191 for only disorders; for major affective or schizophrenia, 0.007 for all categories, 0.606 for only disorders.
[1]See table 1 for names of categories. Alcohol = alcohol abuse or dependency. Other drug = other drug abuse or dependency (excludes caffeine, tobacco, and cannabis). Major affective = major affective or schizophrenia (includes schizophreniform).

Chapter 7

Using Geographic Information Systems for Small Area Analysis

William F. Wieczorek

KEY WORDS: geographical area; statistical estimation; information source; socio-cultural norms; epidemiology; AOD use; AOD-associated consequences; computer technology; literature review

The epidemiology of alcohol use and problems has a large and apparent geographic component. Alcohol consumption and related problems are known to be affected by a variety of cultural, demographic, and social factors. Many of the factors that influence the level of alcohol use and associated problems are to a major extent a function of geography—culture, region, county, city, and neighborhood. The development of geographic information systems (GIS) offers an innovative approach to the study of alcohol use and problems. A brief overview of cultural, regional, and local factors associated with alcohol use provides the theoretical and empirical rationale for geographic approaches that utilize GIS technology. Information on the development of GIS technology and the capabilities of GIS is essential to the development of appropriate strategies for alcohol research and services.

GEOGRAPHIC AND CULTURAL FACTORS ASSOCIATED WITH ALCOHOL USE AND PROBLEMS

The groundbreaking work by MacAndrew and Edgerton (1969) clearly showed the dramatic influence of culture on drinking and on behaviors associated with drunkenness; the impact of culture is difficult to overestimate. The most readily identified culturally based drinking pattern is

W.F. Wieczorek, Ph.D., is director and research professor, Center for Health and Social Research, Buffalo State College, 1300 Elmwood Ave., Buffalo, NY 14222.

seen in wine-drinking countries. Differences in total alcohol consumption, beverage preference, and problems such as cirrhosis and trauma between the wine-drinking countries (e.g., France, Spain, Portugal, Italy) and other societies are well known and documented (Israel et al. 1991). Cultural impact on drinking may even persist after immigration to other countries. Research by Kitano and colleagues (1988, 1992) on Japanese persons in Japan, Hawaii, and California showed that cultural influences on alcohol consumption and drinking norms have a sophisticated impact, even in different environments over a number of generations. Kitano's research found that drinking practices for Japanese outside of Japan tended to be different from homeland Japanese. However, there were still identifiable differences in drinking practices between persons of Japanese heritage and Caucasians in California, suggesting an interaction of cultural heritage with local factors.

In the United States, regional differences in drinking practices are most apparent in the contrast between the wet regions (mainly the Northeast) and the drier regions of the South (Room 1983; Hilton 1988). Alcohol tends to be more available and abstention rates are lower in the wetter regions, compared with the drier regions. Models of alcohol and other drug use developed from the National Household Survey on Drug Abuse show a large range (36 to 59 percent) in the rate of drinking, with Northern and Midwest States having the highest rates and Southern and Southwestern States having the lowest rates (Substance Abuse and Mental Health Services Administration 1996). The relationship between drinking and problems is more complex in that the "dry" South is characterized by higher alcohol consumption among those who do imbibe, more binge drinking, and more adverse drinking consequences than the wetter areas (Hilton 1988). The reasons for these regional differences are not clear. Welte and Russell (1982) found that regional differences could be accounted for by controlling for urbanization, ancestry, and education. These factors are a large part of what defines "culture," and may be surrogates of the underlying values and norms of different regions. The alcohol field is lacking research that utilizes regions as developed by sociologists and geographers to study regional influences on drinking in the United States.

Research has shown that alcohol and related problems may vary substantially for smaller areas, such as cities and even census tracts, which are small areas with a population averaging 3,500 persons. Scribner and colleagues (1994, 1995) studied the cities within Los Angeles County in southern California and found that local factors, such as alcohol availability, are related to violence and crashes. Gruenewald and colleagues (1996*b*), in a study of drinking and driving and single-vehicle crashes, utilized sophisticated techniques to model spatial effects and alcohol availability, environmental factors, drinking behaviors, and sociodemographic characteristics in areas approximately the size of census tracts. They found in these areas that the frequency of alcohol consumption was positively associated with drinking and driving and that alcohol availability, based on type of outlet, was associated with single-vehicle nighttime crashes. In an analysis based on census tracts, Wieczorek and Coyle (1998) found that the rate of drinking and driving convictions had a significant positive spatial relationship and also was associated with age, race, occupation, education, and sex of the population in the tracts.

This brief review clearly indicates that geography and culture have a major role in the epidemiology of alcohol use and problems. Geographic context is likely to interact with individual-level factors (e.g., family history of drinking, personality, expectancies) to generate various drinking styles and traditions. A major role for geography in epidemiology has been apparent since John Snow removed the handle of the Broad Street pump to stop the spread of cholera. Other areas of epidemiologic research have found that neighborhood and community context are important factors in mortality, coronary disease, and infant health (Anderson et al. 1997; Diez-Roux et al. 1997; Roberts 1997).

Small areas, which may range from about the size of a county down to census block groups and individual points, provide specific social milieus defined by local demographic characteristics, risk factors (e.g., alcohol availability), norms, and consumption patterns. Small area epidemiology is deserving of greater research attention by the alcohol field because it can provide valuable insights into the individual-environment interaction associated with specific drinking traditions and problems. Information on the geographic distribution of heavy drinking and on indicators and risk factors associated with alcohol problems is essential to the development of prevention and treatment strategies, as well as to the allocation of resources for alcohol-related services.

SMALL AREA EPIDEMIOLOGY: GIS AND ALCOHOL

The influence of geography and context on alcohol use is of major importance, but the main topic of interest is what can be done to facilitate the inclusion of geographic factors in alcohol epidemiology. An important role for GIS applications in the broader field of epidemiology is widely recognized. The *Epidemiology Monitor* (1996) cited the emerging use of GIS in epidemiologic research as one of 1995's 10 most notable developments in epidemiology. Geographic information systems have the potential to revolutionize spatial aspects of alcohol epidemiology.

The most relevant topics for understanding the feasibility and capabilities of GIS are (1) GIS as an emerging technology, (2) definitions of GIS, (3) capabilities of GIS, (4) limitations of GIS, and (5) GIS in alcohol small area epidemiology. These concepts provide an essential introduction to GIS, but they cannot provide a full exploration of specific analytic, modeling, and data issues. These topics are beyond the coverage of this chapter, which focuses on the concepts and capabilities of GIS. Other sources that focus on specific types of spatial models in GIS include Goodchild (1987), Garson and Biggs (1992), Fotheringham and Rogerson (1995), and Levine (1996).

GIS as an Emerging Technology

A confluence of developments in computer hardware, software, databases, and data infrastructure tremendously enhanced the feasibility of GIS applications. The computing requirements for GIS are intensive because the amount of data required for digital maps and associated descriptive data is often very large (many times measured in megabytes). This meant that early (pre-1990) GIS required computers with large data storage capacity, substantial internal memory, and powerful processors. These requirements were costly, and usually were provided by mainframe and minicomputers, until the development of high-powered personal computers (PCs). During this period, the computer software for GIS also was expensive because the market was limited to users with access to adequate computer resources and who had a geographic interest (e.g., geography departments in research universities, management of land resources in large corporations) that could support the hardware and software expenses.

The development of low-cost, high-powered PCs provided adequate computing power for GIS, and Windows-based operating systems provided software developers greater access to this computing power. The market for GIS software exploded because almost every PC user had a database containing some level of geographic identification, such as street address, city, county, ZIP Code, or State. This led to a decrease in the cost of PC-based GIS and an increase in the usability and power of such systems.

One final ingredient was necessary to make desktop GIS feasible. This ingredient was the development of a low-cost digital-base map that was standard and provided widespread coverage of the United States. This data infrastructure is known as the TIGER (Topologically Integrated Geographic Encoding and Referencing) system. TIGER was produced for the Census Bureau at a cost of almost $200 million, and it also provides linkage to census data (Marx 1990). The accuracy and scale of TIGER were problematic for engineering uses but ideal for social science and epidemiologic applications.

Geographic information systems would be useless if the phenomenon to be studied did not have spatial dependency within the data. In other words, if the value of a variable did not depend on location, then a geographic approach would not be warranted (Berry 1997*a*). Spatial dependence is also known as spatial autocorrelation, because any specific value (auto or self) is correlated by distance to other values. Simply stated, neighboring values tend to be more similar than the similarity between all of the other values which are more distantly located (Berry 1997*b*).

The spatial dependencies facilitate new conceptualizations of alcohol-related problems. Questions such as where are alcohol-related phenomena, what is the spatial coincidence between multiple measures such as demographics and alcohol problems, and what solutions can be developed to problems related to the geographic pattern of alcohol use are presented in an entirely new, and geographic, perspective. The main form of GIS output—maps—provides a visual medium for analysis and interpretation. GIS also overcomes massive data-handling problems, thus allowing analyses that would not be feasible if done by hand. Thousands of points, such as alcohol outlets, can easily be selected by specific characteristics (type of outlet) and remapped and analyzed, which would take many hours of labor if done using manual cartographic techniques. Although one of the most exciting aspects of GIS is to stimulate new questions and hypotheses, it also is suitable for testing geographic and alcohol-epidemiologic hypotheses (e.g., persons who reside in places with greater alcohol availability will have a higher average consumption than persons in areas with less availability).

Definitions of GIS

There are a number of conceptualizations of the definition of a geographic information system. One of the issues associated with defining GIS is whether one considers GIS to be a tool for spatial research, or a separate science or subscience of the geography or information sciences (Wright et al. 1997). The theoretical development of GIS, refinement of algorithms, and societal implications of the technology may be referred to as geographic information science (Goodchild 1992; Martin 1996). Although these issues of information science are important for future developments in GIS (Pickles 1997), the conceptualization of GIS as a tool for research is most appropriate for epidemiologic applications (Clarke et al. 1996).

Martin's (1996) definition utilizes the meaning of each term from the acronym *GIS. Geographic* pertains to data relating to spatial objects, including coordinate systems and scale. *Information* is a collection of data that pertain to real phenomena, including spatial location and other characteristics associated with location. A *system* is an environment that facilitates management of data and, especially, the ability to query the spatial data. Clarke and colleagues (1996) simply define GIS as "automated systems for the capture, storage, retrieval, analysis, and display of spatial data" (p. 85). These definitions are sufficient for the development of GIS as a general tool, but they are not sufficient for the investigation of specific applications in health or social science research. A GIS without expertise in a specific research area is nothing more than a sophisticated database manager.

GIS as a combination of computer hardware, software, digital-base maps, data with a spatial reference, and expertise in a specific area of research to conduct spatial analysis is a more appropriate definition relevant to epidemiologic, health, and social research. The main idea is that GIS facilitates analysis through maps, visualization, and quantitative models. Some information on the types of data used by GIS is needed to understand the range of applications that may be possible in alcohol epidemiology.

Data used in GIS can be categorized as either spatial objects or descriptive data associated with spatial objects. The basic geographic dimension is length, and spatial objects (also called features) are classified by the number of length dimensions. Points have zero length and are typically represented by x,y coordinates in space. An example of descriptive information associated with a point is type of alcohol license at a specific alcohol outlet. Lines have a single dimension, such as a street, and have names and address ranges associated with them. Polygons are areas that have two dimensions, such as a census tract or a county that can have associated descriptive data. These are the most relevant spatial objects, although other multidimensional features such as three-dimensional surfaces are possible using a GIS.

Capabilities of GIS

The view of GIS as a tool to facilitate spatial analysis is possible only because GIS has set of key, definitive capabilities to manipulate spatial objects and associated attributes. Access to these capabilities is made possible by the GIS hardware, software, and databases. The main functions of GIS are (1) to geocode data by providing a spatial reference (x,y coordinates) based on address; (2) to combine the contents of multiple maps or data layers by overlaying them in a single operation; (3) to reclassify data based on user queries; and (4) to measure distance, adjacency, and connectivity between geographic entities. The following overview of GIS capabilities draws upon the work of Berry (1993) and Martin (1996) and my own experiences.

Geocoding

Geocoding is the process of providing a geographic reference to descriptive data by linking it to a spatial object. Geocoding is the single most important capability of GIS because spatial analysis is impossible without a geographic reference that can be manipulated by the system. All other GIS capabilities become available once data are geocoded. Geocoding is sometimes referred to as address matching, because one of the most common methods of providing a geographic reference is to utilize an address and match it to a database of addresses that are already associated with spatial features.

Figure 1 (see p. 156) shows two alcohol outlets that have been geocoded. The outlets are shown as points and are labeled with their specific addresses. Table 1 (see p. 154) shows a part of the database used to geocode the outlets in figure 1. The database is from the TIGER file for Buffalo, NY, which provides the address ranges of each block length (see Leftadd1, Leftadd2, Rgtadd1, and Rgtadd2 in table 1) for every street. In addition, each street in the TIGER file is already defined as a spatial feature in the GIS. Almost all GIS software allows the user to geocode a list of addresses, and associated descriptive data, by matching with the TIGER or similar type of file. The correct matches for the two alcohol outlets are highlighted in table 1. Next, the GIS interpolates the correct location along the block based on the actual street number and places a point for the feature. The point can then be saved as a specific x,y coordinate, which links the attribute, type of outlet, to a specific geographic coordinate. Cross-street locations, such as Main and Amherst, can be used for a simpler form of geocoding.

Geocoding is not limited to points based on addresses. Map databases of polygon objects such as counties, census tracts, and States are readily available, especially as TIGER boundary files. Many types of geocoding are possible by matching feature names, such as county, with similar-level attribute data, such as alcohol mortality. Some persons fail to recognize this process as a geocoding function; however, it creates a linkage between the geographic location of the polygon and the descriptive information that can be used for spatial analysis.

Geocoding functions of GIS software provide a powerful capability for initiating geographic analysis; however, there are some drawbacks. There is variation in the sophistication of the geocoding algorithms of various GIS packages. Typically, the GIS software creates a score based on the level of the match between your address file and the geocoding address database. Exact matches are not always possible because many addresses will lack some of the specific features (e.g., street prefix or suffix), and may have some spelling errors. Common street names (e.g., Main, Maple) and rural areas can lead to other geocoding errors. Especially when first working in a new geographic or TIGER database, it is worthwhile to perform reliability analysis on geocoded databases by manually checking the location assigned to a random subset of the cases.

GIS Overlay Function

The features of a single map in a GIS are known as a coverage or layer. Two separate coverages are shown by the maps labeled A and B in figure 2 (p. 157). GIS has the capability of combining multiple coverages into a single map. In addition, GIS can create an intersection between multiple coverages so that only the features common to all of the coverages are included in the final map. This capability is shown in figure 2. A coverage of streets and points (alcohol outlets) is overlaid and intersected with a coverage of census tract boundaries. The result of the overlay and intersection is shown by C in figure 2, in which the appropriate streets and outlets are placed into census tracts. The overlay function also facilitates another important GIS capability. Extremely common point features (e.g., outlets, arrests, subject addresses) can be assigned to areas and aggregated. In figure 2, the outlets are now assigned to specific census tracts and can be counted to create rates of alcohol availability. This aggregation of points to areas reinforces the importance of the data-handling capabilities of GIS, because this process is extremely time consuming if done by hand.

GIS Reclassification Function

Another labor-saving feature of GIS is the reclassification function. *Choropleth maps* is the name given to maps with shaded areas to represent different levels of a spatial variable (see figure 3, p. 158, for two examples). Reclassification by GIS facilitates multiple options for representing data. The impact on the visual interpretation of the data is difficult to overestimate. Figure 3 shows the result of the reclassification function on choropleth maps of alcohol availability. Note that the overlay function was utilized to assign and count the outlets in each census tract. A quantile classification in figure 3 (each quantile represents 20 percent of the census tracts) provides a large amount of information and shows substantial details of the geography of alcohol availability. The same data are reclassified to show the tracts with the highest 10 percent of alcohol availability. This map shows much less information, but also is much easier to interpret. For example, it is clear which map would be most useful if interventions were to be directed toward areas with the highest alcohol availability. Reclassification may at first appear to be a simple concept, but without a GIS, it is nearly impossible to accomplish reclassification for places with a substantial number of polygons.

GIS Distance and Adjacency Functions

The calculation of distance between points, centroids of polygons, or distance along network pathway is a capability of all geographic information systems. In addition to distance, a GIS can also recognize that areas are adjacent to one another. Figure 4 (see p. 159) shows the distances between a number of census tract centroids. Note that a GIS can readily calculate the distance between every point or centroid. Furthermore, the fact that area E is adjacent (i.e., shares a common border) to areas D, F, and G, but is not adjacent to areas A, B, and C, is recognized by the GIS. Measure of distances and adjacency can be calculated and output can be directed to data files or matrices. Matrices of spatial distance relationships or spatial contiguity are necessary for modeling spatial autocorrelation. This type of output is an example of a nonvisual product of GIS analysis that can be used in a quantitative model to assess spatial effects (e.g., see Gruenewald et al. 1996*b*). The "map" that is used to calculate the distance and contiguity data exists in the digital GIS environment, but is not usually viewed by the user. Access to alcohol-related services along the road network, or based purely on the relative locations of populations and service locations, is readily calculated using the distance function of a GIS.

GIS Buffer Function

The buffer function utilizes the distance function on a complex set of geographic features, such as a street network. A buffer distance defines the area that will be selected around the network. Figure 5 (see p. 160) shows an example of the buffer function. The map shows the street network, locations of DWI offender residences, and a buffer around the bus routes. The buffer is set at a distance that would allow the offender to walk to public transportation. The buffer selects those DWI offenders who live within the specified distance of public transportation. This is shown by the shaded area around the bus routes and the highlighted points of the DWI offenders in this buffer distance. Ready access to alternative transportation may be an important factor in the process of deciding whether a person with a suspended license will continue to drive. A buffer function could also be used to identify population exposed to corridors of high levels of alcohol availability. The calculation of these types of variables for a large sample is virtually impossible without a GIS.

GIS Neighborhood Function

The neighborhood function provides the capability to assign values to a point or area based on the local characteristics. Neighborhood characterization can take a number of forms, some of which utilize other GIS capabilities and others that allow the assignment of descriptive attributes assigned to a specified area, such as a census tract.

Figure 6 (see p. 161) shows the street network, alcohol outlets, census tract boundaries, and location of a DWI offender's residence. Notice that the DWI residence is located within a specific census tract. The neighborhood capability of the GIS can assign the attributes of the census tract descriptive data, such as census population and housing characteristics, through the recognition that the residence is in a specific tract. This process can be done for an entire database of residences and placed in another database through an automated GIS procedure.

Another method of neighborhood characterization is also shown in figure 6. Notice that the DWI residence is at the center of a circle defined by a 500m radius. The radius defines a neighborhood, or localized area, by using the distance functionality of the GIS. This neighborhood characterization is specific to the DWI residence and does not rely on any other form of information generalized for some other purpose, such as census data. The GIS can calculate the alcohol availability specific to the DWI offender's residence. This operation results in a spatially derived variable, which can be computed for an entire database and utilized in future analyses as an additional variable specific to each individual subject.

Limitations of GIS

Not all data and epidemiologic problems are amenable to a GIS-based approach (Heywood 1990). GIS provides an additional tool for conceptualizing and analyzing epidemiologic problems, especially in small geographic areas, but if the problem has no spatial component, GIS use is inappropriate. Rates for small areas may be based on very small samples, which may result in unstable estimates or other difficulties of interpretation. Some techniques, such as utilizing multiple years of data to provide more stable rates—a method that is used for the National Institute on Alcohol Abuse and Alcoholism (NIAAA) county alcohol problem indicators—should be considered (NIAAA 1994). The size of the polygons in a choropleth map may have an impact on interpretation; small area polygons on maps may have a large population (e.g., urban places) but have less visual impact than a large area polygon with a much smaller population (e.g., rural areas) (Moulton et al. 1994). However, most quantitative spatial analyses are not susceptible to visual bias based on the size of the area shown on a map.

The main issue with quantitative analysis based on areal units other than points is that the results may differ with the scale of the analysis. For example, an analysis performed at the census tract level may not necessarily apply to the same phenomenon at the block group level. Multivariate analysis is most susceptible to this problem, which is known as the modifiable areal unit problem (Fotheringham and Wong 1991). There is a great need for research to determine if some health and social processes are scale dependent, that is, if there are different models for tracts, counties, or areas defined by clusters. Specific neighborhood or small area effects may only occur at certain scales; if the area is too small, only individual factors may be discernible, and if the area is too large, the local neighborhood factor may be lost. An additional possibility for handling the modifiable areal unit problem is to use GIS to develop estimates of the sensitivity of models to changes in scale (Fotheringham and Charlton 1994).

Finally, the availability of accurate digital databases has improved greatly since the advent of TIGER. However, in some areas there are substantial limitations or problems, either with TIGER or with the method of assigning addresses. Geocoding in rural areas may be problematic because of the use of post office boxes and rural delivery routes that do not correspond to the street identifiers in the spatial data. In areas undergoing substantial new development, streets and subdevelopments may not yet exist in the TIGER system. Finally, some places, such as areas in Delaware, use an idiosyncratic form of addresses for mail delivery, which do not correspond to street addresses found in TIGER. Nonetheless, geocoding and GIS-based analysis is more feasible than ever before.

APPLICATIONS FOR GIS IN ALCOHOL SMALL AREA EPIDEMIOLOGY

The overview of the capabilities of GIS provides a wealth of new techniques to examine and model alcohol use and problems, which is meant to stimulate future utilization of GIS in alcohol research. The epidemiology of some alcohol-related phenomena is particularly appropriate for GIS-based study. Drinking and driving is one problem that has an explicit spatial component. Gruenewald and colleagues (1996*b*) have taken one approach to modeling drinking and driving behavior and related crashes, but many alternative approaches are yet to be examined. Little is known about the travel patterns of specific drinking drivers, and how this may affect the probability of a crash or arrest. Wieczorek and Coyle (1998) examined patterns of drinking and driving offenders from a health services perspective, so that prevention efforts could be targeted.

The geography of alcohol availability and access is another major topic appropriate for GIS applications. My research (Wieczorek 1995) showed that alcohol availability differed significantly between census tracts within a major city, and that persons of lower economic status tended to be exposed to areas with greater levels of alcohol availability. An article by Gruenewald and colleagues (1996*a*) focuses on a number of research issues associated with access to alcohol, and in particular how this research can assist in the prevention of alcohol-related problems. The impact of local variations, customs, and laws regarding the location and licensing of alcohol outlets is likely to provide a complex mosaic of the associations between alcohol availability and problems. The capability of GIS to develop subject-specific and other geographic measures of alcohol availability is essential to further research on the role of alcohol availability in alcohol health epidemiology.

The use of GIS in developing needs assessments for alcohol-related treatment and prevention services coincides with the previously recognized value of social indicator approaches (Wilson et al. 1983; Goldsmith et al. 1992). GIS facilitates the use and calculation of additional indirect indicators of alcohol problems, such as overcrowding and area age structure. Locally derived social indicators based on available information and GIS geocoding capabilities are now feasible. Rate measures are more readily calculated because GIS provides access to population denominators through linkage with census data. Almost all forms of alcohol-related services research and models are developed for service areas, which by definition, are the domain of geographic methods (Ricketts et al. 1994). Too often the role of spatial autocorrelation is overlooked in regression-based models of geographic areas. Spatial autocorrelation in the data invalidates the significance testing associated with regression variables because independence of the cases is violated (Greene 1990). GIS, however, can provide the spatial weights and contiguity information need to detect and model spatial autocorrelation.

Finally, GIS is often used to identify optimal sites for locating new businesses or services (Environmental Systems Research Institute 1995). To date there are no studies that utilize GIS to locate new treatment sites and examine the impact of location on the provision of services. Improvements in treatment site selection could result in treatment for a larger proportion of the population at need. Research could compare communities that utilize GIS for treatment site selection with those that do not, to discern if this level of decision analysis results in improved public health.

Spatial Clustering

Spatial cluster analysis is a technique facilitated by GIS that is widely applicable to a broad number of research issues in alcohol small area epidemiology. A cluster is a greater than expected group of similar items or occurrences (e.g., outlets, DWI offenders, deaths) that are geographically close. Spatial clustering is similar to other types of cluster analysis (e.g., Hartigan 1975), with the exceptions that many spatial clustering techniques utilize significance testing and that space-time clusters can also be investigated. Specific spatial cluster analytic techniques are suitable for use with point or geographic area data.

Overviews of spatial cluster techniques are provided by Boots and Getis (1988), Jacquez (1994), Ricketts and colleagues (1994), Anselin (1995*a*), and a special issue of the *American Journal of Epidemiology* (1990). Jacquez and Ricketts and colleagues provide general overviews of the capabilities of a variety of spatial clustering algorithms, including a discussion of which are designed for spatial and/or temporal clustering. Software for spatial cluster analysis is available from Aldrich (1990), Jacquez (1994), and Anselin (1995*b*).

The main reason to be excited about spatial cluster analysis is that it offers a wealth of research opportunities for small area analysis in alcohol studies. Cluster analysis can be used to identify "hot spots" for targeting alcohol-related services (Wieczorek and Hanson 1997) by examining patterns of indicators of service need, such as alcohol-related mortality, crashes, and alcohol outlets. Alcohol health service areas could be defined by the boundaries of spatial clusters, rather than limited to the predefined boundaries of already existing service areas that often just follow political boundaries.

Space-time clustering could be used to identify the spatiotemporal patterns of alcohol-related crashes. Research can examine whether these patterns are universal, or whether they are affected by local cultural factors or by environmental factors such as highway design and traffic patterns. Cluster analysis also may be able to identify natural communities, or neighborhoods, which may have sociodemographic, cultural, drinking-norm, or other similarities. This approach may help to identify whether specific drinking behaviors and norms are associated with specific spatial scales. Within a regional context, can heavy-drinking communities be identified? Exposure to high alcohol availability as a risk factor for alcohol problems could be examined with spatial clustering. The opportunities presented by GIS and spatial cluster analysis provide a rich agenda for future research.

An Example of Spatial Clustering

This example is from Wieczorek and Coyle's (1996) analysis of DWI offenders—persons convicted of drinking and driving—in Erie County, NY. DWI is an especially useful indicator of heavy-drinking areas and of places in need of additional or enriched services, for several reasons. DWI is one of the most common crimes in the United States, with about 1.5 million arrests each year (Maguire and Pastore 1996). This provides a large number of cases for analysis, especially if multiple years of data are used. DWI is one of the only offenses defined specifically by alcohol misuse. Also, research has shown that a large proportion of DWI offenders qualify for an alcohol diagnosis of abuse or dependence (Vingilis 1983). The one drawback is that DWI tends to underrepresent African Americans, as 90 percent of DWI offenders are white (Breer et al. 1996; Maguire and Pastore 1996). This does not lessen the appropriateness of DWI for most areas, but suggests that other indicators are needed for places with a high percentage of African Americans.

The analysis utilized 14,292 geocoded addresses of DWI offenders. The home address was geocoded because the clusters are meant to identify neighborhoods that have both a high rate of heavy drinking and a high rate of drinking and driving. However, future research should examine the travel patterns of DWI offenders in greater detail. Little is known about the relationship between the area of residence and area of the DWI occurrence, although some research suggests that many offenders are caught near their residences (Wieczorek and Coyle 1998). The analysis utilized software from Jacquez (1994) and the Grimson (1991) spatial clustering technique. The geocoded addresses were allocated to 5,000-square-foot cells by overlaying a grid on the geocoded points and counting the offenders in each cell. High-risk cells were defined as the upper 15 percent of the distribution.

The Grimson method is designed to identify spatial clustering of high-risk areas. The test statistic is based on the total number of objects, number of high-risk areas, average number of borders between objects, variance in number of borders, and adjacency among high-risk areas. A GIS provided all of this necessary information to calculate the Grimson test statistic. The null hypothesis is that the high-risk areas are randomly distributed.

Figure 7 (see p. 162) shows the grid cells and high-risk areas for this example. By visual inspection, there appears to be many adjacencies among the high-risk areas. The p level of the resulting statistic was < 0.0001, which strongly supports the interpretation that the high-risk DWI areas are spatially clustered. The clustered, or adjacent, high-risk cells define areas where DWI-related behaviors are particularly common. Case-finding efforts as well as additional DWI-focused prevention would be appropriate for these locations.

CONCLUSION

Geographic information systems have come of age and offer bountiful opportunities for new methods of conducting alcohol research in small areas. GIS also provides a tool for exploratory forms of research, which can generate new hypotheses in alcohol research. Alcohol researchers should heed Berry's statement (1996) that "effective GIS applications have something to do with data and everything to do with understanding, creativity, and perspective" (p. 26).

Scientists and epidemiologists who conduct alcohol-related research have access to a massive pool of data, much of which has a geographic component. Information is data with some level of explanation, which is the basis for much research. Knowledge is information set within a context that explains a phenomenon, which is a relatively rare commodity, even in research. The tools made available through GIS provide an opportunity to facilitate the process of understanding alcohol use and problems by developing new forms of information and knowledge that are subjected to a dialog of ideas based on research. There is a great potential for meaningful contributions to alcohol research by utilizing GIS; the responsibility is on alcohol researchers to respond to the challenge.

ACKNOWLEDGMENTS

This research was supported by grants K02 AA00154, P50 AA09802, and R01 AA10305 from the National Institute on Alcohol Abuse and Alcoholism.

REFERENCES

Aldrich, T.E. *CLUSTER: User's Manual for Software To Assist With Investigations of Rare Health Events.* Atlanta, GA: Agency for Toxic Substances and Disease Registries, 1990.

Anderson, R.T.; Sorlie, P.; Backlund, E.; Johnson, N.; and Kaplan, G.A. Mortality effects of community socioeconomic status. *Epidemiology* 8(1):42–47, 1997.

Anselin, L. Local indicators of spatial association—LISA. *Geographical Analysts* 27(2):93–115, 1995*a*.

Anselin, L. *SpaceStat Version 1.80 User's Guide.* Morgantown: West Virginia University, 1995*b*.

Berry, J.K. Cartographic modeling: The analytical capabilities of GIS. In: Goodchild, M.F.; Parks, B.O., and Steyaert, L.T., eds. *Environmental Modeling With GIS.* Oxford, England: Oxford University Press, 1993. pp. 58–74.

Berry, J.K. Developing and understanding GIS. *GIS World* 9(8):26, 1996.

Berry, J.K. Spatial dependencies define the data. *GIS World* 10(5):26–27, 1997*a*.

Berry, J.K. Uncover the mysteries of spatial autocorrelation. *GIS World* 10(6):30–31, 1997*b*.

Boots, B.N., and Getis, A. *Point Pattern Analysis.* Newbury Park, CA: Sage Publications, 1988.

Breer, P.; McAuliffe, W.E.; and Levine, E.B. Statewide substance abuse prevention planning. *Evaluation Review* 20(5):596–618, 1996.

Clarke, K.C.; McLafferty, S.L.; and Tempalski, B.J. On epidemiology and geographic information systems: A review and discussion of future directions. *Emerg Infect Dis* 2(2):85–92, 1996.

Diez-Roux, A.V.; Nieto, F.J.; Muntaner, C.; Tyroler, H.A.; Comstock, G.W.; Shahar, E.; Cooper, L.S.; Watson, R.L.; and

Szklo, M. Neighborhood environments and coronary heart disease: A multilevel analysis. *Am J Epidemiol* 146:48–63, 1997.

Epidemiology Monitor. 1995's 10 most notable developments in epidemiology. *Epidemiology Monitor* 17(2):1–3, 1996.

Environmental Systems Research Institute. *Understanding GIS.* New York: John Wiley & Sons, 1995.

Fotheringham, A.S., and Charlton, M. GIS and exploratory spatial data analysis: An overview of some research issues. *Geographical Systems* 1:315–327, 1994.

Fotheringham, A.S., and Rogerson, P. *Spatial Analysis and GIS.* London: Taylor & Francis, 1995.

Fotheringham, A.S., and Wong, D.W.S. The modifiable areal unit problem in multivariate statistical analysis. *Environment and Planning A* 23:1025–1044, 1991.

Garson, G.D., and Biggs, R.S. *Analytic Mapping and Geographic Databases.* Newbury Park, CA: Sage Publications, 1992.

Goldsmith, H.F.; Bell, R.A.; and Warheit, G. Indirect needs assessment for mental health services planning. *Evaluation and Program Planning* 15:111–113, 1992.

Goodchild, M.F. A spatial analytical perspective on geographical information systems. *International Journal of Geographical Information Systems* 1(4):327–334, 1987.

Goodchild, M.F. Geographical information science. *International Journal of Geographical Information Systems* 6:31–45, 1992.

Greene, W.H. *Econometric Analysis.* New York: Macmillan, 1990.

Grimson, R.C. A versatile test for clustering and a proximity analysis of neurons. *Methods Inf Med* 30:299–303, 1991.

Gruenewald, P.J.; Millar, A.; and Roeper, P. Access to alcohol: Geography and prevention for local communities. *Alcohol Health Res World* 20(4):244–251, 1996*a*.

Gruenewald, P.J.; Millar, A.B.; Treno, A.J.; Ponicki, W.R.; Yang, Z.; and Roeper, P. The geography of availability and driving after drinking. *Addiction* 91(7):967–983, 1996*b*.

Hartigan, J.A. *Clustering Algorithms.* New York: John Wiley & Sons, 1975.

Heywood, I. Commentaries: Geographic information systems in the social sciences. *Environment and Planning A* 22:849–854, 1990.

Hilton, M.E. Regional diversity in United States drinking practices. *British Journal of Addiction* 83:519–532, 1988.

Israel, Y.; Orrego, H.; Schmidt, W.; Popham, R.E.; Escartin, P.; Ishi, H.; Kelly, D.; Long, J. P.; Malizia, G.; Mezey, E.; Pagliaro, L.; Poynard, T.; Salaspuro, M.; and Tanikawa, K. Trauma in cirrhosis: An indicator of the pattern of alcohol abuse in different societies. *Alcohol Clin Exp Res* 15:433–437, 1991.

Jacquez, G.M. *Stat! Statistical Software for the Clustering of Health Events.* Ann Arbor, MI: BioMedware, 1994.

Kitano, H.H.L.; Chi, I.; Law, C.K.; Lubben, J.; and Rhee, S.-Y. Alcohol consumption of Japanese in Japan, Hawaii, and California. In: *Cultural Influences and Drinking Patterns: A Focus on Hispanic and Japanese Populations.* Research

Monograph No. 19. Rockville, MD: National Institute on Alcohol Abuse and Alcoholism, 1988. pp. 99–133.

Kitano, H.H.L.; Chi, I.; Rhee, S.; Law, C.K.; and Lubben, J.E. Norms and alcohol consumption: Japanese in Japan, Hawaii and California. *J Stud Alcohol* 53:33–39, 1992.

Levine, N. Spatial statistics and GIS. *Journal of the American Planning Association* 62(3):381–391, 1996.

MacAndrew, C., and Edgerton, R. *Drunken Comportment.* Chicago: Aldine, 1969.

Maguire, K., and Pastore, A.L., eds. *Sourcebook of Criminal Justice Statistics 1995.* Washington, DC: U.S. Department of Justice, Bureau of Justice Statistics/U.S. Government Printing Office, 1996.

Martin, D. *Geographic Information Systems.* London: Routledge, 1996.

Marx, R.W., ed. The Census Bureau's TIGER System. [Special Issue.] *Cartography and Geographic Information Systems* 17(1), 1990.

Moulton, L.H.; Foxman, B.; Wolfe, R.A.; and Port, F.K. Potential pitfalls in interpreting maps of stabilized rates. *Epidemiology* 5:297–301, 1994.

National Institute on Alcohol Abuse and Alcoholism (NIAAA). *U.S. Alcohol Epidemiologic Data Reference Manual.* Volume 3, Fourth Edition: County Alcohol Problem Indicators, 1986–1990. Washington, DC: NIAAA, 1994.

Pickles, J. Tool or science? GIS, technoscience, and the theoretical turn. *Annals of the Association of American Geographers* 87(2):363–372, 1997.

Ricketts, T.C.; Savitz, L.A.; Gesler, W.M.; and Osborne, D.N., eds. *Geographic Methods for Health Services Research.* New York: University Press of America, 1994.

Roberts, E.M. Neighborhood social environments and the distribution of low birthweight in Chicago. *Am J Public Health* 87:597–603, 1997.

Room, R. Region and urbanization as factors in drinking practices and problem. In: Kissin, B., and Begleiter, H., eds. *The Biology of Alcoholism.* New York: Plenum Press, 1983. pp. 555–604.

Scribner, R.A.; MacKinnon, D.P.; and Dwyer, J.H. Alcohol outlet density and motor vehicle crashes in the Los Angeles County cities. *J Stud Alcohol* 55:447–453, 1994.

Scribner, R.A.; MacKinnon, D.P.; and Dwyer, J.H. The risk of assaultive violence and alcohol availability in Los Angeles County. *Am J Public Health* 85:335–340, 1995.

Substance Abuse and Mental Health Services Administration. *Model Based Estimates From the 1991–1993 National Household Surveys on Drug Abuse Summary Report.* Rockville: U.S. Department of Health and Human Services, 1996.

Vingilis, E. Drinking drivers and alcoholics. In: Smart, R.G.; Glaser, F.B.; Israel, Y.; Kalant, H.; Popham, R.E.; and Schmidt, W., eds. *Research Advances in Alcohol and Drug Problems.* New York: Plenum Press, 1983. pp. 99–141.

Welte, J.W., and Russell, M. Regional variations in the consumption of alcohol in the U.S.A. *Drug Alcohol Depend* 10:243–249, 1982.

Wieczorek, W.F. Spatial variation in alcohol availability in Buffalo, New York. In: *CDC/ATSDR 5th Biennial Symposium on Statistical Methods, Small Area Statistics in Public Health: Design, Analysis, Graphic and Spatial Methods, Program and Abstracts.* Atlanta, GA: Centers for Disease Control and Prevention/Agency for Toxic Substance and Disease Registry, 1995. p. 79.

Wieczorek, W.F., and Coyle, J.J. Spatial analysis of DWI offenders for alcohol-related services. In: *Abstracts: Association of American Geographers 92nd Annual Meeting.* Washington, DC: Association of American Geographers, 1996. p. 314.

Wieczorek, W.F., and Coyle, J.J. Targeting DWI prevention. *Journal of Prevention and Intervention in the Community* 17:17–32, 1998.

Wieczorek, W.F., and Hanson, C.E. Spatial analysis of alcohol-related mortality for identification of alcohol service areas. In: *The Association for Health Services Research Program and Abstracts.* Chicago: Association for Health Services Research, 1997. p. 321.

Wilson, R.; Malin, H.; and Lowman, C. Uses of mortality rates and mortality indexes in planning alcohol programs. *Alcohol Health Res World* 8(1):41–53, 1983.

Wright, D.J.; Goodchild, M.F.; and Proctor, J.D. GIS: Tool or science? *Annals of the Association of American Geographers* 87(2):346–362, 1997.

Table 1. TIGER Data for Geocoding.

Recnum	Fdpre	Fname	Ftype	Fdsuf	Cfcc
48295912		Hertel	Ave		A41
48295852		Hertel	Ave		A41
48295915		**Hertel**	**Ave**		**A41**
48295931		Hertel	Ave		A41
48289574		Hertel	Ave		A41
48296217		Main	St		A31
48296050		Main	St		A31
48296036		**Main**	**St**		**A31**
48296148		Main	St		A31
48295996		Main	St		A31

Note: Data in bold refers to the alcohol outlets depicted in Figure 1.

Recnum = record number (provides link to geographic coordinates); Fdpre = prefix for street name; Fname = street name; Ftype = street type; Fdsuf = street suffix information; Cfcc = census feature class code; Leftadd1 = beginning of address range, left side of street; Leftadd2 = end of address range, left side of street; Rgtadd1 = beginning of address range, right

Leftadd1	Leftadd2	Rgtadd1	Rgtadd2	Zipcolef	Zipcorgt
1818	1840	1823	1829	14216	14216
1656	1728	1657	1729	14216	14216
1842	**1864**	**1831**	**1865**	**14216**	**14216**
1902	1922	1893	1917	14214	14214
1576	1608	1577	1609	14216	14216
2820	2846	2819	2841	14214	14214
2760	2780	2757	2781	14214	14214
2576	**2620**	**2577**	**2619**	**14214**	**14214**
2994	2998	2981	3003	14214	14214
2496	2504	2471	2495	14214	14214

side of street; Rgtadd2 = end of address range, right side of street; Zipcolef = ZIP Code on left side of street; Zipcorgt = ZIP Code on right side of street.

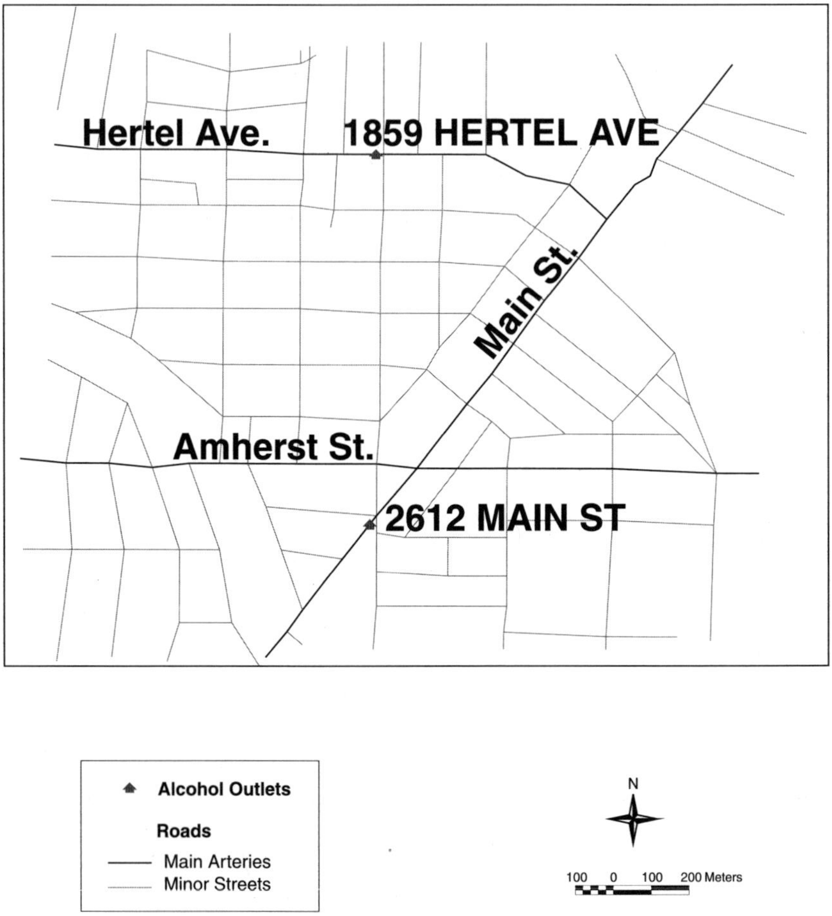

Figure 1. GIS geocoding function.

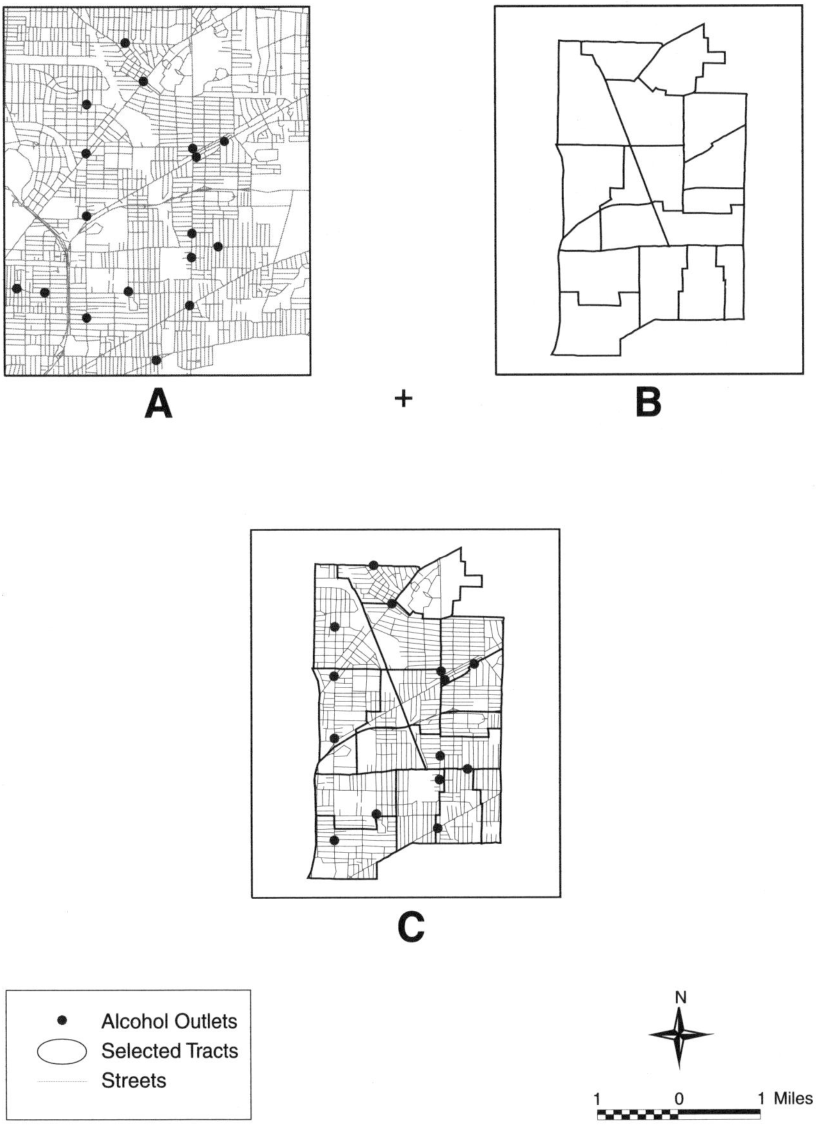

Figure 2. GIS overlay function.

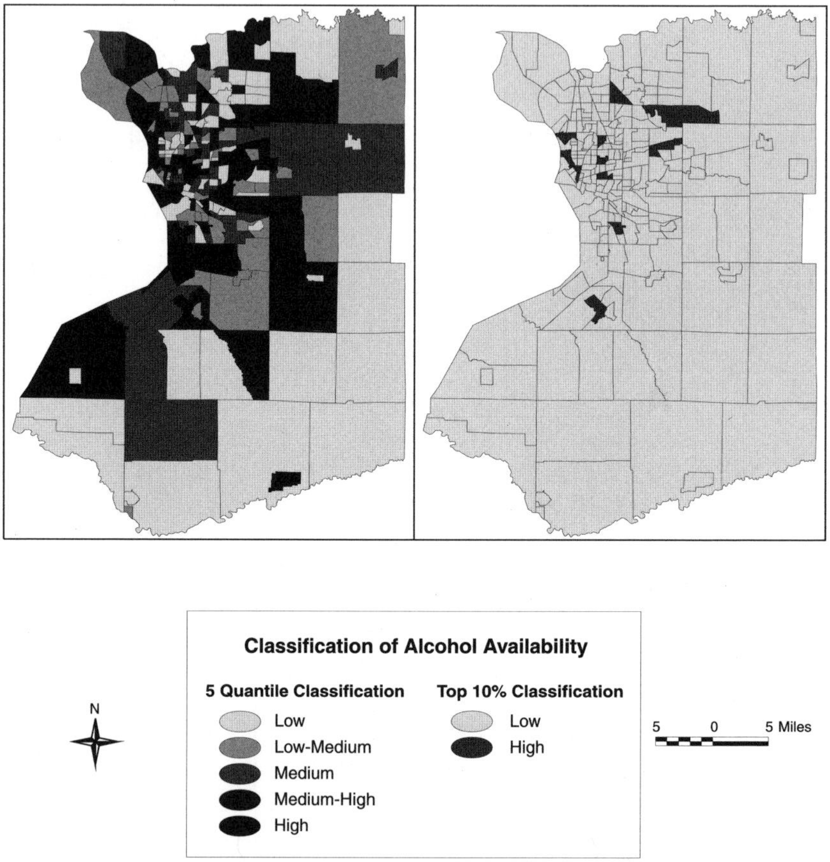

Figure 3. GIS reclassification function.

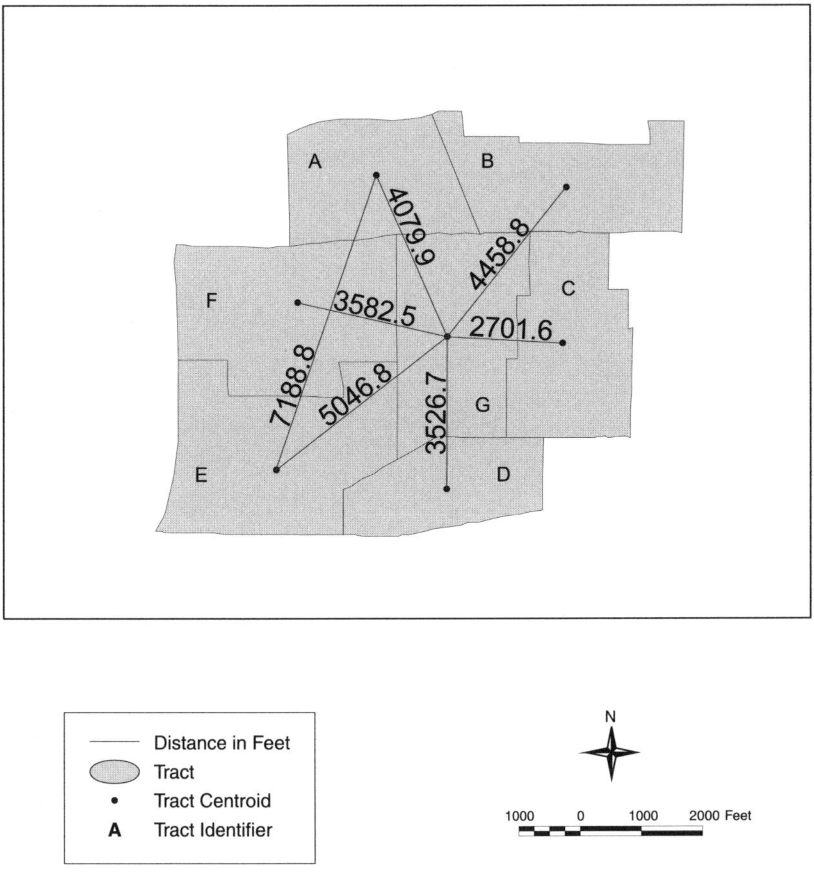

Figure 4. GIS distance and adjacency function.

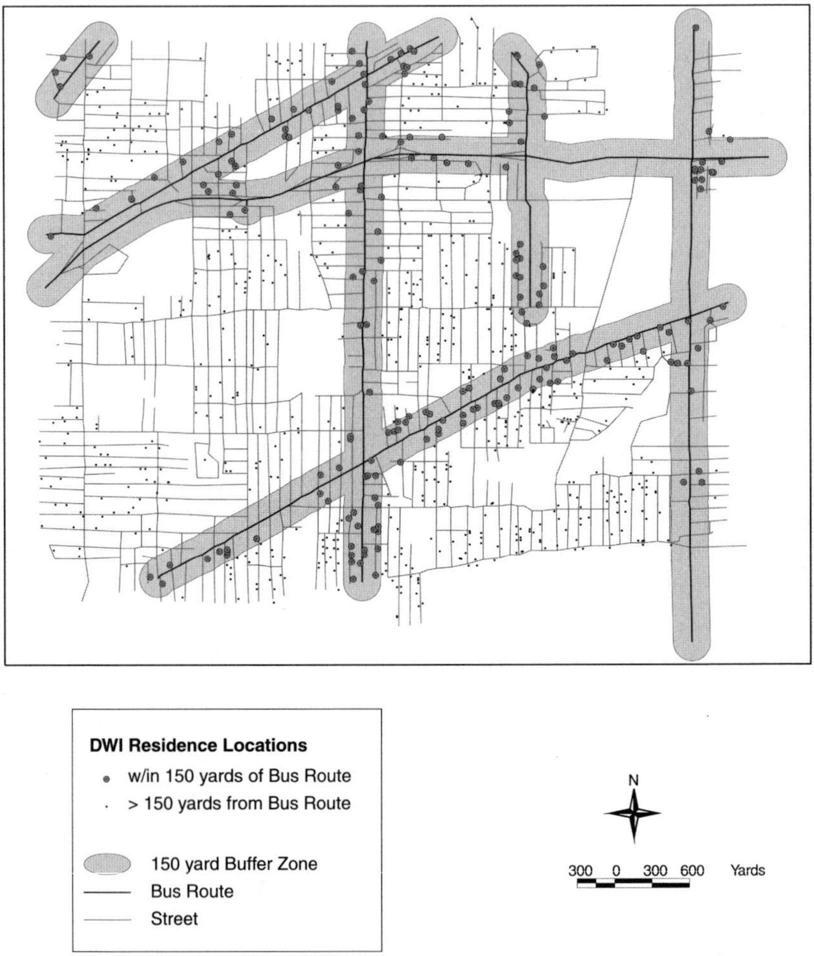

Figure 5. GIS buffer function.

Figure 6. GIS neighborhood function.

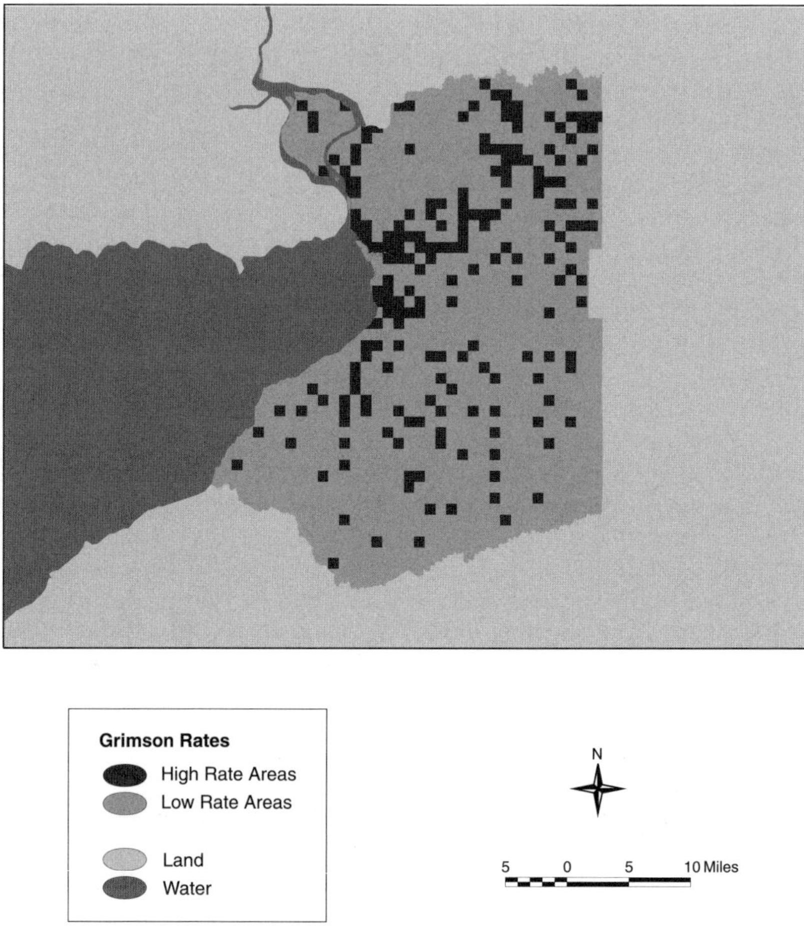

Figure 7. Grimson clustering of DWI offenders.

Chapter 8

Physical and Economic Access to Alcohol: The Application of Geostatistical Methods to Small Area Analysis in Community Settings

Paul J. Gruenewald, Ph.D., Alexander Millar,
William R. Ponicki, M.S., and Garland Brinkley, Ph.D.

KEY WORDS: AOD availability; statistical estimation; geographical area; supply and demand; AOD price; alcoholic beverage sales outlet; AOD use pattern; data collection; literature review

The classical microeconomic theory of consumer demand suggests that should the physical availability of alcohol fall to zero or the price of alcohol rise to infinity, all drinking would be eliminated; the costs of finding and then purchasing alcohol would far exceed the time-energy and economic budgets of consumers (Pindyck and Rubinfeld 1989). Barring the creation of an illegal alcohol market, these two environmental approaches to the control and regulation of alcohol use would eliminate drinking and reduce rates of alcohol problems to zero. It is a testament to the endurance of this classically based view that empirical investigations have continued to examine both of these determinants of alcohol use despite the conceptual and analytic problems confronting these areas of research (Gruenewald et al. 1996*a;* Kenkel and Manning 1996). The conceptual problem central to the issue of the effects of price on alcohol use and problems is the ability of consumers to make quality substitutions between beverage brands (Treno et al. 1993; Gruenewald et al. 1995), potentially mitigating price

---

P.J. Gruenewald, Ph.D., is a senior research scientist, A. Millar and W.R. Ponicki, M.S., are research analysts, and G. Brinkley, Ph.D., is a postdoctoral trainee at the Prevention Research Center, 2150 Shattuck Ave., Suite 900, Berkeley, CA 94704.

effects; consumers could simply shift their purchases to cheaper beverages.[1] The conceptual problem central to the issue of the effects of availability on alcohol use and problems is the ability of consumers to pursue alcohol as part of daily routine activities (e.g., grocery shopping and eating at restaurants [Abbey et al. 1993]), potentially mitigating the effects of changes in availability; consumers could simply purchase and use alcohol elsewhere.[2] Indeed, under these circumstances, it is possible to argue that changes in average prices and typical levels of availability will have no effect whatever on the use of alcohol per se. Consumers could compensate for higher prices by purchasing cheaper forms of alcohol and could compensate for reduced availability by combining alcohol purchases with other activities (e.g., grocery shopping). The central questions for research in both these areas are whether, and if so to what extent, quality substitutions and changes in routine activities alter price and availability effects.

Most studies of the effects of alcohol beverage prices and the physical availability of alcohol on alcohol use and problems have been conducted at very high levels of aggregation or relied upon substantial individual-level data sets from broad samples of respondents. Typically, aggregate studies demonstrating price and availability effects have been conducted at the level of States within the United States (Gruenewald 1993; Gruenewald et al. 1993*b;* Leung and Phelps 1993). The power of these studies to detect impacts of changes in price and availability rests upon the substantial variation in alcohol regulation and pricing patterns observed between States over time. Substantial State and regional variations in price and availability cannot be easily overcome by changes in individual choice or mobility. Individual-level studies have relied upon very large samples available from national data sources (e.g., the National Health Interview Survey [Kenkel 1996]) or developed as part of large-scale survey projects (e.g., the California Availability Survey [Gruenewald et al. unpublished manuscript 1996]). The power of these studies to detect effects rests upon the broad geographic dispersion of respondents across States and regions with widely differing levels of price and availability. Again, the ability of respondents to mitigate price and availability effects through alterations in patterns of beverage choice and venue use is minimized; to take advantage of these differences, respondents would have to travel substantial distances.

With respect to these observations, the two most important empirical questions to ask at this juncture of the research enterprise are whether geographic variations in price and availability make a difference and, if so, at what geographic scale do these variations cease to make a difference. Can the effects of variations in availability observed at State and county levels also be observed at the level of local communities, with neighborhood availability related to neighborhood patterns of use? Can the effects of variations in beverage prices observed at the State level also be observed at county and community levels, with neighborhood prices related to neighborhood patterns of use? In an effort to begin to address these questions, the empirical focus of the current work will be upon the development of issues regarding the relationships of alcohol beverage prices and the physical availability of alcohol to patterns of alcohol use in "small" community settings. Concerns about the relationships between beverage prices and availability and various forms of harm related to the use of alcohol will be set aside. Thus, the substantial literature on the relationship of beverage prices to alcohol-related harm (Leung and Phelps 1993; Kenkel and Manning 1996) and the growing literature on the relationship of specific forms of availability to alcohol-related harm (Gruenewald 1993; Scribner et al. 1994, 1995; Gorman et al. 1998) will not be reviewed.

APPLYING GEOGRAPHICALLY BASED TECHNIQUES TO DATA ANALYSIS

The analytic emphasis of this chapter will be upon the application of a set of specific geographically based techniques to the analysis of small area data on prices, availability, and alcohol use. The discussion of these methods has been developed for three purposes:

- to elucidate the geostatistical issues confronted by all researchers performing small area analyses at low levels of aggregation,
- to explore the degree to which measures of prices and availability may serve as statistical instruments by which to better understand geographic patterns of alcohol use, and
- to test empirical expectations regarding the relationships of prices and availability to alcohol use in the context of community demographics.

Thus, the primary goals of this chapter are to encourage a better understanding of the analytic issues involved in the analysis of small area data on alcohol use and to elucidate the implications of these issues for studies of the geographic patternings of such use. The content focus of the study, although of profound importance to students of availability and problems, is secondary to these goals.

"Small" Ecologies for "Small" Areas

An obvious ambiguity lingers at the heart of small area analysis. This ambiguity is summarized by the questions, "What is a small area?" and "What makes it small?" The answers to these questions are both characterized by the nature of the study and the empirical problem at hand. For example, when attempting to assess rates of mortality related to different forms of cancer, the researcher may determine that a small area will be any of the smallest observable geographic units in a study (e.g., ZIP Codes) that contain the minimum number of necessary cases for adequate statistical assessment. The small area is determined both by available units of observation (i.e., ZIP Codes) and, as an operational criterion, available sample within units. In the absence of available sample, estimated rates for areas smaller than this may be subject to interpolation from other adjacent small areas (the central interpolation problem in small area analysis). On the other hand, when attempting to assess the rate of drinking and driving crashes related to the distribution of alcohol outlets, the researcher may determine that a small area will be the geographic unit capturing some minimum sample of observations (again an operational criterion) that approximates the scale of the process itself (the spatial distribution of alcohol-related crashes around outlets [Gruenewald et. al. 1996*b*]). In this case, the process under study properly enters into the definition of the small area at hand. A larger area, such as ZIP Codes, may be too large to detect specific relationships between outlets and crashes. Smaller areas may not contain adequate samples of observations and may demand interpolation. In this way the ecology of the problem, the relationship between human activities and the environments in which these activities take place, enters into the definition of small areas. In essence, a small area is that geographic area which is sufficiently small to elucidate the ecology of the spatial process under study. In the case of cancer these will be the small units necessary to elucidate the spatial relationships between carcinogens and cancer risks.[3] In the case of drinking and driving these will be the small units necessary to elucidate the spatial relationships between locations of alcohol use and locations of alcohol-related crashes.[4]

The work by Gruenewald and colleagues (1996*b*) studying the geographic relationships between alcohol outlets and alcohol-related crashes serves as a good example of the process by which small areas come to be defined. The presumption of the study was that the dynamic mechanism linking drinking and impaired driving was a simple one; individuals would consume alcohol at on-premise establishments, get into their cars to drive home, and crash with some probability in the nearby vicinity. Based on previous work it was known that a sensitive characterization of the distribution of outlets within community areas would require units far smaller than those of ZIP Codes. These units would have to be sufficiently small to distinguish densities of different types of outlets (off-premise, bars and restaurants) within quite small community areas (in some cases amounting to an area of some 10 city blocks). These units would also have to be sufficiently large to allow assessment of the drinking, and drinking and driving, patterns of local populations (essential covariates in the study). The solution found by the authors was to develop a clustering algorithm that aggregated point assemblages of respondents (based on cross-street locations) into community neighborhoods based on population density and available sample. Using this technique, a geometric mean number of about 40 respondents per area was obtained within geographic areas defined along population gradients within communities. The units obtained were sufficiently small to partition the distribution of outlets into statistically separable geographic domains while at the same time providing adequate sample within cells.

Within the current study, similar requirements to those stated in the previous research (Gruenewald et al. 1996*b*) arise. Examining the relationships between the economic and physical availability of alcohol and drinking patterns within community settings, it is necessary to define geographic units sufficiently small to capture the different distributions of outlet types across community geographies while at the same time retaining adequate sample to simultaneously portray the geographic distribution of drinking patterns. The units defined in the previous study are of value here, and the reader is referred to the referenced article for further discussion of these issues.

The Small Area Ecology of Alcohol Supply and Demand

The meanings of alcohol supply and demand take on new significance within the context of the small community areas defined in the current study. Naive approaches to classical economic theory suggest a number of relationships one can expect between patterns of distribution of alcohol and patterns of alcohol use. More sophisticated approaches to these issues in a geographic context suggest further, more subtle relationships that may be observed at the community level. These approaches arise through a consideration of the nature of the dynamics of alcohol use within community settings.

Although at the highly aggregated geographic levels of whole States, counties within States, and cities within counties, the geographic distribution of the supply of alcohol is usually treated as relatively homogeneous, within individual cities or communities the distribution of alcohol outlets is highly heterogeneous and, within some neighborhoods, highly concentrated. At any geographic point in a community, one may be very close to a source of alcohol (e.g., standing outside a bar or restaurant) or very far from a source of alcohol (e.g., standing in an outlying park in a residential area). Similarly, prices charged for alcoholic beverages, while presumptively homogeneous across the geographic units customarily observed by economists (Leung and Phelps 1993), may be quite heterogeneous across community neighborhoods. At any geographic point in a community one may be near a source of alcohol at which prices charged are very high (e.g., in a high-income area) or very low (e.g., in a low-income area). Complementarily, the demand for alcohol, as represented by geographic patterns of alcohol use, may also vary substantially across community settings. At any point within a community one may find oneself in an area where drinking is common (e.g., areas in which a substantial number of young people are resident) or infrequent (e.g., areas in which a substantial number of older people are resident). All depends on location.

From an empirical point of view, the obvious questions are (1) whether the distributions of availability, price, and patterns of drinking are indeed heterogeneous across communities; (2) whether the geographic distributions of measures of these constructs covary across communities; and (3) whether these distributions reflect other characteristics of community environments or human populations. In order to provide preliminary answers to these questions, a brief theoretical examination of some of the socioeconomic bases of drinking must be undertaken.

The primary underlying behavioral dynamic assumed in the current study is a simple one: that alcohol consumers must purchase alcohol either at an off-premise establishment (e.g., grocery or convenience store) for consumption elsewhere (e.g., at home, at a friend's or relative's home) or at an on-premise establishment (e.g., bar or restaurant) for use at the point of purchase. The underlying economic constraints on drinking assumed here are also relatively simple: that drinkers with less money and time-energy budgets for drinking drink less, that they factor the costs of drinking into their drinking behaviors (e.g., the degree to which they use different establishments for drinking [Gruenewald et al. 1995]), and that alcohol prices and physical availability are part of these costs. As part of the full costs of alcohol use (Grossman 1988; Gruenewald 1993), reduced availability increases costs of travel to and from outlets and, therefore, increases the full costs of alcoholic beverages.

Dissimilar to previous studies, however, this study also takes into account the actions of alcohol retailers in terms of (1) siting outlets and (2) determining prices to be charged for alcoholic beverages. On the supply side, these issues require consideration as a central part of economic studies of alcohol use in community settings. Presumably, while the drinking behaviors of consumers are determined by, among other things, their geographic relationships to outlets and the full costs of alcohol, the locations of outlets and costs of alcohol are determined by the desire of retailers to maximize profits from sales of alcohol. With this assumption in hand, fairly straightforward arguments from economic geography suggest that retailers should (1) site their locations to minimize distances to consumers (e.g., in areas of high population density) or in areas of communities where there is considerable traffic, (2) site their locations to minimize the costs of operation (e.g., in low-income areas), and (3) charge prices for alcohol that are competitive with the "local" market. In this way, retailers would minimize the full costs of alcohol to consumers by reducing travel time to and from outlets, maximize their own profits by locating in areas where costs of operation are low, and retain a competitive price for alcohol.

The issue of how prices come to be established in this sort of competitive market is a complex one, which cannot be elucidated here. The interested reader is referred to introductory studies in microeconomics (Pindyck and Rubinfeld 1989) and mathematical geography (Thomas and Huggett 1980). From an economic perspective, the determinants of price flow from shifts in demand (e.g., changes in the number of consumers, changes in income levels, and changes in the prices of substitute and complementary goods), shifts in supply (e.g., changes in input prices, changes in technology, and changes in the number of competing establishments), and pricing strategies taken by geographically limited firms striving to capture maximum market share. With regard to the last issue, the classic literature on spatial competition in economic geography dates back to Hotelling's (1929) demonstration that a competitive advantage can be had by any firm that sites itself closer to the locations of consumers than any other (suggesting that there are optimal locations for the placement of alcohol outlets). More recent work demonstrates that optimal locations may be found by taking into account the geographic determinants of input prices, and the geographic locations of competitors and consumers (Eaton and Wooders 1985).

Simplifying the theoretical points of this literature, three basic observations can be made. First, considering the nature of full prices as reflecting the nominal costs of alcohol and costs of travel to and from outlets, as a general rule an outlet sited closer to a pool of consumers with greater demand will have a competitive advantage over an outlet sited further away. From the perspective of the consumer, alcohol sold in "nearby" outlets costs less than alcohol sold in "distant" outlets. From the perspective of the retailer, in order to remain full price competitive ("full price" refers to nominal costs plus travel time costs relative to the value of time) "distant" outlets should charge less than "nearby" outlets to make up this difference. Second, under conditions of pure competition it is reasonable to assume that alcohol beverage prices will be lower where the greatest densities of outlets exist. With greater numbers of outlets competing for limited market shares, prices should fall relative to other areas with fewer competitors. Assuming a constant demand, the increased supply due to increased competition from more outlets should result in lower prices. Third, under conditions in which it is assumed that alcohol supply in a sense creates its own demand, it is also possible that alcohol beverage prices will be greater where densities of outlets are greatest. In this case it is assumed that prices will be established on the basis of the flow of consumers through market areas established by collectives of retailers; geographic clusters of restaurants, for example, attract greater numbers of consumers over time than individual outlets, collectively reducing the aggregate travel time to each individual outlet in the face of increased competition between outlets (the second point above).[5]

As a result of these considerations the following exploratory hypotheses can be put forward:

Prices

1. Prices for alcohol should be greater in areas of communities

with the greatest demand for alcohol (i.e., high-income areas with greatest densities of consumers).
2. Prices for alcohol should be lower in areas where there are greater densities of outlets.
3. Prices for alcohol should be greater in areas where there are greater densities of outlets.

Availability

1. Greater densities of outlets should be found in community areas within or adjacent to areas with greater demand for alcohol (i.e., high-income areas with greatest densities of consumers).
2. Greater densities of outlets should be found in community areas within or adjacent to areas with greater traffic flow.
3. Greater densities of outlets should be found in low-income neighborhoods where costs of operation can be kept to a minimum.

Drinking Patterns

1. Greater use of alcohol should be observed in community areas where prices are lower.
2. Greater use of alcohol should be observed in community areas where availability is greater.

It is important to note at this juncture that some of these hypotheses are superficially contradictory. It is suggested, for example, that prices will be either greater or lower in areas with greater densities of outlets. Prices will be greater relative to other areas of a community because distal outlets must charge less than nearby outlets to successfully compete for market share. Prices will be lower relative to other areas of a community because of increased competition. Both outcomes are predicted by economic theory since both processes are aspects of the market that determines alcohol beverage prices. The question within a community context is which, if either, process dominates? More generally, the descriptive goal of the current study is to statistically assess the empirical observed geographic patternings of prices, outlets, and use in a theoretical context in which multiple hypothetical outcomes are possible. It is expected that the observations made on the communities in the current study will reflect the general patternings of alcohol availability and use within moderate-sized communities in the United States. Using data obtained from a database similar to that used by Gruenewald and colleagues (1996*b*), the current study will test these hypotheses using geostatistical software specifically designed to handle tests of spatial effects among geographic objects (Ponicki and Gruenewald 1997).

The Methodological Approach of Geostatistics

As the previous discussions suggest, within the context of community-based studies of economic and physical access to alcohol and alcohol use there is much to be said about the spatial arrangement of outlets, the geographic distribution of prices, and their relationships to the geographic distributions of consumers within the marketplace. Measures from diverse archival and survey sources must be integrated into geographic areas somehow characteristic of the communities under study. In the current case, archival data on the geographic distribution of alcohol outlets must be mapped onto the same geographic frame as price data from sampled alcohol retailers and drinking data from surveyed respondents. The geographic frame of the study serves as the basis upon which these diverse data sources can be coupled in space and time. In addition, the hypotheses themselves demand that the researcher develop spatial formulations of relationships among the studied objects (i.e., measured variables within and between geographic areas) that are both empirically tractable and statistically testable within some analytic context. The methodological approach of geostatistics provides the framework for such tests.

The analysis of area data is the particular province of geostatistics, the statistical analysis of geographically mappable data structures. The unique features of such data are as follows: (1) they may represent rates, proportions, or quantities of observed measures within two or more dimensional areas; (2) the geographic areas are defined to be contiguous in space; and (3) observations are not necessarily independent of one another. Historically, the statistical analysis of area data grew out of the scientific need to assess the reliability of observed relationships between variables naturally measured at the aggregate level: voting patterns in public policy studies, money flow between countries in economic geography, human migration patterns in demography, avian migration patterns in ethology, and so on. There were two central analytic concerns for such studies. First, within each content area an explicit spatial dynamic related the units under consideration. The empirical exploration of these dynamics had to rely upon an explicit modeling of geographic relationships among study units. For example, studies of avian migration patterns required the examination of species' use of different land areas in different seasons and the correlation of measures of population growth (and decline) along migratory paths. The size of a wintering population in one geographic area is a direct function of the size of the mating population in another (Maurer 1994). Second, within each content area the geographic units under study could not be assumed independent of one another. Exogenous conditions affecting one area would likely affect adjacent areas, inducing correlations between spatially contiguous areas. For example, the local growth of avian populations could be commonly traced to local weather conditions affecting both target areas and their immediate surroundings.

Techniques for the geostatistical analysis of area data were developed to provide a mathematical approach to the estimation of empirical relationships between observations taken on geographic units. The techniques allow researchers interested in geographic relationships among study objects to explicitly model spatial relationships among such objects without bias. The statistical basis of these techniques was developed by Cliff and Ord (1981). Developments since that time are well represented in the works of Griffith (1988) and Anselin (1988). A useful introduction to issues involved in the analysis of area data can be found in Griffith (1987), and a general introduction to geostatistics is best provided by Bailey and Gatrell (1995). Within the social sciences, fundamental developments in the application of these techniques have been provided by Doriean (1980*a*, 1980*b*) and Loftin and Ward (1983).

In outline, the primary goal for analyses of area data is to relate one set of observations on *n* areal units, y_i, $i = 1, \ldots, n$, to another set of k measures taken on the same units, X_{ij}, with $j = 1, \ldots, k$. The standard linear regression formulation of these relationships, $y_i = \Sigma\beta_j X_{ij} + \varepsilon_i$, for $i = 1, \ldots, n$ and $j = 1, \ldots, k$, expressed in matrix notation $\mathbf{y} = \mathbf{X}\beta + \varepsilon$, shows that it is assumed that all effects are "intrinsic" to the units examined. It is assumed that the effect of each independent measure within any unit, for example, X_{1j}, is specific to the dependent measure within that unit, y_1, and has no relationship to any unit outside of y_1, (i.e., $y_{i \neq 1}$). It is assumed that there are no spatial relationships between units; all ε_i are assumed independent and identically distributed.

If one assumes that there are spatial relationships between different observations **X** taken on some units and the dependent measure **y** taken on other units, then the standard linear regression formulation requires restatement. In this case, it is necessary to construct a matrix representing the spatial relationships between measures taken on different units, **L**, and relate the "spatial lagged" effects of exogenous measures, **LX**, to **y**:

$$\mathbf{y} = \mathbf{X}\beta + \mathbf{LX}\lambda + \varepsilon \qquad (1)$$

where **L** is an $n \times n$ matrix of hypothesized connections between spatial units; for example, a matrix of zeros and ones in which zero represents no connection between units and one represents a connection between units.[6] λ is the vector of coefficients relating the effects of distal observations in **X** to local observations in **y**. This modeling step resolves the first analytic issue; how to model the extrinsic distal effects of exogenous measures upon observations within geographic units. Generally referred to in the literature as "spatial effects" or "spatial lags," the study of these relationships is central to area analyses.

The role of matrix **L** in modeling spatial data needs some further explanation at this point. As presented here, **L** represents hypothetical spatial relationships between observations in **X** and observations in **y**. For example, **L** could be used to relate weather conditions in one area of a country (**X**) to growth of avian populations in another (**y**). This analysis would thereby take into account the effects of weather patterns in mating territories on observed populations of birds in wintering territories. As such, the modeling of spatial effects through **L** provides a means of testing hypothetical relationships. It does not, however, take into account the general failure of unit independence in geographic studies, the second point made above. In order to account for failures of unit independence, the model expressed in equation 1 must be modified to take into account potential correlated error between adjacent geographic units.[7] This is accomplished through the construction of a connection matrix **C**, another n × n matrix relating errors in observation in each unit to errors in observation among its connected (e.g., adjacent) units. Reweighted to have unit row sums in matrix **W**, equation (1) may be expressed:

$$\mathbf{y} = \mathbf{X}\beta + \mathbf{LX}\lambda + (\mathbf{I} - \rho\mathbf{W})\varepsilon \qquad (2)$$

where **I** is an n × n identity matrix and ρ is the correlation in errors observed between spatially connected units (the spatial autocorrelation coefficient). As a matter of convenience, the reweighting of **C** to **W** constrains the value of the spatial autocorrelation coefficient to $-1 \leq \rho \leq +1$. As a matter essential to the analysis of area data, when ρ is greater than 0, Type I errors in analysis occur; the null hypothesis is too often rejected. When ρ is less than 0, Type II errors in analysis occur; the null hypothesis is too often accepted. Simplifying equation 2 somewhat, these impacts of spatially autocorrelated measurement error can be more directly observed:

$$\mathbf{y} = \mathbf{X}\beta + \mathbf{LX}\lambda + (\varepsilon - \rho\mathbf{W}\varepsilon) \qquad (2a)$$

When $\rho > 0$, standard errors of estimate are reduced. When $\rho < 0$, standard errors of estimate are amplified.

Equation 2 may be adapted to data including observations that vary over both space and time by including appropriate terms for temporal in addition to spatial autocorrelation:

$$\mathbf{y} = \mathbf{X}\beta + \mathbf{LX}\lambda + (\mathbf{I} - \rho_s\mathbf{W} - \rho_t\mathbf{T})\varepsilon \qquad (3)$$

where ρ_s and ρ_t distinguish between spatial and temporal autocorrelated error. The temporal structure of autocorrelated errors is captured by another sort of connection matrix, matrix **T**, which identifies connections within units over time. Since, typically, units are assumed to connect only to themselves across time, but to others across space, a Cochrane-Orcutt adjustment serves as a suitable correction for temporal autocorrelated error (Greene 1993): A first-stage spatial autoregressive model is estimated (equation 2), temporal autoregressive effects among residuals from this model are used to calculate a value for ρ_t, and this value is used to transform **y** and **X** to $\mathbf{y}^*$and $\mathbf{X}^*$.[8] The analysis model is then reestimated using these transformed data and equation 2 to provide model estimates corrected for temporal autocorrelated error.[9]

The use of these models for the geostatistical analysis of area data is computationally quite demanding. Since the creation of these analytic techniques in the late 1970's, the development of software implementing statistical models that account for spatial and temporal autocorrelation has awaited growth in both computerized geographic information systems (GIS) and numerical modeling software. GIS technology has seen exponential growth over the past 20 years, leading to the current wide availability of mapping technology (MapInfo 1994). Among other elements of this technology are processes capable of defining spatial relationships among geographic units using original map elements (e.g., a map of all counties in the United States) and processes allowing the representation of area data in a multilayered format (Tomlin 1990; Fotheringham and Rogerson 1994). This new class of software allows the user to easily construct connection matrices describing spatial relationships among area units (**L** and **C** above) and provides mapping procedures that allow one to visually compare the geographic distributions of different map elements (e.g., the distribution of alcohol outlets and alcohol-related crashes [Gruenewald et al. 1993*a*]). Similar growth has occurred in numerical analysis software, so much so that models of much greater complexity than those anticipated by the authors of the techniques are now feasible. Although many analysis procedures are still implemented by and for individual research institutions (e.g., the Spatial Statistical System package [S^3] [Ponicki and Gruenewald 1997]), powerful commercial packages for the analysis of spatial data are becoming available (e.g., SpaceStat [Anselin 1990]).

METHODS

Data Collection

Data for the study were collected as part of an efficacy trial of the effects of a set of preventive interventions upon alcohol-related traffic and nontraffic injuries in the United States (Holder et al. 1997). The efficacy trial studied the degree to which the interventions were effective in reducing alcohol-related harm over the course of a 4-year study in six communities: three experimental communities in which the preventive programs were implemented and three matched comparison communities in which no preventive programs were implemented. A great deal of data was collected in all six communities to provide a broad and statistically efficient evaluation of intervention effects. Focusing upon the data sets specific to the current study, within each of the six communities archival data were collected on locations of retail alcohol outlets and on road network lengths and cross-street densities, on- and off-premise alcohol beverage price data were collected using annual telephone surveys of randomly selected alcohol outlets, and individual-level data were collected using a random-digit dial telephone survey of adults 18 years of age and older within each community. The data collection period spanned April 1992 through March 1996.

Numbers and locations of active retail alcohol outlets were obtained in April at the beginning of each of the 4 years of the study. Premise addresses of all active retail alcohol outlets were obtained from California Alcohol Beverage Control (four sites) and the South Carolina Department of Revenue, Alcoholic Beverage Information (two sites). Active licenses represent premises which, to the knowledge of the departments, are open and legally licensed to do business in the State. Retail outlet types were categorized as off-premise (mainly liquor, grocery, and convenience stores) and on-premise (bars and restaurants). Although it was possible to distinguish between bars and restaurants using the California licensing data, it was not possible to distinguish consistently between all types of bars and restaurants using the South Carolina licensing data. The premise address of each outlet was used to locate retail establishments within each community using TIGER (Topologically Integrated Geographic Encoding and Referencing) files available from the U.S. Census and coded into a MapInfo (1994) GIS for each of the six sites. Of the 1,188, 1,175, 1,255, and 1,276 on-premise outlets identified in each year, 88.1 percent were geocoded to their exact address. Of the 835, 801, 823, and 813 off-premise outlets identified in each year, 91.3 percent were geocoded to their exact address. Those licenses not geocoded included premises with multiple licenses representing outlets in the same location (24 percent and 28 percent of the remainder), outlets with addresses that placed them outside of the geographic range of the study (13 percent and 4 percent), and outlets that had uninterpretable addresses (63 percent and 68 percent). Uninterpretable addresses included those with invalid numbers (e.g., a 1000 address on a street that spanned numbers from 1 to 100) or with street names that did not exist within either the target or any nearby geographic area. Reflecting the importance of the roadway system for access to these outlets, outlet densities within geographic areas were expressed as a function of roadway length (outlets per kilometer of roadway, local and highway). Since the aggregated distributions of outlet densities were highly skewed, log transforms of on- and off-premise densities were used in the current analyses.[10]

Road network lengths and cross-street densities were computed from electronic versions of the TIGER files used to geocode outlet locations. It was assumed that this index would reflect both complex urban roadway systems in areas with considerable retail activity and densely populated residential areas (both to be distinguished from rural areas with few roads and few intersections). It was further assumed that these characteristics of the roadway system would not change substantively over the 4 years of the study. Within the geographic units defined for the study, road network densities were calculated as the ratio of the number of cross-street intersections to kilometers of roadway (also directly estimated from the TIGER files).

Nominal alcohol beverage prices within all six communities were assessed through telephone surveys administered in April 1992, October 1992, October 1993, October 1994, and October 1995. The 5-minute price survey assessed retail prices of a core list of alcoholic beverages by volume by type (beer, wine, and spirits) at on- and off-premise establishments.[11] Within each community a stratified random sample of 15 on-premise and 15 off-premise active retail outlets and their addresses was obtained from the geocoded lists of outlets used to determine outlet densities by community areas (above).

The samples of outlets were stratified by ZIP Code to ensure adequate distribution of sample across the geographic area of each community. Telephone numbers for the sampled outlets were then obtained from local telephone directories. The surveys were administered during periods of low sales volume (on weekdays in the afternoon and early evening between 2:00 and 6:00 p.m. for on-premise establishments; on weekdays in the early morning and afternoon between 10:00 a.m. and 2:00 p.m. for off-premise establishments).

Response rates to the price survey averaged 86.4 percent across both outlet types. Within on-premise establishments, prices were requested for 12-oz beers by bottle (or can), 5-oz glasses or 750 mL bottles of wine, and single 1-oz shots or 750 mL bottles of spirits.[12] Within off-premise establishments, prices were requested for six-packs of beer and 750-mL bottles of wine and spirits. In order to maintain price comparability by volume by beverage type, prices were standardized to units of six-packs of beer and 750-mL bottles of wine and spirits across premise types. Nominal prices were deflated to real 1990 dollars using western and southern regional consumer price indices. The average of prices charged for brands sold by beverage type was used as the index of prices within each retail establishment. Finally, ZIP Code–level price estimates were overlaid on the geographic units used in the current analysis to provide best estimates of prices within the units under study. Units nested within ZIP Codes were assigned that ZIP Code's prices. Units crossing ZIP Code boundaries were assigned the average of those ZIP Code prices.[13] Cross-sectional analyses of the price indices indicated strong correlations between prices by beverage type within establishments (on- vs. off-premise), suggesting that the measures were essentially single factored. Principal components analyses revealed that the first component of on-premise prices explained 85.6 percent of the variance in the ZIP Code–based measures; the first component of the off-premise prices explained 77.8 percent of the variance in the measures. For this reason, on- and off-premise prices were summarized by their first principal components scores, forming two separate price indices for each geographic unit.

To obtain individual-level survey data, households were called on a random-digit dial basis throughout the year (thus avoiding biases due to seasonality [Lemmens and Knibbe 1993]). The adult (18 years of age or older) membership of each household was enumerated, and one potential respondent was selected at random for participation. This candidate was then contacted for interviewing. Households were defined as single dwellings (houses or apartments) in which one or more adults resided as their primary (not vacation) home. All multiple-member institutional settings were excluded from the sample. Among those respondents contacted, the completion rate was 80.6 percent (numbers of completions divided by number of known eligible respondents). Including in the denominator of this estimate the expected number of unknown eligible respondents who could not be contacted, the response rate for the survey was 62.3 percent. Over the 4 years of the study, 34,582 completed interviews were obtained. During this time 0.3 percent (104) interviews were repeated with previously interviewed respondents.

Each survey respondent was asked to report the nearest major cross-streets in his or her neighborhood. Cross-street locations were used to identify the approximate geographic location of each respondent and to serve as the basis for defining the geographic areas used in the current study. Of the 34,478 respondents available for geocoding across the communities, 22,100 (64.1 percent) were successfully located using this procedure. Examinations of the characteristics of those respondents who could and could not be interviewed suggested that abstainers, older individuals, and those with greater education were less likely to have provided adequate cross-street information for geocoding. None of these relationships, however, was significant when tests were corrected using the Bonferroni inequality (see Gruenewald et al. 1996*b*).[14] Noting that the cross-product of the response and geocoding rates reflects the extent to which geocoded respondents represent residents within community areas, the survey-specific geocoding rate was $0.623 \times 0.641 \times 100 = 39.9$ percent. That is, about 40 percent of all eligible respondents were interviewed and located within community areas. For this reason, the nongeocoded respondents were overlaid onto the geographic areas of the study using their ZIP Code identifiers (provided by 97.3 percent of these respondents). These respondents were randomly allocated to study units based on the proportional overlap of ZIP Code and study areas weighted by road network length (assumed to reflect population densities of unit areas). This alternative geocoded data set was used in supplementary analyses of the data presented here. Since the results of these supplementary analyses were very similar to the original analyses using the exact geocoded data, they will not be reported here.[15]

Although the respondents were asked a broad array of questions covering a number of issues relevant to the evaluation of the community preventive interventions, this study focused upon three areas of information. Sociodemographic background variables included age, education, gender, marital status, household composition, ethnic group membership, income, and employment. Drinking variables included abstention (whether or not a full drink of alcohol was consumed at any time in the previous 12 months), standardized 28-day frequencies of drinking, average quantities consumed, and the variance in quantities consumed over time (derived from continued drinking questions using a mathematical model described in Gruenewald et al. 1996*c*). Variables representing individual frequencies of using different venues for drinking were also obtained (frequencies of drinking at home and drinking at a bar or restaurant standardized to a 28-day period). All variables were coded and aggregated within geographic units to provide population-based measures of the most relevant socioeconomic correlates of drinking.[16]

Density Measures

The measure of population density used in the current study was obtained from the household enumerations provided by survey respondents. Within geographic areas, this was the only source of information about changes in population density that was, first, sufficiently geographically specific and, second, responsive to changes in population density over the time of the study. Although cross-sectional measures of population density were available from 1990 census estimates, these measures did not reflect the geographic areas used in the current study. The study areas were, typically, both much smaller (in densely populated areas) and much larger (in sparsely populated areas) than 1990 census blocks, and the boundaries of census blocks and study areas did not coincide with one another. Further, changes in population densities by census blocks were unavailable over the time of the study (annual census estimates of population densities are typically available only down to the county and, more rarely, ZIP Code levels). For these reasons, it was assumed that this measure would be far more responsive to changes in local population distributions than available census estimates.

As a final comment on methods, the choice of roadway length as the denominator for the outlet density, cross-street density, and population density measures was motivated by the need to represent the physical relationships of drinkers to drinking places in as natural a manner as possible. Assuming that access to alcohol is largely along the roadway system, the physical availability of alcohol is best measured along the roadway network. As noted in Gruenewald and colleagues (1996*b*), neither population-based measures nor areal-based measures of outlet densities adequately represent the geographic character of availability. Simply, one's access to alcohol does not vary as a function of the number of one's neighbors, nor as a function of the land area of one's environs. Similar arguments obtain for measures of population and cross-street densities in urban and suburban environments.

Analysis Procedures

The data for the study were aggregated into 144 geographic units across the six communities within each of the 4 years of study. Outline maps of the geographic units in the six communities are presented in figure 1 (see p. 198).

With n = 144 units and t = 4 years, the total number of time series cross-sectional units available for study was 4 × 144 = 576. Thus, both cross-sectional and time series cross-sectional studies were feasible using this extensive database. Since it was suspected that extremely stable cross-sectional relationships might characterize much of the data, with aggregate measures of income, physical availability, and beverage prices related to socioeconomic status within areas of the communities, two strategies were taken to the analysis of these data. First, cross-sectional studies of the first year of 1992–93 data were replicated using the fourth year of 1995–96 data, providing cross-validated estimates of cross-sectional effects. Second, time series cross-sectional studies of the entire data set were used to assess annually based time-ordered effects. Because of wide variations in observed sample sizes within cells from the general population survey ($n = 2$ to $n = 198$, mean = 58, median = 51), the effects of this source of heteroscedasticity on the calculation of standard errors of estimate were controlled using weighted least squares (Greene 1993). Because of the sensitivity of geostatistical area analyses to outlying and highly leveraged observations, Cook's distances and studentized t statistics were examined for all measures (see Gruenewald et al. 1996*b*). Because of the possible inefficiencies in analysis arising from temporal autocorrelated error in the time series cross-sectional analyses, a Cochrane-Orcutt adjustment was used where appropriate (Greene 1993). Of course, estimates of and corrections for spatial autocorrelated error were implemented in all analyses.

RESULTS

Table 1 (see p. 200) provides descriptive statistics for all variables used in the study. The primary outcome measures are described at the top of the table (i.e., measures of physical access, alcohol use, the use of drinking places, and beverage prices). Essential covariates are described at the bottom of the table (i.e., local suburban/urban environment, economic access, ethnic group composition, and other demographics). The minimum and maximum value, mean, and standard error of each measure is presented. Two observations of note are obtainable from this table. First, there was great variation in all measures across community areas. For example, some areas had no on-premise outlets, and some had two or more on-premise outlets per kilometer of roadway; average prices of six-packs of beer varied from \$3.83 to \$6.08 on-premise; some areas had no Hispanics, and others had up to 83 percent Hispanics; some areas were dominated by single populations (up to 45.4 percent), and others by married populations (up to 96.0 percent). Second, these variations were statistically quite discriminable between units. Standard errors of estimate were quite small relative to either the range of observed differences between units or the mean of observations.

Table 2 (see p. 201) provides an overview of the raw spatial autocorrelations observed among the primary outcome measures used in the analyses. The Moran coefficient was used to estimate the degree to which observed values of each dependent measure were correlated with values of the dependent measure in adjacent geographic units (in this case all units sharing a border). The Moran coefficient approximately varies between −1.00 and +1.00, like the Pearson product moment coefficient, and the asymptotic significance of the coefficient can be assessed through a *z*-transformation by comparison with a normal distribution (see Griffith 1987). On the whole the Moran coefficients were positive, suggesting that high (or low) values of these measures in each area were associated with high (or low) values in surrounding areas. In the case of the measures of abstention, frequency of alcohol use among consumers, frequency of drinking at bars/restaurants, and on-premise prices, the observed spatial autocorrelations were significant. In three of these four they were replicated in the 1995–96 data (all but frequency of drinking at bars/restaurants). These preliminary analyses suggest that spatial autocorrelation may be a problem in further analyses of these data. To the extent that spatial autocorrelations are positive and significant, the likelihood of Type I errors (the null hypothesis is too often rejected) in analysis is great.

The final column of table 2 indicates the percentage of cases observed as outliers in the analysis of each outcome measure. Statistically observed significant outlying or highly leveraged cases are a function of both the distribution of observations on the dependent measure and the distribution of observations among the exogenous measures in any given analysis (i.e., the projection matrix [Cook and Weisberg 1982]). Thus, the definition of an outlying or highly leveraged case is context dependent, depending as it does on the mix of measures included in the analysis. Using procedures for the evaluation of outlying and highly leveraged cases adapted to models with spatial autocorrelated error (Gruenewald et al. 1996*b*), and fixing upon that mix of exogenous measures central to the analysis of each outcome measure, outlying and highly leveraged cases were evaluated from the residuals of these analyses using protected studentized *t* statistics and Cook's distances.[17] In each outlying case, the observations on the corresponding dependent measure were smoothed through simple averaging with spatially connected cases. As table 2 shows, there were no highly leveraged cases and relatively few outlying cases observed and so corrected.

Alcohol Beverage Prices

The cross-sectional relationships observed between alcohol beverage prices, measures of consumer demand for alcohol, and outlet densities were evaluated by regressing each of the price indices (on- and off-) over measures specifically related to the demand for alcohol (i.e., population density, income, and drinking patterns) and the availability of alcohol (on- and off-premise). The results of these analyses appear in table 3 (see p. 202). Given the geographic basis of the current study, in addition to the acknowledged expected effects of income, greater demand for alcohol was represented by greater population densities (i.e., greater numbers of drinkers representing more demand) and greater use (i.e., lower rates of abstention, and greater drinking frequency and drinks per occasion representing more aggregate demand). The measure of drinking variance is, by definition, unrelated to total demand and was not included in the analyses.[18]

The assertion that prices may be related to the demand for alcohol from geographic areas in or near the locations of outlets was tested by examining effects within geographic units and across immediately adjacent geographic units. Table 3 presents the results of a model of beverage prices including both the intrinsic effects of each measure within each neighborhood area ("Lag 0" effects) and the extrinsic effects of each measure one neighborhood unit away ("Lag 1" effects). For example, the intrinsic effect of greater population densities upon on-premise prices was $b = 0.2047$; the extrinsic effect of greater population densities one lag away was $b = 1.8793$. The first coefficient represents the direct effects of greater population densities on on-premise prices within neighborhood areas. The second coefficient represents the direct effects of greater population densities in surrounding areas on on-premise prices within neighborhood areas.

As the table shows, quite strong spatial autocorrelations, ρ, appeared in both analyses. At least to some extent, the observed positive spatial autocorrelations arose from the smoothing operations used to obtain the neighborhood area price estimates from ZIP Code price data. The extent to which these positive autocorrelations are related to natural pricing patterns within communities remains unknown. It is important to note, however, that without the statistical controls for spatial autocorrelated errors used in the current analyses, substantial Type I errors would have occurred in the estimation of these models. That is, a number of effects would have appeared significant even though they were not. As it is, there were few observed significant effects and no successful replication of effects using the 1995–96 data. As shown in table 3, the analyses of the 1992–93 data suggest that on-premise densities were positively related to on-premise prices and off-premise densities were negatively related to on-premise prices, with some evidence that greater demand in nearby areas was negatively related to prices (drinks per occasion at lag 1). Greater population densities were positively related to greater off-premise prices and greater on-premise outlet densities were related to lower off-premise prices. Again, these effects failed to replicate in the 1995–96 data.

It is instructive to note the importance of accounting for spatial autocorrelated error in analyses of these data. Table 4 (see p. 203) presents the results of an ordinary least squares (OLS) analysis of the on-premise price data analyzed in table 3. Reported at the bottom of the table, in place of ρ, is the Moran coefficient calculated from the residuals of the OLS model (MC_r). As expected, a greater number of OLS coefficients appeared significant in the 1992–93 data. Greater off-premise densities appeared related to reduced on-premise prices, while greater demand (abstention and frequency) was related to greater on-premise prices. Also as expected, the Moran coefficient on the residuals indicated that there was a significant problem with spatial autocorrelated errors.

Alcohol Availability

The cross-sectional relationships to be observed between locations of alcohol beverage outlets, measures of consumer demand for alcohol, a surrogate for areas of communities with greater traffic, and income were evaluated by regressing each of the outlet density indices (on- and off-) over measures specifically related to the demand for alcohol (i.e., population density, income, and drinking patterns), a surrogate for high-density retail areas (i.e., cross-street density), and measures of income. The results of these analyses appear in table 5 (see p. 204).

The top part of table 5 shows the results of regressing on-premise outlet densities over the environmental measures, measures of economic access, and measures of alcohol use. Significant unit intrinsic effects were found for the measures of population density and the percentage of respondents with incomes greater than or equal to $60,000. Significant first-order spatial lagged effects were found for percentage of respondents with incomes less than $20,000, for percentage of abstainers, and for average frequency of drinking and average drinks per occasion among drinkers. Only the effects for population density and percentage of respondents with income greater than or equal to $60,000 replicated in the 1995–96 data. These effects show that greater densities of on-premise outlets were to be found in areas with greater population density and fewer high-income respondents.

The bottom part of table 5 shows the results of regressing off-premise outlet densities over the environmental measures, measures of economic access, and measures of alcohol use. Significant unit intrinsic effects were found for the measures of population density and cross-street density. Significant first-order spatial lagged effects were found for the measures of population density, percentage of respondents with incomes less than $20,000, and frequency of use among drinkers. The intrinsic effects for population density and cross-street density and the extrinsic effects for areas with more lower income respondents replicated in the 1995–96 data. These effects show that greater densities of off-premise outlets were to be found in areas with greater population density and greater daily traffic (represented by cross-street densities). Greater densities of off-premise outlets were also to be found near areas with greater percentages of low-income residents.

Drinking Patterns

Central to the consideration of the impact of differences in economic and physical access to alcohol upon alcohol use is the issue of the spatial geography of availability. As argued in the introduction, within individual communities alcohol may be more or less expensive and more or less physically available within neighborhoods and their surrounding areas. Thus, the questions of whether and to what extent availability affects use must include considerations of the spatial geography of drinkers and drinking places. That is, both the intrinsic and extrinsic effects of availability upon use are of interest.

Table 6 (see p. 205) presents the results of a geostatistical assessment of the relationships between the measures of alcohol access (on- and off-premise densities) and the six measures of drinking patterns. Likelihood ratio chi-square tests were used to test whether unit intrinsic effects were statistically significant (lag 0), whether first-order lagged effects were significant (between nearest neighbor units, lag 1), and whether second-order lagged effects were significant (between second nearest neighbors, those twice removed from each target unit, lag 2). The reported chi-square tests originated in analyses of the 1992–93 data and were validated in analyses of the 1995–96 data. As shown in the table, only the first-order lagged effects of outlet densities upon rates of abstention from alcohol use and frequency of use among consumers were significant and replicated in the 1995–96 data. Cross-validated effects were not observed for the measures of drinks per occasion and drinking variance, nor for the measures of use of different drinking places. No significant effects were found in a similar analysis of the relationships between alcohol beverage prices and drinking patterns.

Tables 7 and 8 (see pp. 206 and 208) present comprehensive spatial analyses of the measures of rates of abstention and drinking frequency, sequentially stepping into each analysis the measures of physical access, its first-order lag, economic access, and sociodemographic variables. These analyses reveal the extent to which the observed marginal relationships between physical availability and use may be explained by alternative explanatory measures. In each table, each of the sets of measures is stepped into the analysis, and the observed spatial autocorrelation, ρ, and improvement in model fit (likelihood ratio chi-square) are reported, along with *b* values and corresponding *t* tests from the weighted generalized least squares solution. On the right side of each table the "simultaneous tests" are presented for each variable group. These tests statistically assess the degree to which each group of measures is associated with rates of abstention and drinking frequency independent of all other measures in model V.

Table 7 shows, first, that there were very large differences between communities in rates of abstention from alcohol (model I, $\Delta G^2 = 29.361$, $\Delta df = 5$; replicated in the 1995–96 data). Model II shows that the unit intrinsic effects of physical access were not significantly related to abstention ($\Delta G^2 = 0.224$, $\Delta df = 2$), but model III shows that the first-order lagged effects of physical access were significantly related to abstention ($\Delta G^2 = 7.647$, $\Delta df = 2$; replicated in the 1995–96 data). Adding the measures of economic access, model IV shows that these variables explained a yet again significant proportion of deviance in the dependent measure ($\Delta G^2 = 30.435$, $\Delta df = 4$; replicated in the 1995–96 data). Adding the sociodemographics, model

V shows that these measures also explained a significant proportion of deviance in rates of abstention (ΔG^2 = 22.703, Δdf = 10; replicated in the 1995–96 data). From the point of view of providing statistically unbiased estimates of the significance of effects in these models, it is important to note that there were strong positive spatial autocorrelated errors observed in models I through III and weak positive spatial autocorrelated errors observed in models IV and V. These would encourage the appearance of Type I errors in analysis if left uncorrected.

A very similar picture emerges with regard to drinking frequency (table 8). Again there were large differences between communities (model I), no unit intrinsic effects of availability (model II), and significant replicated effects related to first-order lags of physical access (model III), economic access (model IV), and sociodemographic measures (model V).

It is of considerable significance to note that the effects of physical availability on rates of abstention and frequency of use were not robust to alternative model specifications. The apparently significant effects of on- and off-premise densities on rates of abstention (table 7, model III) are reduced by the inclusion of economic measures (model IV; not replicable in the 1995–96 data) and virtually eliminated with the inclusion of sociodemographic measures (model V). Looking at the results for the model V simultaneous case, only the sociodemographic variables presented a significant (and replicated) independent contribution to explaining rates of abstention from alcohol. Once again, the models of drinking frequency in table 8 are quite similar. The suggestive significant simultaneous effects of physical availability on abstinence (table 7, model V, p = 0.050) and frequency of use (table 8, model V, p = 0.030) were not replicated in the 1995–96 data.

Simultaneous Equations

A review of the analyses presented in tables 5, 6, 7, and 8 suggests a few summary statements that may be made about physical availability and alcohol use. First, locations of alcohol outlets appeared largely determined by general features of the urban/suburban environments of these communities; outlets were most dense in or near those areas of communities having greater population densities and/or greater cross-street densities. Second, outlets were placed in or near areas of communities where incomes were relatively low and, only suggestively, where alcohol use was greatest. Conversely, although the geographic distributions of on-and off-premise outlets appeared to be related to patterns of alcohol use, these relationships were not robust to alternative model specifications; the observed effects of availability on use could not be replicated in models including economic and sociodemographic variables. These analytic observations, although superficially straightforward, may be statistically misleading; the inclusion of the measures of physical availability and alcohol use as complementary dependent and independent measures in both sets of models may have created simultaneous equation bias. The coefficients and standard errors of estimate from the models may be biased by correlated errors in equations (Greene 1993).

Figure 2 (see p. 199) presents a conceptual outline of the situation. As a general assertion central to this chapter, it is assumed that physical access to alcohol is related to alcohol use in two ways. Greater densities of outlets may appear in or about neighborhood areas where demand for alcohol is greatest *and* greater alcohol use may appear in or about neighborhood areas where physical access to alcohol is greatest. This simultaneous causal relationship is graphically indicated by the reciprocal pair of arrows drawn between the circles labeled "Physical Access" and "Alcohol Use." The indicators of these two measures are noted by the arrows descending from these circles; physical access is indexed by on- and off-premise densities, alcohol use is indexed by rates of abstention and frequency of use. A pair of purely environmental measures appear to be related exclusively to the distribution of alcohol outlets in the communities under study: population density and cross-street density. Another pair of purely idiographic sociodemographic measures appear to be related exclusively to the distribution of alcohol use: average age and educational levels. The measures of income are arguably related to both the geographic distributions of outlets (where outlet densities respond to greater demand) and alcohol use (where use is a function of disposable income).

Given these assertions about the underlying processes that form the supply of and demand for alcohol, it is possible to reestimate smaller versions of the models presented in tables 5, 7, and 8 using simultaneous equation modeling techniques. In this case, focus will be upon those measures which appeared statistically most related to the outcomes of interest in the previous analyses and which, for theoretical and empirical reasons, can be justifiably used to identify and estimate a simultaneous equation model that best reflects the cross-sectional data obtained in the current study. For this purpose it was assumed that population and cross-street densities were, as empirically observed, related to outlet densities, but excluded from the equations for aggregate measures of alcohol use. It was assumed that these environmental measures would have no direct effects on drinking. It was also assumed that the age and education of local populations were, again as empirically observed, related to measures of alcohol use (i.e., rates of abstention and frequency), but excluded from the equations for measures of outlet densities. In essence, it was assumed that alcohol retailers locate outlets on the basis of local knowledge of the size of the potential consumer pool (population density), the extent of local traffic (cross-street density), the ability of consumers to purchase alcohol (i.e., income), and local demand (i.e., abstention and frequency), but not on the basis of the particular sociodemographics of local populations (e.g., age, education, ethnic group composition). Complementarily, it was assumed that alcohol use would be responsive to background normative determinants of use (i.e., the sociodemographic measures of age and education), the ability of consumers to afford alcohol (i.e., income), and physical availability, but not to the numbers of individuals or densities of urban/suburban areas within users' environments.

Table 9 (see p. 210) presents the results of the two-stage least squares (2SLS) analyses of the relationships of availability to use. The measures of abstention and frequency of use were regressed over measures representing differences between communities, economic access, the excluded sociodemographic measures (age and education) presumed related to use but not related to physical availability (exclusion restrictions necessary to identify the model [Greene 1993]), and measures of physical access to alcohol estimated from first-stage regressions.[19] As expected from previous analyses, the sociodemographic measures were significantly related to both abstention and frequency of use (replicated in the 1995–96 data). However, neither the measures of economic access nor the measures of physical access were related to either abstention or frequency of use.

Table 10 (see p. 211) presents the results of the 2SLS analyses of the relationships of use to availability. The measures of on- and off-premise densities were regressed over measures representing differences between communities, environmental conditions pertinent to the locations of outlets (population and cross-street density), economic access, and measures of alcohol use (abstention and frequency) estimated from first-stage regressions. As expected from previous analyses, the environmental and economic measures were significantly related to both on- and off-premise densities (replicated in the 1995–96 data). In addition, the measures of alcohol use were also significantly related to locations of outlets. In particular, outlet densities appeared greatest in neighborhoods contiguous to residential areas with lesser rates of abstention and greater frequency of use.

Spatial Panels

The results of the simultaneous equation analyses suggest that a model in which on-premise and off-premise outlet densities reflect patterns of environmental conditions, economic access, and alcohol use within communities is consistent with the replicated cross-sectional data obtained in the current study. The results also suggest that a model in which availability affects use is inconsistent with these data. All said, the results indicate that the retail market for alcohol is, over the long run, sensitive to geographic patterns of alcohol use. How sensitive the market is to usage patterns in the short term can be determined through an examination of all the data from the study in a panel model of alcohol availability and use. The question to be asked is whether, over the 4 years of study, shifts in environmental conditions, economic access, and patterns of alcohol use were related to shifts in availability.

Table 11 (see p. 212) presents the results of a time series cross-sectional analysis of the geographic data over the 4 years of the study. These analyses represent what are referred to as "spatial panels"—classical panel models with spatial components. As per the previous analyses, the spatial components include lagged effects of independent on dependent measures and corrections for spatial autocorrelated errors between units. In addition, spatial panel models include an examination of time series effects within units over time independent of cross-sectional differences between units. This is accomplished through application of a variant of least squares dummy variable (LSDV) regression techniques to these geographic data. Classical analyses of panel data rely upon LSDV regressions to provide asymptotically unbiased estimates of the effects of independent measures upon dependent measures in panel designs (Hsiao 1986). Simply, these models regress out all cross-sectional effects related to the observed units using dummy variables in the regression equation. The residual variance then, by definition, represents changes in the dependent variable over time. Additional independent measures included in the regression model will, presumably, account for some of this residual variance, indicating temporal effects of independent measures upon dependent measures in the model.

Although the technical complications of analyzing panel data are too numerous to go into here, it is important to note two features of these designs that may significantly interfere with direct interpretation of LSDV results. First, temporal autocorrelated error will account for some additional unknown variance within units over time. That is, to some extent errors in estimation may be correlated from one wave of the panel to the next. Second, as noted for the previous models, spatial autocorrelated error may account for some additional unknown variance between units over time. Failures of cross-unit independence must still be taken into account. To the extent that these problems are substantive features of the analysis, they will reduce efficiencies of the analytic technique. Thus, it is of considerable importance to diagnose and control for both spatial and temporal autocorrelated error in analyses of panel data.

As shown in table 11, these additional sources of bias were evaluated in the examination of the relationships between alcohol use and availability. The analyses were once again restricted to that core set of measures which appeared related to access to alcohol in previous tables. The measures of on- and off-premise outlet densities were regressed over 3 dummy variables representing time trend effects (effects coded), 144 dummy variables representing the constant term and cross-sectional unit effects (effects coded), one environmental measure (population density), and the measures of economic access and alcohol use. Since any purely cross-sectional measure would be collinear with the dummy variables representing unit effects, the measure of cross-street densities was not included as a second environmental variable. As shown in the table, each of the analyses included a control for spatial autocorrelation, ρ_s, and a test for temporal autocorrelation, ρ_t[20]. Since the tests for temporal autocorrelation were not significant, Cochrane-Orcutt adjustments were unnecessary.

Controlling for a general decline in outlet densities observed over the years of the study, the results of these analyses show that shifts in population densities were reflected in altered densities of on- and off-premise outlets. Changes over time in both the sets of measures of economic access and alcohol use had relatively little impact upon the distribution of on- and off-premise outlets within these communities. A significant effect did appear, however, with respect to the first-order spatial lagged effect of income; growth in higher income populations was related to declines in off-premise outlet densities in nearby areas. This reflects the same pattern of (not significant) effects of high income on access to alcohol observed in the cross-sectional analyses (table 10).

DISCUSSION

Interpretation and analysis of data within "small" geographic settings require considerable sensitivity to two central issues, the geographic scale of the process being measured and the resolution of the geographic units being studied. The relative size of a specific ecological process to the observed geographic units will affect the patterns of outcomes obtained in geostatistical studies. In the context of the current analyses, a similar comment may be made with respect to time. The relative temporal scale of a specific ecological process to the resolution of the temporal units observed will affect the temporal patterns obtained. The results of the research presented here must be viewed with these considerations in mind. Thus, as a central feature of the current study, the results of the replicated cross-sectional analyses of alcohol beverage prices, availability, and drinking patterns reflect the long-term stable patterns of relationships between the independent and dependent measures used in these analyses. Presumably, results of analyses of data collected in 1992–93 that were replicated using data collected 3 years later, in 1995–96, reflect aspects of community ecologies for alcohol that are relatively stable in time. As a secondary feature of the current study, the results of spatial panel analyses were used to index the responsiveness of the outcomes to change in time.

The cross-sectional analyses of the relationships between alcohol beverage prices, alcohol use, and economic and physical access to alcohol supported a few of the original hypotheses of the study. After a brief discussion of these results, the more general methodological contributions of the current study will be discussed.

Prices

To review, the three hypotheses regarding prices were as follows: (1) Prices for alcohol should be greater in areas of communities with the greatest demand for alcohol (i.e., high-income areas with greatest densities of consumers); (2) prices for alcohol should be lower in areas where there are greater densities of outlets; and (3) prices for alcohol should be greater in areas where there are greater densities of outlets.

There was no support provided for any of these hypotheses. As shown in table 3, prices for alcohol were clearly not related to consumer demand or outlet densities. Retailers' prices for alcohol did not appear to be greater in areas of communities with greater demand, nor were they greater (or lesser) in areas in which greatest competition among outlets (or greater through traffic of consumers) occurred. It would appear that, at least in these sites, prices at the community level are insensitive to local variations in competition and demand. One explanation for this observation is that price competition may be relatively ineffective in local alcohol markets. In local areas in which breadth of beverage qualities is very great and alternative sources of alcohol common, price competition between retailers may be relatively ineffective in altering consumer behavior. Consequently, alcohol beverage prices at any particular retail outlet may reflect broad community demand (through wholesale prices) and costs of operation, but not local demand (e.g., through variations in neighborhood use of alcohol) nor local competition (e.g., through variations in local outlet densities).

AVAILABILITY

The three hypotheses regarding availability were as follows: (1) Greater densities of outlets should be found in community areas within or adjacent to areas with greater demand for alcohol (i.e., high-income areas with greatest densities of consumers); (2) greater densities of outlets should be found in community areas within or adjacent to areas with greater traffic flow; and (3) greater densities of outlets should be found in low-income neighborhoods where costs of operation can be kept to a minimum.

The cross-sectional analyses of the relationships between outlet densities, the demand for alcohol, and environmental measures of sources and flows of drinkers (population and cross-street density) suggest a quite different picture. As shown in table 5, greater densities of on- and off-premise outlets were found within areas of communities where larger pools of potential consumers were located (on- and off-premise outlets related to population density), where greater local traffic was expected (off-premise outlets related to cross-street density), and within areas with fewer high-income residents (on-premise) and near areas with more low-income residents (off-premise). Thus, it would appear that retailers select locations that maximize access to larger pools of potential consumers and in which the overhead of operations is likely to be lower (away from high-income areas of the community). Specific effects for the measures of demand (abstention, frequency, and drinks per occasion) were not replicable, but suggested that outlet densities might be somewhat greater near areas with fewer abstainers and higher frequency drinkers. Noting that the effect of greater population density is to increase the pool of consumers of alcohol in any geographic area (all else being equal), it would appear that retailers site their businesses in locations likely to tap into this market.

It is of particular significance at this point to note that the simultaneous equation model of the causal relationships of the environmental measures, economic access, and alcohol use to physical availability (table 10) strongly supported these observations. Effects similar to those observed for the environmental and economic access measures in the earlier analyses still obtained. However, the effects of alcohol use on availability became much clearer. In particular, greater densities of on-premise outlets were to be observed in areas of the communities near to residential areas with fewer abstainers and higher frequency drinkers. Greater densities of off-premise outlets were to be observed in areas of the communities near to residential areas with higher frequency drinkers. Pushing this point still further, the spatial panel model used to study the time series effects of these measures on the geographic distribution of availability (table 11) indicated that increases in population density were accompanied by increases in on- and off-premise outlet densities throughout the period of study.

Drinking Patterns

The two hypotheses regarding drinking patterns were as follows: (1) Greater use of alcohol should be observed in community areas where prices are lower, and (2) greater use of alcohol should be observed in community areas where availability is greater.

The cross-sectional analyses of the relationships between economic and physical access to alcohol and alcohol use demonstrated that some marginal relationships did exist between physical availability and drinking (table 6), but that these effects eroded when additional sociodemographic covariates were included in the model (tables 7 and 8). At no point did prices of alcoholic beverages appear related to alcohol use. As the detailed analyses of these relationships revealed, significant bivariate relationships were to be observed between on- and off-premise outlet densities and the measures of rates of abstention from alcohol and frequency of drinking among drinkers. Less abstention and greater frequency of drinking were observed in neighborhoods near to areas with greater densities of on-premise outlets. However, the inclusion of measures of income and other sociodemographic variables in the analysis model rendered these apparently direct significant effects of availability not significant. Quite reasonably, lesser rates of abstention and greater frequencies of use were related to higher incomes, lower age, and greater education, replicating previous studies of alcohol use. The simultaneous equation model of availability and use (table 9) supported these observations.

The current study represents the largest, most detailed community-level study of the relationships of the availability of alcohol to patterns of alcohol use conducted to date. To our knowledge at least, no other study has directly measured the spectrum of beverage prices at a geographic level appropriate to the scale at which individual purchases and use take place, neighborhoods in the local community. At this level, much like previous studies at the State level (Gruenewald et al. 1995), the range of prices within beverage and premise types varied enormously across community areas (i.e., ranges of prices differing by factors from 1.5 to 6.1). Similarly, the observed ranges of physical access to alcohol varied enormously from one place in the community to another (i.e., factors in excess of 416 on-premise and 265 off-premise). Thus, cross-sectional variations in these important ostensive determinants of use were substantive. Noting also that patterns of alcohol use were very precisely measured within units (e.g., with coefficients of variation approximating 0.02), one would expect to see significant effects of price and availability on use *if* such effects were to be obtained in either simple recursive models relating availability to use (tables 7 and 8) or more appropriate simultaneous equation models (table 9). These effects were not obtained, nor were significant effects obtained in the spatial panel model of availability and use presented in table 11. The conclusion of this study then is that *economic and physical availability are not determinants of use at the local community level.* To the extent that substantive effects of physical availability on use were obtained in the study, they are revealed in elasticities calculated from table 9. Based on the analyses presented there, a 10-percent increase in outlet densities was related to a not significant 1.7-percent decrease in abstentions and a not significant 0.7-percent increase in average drinking frequencies.

Spatial Effects and Spatial Autocorrelations

From a methodological perspective, one of the abiding concerns of the current study has been to demonstrate the application of geostatistical methods to the analysis of small area data. Within the small areas defined in the current study, the importance of taking into account both spatial effects (i.e., statistical relationships between variables within and between spatial units) and spatial autocorrelated error (i.e., correlated error between spatially related units) has been amply demonstrated. Of the analyses presented here, spatial effects have been a central issue in all, and significant replicated spatial effects were found in several analyses (e.g., spatial lagged effects in the analyses of off-premise densities and alcohol use). Thus, the geographic relationships among variables measured within and between spatially related geographic units have proven to be of statistical and empirical importance in this study. The content of these observations is largely to suggest that spatial effects matter in small area studies of community ecologies for alcohol.

In addition to spatial effects, the statistical issue of geographic unit independence in geostatistical studies has proven to be of central importance in the study. Raw measures of a number of the primary outcomes were observed to have significant spatial autocorrelations (abstention, frequency of use, on-premise prices), and significant replicated spatial autocorrelated errors appeared in 7 of the 20 spatial analyses. Significant positive spatial autocorrelated errors were obtained in all 7 of these analyses. This indicates that Type I errors would be very likely using OLS analyses uncorrected for this source of bias. To date, with the exception of Gruenewald and colleagues (1996*b*), no geographically based alcohol study in the literature has taken into account this source of bias.

Taking a broader view of the current study, the observed spatial effects and spatial autocorrelations suggest several implications for any study that relies upon geographically organized ecological units as the primary sources of data. Beyond the obvious recommendations that both spatial effects and spatial autocorrelations will be relevant to analyses of such data, it is possible to further suggest that these sources of specification error in geographic models may also be primary means of improving the predictive accuracy of ecologically based imputation techniques. Thus, both the spatial effects observed in these studies and the spatial autocorrelations observed as "nuisances" in these studies can be used to inform predictive models of the geographic patterns of alcohol use.

Acknowledging that little is known about the geographic distribution of alcohol use in the typically "small" areas with which local public health agencies are typically concerned (e.g., neighborhoods, communities, and cities within counties), these patterns may be inferred from the geographic distributions, spatial lags, and spatial autocorrelations to be observed among a number of measures in the current study. For example, in the absence of any other surrogate for alcohol use, measures of physical access to alcohol may be used to geographically index rates of abstention and frequency of alcohol use (table 6), and the measure of abstention appears strongly spatially autocorrelated across units (table 7). Importantly, none of these effects are intrinsic to the units studied, but rather reflect spatial lags across adjacent geographic units. Thus, measures of on- and off-premise outlet densities would prove of little value in indexing use within local areas, providing a poor fit to local rates of abstention and frequency of drinking (tables 7 and 8). However, the same measures would be of great value in indexing use in adjacent geographic areas. Including spatial autocorrelated lagged effects related to errors in estimate of rates of abstention would prove of further use in geographically indexing drinking (see table 7). The geostatistical techniques for incorporating this sort of spatial information into models for spatial prediction and interpolation are well reviewed in the important texts by Bailey and Gatrell (1995) and Isaaks and Srivastava (1989). Combined with the results of analyses such as presented here, these models provide considerable hope for future improvements in the technologies necessary to identify areas of health need for the targeted delivery of health services.

ACKNOWLEDGMENTS

Research for and preparation of this manuscript were supported by the

National Institute on Alcohol Abuse and Alcoholism (NIAAA) under Grant No. AA09146 and NIAAA Center Grant No. AA06282 and by the Center for Substance Abuse Prevention.

NOTES

1. Quality substitution has been a central topic in microeconomic research for decades (see Theil 1952; Prais and Houthakker 1955) and continues to be a problem of central importance to the estimation of price elasticities (Deaton 1989).

2. The related topic of the substitution of amenities (e.g., off- for on-premise drinking) has been noted by Godfrey (1989) and empirically examined by Gruenewald and colleagues (1995).

3. One of the central problems of small area analysis has been the detection of cancer clusters. The etiologic context of this search supports the definition of small areas provided here; cancer clusters are assumed to be related to a local confluence of risk factors for this disease.

4. A large literature regarding the important issues of "scale" (unit size) and "resolution" (unit size relative to process size) in geostatistical/ecological studies exists and bears directly on the problem of working with "small" geographic units. The scale and resolution of maps affect the geostatistical properties of spatial analyses (Chou 1991), must be sensitive to the spatial extent of biological processes (Sokol and Oden 1978), and require specific treatment in GIS displays (Valenzuela and Baumgardner 1990).

5. This is the way retailers within shopping malls maximize profits. Despite the increased competition presented by greater proximity to similar retailers, the individual shops all experience a compensatory increased flow of consumers through the marketplace.

6. The effect of such a matrix is to weight distal observations on **X** with regard to their proximal effects on **y** through **L**. The use of zeros and ones assumes equal weighting, an assumption not central to the current argument.

7. Correlated errors in estimation arise in both time and spatial domains. Temporal autocorrelated error refers to sequential correlated error in time. Given the unidimensional unidirectional nature of time, temporal autocorrelated errors can be represented by relatively simple vector processes. Spatial autocorrelated error refers to correlated errors between spatially "adjacent" units. Given the multidimensional multidirectional nature of spatial effects, spatial autocorrelated errors must be represented by complex multivectorial processes.

8. The transformation regime requires differencing the cross-sectional vectors of observations with respect to lagged values of endogenous, $\mathbf{y}_t - \rho_t\mathbf{y}_{t-1}$, and exogenous, $\mathbf{X}_t - \rho_t\mathbf{X}_{t-1}$, model terms. This results in the loss of one full wave of data, necessitating the collection of a minimum of four or more waves for the procedure to provide relatively stable estimates of and corrections for ρ_t. At four waves of data collection the procedure provides somewhat unstable corrections for temporal autocorrelated error. The asymptotic properties of the procedure are such that the collection of more temporal waves will quickly stabilize the estimate of ρ_t, providing further improvements in model fit.

9. This procedure assumes the orthogonality of space-time autocorrelation. This is not a necessary assumption. Alternative formulations of space-time effects are possible. However, the assumption considerably simplifies the estimation process, a nontrivial issue in the estimation of these models.

10. More precisely, log transforms for density x were equal to ln(x + 1). This provided a transformation suitable for the 116 on-premise units and 98 off-premise units that had no outlets.

11. Core beverage lists were based upon those having greatest market share across the United States (reported in Treno et al. 1993).

12. Among the questions asked on the survey, assessments of the size of drinks served at on-premise establishments were most varied, requiring considerable adjustment of survey responses. Volume of units sold at off-premise establishments was far more homogeneous.

13. Although the precision of these price data far exceeded that collected in any prior study, it should be noted that this procedure artificially reduced the observed variance in the price measures. This could prove a source of bias in coefficient estimates (Geronimus et al. 1996).

14. While this analysis suggests that there were, overall, no statistically significant differences between respondents who could or could not be geocoded, it does not protect against the possibility that non-geocodable respondents came from specific community areas—a bias that could affect the observed spatial relations among the variables measured here. This source of bias cannot be ascertained without location information for the unlocated respondents.

15. Signs and effect sizes of all replicable significant effects reported in the tables in this chapter were generally repeated in analyses including the overlaid general population data. These supplementary analyses did, however, exhibit greater degrees of spatial autocorrelation (created by the random allocation of respondents across geographic boundaries) and were somewhat inefficient (greater standard errors of estimate).

16. All general population data were weighted by number of adults within households, number of residential phone lines, and poststratification weights constructed from census data. Poststratification weights based upon census estimates of population gender, ethnic group composition, and age were implemented at the community level using county demographics, the geographically common unit of observation across communities.

17. The central analyses for each measure appear in the tables in this chapter. Central analyses for abstention and frequency appear in tables 7 and 8 (identically composed models were used for assessments of outliers for drinks per occasion, drinking variance, and drinking at home and bars/restaurants). Central analyses for outlet densities appear in table 5. Central analyses for beverage prices appear in table 3.

18. Total demand is reflected in the total volume of goods or services used or sold. Variance in drinking quantities is unrelated to the total volume of alcohol used but, rather, reflects temporal variation in this volume related to changes in the average quantity consumed per occasion (average drinks per occasion; see Gruenewald et al. 1996*c*).

19. First-stage estimates were obtained from spatial regression models in which

each endogenous measure (rates of abstention, frequency of use, on-premise densities, off-premise densities) was regressed over all exogenous measures (see figure 2). This procedure provides estimates of the endogenous measures, which can be used in second-stage regressions in place of the original observations (in essence replacing original observations containing correlated measurement error with estimates purged of correlated measurement error). This procedure has been part of standard statistical practice for many years (see Duncan 1975 for a historical review).

20. The asymptotic test of first-order autoregressive errors presented in Judge et al. (1988) was used. Degrees of freedom for the test are $df = (n^*t) - k - k_u$; n*t are the total number of observations (144 * 4 = 576), k is the number of model degrees of freedom (here k = 16, including 1 df for ρ_s), k_u is the number of cross-sectional units.

REFERENCES

Abbey, A.; Scott, R.O.; and Smith, M.J. Physical, subjective, and social availability: Their relationship to alcohol consumption in rural and urban areas. *Addiction* 88:489–499, 1993.

Anselin, L. *Spatial Econometrics: Methods and Models.* Dordrecht, The Netherlands: Kluwer Academic Publishers, 1988.

Anselin, L. *SpaceStat: A Program for the Statistical Analysis of Spatial Data.* Santa Barbara: Department of Geography, University of California, Santa Barbara, 1990.

Bailey, T.C., and Gatrell, A.C. *Interactive Spatial Data Analysis.* Essex, England: Longman Group, 1995.

Chou, Y.H. Map resolution and spatial autocorrelation. *Geographical Analysis* 23:228–246, 1991.

Cliff, A.D., and Ord, J.K. *Spatial Processes: Models and Applications.* London: Pion, 1981.

Cook, R.D., and Weisberg, S. *Residuals and Influence in Regression.* New York: Chapman and Hall, 1982.

Deaton, A. Quality, quantity, and spatial variation of price. *American Economic Review* 78:418–430, 1989.

Doriean, P. Estimating linear models with spatially distributed data. In: Leinhardt, S., ed. *Sociological Methodology 1980.* San Francisco: Jossey Bass, 1980*a*. pp. 359–385.

Doriean, P. Linear models with spatially distributed data: Spatial disturbance or spatial effects? *Sociological Methods and Research* 9:29–60, 1980*b*.

Duncan, O.D. *Introduction to Structural Equation Models.* New York: Academic Press, 1975.

Eaton, B.C., and Wooders, M. Sophisticated entry in a model of spatial competition. *Rand Journal of Economics* 16:282–297, 1985.

Fotheringham, S., and Rogerson, P. *Spatial Analysis and GIS.* Bristol, PA: Taylor & Francis, 1994.

Geronimus, A.T.; Bound, J.; and Neidert, L.J. On the validity of using census geocode characteristics to proxy individual socioeconomic characteristics. *Journal of the American Statistical Association* 91:529–537, 1996.

Godfrey, C. Factors influencing the consumption of alcohol and tobacco: The use and abuse of economic models. *Br J Addict* 84:1123–1138, 1989.

Gorman, D.M.; Speer, P.W.; Labouvie, E.W.; and Subaiya, A.P. Risk of assaultive violence and alcohol availability in New Jersey. *Am J Public Health* 88:97–100, 1998.

Greene, W.H. *Econometric Analysis.* 2d ed. New York: Macmillan, 1993.

Griffith, D.A. *Spatial Autocorrelation.* Washington, DC: Association of American Geographers, 1987.

Griffith, D.A. *Advanced Spatial Statistics.* Dordrecht, The Netherlands: Kluwer Academic Publishers, 1988.

Grossman, M. Health economics of prevention of alcohol-related problems. Paper presented at the workshop on Health Economics of Prevention and Treatment of Alcohol-Related Problems, National Institute on Alcohol Abuse and Alcoholism, Washington, DC, 1988.

Gruenewald, P.J. Alcohol problems and the control of availability: Theoretical and empirical issues. In: Hilton, M.E., and Bloss, G., eds. *Economics and the Prevention of Alcohol-Related Problems.* Research Monograph No. 25. NIH Pub. No. 93–3513. Bethesda, MD: National Institute on Alcohol Abuse and Alcoholism, 1993. pp. 59–90.

Gruenewald, P.J.; Millar, A.; and Treno, A.J. Alcohol availability and the ecology of drinking. *Alcohol Health Res World* 17:39–45, 1993*a*.

Gruenewald, P.J.; Ponicki, W.R.; and Holder, H.D. The relationship of outlet densities to alcohol consumption: A time series cross-sectional analysis. *Alcohol Clin Exp Res* 17:38–47, 1993*b*.

Gruenewald, P.J.; Treno, A.J.; Nephew, T.M.; and Ponicki, W.R. Routine activities and alcohol use: Constraints on outlet utilization. *Alcohol Clin Exp Res* 19:44–53, 1995.

Gruenewald, P.J.; Millar, A.B.; and Roeper, P. Access to alcohol: Geography and prevention for local communities. *Alcohol Health Res World* 20:244–251, 1996*a*.

Gruenewald, P.J.; Millar, A.B.; Treno, A.J.; Ponicki, W.R.; Yang, Z.; and Roeper, P. The geography of availability and driving after drinking. *Addiction* 91:967–983, 1996*b*.

Gruenewald, P.J.; Treno, A.J.; and Mitchell, P.R. Drinking patterns and drinking behaviors: Theoretical models of risky acts. *Contemporary Drug Problems* 23:407–440, 1996*c*.

Holder, H.D.; Saltz, R.F.; Grube, J.W.; Voas, R.B.; Gruenewald, P.J.; and Treno, A.J. A community prevention trial to reduce alcohol-involved accidental injury and death: Overview. *Addiction* 92 (Suppl 2):155–171, 1997.

Hotelling, H. Stability and competition. *Economic Journal* 39:41–57, 1929.

Hsiao, C. *Analysis of Panel Data.* New York: Cambridge University Press, 1986.

Isaaks, E.H., and Srivastava, R.M. *An Introduction to Applied Geostatistics.* New York: Oxford University Press, 1989.

Judge, G.G.; Hill, R.C.; Griffiths, W.E.; Lütkepohl, H.; and Lee, T.-C. *Introduc-*

tion to the Theory and Practice of Econometrics. 2d ed. New York: John Wiley, 1988.

Kenkel, D.S. New estimates of the optimal tax on alcohol. *Economic Inquiry* 34:296–319, 1996.

Kenkel, D.S., and Manning, W. Perspectives on alcohol taxation. *Alcohol Health Res World* 20:230–238, 1996.

Lemmens, P.H.H.M., and Knibbe, R.A. Seasonal variation in survey and sales estimates of alcohol consumption. *J Stud Alcohol* 54:157–163, 1993.

Leung, S.F., and Phelps, C.E. "My kingdom for a drink . . . ?": A review of estimates of the price sensitivity of demand for alcoholic beverages. In: Hilton, M.E., and Bloss, G., eds. *Economics and the Prevention of Alcohol-Related Problems.* Research Monograph No. 25. NIH Pub. No. 93–3513. Bethesda, MD: National Institute on Alcohol Abuse and Alcoholism, 1993. pp. 1–31.

Loftin, C., and Ward, S. A spatial autocorrelation model of the effects of population density on fertility. *Am Sociolog Rev* 48:121–128, 1983.

MapInfo. *MapInfo for Windows 3.0: Reference Manual.* Troy, NY: MapInfo Corporation, 1994.

Maurer, B.A. *Geographical Population Analysis: Tools for the Analysis of Biodiversity.* Oxford, England: Blackwell Scientific Publications, 1994.

Pindyck, R.S., and Rubinfeld, D.L. *Microeconomics.* New York: Macmillan, 1989.

Ponicki, W.R., and Gruenewald, P.J. *S^3: Spatial Statistical System, V3.20, Program User's Guide.* NIAAA Center Grant No. AA06282. Berkeley, CA: Prevention Research Center, Pacific Institute for Research and Evaluation, May 1997.

Prais, S.J., and Houthakker, H.S. *The Analysis of Family Budgets.* Cambridge, England: Cambridge University Press, 1955.

Scribner, R.A.; MacKinnon, D.P.; and Dwyer, J.H. Alcohol outlet density and motor vehicle crashes in Los Angeles County cities. *J Stud Alcohol* 55:447–453, 1994.

Scribner, R.A.; MacKinnon, D.P.; and Dwyer, J.H. The risk of assaultive violence and alcohol availability in Los Angeles County. *Am J Public Health* 85:335–340, 1995.

Sokol, R.R., and Oden, N.L. Spatial autocorrelation in biology. 1. Methodology. *Biological Journal of the Linnean Society* 10:199–228, 1978.

Theil, H. Qualities, prices, and budget enquiries. *Review of Economic Studies* 19:129–147, 1952.

Thomas, R.W., and Huggett, R.J. *Modelling in Geography: A Mathematical Approach.* New York: Harper & Row, 1980.

Tomlin, C.D. *Geographic Information Systems and Cartographic Modeling.* Englewood Cliffs, NJ: Prentice-Hall, 1990.

Treno, A.J.; Nephew, T.M.; Ponicki, W.R.; and Gruenewald, P.J. Alcohol beverage price spectra: Opportunities for substitution. *Alcohol Clin Exp Res* 17:675–680, 1993.

Valenzuela, C.R., and Baumgardner, M.F. Selection of appropriate cell sizes for thematic maps. *ITC Journal* 3:219–224, 1990.

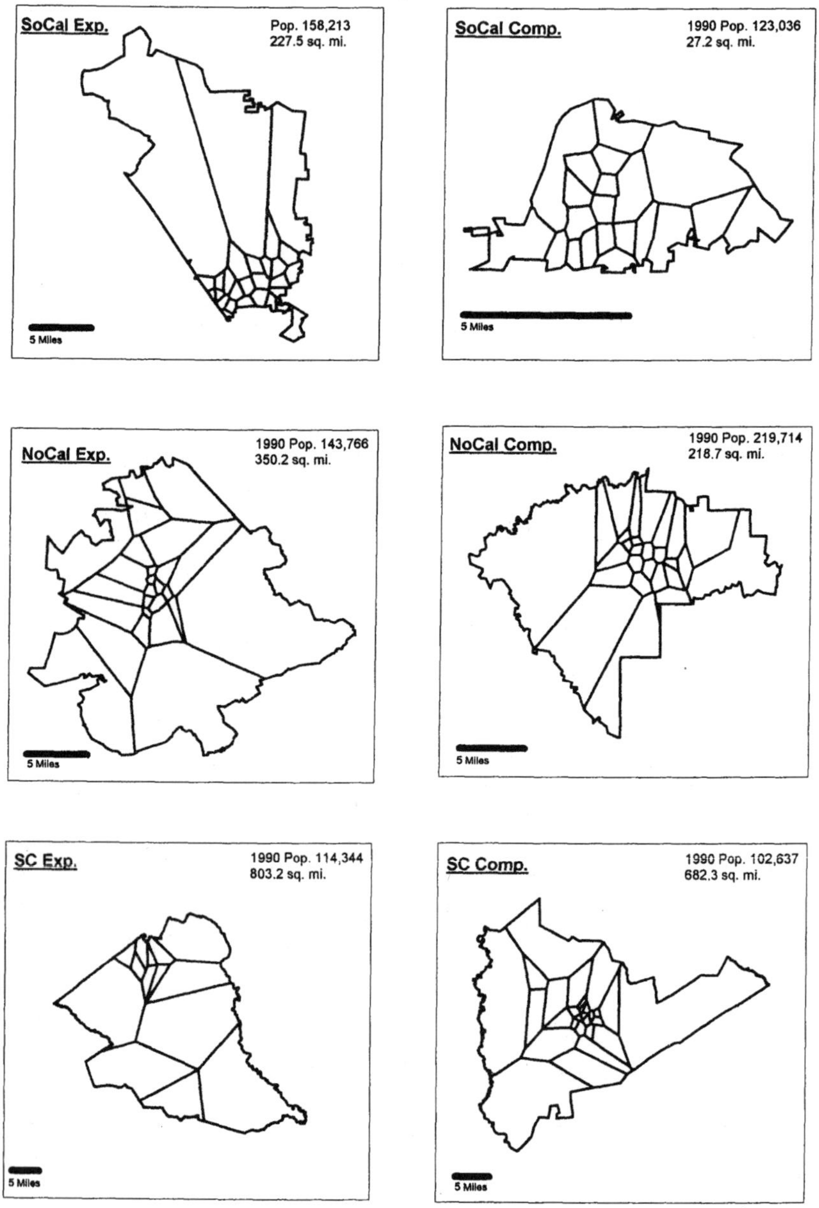

Figure 1. Community boundary units.

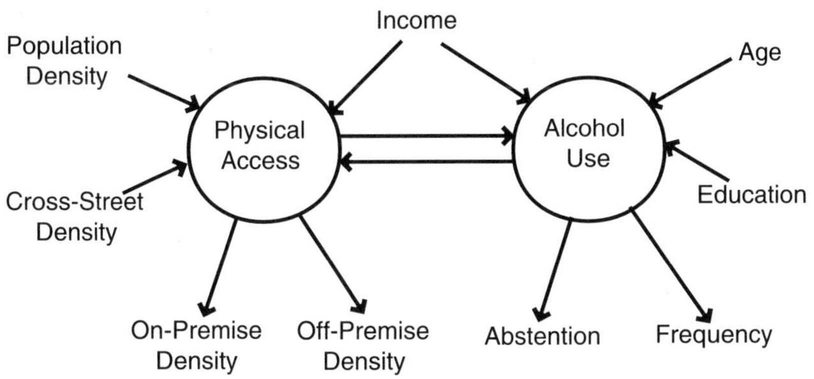

Figure 2. Conceptual outline of simultaneous equation model of physical access and alcohol use.

Table 1. Descriptive Statistics: Wave 1 Cross-Section ($N = 144$ units, 1992 data).

Variable Group	Variable Name	Range Minimum	Range Maximum	Mean	SE
Physical access	On-premise[1]	0.000	2.078	0.269	0.030
	Off-premise[1]	0.000	1.323	0.184	0.019
Alcohol use	Abstention[2]	5.714	64.286	30.552	1.016
	Frequency[3]	0.484	9.063	3.661	0.132
	Drinks per occasion[3]	0.629	4.610	1.584	0.052
	Variance[3]	0.342	120.774	5.478	1.067
Drinking places	Home[4]	0.520	7.008	2.815	0.090
	Bar/Restaurant[4]	0.000	3.392	1.204	0.053
Beverage prices					
Beer (on-premise)[5]		3.83	6.08	4.74	0.036
Beer (off-premise)		0.85	2.58	1.69	0.039
Wine (on-premise)[5]		5.07	31.10	17.34	1.143
Wine (off-premise)		1.20	6.70	3.34	0.121
Spirits (on-premise)[5]		6.75	14.16	10.95	0.165
Spirits (off-premise)		2.25	4.50	3.09	0.058
Environment	Cross-street density[6]	0.704	6.647	3.365	0.118
	Population density[7]	0.188	50.982	5.147	0.571
Economic access	Income < 20K[2]	0.000	84.615	29.986	1.428
	Income ≥ 60K[2]	0.000	78.261	17.201	1.243
Ethnic groups	Black[2]	0.000	63.077	9.006	1.148
	Hispanic[2]	0.000	82.759	10.686	1.245
	Other[2]	0.000	27.586	6.759	0.475
Demographics	Number of children[3]	0.250	1.923	0.859	0.027
	Age[3]	31.821	55.912	42.581	0.368
	Education < high school[2]	0.000	61.538	12.502	0.868
	Education ≥ college[2]	13.793	90.000	55.259	1.325
	Male[2]	21.429	83.333	43.728	0.770
	Married[2]	16.667	96.000	60.586	1.121
	Single[2]	0.000	45.455	18.588	0.752

[1]Outlets per kilometer of roadway (local and highway).
[2]Percentage of adult respondents greater than or equal to 18 years of age.
[3]Averaged over range of variable.
[4]28-day standardized frequencies of venue use for drinking alcohol.
[5]Average real prices per unit volume. Beer: six-pack of 12-oz cans or bottles; wine: 750-mL bottle; spirits:750-mL bottle. Deflated to 1990 dollars using regional consumer price index.
[6]Number of intersections per kilometer of roadway (local and highway).
[7]Estimated from population survey: households responding × household size expressed per kilometer of roadway (local and highway).

Table 2. Spatial Correlations of Raw Dependent Measures.

Dependent Measure	Moran Coefficient	*z*	*p*	Percent Outliers
Abstention	0.296	2.580	0.005*	0.0
Frequency	0.272	2.376	0.009*	0.0
Drinks per occasion	0.057	0.543	0.294	1.4
Variance	0.027	0.285	0.388	0.7
Drinking at				
Home	–0.016	–0.073	0.471	0.0
Bar/restaurant	0.193	1.706	0.044**	0.0
On-premise density[1]	0.149	1.331	0.092	1.4
Off-premise density[1]	0.144	1.284	0.099	1.4
On-premise price index	0.329	2.860	0.002*	3.5
Off-premise price index	0.162	1.443	0.075	2.8

[1]Logarithm of value of original measure plus 1.000 for reduced skew in conditional errors.
*Replicated in 1995 validation wave; $p < 0.05$.
**$p < 0.05$.

Table 3. Correlates of Alcohol Beverage Prices.

Variable Group	Variable Name	Lag 0 *b/(t)*	Lag 1 *b/(t)*
On-Premise			
Communities[1]	—	—	—
Environment	Population density	0.2047	1.8793
		(0.218)	(0.882)
Economic access	Income < 20K	0.0450	0.0751
		(0.835)	(0.656)
	Income ≥ 60K	–0.0469	–0.0442
		(–0.738)	(–0.366)
Physical access	On-premise	7.1667*	11.9454
		(1.728)	(1.014)
	Off-premise	–17.3409*	–25.2074
		(-2.728)	(–1.404)
Alcohol use	Abstention	0.0511	0.0691
		(0.571)	(0.528)
	Frequency	0.6897	1.2696
		(1.132)	(1.087)
	Drinks per occasion	–0.3284	–4.1219*
		(–0.343)	(–1.715)
ρ		0.6750**	
		(9.174)	
Off-Premise			
Communities[1]	—	—	—
Environment	Population density	0.4627*	0.3533
		(2.221)	(0.794)
Economic access	Income < 20K	0.0056	0.0318
		(0.462)	(1.292)
	Income ≥ 60K	–0.0133	0.0040
		(–0.934)	(0.159)
Physical access	On-premise	–2.2321*	0.0627
		(–2.416)	(0.024)
	Off-premise	0.6140	–4.5569
		(0.438)	(–1.179)

Table 3. *Continued*

Variable Group	Variable Name	Lag 0 *b/(t)*	Lag 1 *b/(t)*
	Off-Premise		
Alcohol use	Abstention	0.0031	–0.0033
		(0.150)	(–0.118)
	Frequency	0.1401	0.2176
		(1.102)	(0.862)
	Drinks per occasion	–0.3601	–0.6300
		(–1.406)	(–1.187)
ρ		0.5027**	
		(5.140)	

[1] *b* values suppressed in table.
**p* < 0.05.
**Replicated in 1995 validation wave; *p* < 0.05.

Table 4. OLS Analyses of Correlates of Alcohol Beverage Prices (On-Premise).

Variable Group	Variable Name	Lag 0 *b/(t)*	Lag 1 *b/(t)*
Communities[1]	—	—	—
Environment	Population density	0.3334	2.0017
		(0.321)	(1.031)
Economic access	Income < 20K	0.0497	0.0468
		(0.803)	(0.405)
	Income ≥ 60K	–0.0528	–0.0716
		(–0.707)	(–0.631)
Physical access	On-premise	6.9273	10.881
		(1.520)	(0.921)
	Off-premise	–18.0483*	–30.0822*
		(–2.694)	(–1.760)
Alcohol use	Abstention	0.2050*	0.1427
		(1.986)	(1.020)
	Frequency	1.3846*	2.1584*
		(2.029)	(1.851)
	Drinks per occasion	–0.0766	–6.4068
		(–0.070)	(–2.583)
MC_r		0.3275**	
		(7.898)	

[1] *b* values suppressed in table.
**p* < 0.05.
**Replicated in 1995 validation wave; *p* < 0.05.

Table 5. Correlates of Outlet Locations.

Variable Group	Variable Name	Lag 0 *b/(t)*	Lag 1 *b/(t)*
On-Premise			
Communities[1]	—	—	—
Environment	Population density	0.1851**	–0.0074
		(11.062)	(–0.201)
	Cross-street density	0.0023	0.0156
		(0.179)	(0.672)
Economic access	Income < 20K	0.0010	0.0059*
		(0.764)	(2.352)
	Income ≥ 60K	–0.0035**	–0.0015
		(–2.214)	(–0.594)
Alcohol use	Abstention	0.0003	–0.0070*
		(0.114)	(–2.286)
	Frequency	0.0092	0.0752*
		(0.605)	(2.888)
	Drinks per occasion	–0.0321	–0.1705*
		(–1.374)	(–3.064)
ρ		0.1805	
		(1.412)	
Off-Premise			
Communities[1]	—	—	—
Environment	Population density	0.1208**	–0.0560*
		(11.503)	(–2.508)
	Cross-street density	0.0353**	–0.0079
		(4.378)	(–0.551)
Economic access	Income < 20K	0.0006	0.0033**
		(0.739)	(2.108)
	Income ≥ 60K	–0.0017	–0.0010
		(–1.715)	(–0.663)

Table 5. *Continued*

	Off-Premise		
Variable Group	**Variable Name**	**Lag 0** *b/(t)*	**Lag 1** *b/(t)*
Alcohol use	Abstention	0.0014	–0.0027
		(0.977)	(1.423)
	Frequency	0.0019	0.0285*
		(0.203)	(1.807)
	Drinks per occasion	0.0042	–0.0231
		(0.285)	(–0.673)
ρ		0.0031	
		(0.022)	

[1]*b* values suppressed in table.
*$p < 0.05$.
**Replicated in 1995 validation wave; $p < 0.05$.

Table 6. Likelihood Ratio Chi-Square Tests of Associations of Alcohol Access to Drinking Patterns and Places.

	Alcohol Access Lag		
Measure	**Lag 0**	**Lag 1**	**Lag 2**
Drinking patterns			
Abstention	0.224	7.647**	1.404
Frequency	1.540	6.195**	2.428
Drinks per occasion	1.814	2.140	1.016
Variance	0.952	0.341	1.076
Drinking places			
Home	6.440*	3.051	0.903
Bar/restaurant	1.794	1.145	6.382*

Note: Community dummy variables included as regional controls for community differences.
*$p < 0.05$.
**Replicated in 1995 validation wave; $p < 0.05$.

Table 7. Cross-Sectional Correlates of Drinking Abstention.

Variable Group	Variable Name	Model I $b/(t)$	Model II $b/(t)$
Communities	—	—	—
Physical access	On-premise		−1.3107 (−0.255)
	Off-premise		3.1685 (0.432)
Physical access lag 1	On-premise		
	Off-premise		
Economic access	Income < 20K		
	Income ≥ 60K		
	On-price		
	Off-price		
Sociodemographics	Age		
	Education < high school		
	Education ≥ college		
	Married		
	Single		
	Male		
	Black		
	Hispanic		
	Other		
	Number of children		
ρ		0.3937** (3.803)	0.3842** (3.651)
ΔG^2 (Δdf)		29.361** (5)	0.224 (2)

[a]Tested against all exogenous terms absent of lagged effects.
*$p < 0.05$.
**Replicated in 1995 validation wave; $p < 0.05$.

Model III *b/(t)*	Model IV *b/(t)*	Model V *b/(t)*	Model V Simultaneous Test ΔG2	 *p*
—	—	—	26.279	< 0.001**
–5.7136	–5.6150	–4.6908	0.633	0.729[a]
(–1.094)	(–1.131)	(–0.942)		
10.6433	4.6281	1.9565		
(1.394)	(0.625)	(0.272)		
–36.5508**	–27.0921*	–22.2031*	5.969	0.050*
(–2.649)	(–2.150)	(–1.821)		
52.6355**	34.7880*	22.6917		
(2.759)	(1.992)	(1.343)		
	0.2066**	–0.0257	3.047	0.693
	(3.263)	(–0.282)		
	–0.1158	–0.0666		
	(–1.556)	(–0.832		
	0.0740	0.1305		
	(0.719)	(1.286)		
	0.2053	0.1026		
	(–0.424)	(0.2102)		
		0.5798**	22.703	0.012**
		(2.593)		
		0.0782		
		(0.570)		
		–0.1879**		
		(–2.301)		
		–0.0772		
		(–0.708)		
		0.1046		
		(0.748)		
		–0.0182		
		(–0.193)		
		0.0406		
		0.1372		
		(1.242)		
		0.0209		
		(0.137)		
		4.020		
		(1.240)		
0.3149**	0.1304	0.0097		
(2.802)	(1.015)	(0.069)		
7.647**	30.435**	27.703**		
(2)	(4)	(10)		

Table 8. Cross-Sectional Correlates of Drinking Frequency.

Variable Group	Variable Name	Model I b/(t)	Model II b/(t)
Communities	—	—	—
Physical access	On-premise		−0.0223 (−0.030)
	Off-premise		−0.6808 (−0.641)
Physical access lag 1	On-premise		
	Off-premise		
Economic access	Income < 20K		
	Income ≥ 60K		
	On-price		
	Off-price		
Sociodemographics	Age		
	Education < high school		
	Education ≥ college		
	Married		
	Single		
	Male		
	Black		
	Hispanic		
	Other		
	Number of children		
ρ		0.1200 (0.961)	0.1239 (0.987)
ΔG^2 (Δdf)		21.060** (5)	1.540 (2)

[a]Tested against all exogenous terms absent of lagged effects.
*$p < 0.05$.
**Replicated in 1995 validation wave; $p < 0.05$.

	Model III	Model IV	Model V	Model V Simultaneous Test	
	$b/(t)$	$b/(t)$	$b/(t)$	ΔG^2	p
	—	—	—	13.476	0.019**
	0.0724	–0.1401	–0.5750	1.318	0.517[a]
	(0.099)	(–0.199)	(–0.806)		
	–0.8518	0.4566	1.1098		
	(–0.802)	(0.440)	(1.092)		
	3.9261**	2.2233	1.4664	7.020	0.030*
	(2.121)	(1.291)	(0.871)		
	–3.8913	–0.7576	0.2070		
	(–1.521)	(–0.317)	(0.089)		
		–0.0230**	0.0018	5.088	0.405
		(–2.616)	(0.141)		
		0.0223	0.0204**		
		(–0.758)	(1.870)		
		0.0125	0.0141		
		(0.918)	(1.054)		
		0.0404	0.0150		
		(0.613)	(0.225)		
			0.0089	20.844	0.022**
			(0.282)		
			–0.081		
			(–0.414)		
			0.0209**		
			(1.803)		
			0.0133		
			(0.865)		
			(0.0241)		
			(1.223)		
			(0.0154)		
			(1.139)		
			–0.0159		
			(–1.246)		
			–0.0066		
			(–0.427)		
			0.0261		
			(1.229)		
			–0.6189		
			(–1.335)		
	0.0987	–0.0717	–0.243		
	(0.771)	(–0.517)	(–1.629)		
	6.195**	30.562**	20.844**		
	(2)	(4)	(10)		

Table 9. 2SLS Models Predicting Alcohol Use From Physical Availability.

Variable Group	Variable Name	Abstention *b/(t)*	Frequency *b/(t)*
Communities	—	—	—
Economic access	Income < 20K	0.1085	–0.0039
		(1.452)	(–0.363)
	Income ≥ 60K	–0.0664	0.0136
		(–0.869)	(1.255)
Sociodemographics	Age	0.2879**	0.0048
		(1.650)	(–0.190)
	Education < high school	0.2024*	–0.0180
		(1.690)	(–1.027)
	Education ≥ college	–0.1359**	0.0236**
		(–1.727)	(2.038)
Physical access[1]	On-premise	3.2973	0.4779
		(0.197)	(0.196)
	Off-premise	–12.9244	–0.4160
		(–0.534)	(–0.119)
Lag 1	On-premise	–21.6276	2.1473
		(–0.994)	(0.672)
Lag 1	Off-premise	29.9159	–1.1930
		(1.027)	(–0.278)
ρ		0.1202	–0.0574
		(0.931)	(–0.416)

[1]Estimated values based on first-stage regressions in 2SLS.
*$p < 0.05$.
**Replicated in 1995–96 validation wave; $p < 0.05$.

Table 10. 2SLS Models Predicting Physical Availability From Alcohol Use.

		Outlet Densities	
		On-Premise	Off-Premise
Variable Group	Variable Name	*b/(t)*	*b/(t)*
Communities	—	—	—
Environment	Population density	0.1957**	0.1212
		(10.456)	(10.344)
	Cross-street density	0.0075	0.0382**
		(0.583)	(4.616)
Lag 1	Population density	–0.0514	–0.0652*
		(–1.328)	(–2.852)
Lag 1	Cross-street density	0.0102	–0.0143
		(0.402)	(–0.934)
Economic access	Income < 20K	0.0009	0.0010
		(0.497)	(0.917)
	Income ≥ 60K	–0.0034**	–0.0018
		(–1.988)	(–1.643)
Lag 1	Income < 20K	0.0072	0.0032**
		(2.402)	(1.744)
Lag 1	Income ≥ 60K	–0.0035	–0.0031
		(–1.163)	(–1.191)
Alcohol use[1]	Abstention	0.0122	0.0001
		(1.435)	(0.022)
	Frequency	0.1134*	0.0054
		(1.725)	(0.132)
Lag 1	Abstention	–0.175**	–0.0037
		(–3.976)	(–1.330)
Lag 1	Frequency	(0.0869)**	0.0427**
		(2.360)	(1.881)
ρ		0.2842**	0.0355
		(2.397)	(0.262)

[1]Estimated values based on first-stage regressions in 2SLS.

*$p < 0.05$.

**Replicated in 1995-96 validation wave; $p < 0.05$.

Table 11. Spatial Panel Models of Alcohol Use and Availability.

Variable Group	Variable Name	On-Premise *b/(t)*	Off-Premise *b/(t)*
Years	1992–93	0.0094*	0.0037*
		(2.594)	(1.876)
	1993–94	0.0060*	0.0025
		(1.859)	(1.418)
	1994–95	0.0011	–0.0015
		(0.344)	(–0.932)
Environment	Population density	0.0949*	0.0606*
		(9.062)	(8.974)
Lag 1	Population density	–0.0028	–0.0051
		(–0.120)	(–0.374)
Economic access	Income < 20K	–0.001	–0.0001
		(–0.342)	(–0.831)
	Income ≥ 60K	0.0001	–0.0001
		(0.111)	(–0.659)
Lag 1	Income < 20K	0.0002	0.0002
		(0.369)	(0.734)
Lag 1	Income ≥ 60K	–0.0006	–0.0008*
		(–0.964)	(–1.920)
Alcohol use	Abstention	0.0002	0.0003
		(0.742)	(1.464)
	Frequency	0.0026	0.0010
		(1.353)	(0.808)
	Drinks per occasion	–0.0043	–0.0010
		(–1.096)	(–0.408)
Lag 1	Abstention	–0.0004	0.0001
		(–0.888)	(0.397)
Lag 1	Frequency	0.0022	0.0013
		(0.516)	(0.498)
Lag 1	Drinks per occasion	–0.0079	–0.0020
		(–0.932)	(0.384)
ρ_s		0.1958*	–0.0293
		(2.833)	(–0.384)
ρ_t		–0.0662	–0.0015
		(–1.092)	(–0.026)

*$p < 0.05$.

Chapter 9

Measuring Interstate Variations in Problems Related to Alcohol Use Disorders

William E. McAuliffe, Ph.D., Richard LaBrie, Ed.D., Nicoletta A. Lomuto, Nancy E. Pollock, M.S., Rebecca Betjemann, and Elizabeth Fournier

KEY WORDS: validation study; alcohol use test; AODR mortality; AODD; geographical area; social indicators; population dynamics; United States

This chapter details the development and validation of the Alcohol Problem Index (API), an indicator-based measure created to compare States with regard to problems related to alcohol use disorders (abuse and dependence) as defined by the American Psychiatric Association (1994). Operationally defined, the API is an unweighted linear composite of alcohol-related mortality, arrest, and treatment client rates per 100,000 State residents. Elsewhere (McAuliffe et al. 1999), we have described a parallel measure for other drugs, the Drug Problem Index (DPI). The API and DPI assess dimensions of the quality of social life in States. Indexes of this type gauge the overall

W.E. McAuliffe, Ph.D., is an associate professor at Harvard Medical School and director of the National Technical Center for Substance Abuse Needs Assessment, North Charles Research and Planning Group, 875 Massachusetts Ave., 7th Floor, Cambridge, MA 02139. R. LaBrie, Ed.D., is an instructor in psychiatry at Harvard Medical School and deputy director of the National Technical Center for Substance Abuse Needs Assessment, North Charles Research and Planning Group. N.A. Lomuto is a graduate student in the Department of Economics, Queen's University, Dunning Hall, Kingston, ON, Canada K7L 3N6. N.E. Pollock, M.S., is an ARCH project scientist at the Harvard Institute for International Development, Harvard University, 14 Story St., Cambridge, MA 02138. R. Betjemann is a graduate student in the Department of Psychology, University of Denver, Frontier Hall, 2155 S. Race St., Denver, CO 80208. E. Fournier is an independent consultant, 119 Slade St., Belmont, MA 02478.

level of health or economic well-being in a population. Examples in other topic areas include the Uniform Crime Index of the Federal Bureau of Investigation (FBI) and the Air Quality Index. Policymakers could use the API and DPI to evaluate the adequacy of State alcohol and other drug prevention and treatment policies.

EXISTING MEASURES AND THEIR VALIDITY

Our review of the literature revealed surprisingly little relevant research on measurement of the variations among States in the severity of problems related to alcohol use disorders. Most Federal epidemiologic studies have focused on obtaining national or regional estimates of alcohol and other drug use and related disorders. Approaches that have been used to assess interstate variations include a population-at-risk index, social indicator methods, household surveys, and an estimation technique that combines all three.

The current Substance Abuse Prevention and Treatment (SAPT) Block Grant allocation formula employs a population-at-risk approach. Federal regulations require that SAPT Block Grant funds be allocated on the basis of relative need (Substance Abuse Funding News 1997*b*). The index measures each State's need for alcohol prevention and treatment services by the proportion of the national population ages 25–64 years that resides in the State. That age cohort was chosen because it had been found to be at high risk of alcohol abuse and dependence in survey research (Burnam et al. 1994). Although designed to improve on population size as the basis for distributing resources, the index nevertheless correlates highly with population size (r = 0.99). It seems therefore unlikely that the Block Grant need allocation index adequately reflects variations in the relative *rates* of alcohol problems among the States.

In the earliest effort at constructing a measure from alcohol indicators, Keller and Efron (1955) used the Jellinek cirrhosis mortality–based estimation method to compare States with each other in 1940 and 1953. Nearly three decades later, Wilson and colleagues (1983) refined the use of mortality-based indicators for this purpose. Closest to the concerns of this chapter was their composite, the Alcohol Chronic Health Index, which included deaths from five causes (cirrhosis, alcoholic psychosis, alcoholism, alcohol poisoning, and homicide) (Wilson et al. 1983). The authors selected these indicators on the basis of a factor analysis plus "their statistical independence and summary capacity, their reliability and face validity. . ., and their overall descriptive scope" (p. 42). Wilson and colleagues noted that mortality statistics were more valid than arrest and treatment statistics, but presented no specific evidence on this point.

In another social indicator study, Ford and Schmittdiel (1983) developed a series of stepwise multiple regression models to estimate variations in State utilization statistics for each of six alcohol treatment modalities from the 1980 National Drug and Alcoholism Treatment Unit Survey (NDATUS). There was no overall service model. The models included alcohol-related mortality as well as alcohol-related arrests and general demographic characteristics (e.g., percentage nonwhite) in varying combinations. The six statistical models explained a substantial percentage of the variance in utilization of the respective modalities (ranging from 46 to 89 percent).

To our knowledge, the only surveys that currently measure State variations in alcohol use and related phenomena are the Centers for Disease Control and Prevention's (CDC) Behavioral Risk Factor Surveillance System's (BRFSS) telephone surveys and the CDC's Youth Risk Behavior Surveillance System's (YRBSS) self-administered school surveys. Each year, the BRFSS surveys persons 18 and older to measure quantity and frequency of alcohol use, binge drinking, and driving after drinking for every State (Bradstock et al. 1987; Liu et al. 1997). The YRBSS periodically measures State-level alcohol and other drug use by adolescents in 45 States (CDC 1991; Kolbe et al. 1993; CDC 1995; Gast et al. 1995; Kann et al. 1996). The studies that have attempted to validate the estimates produced by these surveys have reported mixed findings (e.g., Smith et al.1990; Thompson et al. 1993; Gast et al. 1995; Stein et al. 1995).

To satisfy the growing demand for State-level alcohol and other drug data as a basis for policymaking, the Federal government announced plans to expand the National Household Survey on Drug Abuse (NHSDA) (Substance Abuse Funding News 1997*a*). Previously, the NHSDA estimated alcohol and other drug use for only one State, California (Gfroerer and Brodsky 1991). The current NHSDA sample fails to adequately cover New England States and large parts of the West (see figure 2 and the next paragraph). The Request for Proposal (RFP) that described the NHSDA expansion specified one possible sample design in which there would be a minimum sample of 1,000 face-to-face interviews with persons age 12 and older in each State (Substance Abuse and Mental Health Services Administration [SAMHSA] 1997, p. 44). Also, the RFP included the possibility of a revised design of the NHSDA's multistage area probability sampling plan, which is currently optimized for national estimates but not for State estimates (Folsom and Judkins 1997, p. 1–13).

To enhance the NHSDA's State estimates further, Federal authorities plan to use a new estimation methodology developed by Folsom and colleagues (1996) that combines the survey data with elements of social indicator analysis and synthetic estimation. In that study, the statistical ("survey weighted empirical Bayesian") model estimated the percentage of residents that used alcohol in the last month, were alcohol dependent in the past year, and received alcohol treatment for the 26 States that had the largest number of household interviews (300 or more) in the combined NHSDA samples for 1991, 1992, and 1993 (Folsom et al. 1996). Beginning with the NHSDA survey data, the methodology used indicators (1990 alcohol-related deaths, 1991 Uniform Crime Reports [UCR] arrests for controlled drug possession and sales, and 1991 and

1992 NDATUS alcohol treatment clients) and demographic information (age, race, and gender) to improve the survey estimates, especially the estimates in the States with the smallest number of NHSDA interviews. In support of the model's validity, the authors reported that its estimates for past-month alcohol use correlated highly (over 0.85) with BRFSS telephone survey estimates of the same variable (Folsom et al. 1996, p. 63).

CONCERNS ABOUT RELIABILITY AND VALIDITY

Although several approaches to measuring the severity of alcohol use disorders and related problems among the States have been described in the literature, the lack of independent validation of the measures has resulted in widespread scientific concerns. In a comprehensive review of alcohol and other drug needs assessment models, DeWit and Rush (1996) concluded that models currently used are based on assumptions that have yet to be validated. Almost two decades ago, Furst and colleagues (1981) raised questions about the reliability of drunk-driving statistics, cirrhosis mortality, and treatment-based indicators. The U.S. General Accounting Office (GAO) (1990) pointed out the partial overlap between arrest and treatment data because treatment clients are referred by the criminal justice system. Indicator statistics may reflect changes in funding and activity levels by criminal justice and public health organizations that do not directly or indirectly reflect changes in the prevalence of alcohol and other drug use disorders (DeFleur 1975; GAO 1990; DeWit and Rush 1996). Coding inconsistencies are believed to reduce the reliability of alcohol mortality statistics (Lipscomb and Sulka 1961; Furst et al. 1981; Furst 1983; Wilson et al. 1983; Hopkins et al. 1989; Pollock et al. 1991; Shai 1994; DeBakey et al. 1996).

Wilson and colleagues (1983) noted that indicator measures and survey measures of alcohol and other drug use may not correlate with one another. The authors hypothesized that the two different measurement approaches focused on different aspects of the problem. Folsom and colleagues (1996) found low correlations between social indicators and NHSDA data. Those authors opined that the questionable validity of the indicator-based measures was a possible explanation. Clearly, the lack of agreement between different ways of measuring the same thing can lead to doubts about the approaches, especially when there is no "gold standard" with which to decide among them (McAuliffe et al. 1999).

Another validity issue is whether people with alcohol and other drug use disorders are distinct populations or are merely reflections of an overall "substance use disorder" population. Social indicator researchers want to know whether they should model the prevalence of alcohol and other drug use disorders separately or together. Although the issue is partly conceptual, empirical measurement research is needed to help decide between the two competing theoretical positions.

To evaluate these concerns appropriately, researchers should assess the measures using standard validation methodologies, such as convergent, discriminant, and construct validation (e.g., Campbell and Fiske 1959; Cronbach and Meehl 1967; Nunnally 1978; McAuliffe 1984; Cagle and Banks 1986; Ciarlo et al. 1992). Measurement texts (e.g., Nunnally 1978) define *validity* as the percentage of the variance of measurements that reflects the concept of interest. Validity is a continuous variable that ranges from 0 to 100 percent. Discovery of errors in an indicator or inconsistencies between the indicator and another measure of the same phenomenon does not by itself reveal the indicator's invalidity, that is, what proportion of the measure's variance is due to random or systematic error. Unfortunately, much of the evidence supporting the validity of alcohol and other drug indicators comes from studies of substate areas or measures over time that may not generalize to interstate measurement (e.g., Person et al. 1977; Frank et al. 1978; Cleary 1979; Flaherty et al. 1983; Beshai 1984; Crider 1985; Wilson and Hearne 1985, 1986; Schlesinger and Dorwart 1992; Schlesinger et al. 1993; Simeone et al. 1993; Schlesinger et al. unpublished manuscript 1994; Beenstock 1995; Mammo and French 1996; Pampalon et al. 1996; Sherman et al. 1996).

To address these issues at the interstate level, we used standard psychometric methods to develop and evaluate the validity of a State-level indicator-based measure of alcohol use disorder–related problems. In this effort, we sought to test the following hypotheses:

- A substantially reliable and valid index of these problems among States can be developed from a small number of carefully selected indicators.
- State populations vary substantially in their API scores and in the component variables comprising the API.
- These API scores are empirically distinct from the DPI scores.
- Conclusions based on the API differ substantially from conclusions based on the survey and population-at-risk approaches currently being used in research and policy studies.

METHODS

In the absence of a widely accepted gold standard (Burnam et al. 1994), we sought to ensure that the API would be valid by constructing it with a strong theoretical foundation and from measures with demonstrated validity. First, we selected only variables that according to theory and empirical evidence were reliable and valid. Ultimately, all measurement hinges on theoretical propositions concerning the relationship between the candidate measure(s) and the concept being measured. Accordingly, we selected only variables that were "alcohol-defined" or "alcohol-coded," where the original data collection process established the data's connection with alcohol use. For example, our theoretical and empirical analyses presented below led us to use an alcohol mortality composite that included only "direct" or "explicit mention of alcohol" diagnoses, rather than all deaths that may be associated with alcohol use disorders. Besides wanting to develop an index that did not require inordinate efforts obtaining and cleaning a large number of marginal indicators, we reasoned that measures that were most closely related theoretically to the concept of interest would be most strongly correlated empirically with each other. We did not include risk factors (e.g., alcohol consumption rates) in the index. By limiting the content of the index, we sought to include only components with a high proportion of variance associated with the concept of interest, alcohol use disorders. If our strategy was successful, we would then be more likely to obtain empirical confirmation of the explicit theoretical links among these measures using data from only 50 States, and we would have a more manageable task interpreting our results and investigating data problems or devising appropriate adjustments if the empirical behavior of our index did not confirm theoretical expectations.

In construction of the index, we sought to minimize the danger that indicators would correlate spuriously with each other because they measured some other common concept (e.g., unhealthy lifestyles or socioeconomic status) rather than alcohol use disorders, and we sought to minimize the amount of methodological overlap among the indicators due to using the same data collection system (e.g., the indicators were not all based on mortality data). Consequently, we included only one measure (or composite measure) from each of these three types of data—mortality, arrests, and treatment utilization.

Population Age Structure

The optimal design of an indicator depends on the purpose for which it is to be used. Selection of the appropriate population base for statistical rates is important when measuring the severity of problems related to alcohol use disorders in a State. The indicators that we have used vary with regard to the segments of the population age structure that they cover. Population age structure has a major effect on the number of persons with alcohol use disorders in a State (National Institute on Alcohol Abuse and Alcoholism [NIAAA] 1994). Other things being equal, States with disproportionately large populations of elderly and children should naturally have relatively fewer persons needing alcohol treatment or persons who might be involved in accidents. The Block Grant alcohol need allocation index focuses entirely on this factor. The index eliminates the very young and the very old entirely, and it implicitly assumes that the State populations ages 25–64 years all have the same high risk of alcohol abuse. The NHSDA has described the alcohol dependence rates of persons 12 and older, and the National Longitudinal Alcohol Epidemiologic Survey (Grant et al. 1994) and the BRFSS have covered the population 18 and older. Social indicator studies we have reviewed varied in the population base that they selected (e.g., total population, persons 15–74, persons 20 and older). These differences may be justified by the goals of the different studies. For example, etiologic studies that primarily seek to investigate nondemographic causes of alcoholism among the at-risk population might want to control the effect of age structure on alcoholism rates (NIAAA 1994). However, a measure of the burden of alcoholism on society (e.g., morbidity, mortality, and the cost of services that include the very young and the elderly) would not want to eliminate the effects of a State's age structure. Accordingly, we used the total population as the denominator for the rates included in our API, and we did not use age-adjusted rates.

Reliability and Validity of Index Components

Constructing an API that would possess adequate validity included assessing both the reliability of the index's components and the reliability of the composite. Random errors can plague indicator data, and reliability sets an upper limit of validity (Nunnally 1978). We inspected the raw counts and rates of multiple years of each indicator to minimize random errors in individual variables. When there were values that appeared to be outliers (e.g., a State's rate for 1 year was 10 times smaller than the other 2 years), we called the State or Federal agency that collected or processed the data. Occasionally, we obtained corrected values and substituted them for the published values before assessing reliability of the data for that year. To obtain reliable measures of each indicator, we averaged together 3 years of data (1991–93) for every variable (see discussion of this approach by Wilson et al. 1983). To assess the reliability of the sum of 3 years of data for each variable (e.g., driving under the influence [DUI] arrests), we calculated Cronbach's alpha (1951).

We used *convergent validation* to assess whether the theoretically selected, empirically reliable variables reflected the same underlying concept (Campbell and Fiske 1959; Scherpenzeel and Saris 1997). Convergent validation involves correlating multiple measures of the same concept with each other. We also evaluated the *discriminant validity* of the indicators in a multitrait-multimethod (MTMM) matrix that included parallel measures of alcohol and other drugs (Campbell and Fiske 1959; Scherpenzeel and Saris 1997). Discriminant validity is evident in this context if the alcohol-related indicators correlate more highly with each other than with parallel other drug–related indicators. We also examined whether the correlations among alternative alcohol indicators might be due to "method effects" (e.g., two conceptually distinct mortality-based indicators might correlate with each other to some degree because they share biases built into the way in which mortality data were collected in different States). Although we designed our composite index to "average out" method effects by including just one measure based on as many different methods as possible, the success of this strategy depends on the amount of independence among the three different data collection approaches that we used.

Index Construction

We calculated the API by summing the variables' *z*-scores ($Z_1 + Z_2 + Z_3$). By converting the variables to *Z*-scores, we removed the influence of the variables' absolute magnitude and variance. To aid interpretation of the resulting API, we scaled the index so that the lowest value was 0 and the highest possible value was 100. We constructed the DPI using a parallel approach.

Validation of the API

To assess the validity of the resulting API scores, we used *construct validation.* Cronbach and Meehl (1967) developed construct validation for situations in which there is no gold standard against which a new measure could be compared. The composite API scores are validated by their empirical behavior in models of substantive hypotheses involving the concepts that the scores presumably reflect. Therefore, we examined the hypothesized relationships between the API scores and several sets of variables.

First, we tested relationship of the API to other "alcohol-defined" indicators: fetal alcohol syndrome and drinking by mothers as reported on birth certificates. Although statistics on fetal alcohol syndrome have the theoretical legitimacy that we desire, these measures clearly underestimate the magnitude of alcohol use disorders in a State. Nevertheless, they can be useful as indicators of relative differences among States if the downward bias due to underreporting is relatively constant across States. Most alcohol and other drug indicators have this feature. Because these data were available for only 41 States, they could not be used in the API. However, we assumed that the available data would be useful in our investigation of the construct validity of the API. It is important to bear in mind that when no widely accepted measure or gold standard exists, investigators developing a new measure must inevitably validate it by comparing their candidate for the gold standard with existing measures that are presumed to be inferior. In the logic of construct validation, the pattern and consistency of relationships in the nomological network of findings ultimately serve as the basis for judging the API's validity (Cronbach and Meehl 1967).

Next, we related the API scores with indicators of concepts that have been associated with alcohol use disorders and that come from data systems other than those incorporated in the API. We investigated the relationship between the API and the percentage of American Indians, Eskimos, and Aleuts in States. Several literature reviews and statistical studies as well as data from the Indian Health Service suggest that American Indians and Alaskan Natives have been at high risk of alcohol use disorders (Beauvais and LaBoueff 1985; Sugarman and Smith 1992; Arredondo et al. 1993; Hisnanick and Erickson 1993; Edwards et al. 1995). We also investigated the correlation between the API and motor vehicle fatalities in which the driver's blood alcohol concentration (BAC) was over 0.10. Most States use a blood alcohol level of 0.08 or 0.10 to define drunk driving. Repeated arrests for drunk driving are one of the criteria for alcohol abuse according to the DSM-IV criteria (American Psychiatric Association 1994), and studies have found that a substantial percentage of drunk drivers meet criteria for a variety of alcohol-related problems, including alcohol use disorders (Borges and Hansen 1993; Yu and Williford 1993; CDC

1994; Kennedy et al. 1996; Mancino et al. 1996; Duncan 1997; Myerholtz and Rosenberg 1997). It would be reasonable therefore to hypothesize that a valid indicator-based measure of variations in rates of alcohol use disorders would be statistically associated with those two statistical measures.

After assessing the construct validity of the indicator-based API, we compared it with three other approaches to assessing the severity of alcohol problems, namely, the BRFSS survey measures of alcohol use, the survey-based model alcohol dependence estimates developed by Folsom and colleagues (1996), and the Block Grant alcohol need allocation index.

Variable Data Sources

The sources for data analyzed in this chapter are described in the appendix.

RESULTS

Indicator Selection

We selected the rates per 100,000 of alcohol-coded mortality (deaths coded with at least one multiple cause from the list of diagnoses with an explicit mention of alcohol), UCR DUI arrests, and NDATUS alcohol-only treatment clients as the constituent indicators of the API. In part, we selected these measures because there were parallel measures that we could use to create the API's other drug counterpart, the DPI. Having two sets of parallel measures was highly useful from a methodological perspective. All three alcohol indicators met the theoretical criteria already described, were available for nearly all States, and had been validated to some extent in the literature. Evidence of the validity of one or more of these variables or related measures as indicators of alcohol use disorders has been described by Cleary (1979), Ford and Schmittdiel (1983), Wilson and colleagues (1983), and Beshai (1984).

We selected the NDATUS alcohol-only client measure instead of the NASADAD (National Association of State Alcohol and Drug Abuse Directors, Inc.) alcohol admissions statistics because the former counts individuals in treatment on a single day in both public and private facilities, whereas the latter counts annual admissions in only publicly funded facilities. Also, NASADAD data were missing for Oregon (1992), Washington (1991, 1992), and Wyoming (all 3 years).

From the available NDATUS statistics, we selected alcohol-only clients as our index component. NDATUS categorizes client statistics into three groups: alcohol-only clients (35 percent nationally), alcohol-and-drug clients (40 percent), and drug-only clients (25 percent). Inspection of NDATUS statistics revealed that Massachusetts, Texas, Hawaii, Louisiana, Oklahoma, and New Jersey were especially more likely to report alcohol-and-drug clients than alcohol-only clients. West Virginia, California, Arizona, New Mexico, South Carolina, and South Dakota were especially more likely to report alcohol-only clients rather than alcohol-and-drug clients. We were also well aware of the large number of persons who have both alcohol and other drug use disorders. These considerations suggested that we use the combined category of "alcohol-only-plus-alcohol-and-drug clients." However, we were concerned that coding of the alcohol-and-drug category was less reliable than the alcohol-only and drug-only categories. We felt confident that the clients in the alcohol-only category had an alcohol use disorder.

The relationships of other indicators with the alcohol-only client measure and the combined alcohol-only-plus-alcohol-and-drug client measure were mostly consistent with our rationale. Although the two treatment client measures correlated highly with each other (0.84), DUI arrest rates correlated more strongly with alcohol-only client rates (0.28, $p < 0.05$) than with the combined client rates (0.11). Alcohol-coded mortality rates also correlated more strongly (0.49, $p < 0.05$) with alcohol-only client rates than with the combined client group rates (0.34, $p < 0.05$). The NHSDA model estimates of past-year alcohol treatment correlated slightly less negatively with the alcohol-only client rates (–0.13) than with the combined rates (–0.17); neither was significant. Finally, in the only contradictory evidence, the NASADAD alcohol admissions rate correlated slightly but not significantly less with the alcohol-only client rate (0.34, $p < 0.05$) than with the combined treatment client rate (0.40, $p < 0.05$).

We decided that the alcohol-only client measure was preferable on theoretical and empirical grounds, and we reached a similar conclusion regarding use of the drug-only client measure for the DPI. We also felt that use of the alcohol-only client rates and the drug-only client rates as our treatment indicators would be more informative in our analysis of convergent and discriminant validity than would measures that included the same drug-and-alcohol client data (see table 2 and the discussion in the section Convergent and Discriminant Validity later in this chapter). We plan to combine all three NDATUS client categories in subsequent research that will attempt to merge the DPI and the API into a substance abuse index.

As our mortality indicator, we used a composite of cases having diagnoses with explicit mentions of alcohol as a cause of death rather than just cirrhosis or a much longer list that also included many "indirect" causes. We chose this direct cause or "explicit" mortality composite because we felt that it captures a sufficiently broad spectrum of cases, but is not too broad. Using selections of alcohol-related diagnoses and data described in NIAAA's *County Alcohol Problem Indicators* (1994, p. 4), we conducted methodological and empirical analyses of the two candidate measures: (1) total alcohol mortality that included "all alcohol-related causes of death" and (2) one of its three constituents, "causes of death with explicit mention of alcohol" (Explicit Mention for short). We decided in favor of the second measure.

Selection of the Explicit Mention measure was consistent with our preference for theoretically "pure" indicators even if they were not inclusive. In this instance, we were concerned that the other two components of the total mortality indicator were too inclusive. In particular, the "other alcohol-related diseases" (Other Diseases for short) component included deaths due to diabetes mellitus, essential hypertension, cerebrovascular disease, tuberculosis, pneumonia and influenza, and diseases of esophagus, stomach, and duodenum. According to the alcohol-attributable fractions (AAFs) presented in *County Alcohol Problem Indicators*, these deaths were due primarily to causes besides alcohol. Although the counts were weighted by the AAFs derived from the literature, the weights are constant over States. We were concerned that a composite of these deaths would primarily reflect general health rather than alcohol-related health effects. As a result, we hypothesized that the interstate variance of the Other Diseases component would not be strongly related to the State rate of alcohol use disorders. The third component, "other alcohol-related injuries or adverse effects" (Other Injuries for short) may suffer from the same shortcoming, although perhaps somewhat less so because the AAFs are generally higher. In the country as a whole and in every State, the number of deaths due to Other Disease and Other Injuries far outnumbered the number of Explicit Mention deaths. If these concerns were correct, the total mortality measure would not be useful for our purpose of estimating the relative prevalence of alcohol use disorders among States. It could be quite suitable for the purpose of estimating the total impact of alcohol use on health in the United States.

Analysis of data presented in Table 1 of *County Alcohol Problem Indicators* (p. 32) seemed to confirm our concerns. The Other Diseases rate correlated negatively (–0.22) with the Explicit Mentions rate and with the Other Injuries rate (–0.14). The Other Diseases component also correlated negatively with DUI arrest rates (–0.50, $p < 0.05$), NDATUS alcohol-only client rate (–0.17), and motor vehicle fatalities in which the BAC exceeded 0.10 (–0.23). Because the Other Injuries rate included all motor vehicle accidents, we were not surprised that it correlated strongly positively with the DUI and traffic fatality variables, but the Other Injuries rate had a low, negative correlation (–0.03) with the NDATUS alcohol-only treatment client rate. The Explicit Mentions variable correlated positively with all of these variables (0.23 with UCR, 0.48 with NDATUS alcohol clients, 0.18 with motor vehicle fatalities with BAC over 0.10, and 0.37, $p < 0.05$, with Other Injuries), except the Other Diseases measure. Age adjustments had little effect on these measures or relationships, except with the Other Diseases measure. These empirical results suggested that the Explicit Mentions mortality indicator was our best choice.

We selected the State DUI arrest rate from the available UCR alcohol-defined arrest statistics because DUI rates are associated with problem drinking and severe consequences of drinking, including motor vehicle accidents and fatalities (Borges and Hansen 1993; Yu and Williford 1993; CDC 1994; Kennedy et al. 1996;

Mancino et al. 1996; Duncan 1997; Myerholtz and Rosenberg 1997). The exact proportion of DUI offenders who have an alcohol use disorder is difficult to measure because of underreporting by arrestees and differences in diagnostic methods used in published studies (Chalmers et al. 1993; Lapham et al. 1995; Chang and Lapham 1996). Lapham and colleagues (1995) found that the rate of alcohol-related problems among drunk drivers varied depending on how one measured them. Using the Michigan Alcoholism Screening Test (MAST), these researchers placed 48 percent of male DUI offenders and 37 percent of female DUI offenders in the "alcoholic" category. The same study found that when substance abuse counselors assigned the offenders a DSM-III-R diagnosis (American Psychiatric Association 1987), 21 percent received a diagnosis of alcohol abuse and 19 percent received a diagnosis of alcohol dependence. We decided not to use arrests for drunkenness because several States do not have this category of arrest, and they record this offense as disorderly conduct or as a liquor law violation (Sterne et al. 1967; Royce 1981, p. 310). We did not use arrests for disorderly conduct in the API because disorderly conduct encompasses more than alcohol abuse problems, and we decided against using liquor law violations because violators include retailers and other individuals engaged in activities that may not necessarily reflect having an alcohol use disorder (e.g., bootlegging or furnishing liquor to a minor).

Descriptive Characteristics, Reliability, and Validity of Index Components

The descriptive characteristics of the selected measures indicate that all three were slightly skewed (table 1, p. 237). As expected, the correlations between 1991 and 1993 were slightly lower than the correlations among adjacent years. All three indicators were substantially reliable, with Cronbach's alphas exceeding 0.90. The reliability of the DUI data was calculated without using corrected or imputed values.

Convergent and Discriminant Validity

The correlations in the MTMM matrix are consistent with the assumption that the selected variables measure the underlying concept of alcohol use disorder prevalence (table 2, p. 238). The Pearson correlations among the alcohol variables were significant at the 0.05 level and 0.28 or higher, and the average Pearson intercorrelation among the alcohol variables was 0.41. The Spearman rank-order correlations were in the same direction, but two were slightly lower in magnitude. Two of three Spearman correlations were significant.

Significant "method effects" were found for only the treatment client data. That is, the rates of NDATUS alcohol-only clients correlated significantly (0.46) with the rates of NDATUS drug-only clients, even though clients with both drug and alcohol problems had been removed. The other two "method" correlations involving mortality rates and arrest rates were not significant. The remaining correlations in table 2 share neither the substance nor the method, and therefore they reflect the amount of overlap among the different methods and substances. The average of six Pearson cross-correlations between measures with both different methods and different substances (e.g., alcohol deaths with drug arrests) was –0.05. Two of the correlations were significant: NDATUS alcohol-only treatment client rates correlated with drug-coded mortality, while the DUI arrest rate correlated negatively with the NDATUS drug-only treatment client rate. The two parallel Spearman correlations were in the same direction, but only one of these correlations was significant (drug-only treatment client rate with DUI arrest rate).

The correlations in table 2 also suggest that the parallel alcohol and drug indicators measured somewhat distinct underlying concepts. Although the alcohol measures had lower average intercorrelations among themselves than the drug variables had among themselves (0.41 vs. 0.71), the alcohol variables correlated with each other and the drug variables correlated with each other substantially more than would be expected on the basis of overlap among the methods or substances. For example, alcohol-only client rates correlated 0.49 with alcohol-coded mortality rates. By comparison, alcohol-only client rates correlated 0.37 with drug-coded mortality, and alcohol-coded mortality rates correlated 0.03 with drug-only client rates.

Factor analysis of the three alcohol indicators resulted in similar weights on the first principal component (0.85 for alcohol-coded mortality rates, 0.75 for NDATUS alcohol-only client rates, and 0.73 for DUI arrest rates). The corrected item-total correlations with the API scores describe a similar set of relationships: 0.60 for alcohol-coded mortality rates, 0.45 for NDATUS alcohol-only client rates, and 0.43 for DUI arrest rates. The first principal component explained 61 percent of the variance in the indicators. As measured by Cronbach's alpha, the reliability of the unweighted three-item composite API was 0.68. (This value slightly overestimates the reliability of the index scores because the values for the DUI in 1 year for four States were estimated from the other years.)

Interstate Variations in the API Scores

As shown in table 3 (p. 239), there are substantial variations among the States' populations in the severity of alcohol problems. The variation across States in the alcohol-only client rate was greater than the DUI and alcohol-coded mortality rates. The coefficients of variation for alcohol-only client, mortality, and DUI arrest rates are 58, 32, and 36, respectively. The difference between the highest and lowest alcohol-only client rate was fifteenfold. There were fourfold differences between the highest and lowest rates for the other two indicators. When responding to alcohol problems, some States appeared to emphasize treatment (e.g., Rhode Island and New York), while others appeared to emphasize criminal justice (e.g., Texas and Idaho).

The geographic distribution of the API scores is presented in figure 1 (p. 241). The highest quartile API scores are found mainly in the West (Alaska, Washington,

Oregon, California, New Mexico, Wyoming, and Colorado) and the Southeast (North Carolina, South Carolina, and Kentucky). With the exception of Hawaii, Utah, and Texas, the States in the lowest API quartile are mostly scattered throughout the eastern half of the country.

Correlations With Variables Associated With Risk of Alcohol Use Disorders

To investigate the API's construct validity, we correlated it with a series of variables from other data systems that measure concepts theoretically associated with the rate of alcohol use disorders (table 4, p. 240). The API correlated significantly with data from birth certificates on fetal alcohol syndrome and drinking by mothers. There was an especially strong relationship between these measures and the alcohol-mortality component of the API (0.50 for fetal alcohol syndrome and 0.41 for mothers who reported drinking).

The construct validity of the API was also assessed by its correlations with theoretically relevant demographic and traffic safety data. The percentage of American Indians, Eskimos, and Aleuts in a State correlated significantly with the API. The API correlated significantly with rates obtained from the National Highway Traffic Safety Administration (NHTSA) on occupant and nonoccupant crash fatalities with BAC over 0.10.

Comparisons With Other Methods of Estimating Alcohol Use and Alcohol Use Disorders

We compared the indicator-based API to the BRFSS survey estimates of chronic alcohol use, the model-based estimates of State alcohol dependence developed by Folsom and colleagues (1996) and Folsom and Judkins (1997), and the Block Grant alcohol need allocation index per capita (table 5, p. 241). None of the correlations were statistically significant. The model estimates of alcohol dependence for 26 States developed by Folsom and colleagues (1996) correlated most strongly with our alcohol index, which is to be expected since their estimates included alcohol mortality and treatment client data from the same sources.

Inspection of the maps in figures 1–4 (pp. 241-243) reveals wide differences in the patterns of the State alcohol indicators. Although comparison of the patterns in figures 1 and 2 is made difficult by the amount of missing data in figure 2, the overlap measured by the correlation between the API and Folsom et al. measures appears to reflect agreement regarding the States that shared "high problem" status, such as Washington, California, and New Mexico. There are many minor differences in the relative rankings of States by those two measures, but the greatest differences involved Louisiana and Oklahoma. Texas, Kentucky, and Oregon also have substantially different rankings.

It is noteworthy that the 0.27 correlation between BRFSS survey estimates regarding chronic alcohol use and the Folsom et al. measure of alcohol dependence was much lower than the 0.85 correlation reported by Folsom et al. (1996) between the two surveys with regard to alcohol use in the last month. The largest differences between NHSDA's measure of dependence and the BRFSS chronic alcohol use measure involved Florida, Georgia, and Oklahoma (compare figures 2 and 3). The greatest differences between the API in figure 1 and the BRFSS estimates in figure 2 concern Hawaii, Florida, Texas, South Dakota, Pennsylvania, and Massachusetts.

The most pronounced differences in the four maps involve the Block Grant measure (figure 4). The Block Grant measure depicts the greatest needs for alcohol services occurring, with the exception of Hawaii and Alaska, entirely in the States of New England and the Middle Atlantic. The other measures point to the West as a region with a high level of need for alcohol treatment and prevention services.

SUMMARY AND CONCLUSIONS

We developed a three-variable, social indicator–based measure of problems related to rates of alcohol use disorders in States. This measure was designed to assess the burden of alcohol use disorders on the total State population. The API included only indicators (rates of alcohol-coded treatment utilization, deaths, and arrests) that were available for all States and were theoretically closely related to the concept of alcohol abuse and dependence (i.e., the rate of consequences of alcohol use disorders in the State). After cleaning the data obtained from official sources, we found that the component measures possessed substantial reliability, and there was modest evidence of convergent validity. It appeared that the relatively low correlation between treatment and arrest indicators reflected differences among States in how they chose to respond to the alcohol use disorders among their residents. Having both treatment and criminal justice indicators in the composite index may have allowed it to "average out" these idiosyncrasies.

The API was reliable and was validated to some degree by its correlations with other measures (fetal alcohol syndrome and heavy drinking by mothers) that were theoretically linked to alcohol use disorders but were excluded from the index because of lack of complete data. The API's validity was also investigated by its statistical association with distinctly different indicators that have been found to be related to the risk of alcohol use disorders (percentage of American Indians, Eskimos, and Aleuts; traffic accidents with BAC over 0.10).

Examination of the API and its components revealed that there are wide variations among the States in the rates of problems related to alcohol use disorders. Elsewhere (McAuliffe et al. 1999), we found that there was virtually no correlation (0.02) between the API and the parallel DPI based on the other-drug indicators in table 2. This finding is consistent with the lack of correlation between alcohol and drug mortality in table 2. Thus, the evidence suggests that State populations may vary substantially in both the rates of alcohol use disorders and the rates of other drug use disorders. Analyses that lump indicators of alcohol and other drugs together may therefore miss important differences among States.

Another finding was the lack of correlation between the major approaches to measuring the extent of alcohol problems: the population-at-risk Block Grant measure, the BRFSS survey estimates, the indicator-based API, and the Folsom et al. model that attempts to combine all three approaches. Either these measures focus on different aspects of alcohol use disorder prevalence (Wilson et al. 1983), or they measure something other than what we think they measure. We found similar results for measures of other drug use disorder variations (McAuliffe et al. 1999). This finding was surprising and underscores the scientific importance of conducting further small area research on the validity of alcohol epidemiologic methods.

These results also have practical implications for policy issues. Congress has debated how fiscal aspects of the Block Grant formula are computed (Substance Abuse Funding News 1997*c*), but we know of no plans to revisit the validity of the measure of alcohol treatment need. Our findings showed that the Block Grant allocations are not consistent with any of the other alcohol measures. Perhaps a broadening of the debate may be in order. The evidence we examined regarding the Folsom et al. estimates also suggests that the current program of expansion of the NHSDA and the plans to use the Folsom et al. modeling estimates for assessing State treatment needs in small areas (States and counties) should include a program of validation research.

ACKNOWLEDGMENTS

The authors wish to thank Robert Wilson, William Cartwright, and Mary Dufour for helpful comments on earlier versions of this chapter, and Tristan Robinson for her work preparing the manuscript.

APPENDIX

NDATUS Treatment Client Rates

NDATUS is administered by SAMHSA's Office of Applied Studies (1993, 1995*a*, 1995*b*). In the 3 years used in this chapter, the sampling frame included 12,303 specialty providers of alcohol and other drug treatment, including public and private freestanding units and units in multipurpose institutions. Identified mostly by State and Federal agencies, these providers report information about all active clients in treatment on a specific reference day in the previous year (September 30, 1991 and 1992, and October 1, 1993). Mailed questionnaires sent out on September 15 collect the data. The response rate was 93 percent in the 1993 survey (Office of Applied Studies 1995*b*).

NASADAD Alcohol Treatment Admission Rates

NASADAD reports treatment admissions data annually from State agencies (SAMHSA 1993; Butynski et al. 1994; Gustafson et al. 1995). This survey includes data from only those programs that received at least some funds administered by the State alcohol and other drug agency. The admissions statistics were derived by NASADAD analysts from the Client Data System (CDS), and State officials had an opportunity to review the statistics for accuracy prior to their publication by NASADAD. The NASADAD Alcohol Treatment Admissions Rate was reported as the number of admissions per 100,000 State residents.

Alcohol- and Drug-Defined Arrest Rates

The FBI's UCR system reports statistics on arrests for violations of State and local laws that are associated with alcohol, including DUI arrests, drunkenness, disorderly conduct, and liquor law violations (FBI 1994). The arrest statistics count only those cases in which the alcohol charge was the most serious (GAO 1990). Because the number of units within a State reporting to the UCR varies from year to year, the alcohol-related arrest rates were defined as these arrests per 100,000 State residents covered by the statistics for the year in question. When several apparent discrepancies were noted in the published UCR DUI data, we called the State offices handling the UCR statistics. Entries were corrected for three States. In one State (Delaware), all 3 years were corrected. In both 1991 and 1993, there were two States with missing data. Since they are different States, all four States reported data for at least 2 out of 3 years. Because there were high correlations among the years (see table 1), we used multiple regression analysis to estimate the four missing observations from the other 2 years.

The UCR also reports statistics on arrests for violations of State and local laws pertaining to possession, sale, growing, manufacturing, and making of narcotic drugs (FBI 1994). In both 1991 and 1993, two States had missing observations, although every State had data for at least 2 out of 3 years. As with the DUI arrests, we employed regression analysis to estimate the missing observations.

Alcohol- and Drug-Coded Mortality Rates

The National Center for Health Statistics (NCHS) of the CDC published the Multiple Cause-of-Death Files for 1991, 1992, and 1993 on CD-ROM (NCHS 1997*a*, 1997*b*, 1997*c*). Coded by State or NCHS nosologists from death certificates (Hopkins et al. 1989), each record contains multiple causes (up to 20) and demographic characteristics for each death. We identified all death records that included at least one alcohol-coded cause. We included only causes of death with explicit mention of alcohol according to the coding scheme used by NIAAA's (1994) *County Alcohol Problem Indicators*. The diagnoses (with ICD-9 codes listed in parentheses) include alcoholic psychoses (291), alcohol dependence syndrome (303), nondependent abuse of alcohol (305.0), alcoholic polyneuropathy (357.5), alcoholic cardiomyopathy (425.5), alcoholic gastritis (535.3), alcoholic fatty liver (571.0), acute alcoholic hepatitis (571.1), alcoholic cirrhosis of the liver (571.2), unspecified alcoholic liver damage (571.3), excess blood alcohol level (790.3), and accidental poisoning by ethyl alcohol (E860.0, E860.1). We counted only alcohol-related deaths for persons 12 or older to eliminate accidental deaths by persons who did not have an alcohol use disorder. The denominator of the alcohol mortality rate is based on the entire population.

We defined *drug-coded deaths* as including diagnoses of drug dependence, nondependent abuse, and accidental poisoning associated with drugs commonly leading to diagnoses of abuse or dependence (for specific diagnostic codes, see McAuliffe et al. 1999). The largest proportion of cases was due to poisoning. We counted only drug-coded deaths that occurred in persons ages 12–64 in an effort to eliminate accidental poisoning of children and elderly—groups that rarely if ever need drug treatment. However, the drug-coded mortality rate used the entire population in the denominator.

NHSDA Model Dependence Rate Estimates

Folsom and colleagues (1996; Folsom and Judkins 1997) reported model-based estimates of the percentage of residents in each of 26 States that were dependent on alcohol but not illicit drugs and received treatment in the past year for alcohol use disorders.

Population Size Estimates

The rates analyzed in this chapter are based on census estimates of the entire population for 1991, 1992, and 1993 (U.S. Bureau of the Census 1996).

BRFSS Chronic User Rates

We used data from 1991, 1992, and 1993 on "chronic use," which the CDC has defined as 60 or more drinks during the previous month (CDC unpublished report 1993; Siegel et al. 1993; CDC unpublished report 1994). In the years 1991 to 1993, four States (Arkansas, Kansas, Nevada, and Wyoming) lacked complete data, and therefore they were not included in the analyses in this chapter.

Fetal Alcohol Syndrome and Drinking During Pregnancy Rates

We obtained unpublished birth certificate data from NCHS. The number of birth certificates with fetal alcohol syndrome noted was available for 41 States in 1992. The number of birth certificates noting that the mother drank three or four drinks per week in 1992 was available for 47 States. The denominators of both of these measures were the total State populations.

Alcohol-Related Traffic Fatalities

Using data from the Fatal Accident Reporting System (FARS), NHTSA published State-level estimates of alcohol involvement in fatal crashes for 1993 (U.S. Department of Transportation 1993). NHTSA enhanced the FARS data on the BAC of drivers and nonoccupants by estimating missing blood alcohol levels. We used NHTSA's estimates of the number of drivers involved in fatal crashes with BAC of 0.10 or greater. We divided these statistics by the total State population to obtain the State's rate.

Block Grant Alcohol Need Allocation Index per Capita

The Block Grant allocation formula's alcohol need index is expressed as a proportion of the total Block Grant funds that should go to the State. The alcohol need allocation index equals the proportion of the national population ages 25–64 that resides in the State. For this chapter, we used 1992 population data, which is what we inferred that the Government used to calculate 1995 Block Grant allocations. The Block Grant allocations are based on the latest available data, which usually has several years of lag. We guessed therefore that the need measures that we used in this chapter would have been used for the 1995 allocation. We excluded the District of Columbia. To make this measure comparable to the other rate-based measures in this study, we multiplied each State's proportion by half of the current total Block Grant amount and divided the dollars by the size of the State's total population in 1995. Because these population estimates are periodically updated, there may be small differences between the population figures that we used and those used in the actual calculation of the Block Grant formula in 1995. Our index ignores adjustments for cost of living and State fiscal capacity that also determine the actual Block Grant allocations.

REFERENCES

American Psychiatric Association. *Diagnostic and Statistical Manual of Mental Disorders.* 3d ed., rev. Washington, DC: the Association, 1987.

American Psychiatric Association. *Diagnostic and Statistical Manual of Mental Disorders.* 4th ed. Washington, DC: the Association, 1994.

Arrendondo, R.; Streit, K.; Springer, N.; and Murray, C.K. Ethnic and cultural factors in substance abuse: Diagnosis, treatment, and prevention. *Adolescent Medicine: State of the Art Reviews* 4:263–276, 1993.

Beauvais, F., and LaBoueff, S. Drug and alcohol abuse intervention in American Indian communities. *International Journal of the Addictions* 20:139–171, 1985.

Beenstock, M. An indicator model of drug use in Israel. *Addiction* 90:425–433, 1995.

Beshai, N. Assessing needs of alcohol-related services: A social indicators approach. *Am J Drug Alcohol Abuse* 10:417–427, 1984.

Borges, N.J., and Hansen, S.L. Correlation between college students' driving offenses and their risks for alcohol problems. *J Am Coll Health* 42:79–81, 1993.

Bradstock, M.K.; Marks, J.S.; Forman, M.R.; Gentry, E.M.; Hogelin, G.C.; Binkin, N.J.; and Trowbridge, F.L. Drinking-driving and health lifestyle in the United States: Behavioral risk factors surveys. *J Stud Alcohol* 48:147–152, 1987.

Burnam, M.A.; Reuter, P.; Adams, J.; Palmer, A.; Model, K.; Rolph, J.; Heilbrunn, J.; Marshall, G.N.; McCaffrey, D.; Wenzel, S.L.; and Kessler, R. *Review and Evaluation of the Substance Abuse and Mental Health Services Block Grant Allotment Formula.* Santa Monica, CA: RAND Drug Policy Research Center, 1994.

Butynski, W.; Reda, J.L.; Bartosch, W.; McMullen, H.; Nelson, S.; Anderson,

R.L.; Ciaccio, M.; Sheehan, K.; Fitzgerald, C.; National Association of State Alcohol and Drug Abuse Directors (NASADAD); and SAMHSA. *State Resources and Services Related to Alcohol and Other Drug Problems: Fiscal Year 1992: An Analysis of State Alcohol and Drug Abuse Profile Data*. Rockville, MD: U.S. Department of Health and Human Services, 1994.

Cagle, L.T., and Banks, S.M. The validity of assessing mental health needs with social indicators. *Evaluation and Program Planning* 9:127–142, 1986.

Campbell, D.T., and Fiske, D.W. Convergent and discriminant validation by the multitrait-multimethod matrix. *Psychol Bull* 56:833–853, 1959.

Centers for Disease Control and Prevention (CDC). Alcohol and other drug use among high school students—United States, 1990. *MMWR Morb Mortal Wkly Rep* 40:776–777, 783–784, 1991.

Centers for Disease Control and Prevention (CDC). Drivers with repeat convictions or arrests for driving while impaired—United States. *MMWR Morb Mortal Wkly Rep* 43:759–761, 1994.

Centers for Disease Control and Prevention (CDC). Youth risk behavior surveillance—United States, 1993. *MMWR Morb Mortal Wkly Rep* 44:1–56, 1995.

Chalmers, D.; Olenick, N.L.; and Stein, W. Dispositional traits as risk in problem drinking. *J Subst Abuse* 5:401–410, 1993.

Chang, I., and Lapham, S.C. Validity of self-reported criminal offences and traffic violations in screening of driving-while-intoxicated offenders. *Alcohol Alcohol* 31:583–590, 1996.

Ciarlo, J.A.; Tweed, D.L.; Shern, D.L.; Kirkpatrick, L.A.; and Sachs-Ericsson, N. Validation of indirect methods to estimate need for mental health services. *Evaluation and Program Planning* 15:115–131, 1992.

Cleary, P.D. A standardized estimator of the prevalence of alcoholism based on mortality data. *J Stud Alcohol* 40:408–418, 1979.

Crider, R.A. Heroin incidence: A trend comparison between National Household Survey data and indicator data. In: Rouse, B.A.; Kozel, N.J.; and Richards, L.G., eds. *Self-Report Methods of Estimating Drug Use: Meeting Current Challenges to Validity*. Rockville, MD: National Institute on Drug Abuse, 1985. pp. 125–140.

Cronbach, L.J. Coefficient alpha and the internal structure of tests. *Psychometrika* 16:297–334, 1951.

Cronbach, L.J., and Meehl, P.E. Construct validity in psychological tests. In: Mehrens, W.A., and Ebel, R.L., eds. *Principles of Educational and Psychological Measurement*. Chicago: Rand McNally, 1967. pp. 243–270.

DeBakey, S.F.; Stinson, F.S.; Grant, B.F.; and Dufour, M.C. *Surveillance Report #41: Liver Cirrhosis Mortality in the United States, 1970-93*. Bethesda, MD: National Institute on Alcohol Abuse and Alcoholism, 1996.

DeFleur, L.B. Biasing influences on drug arrest records: Implications for deviance research. *American Sociological Review* 40:88–103, 1975.

DeWit, D.J., and Rush, B.R. Assessing the need for substance abuse services: A critical review of needs assessment models. *Evaluation and Program Planning* 19:41–64, 1996.

Duncan, D.F. Chronic drinking, binge drinking and drunk driving. *Psychol Rep* 80:681–682, 1997.

Edwards, R.W.; Thurman, P.J.; and Beauvais, F. Patterns of alcohol use among ethnic minority adolescent women. In: Galanter, M., ed. *Recent Developments in Alcoholism, Vol. 12: Women and Alcoholism.* New York: Plenum Press, 1995. pp. 369–386.

Federal Bureau of Investigation (FBI). *Uniform Crime Reports for the United States 1993.* Washington, DC: U.S. Department of Justice, 1994.

Flaherty, E.W.; Kotranski, L.; and Fox, E. A model for monitoring changes in drug use and treatment entry. *Prevention in Human Services* 2:89–108, 1983.

Folsom, R.E., and Judkins, D.R. *Substance Abuse in States and Metropolitan Areas: Model Based Estimates From the 1991-1993 NHSDA—Methodology Report.* Rockville, MD: U.S. Department of Health and Human Services, 1997.

Folsom, R.E.; Lessler, J.T.; Witt, M.B.; Gfroerer, J.C.; Wright, D.A.; Gustin, K.; Office of Applied Studies; and Substance Abuse and Mental Health Services Administration. *Substance Abuse in States and Metropolitan Areas: Model Based Estimates From the 1991-1993 National Household Surveys on Drug Abuse Summary Report.* Rockville, MD: U.S. Department of Health and Human Services, 1996.

Ford, W.E., and Schmittdiel, C.J. Predicting alcoholism services needs from a national treatment utilization survey. *International Journal of the Addictions* 18:1073–1084, 1983.

Frank, B.; Schmeidler, J.; Johnson, B.D.; and Lipton, D.S. Seeking truth in heroin indicators: The case of New York City. *Drug Alcohol Depend* 3:345–358, 1978.

Furst, C.J. Estimating alcoholic prevalence. In: Furst, C.J., ed. *Recent Developments in Alcoholism.* Vol. 1. New York: Plenum Press, 1983. pp. 269–284.

Furst, C.J.; Beckman, L.J.; and Nakamura, C.Y. Validity of synthetic estimates of problem-drinker prevalence. *Am J Public Health* 71:1016–1020, 1981.

Gast, J.; Caravella, T.; Sarvela, P.D.; and McDermott, R.J. Validation of the CDC's YRBBS alcohol questions. *Health Values* 19:38–43, 1995.

General Accounting Office (GAO). *Rural Drug Abuse: Prevalence, Relation to Crime, and Programs.* Washington, DC: GAO, 1990.

Gfroerer, J.C., and Brodsky, M.D. Estimation of drug abuse prevalence in California using the national household survey on drug abuse. Paper presented at the Sacramento Statistical Association Meetings, March 27, 1991.

Gustafson, J.S.; Reda, J.L.; McMullen, H.; DiCarlo, M.; Anderson, R.; Brooke, M.; Ciaccio, M.; Foley, L.; Gemma, D.; Nelson, S.; Sheehan, K.; and National Association of State Alcohol and Drug Abuse Directors

(NASADAD). *State Resources and Services Related to Alcohol and Other Drug Problems: Fiscal Year 1993: An Analysis of State Alcohol and Drug Abuse Profile Data*. Washington, DC: NASADAD, 1995.

Grant, B.F.; Peterson, A.; Dawson, D.S.; and Chou, S.P. *Source and Accuracy Statement for the National Longitudinal Alcohol Epidemiologic Survey*. Rockville, MD: National Institute on Alcohol Abuse and Alcoholism, 1994.

Hisnanick, J.J., and Erickson, P.M. Hospital resource utilization by American Indians/Alaska Natives for alcoholism and alcohol abuse. *Am J Drug Alcohol Abuse* 19:387–396, 1993.

Hopkins, D.D.; Grant-Worley, J.A.; and Bollinger, T.L. Survey of cause-of-death query criteria used by State vital statistics programs in the US and the efficacy of the criteria used by the Oregon Vital Statistics Program. *Am J Public Health* 79:570–574, 1989.

Kann, L.; Warren, C.W.; Harris, W.A.; Collins, J.L.; Williams, B.I.; Ross, J.G.; and Kolbe, L.J. Youth risk behavior surveillance—United States 1995. *MMWR Morb Mortal Wkly Rep Suppl* 45:1–85, 1996.

Keller, M., and Efron, V. The prevalence of alcoholism. *Q J Stud Alcohol* 16:619–644, 1955.

Kennedy, B.P.; Isaac, N.E.; and Graham, J.D. The role of heavy drinking in the risk of traffic fatalities. *Risk Anal* 16:565–569, 1996.

Kolbe, L.J.; Kann, L.; and Collins, J.L. Overview of the Youth Risk Behavior Surveillance System. *Public Health Rep* 108:2–10, 1993.

Lapham, S.C.; Skipper, B.J.; Owen, J.P.; Kleyboecker, K.; Teaf, D.; Thompson, B.; and Simpson, G. Alcohol abuse screening instruments: Normative test data collected from a first DWI offender screening program. *J Stud Alcohol* 56:51–59, 1995.

Lipscomb, W.R., and Sulka, E. Some factors affecting the geographic comparison of alcoholism prevalence rates: Implications for the use of the Jellinek estimation formula. *Q J Stud Alcohol* 22:588–596, 1961.

Liu, S.; Siegel, P.Z.; Brewer, R.D.; Mokdad, A.H.; Sleet, D.A.; and Serdula, M.K. Prevalence of alcohol-impaired driving: Results from a national self-reported survey of health behaviors. *JAMA* 277:122–125, 1997.

Mammo, A., and French, J.F. On the construction of a Relative Needs Assessment Scale. *Subst Use Misuse* 31:753–765, 1996.

Mancino, M.; Cunningham, M.R.; Davidson, P.; and Fulton, R.L. Identification of the motor vehicle accident victim who abuses alcohol: An opportunity to reduce trauma. *J Stud Alcohol* 57:652–658, 1996.

McAuliffe, W.E. 1984. A validation theory for quality assessment and other health care measurement. In: Pena, J.J.; Haffner, A.N.; Rosen, B.; and Light, D.W., eds. *Hospital Quality Assurance, Risk Management and Program Evaluation: Tools for Clinicians and Administrators*. Rockville, MD: Aspen Press, 1984. pp. 157–174.

McAuliffe, W.E.; LaBrie, R.A.; Lomuto, N.; Betjemann, R.; and Fournier, E. Measuring interstate variations in drug problems. *Drug Alcohol Depend* 53:125–145, 1999.

Myerholtz, L.E., and Rosenberg, H. Screening DUI offenders for alcohol problems: Psychometric assessment of the Substance Abuse Subtle Screening Inventory. *Psychology of Addictive Behaviors* 11:155–165, 1997.

National Center for Health Statistics (NCHS). *1991 Multiple Cause-of-Death File.* Hyattsville, MD: Centers for Disease Control and Prevention, NCHS, 1997*a*.

National Center for Health Statistics (NCHS). *1992 Multiple Cause-of-Death File.* Hyattsville, MD: Centers for Disease Control and Prevention, NCHS, 1997*b*.

National Center for Health Statistics (NCHS). *1993 Multiple Cause-of-Death File.* Hyattsville, MD: Centers for Disease Control and Prevention, NCHS, 1997*c*.

National Institute on Alcohol Abuse and Alcoholism (NIAAA). *U.S. Alcohol Epidemiologic Data Reference Manual Volume 3, Fourth Edition: County Alcohol Problem Indicators 1986–1990.* NIH Pub. No. 94–3747. Rockville, MD: NIAAA, 1994.

Nunnally, J.C., ed. *Psychometric Theory.* 2d ed. New York: McGraw-Hill, 1978.

Office of Applied Studies. *National Drug and Alcoholism Treatment Unit Survey (NDATUS): 1991 Main Finding Report.* Rockville, MD: US Department of Health and Human Services, 1993.

Office of Applied Studies. *Overview of the FY94 National Drug and Alcoholism Treatment Unit Survey (NDATUS): Data From 1993 and 1980–1993.* Rockville, MD: U.S. Department of Health and Human Services, 1995*a*.

Office of Applied Studies. *Overview of the National Drug and Alcoholism Treatment Unit Survey (NDATUS): 1992 and 1980–1992.* Rockville, MD: US Department of Health and Human Services, 1995*b*.

Pampalon, R.; Saucier, A.; Berthiaume, N.; Ferland, P.; Couture, R.; Caris, P.; Fortin, L.; Lacroix, D.; and Kirouac, R. The selection of needs indicators for regional resource allocation in the fields of health and social services in Quebec. *Soc Sci Med* 42:909–922, 1996.

Person, P.H., Jr.; Retka, R.L.; and Woodward, J.A. *A Method for Estimating Heroin Use Prevalence.* Rockville, MD: National Institute on Drug Abuse, 1977.

Pollock, D.A.; Holmgreen, P.; Lui, K.-J.; and Kirk, M.L. Discrepancies in the reported frequency of cocaine-related deaths, United States, 1983 through 1988. *JAMA* 266:2233–2237, 1991.

Royce, J.E. *Alcohol Problems and Alcoholism.* New York: The Free Press, 1981.

Scherpenzeel, A.C., and Saris, W.E. The validity and reliability of survey questions: A meta-analysis of MTMM studies. *Sociological Methods and Research* 25:341–383, 1997.

Schlesinger, M., and Dorwart, R.A. Institutional dynamics of drug treatment in the U.S.: City and State variation in need and treatment capacity. Paper presented at the 3d Annual Advisory Committee Meeting for the NIDA Center for Drug Abuse Services Research, Tyngsborough, MA, April 28–29, 1992.

Schlesinger, M.; Dorwart, R.A.; Epstein, S.; and Clark, R. *Need, Capacity, and*

Public Choice: Variations in Treatment for Drug Abuse Among the Largest American Cities. NIDA Treatment Services Research Monograph. Rockville, MD: National Institute on Drug Abuse, 1991.

Shai, D. Problems of accuracy in official drug-related statistics. *International Journal of the Addictions* 29:1801–1811, 1994.

Sherman, R.E.; Gillespie, S.; and Diaz, J.A. Use of social indicators in assessment of local community alcohol and other drug dependence treatment needs within Chicago. *Subst Use Misuse* 31:691–728, 1996.

Siegel, P.Z.; Waller, M.N.; Frazier, E.L.; Mariolis, P.; and State Coordinators for Behavioral Risk Factor Surveillance System. Behavioral Risk Factor Surveillance System: Summary of data for 1991. *MMWR Morb Mortal Wkly Rep* 42: 23–30, 1993.

Simeone, R.S.; Frank, B.; and Aryan, Z. Needs assessment in substance misuse: A comparison of approaches and case study. *International Journal of the Addictions* 28:767–792, 1993.

Smith, P.F.; Remington, P.L.; Williamson, D.F.; and Anda, R.F. A comparison of alcohol sales data with survey data on self-reported alcohol use in 21 States. *Am J Public Health* 80:309–312, 1990.

Stein, A.D.; Courval, J.M.; Lederman, R.I.; and Shea, S. Reproducibility of responses to telephone interviews: Demographic predictors of discordance in risk factor status. *Am J Epidemiol* 141:1097–1106, 1995.

Sterne, M.W.; Pittman, D.J.; and Coe, T. Teen-agers, drinking, and the law: A study of arrest trends for alcohol-related offenses. In: Pittman, D.J., ed. *Alcoholism.* New York: Harper & Row, 1967. pp. 55–66.

Substance Abuse and Mental Health Services Administration (SAMHSA). *Request for Proposal (RFP) No. 283-98-9008, 1999–2003 National Household Survey on Drug Abuse (NHSDA).* Rockville, MD: SAMHSA, 1997.

Substance Abuse and Mental Health Services Administration (SAMHSA). *State Resources and Services Related to Alcohol and Other Drug Abuse Problems, Fiscal Year 1991: An Analysis of State Alcohol and Drug Abuse Profile Data.* Rockville, MD: U.S. Department of Health and Human Services, 1993.

Substance Abuse Funding News. Changes in household survey would improve State estimates. *Substance Abuse Funding News,* 1997*a*, p. 9.

Substance Abuse Funding News. House and Senate funding levels for substance abuse-related programs. *Substance Abuse Funding News,* 1997*b*, p. 3.

Substance Abuse Funding News. Proposed change for Substance Abuse Block Grant redistributes $44 million: State directors upset they weren't notified, claim client is the real loser if funds are redirected. *Substance Abuse Funding News,* 1997*c*, pp. 1–2.

Sugarman, J.R., and Smith, E.M. Alcohol-related hospitalizations—Indian Health Service and tribal hospitals, United States, May 1992. *MMWR Morb Mortal Wkly Rep* 41:757–760, 1992.

Thompson, D.C.; Rivara, F.P.; Thompson, R.S.; Salzberg, P.M.; Wolf, M.E.; and Pearson, D.C. Use of behavioral risk factor surveys to predict alcohol-related motor vehicle events. *Am J Prev Med* 9:224–230, 1993.

U.S. Bureau of the Census, Population Division, Population Estimates Program. *ST-96-1 Estimates of the Populations of States: Annual Time Series, July 1, 1990 to July 1, 1996*. Washington, DC: U.S. Bureau of the Census, 1996.

U.S. Department of Transportation, National Highway Traffic Safety Administration (NHTSA). *Traffic Safety Facts 1993, State Alcohol Estimates.* Washington, DC: NHTSA, 1993.

Wilson, R., and Hearne, B.E. *The Feasibility of a Drug Abuse Treatment Profile System*. Washington, DC: U.S. Government Printing Office, 1985.

Wilson, R., and Hearne, B.E. An assessment of the state of the art in drug abuse and alcoholism treatment needs estimation methods. In: Einstein, S., ed. *Treating the Drug User: Selected Planning Models, Issues, Parameters, and Programs.* Danbury, CT: Sandoz Publications, 1986. pp. 186–221.

Wilson, R.A.; Malin, H.J.; and Lowman, C. Uses of mortality rates and mortality indexes in planning alcohol programs. *Alcohol Health Res World* 8:41–53, 1983.

Yu, J., and Williford, W.R. Problem drinking and high-risk drinking: An analysis of official and self-reported drinking-driving in New York State. *Addiction* 88:219–228, 1993.

Table 1. Indicator Variability and Reliability for 1991–93 Composite Variables.

Indicator	Min.	Med.	Mean	Max.	SD	$r_{91,92}$, $r_{92,93}$, $r_{91,93}$	Reliability of 3-Year Composite (Cronbach's Alpha)
NDATUS alcohol-only treatment clients/ 100,000	20	101	112	298	65	0.85, 0.85, 0.81	0.94
DUI arrests/ 100,000	243	649	685	1,366	253	0.89[a], 0.96, 0.85[a]	0.96[a]
Alcohol-coded mortality/ 100,000	7	13	14	28	5	0.96, 0.94, 0.91	0.98

Note: Min. = minimum; Med. = median; Max. = maximum; SD = standard deviation.
[a]To avoid overestimating reliability in these calculations, we did not use the four estimated values or Delaware's corrected values, and therefore the sample sizes varied slightly because of missing data.

Table 2. Multitrait-Multimethod Correlation Matrix of Alcohol and Drug Indicators.

Indicator	Alcohol-Only Treatment Client Rate	Alcohol-Coded Mortality Rate	DUI Arrest Rate	Drug-Only Treatment Client Rate	Drug-Coded Mortality Rate	Drug-Defined Arrest Rate
Alcohol-only treatment client rate	--	0.50*	0.21	0.37*	0.20	-0.11
Alcohol-coded mortality rate	**0.49***	--	0.41*	0.01	0.14	-0.20
DUI arrest rate	**0.28***	**0.47***	--	-0.28	-0.37*	-0.14
Drug-only treatment client rate	0.46*	0.03	-0.31*	--	0.85*	0.68*
Drug-coded mortality rate	0.37*	0.13	-0.26	**0.89***	--	0.55*
Drug-defined arrest rate	0.04	-0.17	-0.16	**0.63***	**0.60***	--

Note: The entries are Pearson product-moment correlations below the diagonal and Spearman rank-order correlations above the diagonal. Numbers in bold are convergent validities measured by Pearson correlations, and underlined Pearson correlations are between measures based on the same measurement methods. All rates are per 100,000 State residents.

*Significant beyond 0.05, two-tailed.

Table 3. API Scores and the Component Rates Per 100,000.

State	API	Alcohol-Only Treatment Client Rate	Alcohol-Coded Mortality Rate	DUI Arrest Rate
1. New Mexico	100	191	23.8	1,366
2. Colorado	97	265	23.7	1,013
3. California	82	298	17.4	867
4. Wyoming	81	217	17.7	1,152
5. Alaska	78	104	28.2	928
6. Oregon	75	226	20.0	837
7. North Carolina	72	114	21.2	1,146
8. Washington	63	177	15.8	974
9. South Dakota	62	117	20.0	958
10. South Carolina	59	187	20.5	580
11. Kentucky	50	135	11.8	1,054
12. Kansas	46	126	11.8	991
13. Montana	46	80	20.7	668
14. Maine	46	138	15.4	733
15. Michigan	44	174	14.6	601
16. Vermont	44	130	19.2	509
17. Arizona	43	119	15.0	766
18. Delaware	43	179	14.7	543
19. Nebraska	43	153	10.7	864
20. North Dakota	39	107	16.0	655
21. Idaho	36	70	10.6	1,034
22. West Virginia	36	140	15.3	492
23. Wisconsin	36	133	11.9	708
24. Georgia	34	49	13.2	925
25. Maryland	33	147	12.9	542
26. New York	33	190	14.9	247
27. Nevada	31	35	19.1	582
28. Mississippi	29	56	12.5	820
29. Tennessee	29	61	13.0	766
30. Missouri	27	59	13.7	701
31. Minnesota	27	39	15.8	656
32. Rhode Island	27	185	12.8	243
33. Virginia	23	97	10.5	632
34. Indiana	22	125	9.5	548
35. Arkansas	22	38	10.0	849
36. New Hampshire	22	41	13.5	642
37. Oklahoma	21	39	11.4	749
38. Illinois	21	91	13.6	421
39. Iowa	18	76	9.9	609
40. Connecticut	16	71	12.4	437
41. Ohio	16	92	10.7	450
42. Florida	14	77	13.2	344

Table 3. API Scores and the Component Rates Per 100,000. *continued*

State	API	Alcohol-Only Treatment Client Rate	Alcohol-Coded Mortality Rate	DUI Arrest Rate
43. Utah	12	99	7.8	495
44. Louisiana	11	61	11.2	440
45. Texas	10	28	9.6	619
46. Alabama	8	34	10.0	533
47. New Jersey	7	71	10.3	351
48. Pennsylvania	4	83	8.5	323
49. Massachusetts	1	42	9.7	364
50. Hawaii	0	20	7.4	540

Table 4. Correlations of the API With Alcohol-Associated Health, Consumption, Population, and Traffic Variables.

Indicator	Correlation With API
Fetal alcohol syndrome recorded on birth certificate/100 birth certificates	0.36*
Mothers who reported drinking 3–4 drinks per week on birth certificate/100 birth certificates	0.29*
% American Indian, Eskimo, and Aleut residents in a State	0.44*
Motor vehicle fatality rate with blood alcohol concentration over 0.10	0.30*

*$p < 0.05$.

Table 5. Correlations With Alternative Measures of Substance Abuse Severity.

Indexes	API	BRFSS	Folsom Alcohol Dependence	Block Grant Alcohol Need Allocation Index Per Capita
API ($n = 50$)	--			
BRFSS chronic alcohol use ($n = 46$)	-0.03	--		
Folsom alcohol dependence model estimates ($n = 26$)	0.29	0.27	--	
Block Grant alcohol need allocation index per capita ($n = 50$)	-0.07	0.26	-0.25	--

$^{*}p < 0.05$.

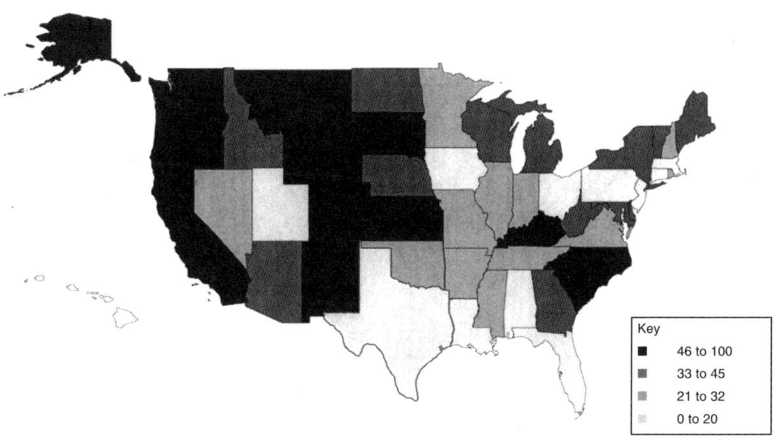

Figure 1. Alcohol Problem Index scores.

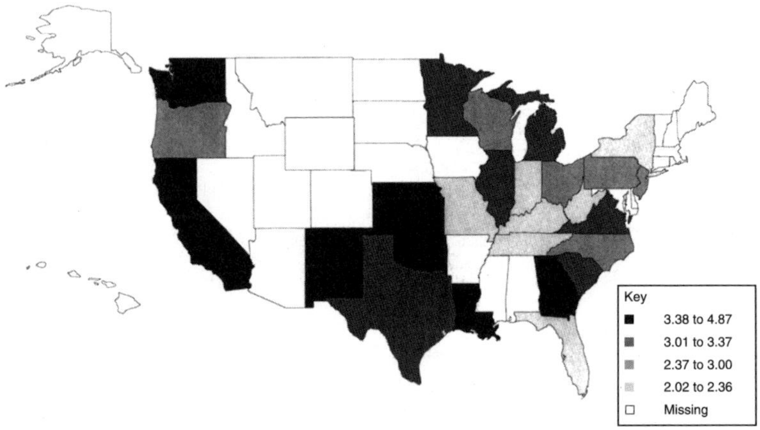

Figure 2. Model estimates of percent alcohol dependent. Reprinted from Folsom, R.E.; Lessler, J.T.; Witt, M.B.; Gfroerer, J.C.; Wright, D.A.; Gustin, K.; Office of Applied Studies; and Substance Abuse and Mental Health Services Administration. *Substance Abuse in States and Metropolitan Areas: Model Based Estimates From the 1991-1993 National Household Surveys on Drug Abuse Summary Report.* Rockville, MD: U.S. Department of Health and Human Services, 1996. p. 36 (exhibit 3.3).

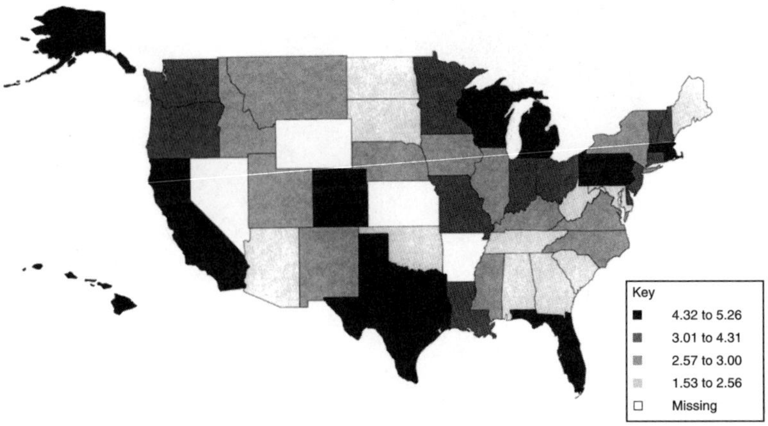

Figure 3. BRFSS chronic drinkers. Data from CDC 1993; Siegel et al. 1993; CDC 1994*a*.

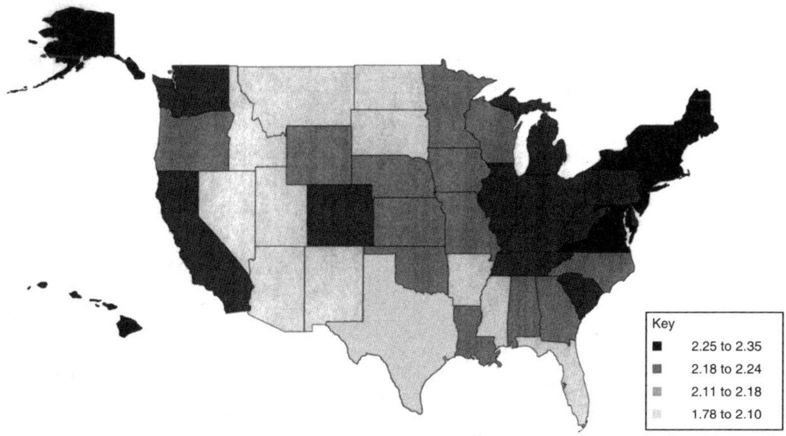

Figure 4. Block Grant alcohol need allocation index per capita.

Chapter 10

Small Area Estimates From a Geostatistical Perspective: Current Status and Future Directions

Paul J. Gruenewald, Ph.D.

KEY WORDS: geographical area; demography; prevalence; AOD consumption; urban area; rural area; statistical estimation; survey; validity (research methods); social indicators

National surveys of alcohol and other drug (AOD) use in the United States have provided invaluable data on the incidence and prevalence of AOD use and abuse across the Nation. Direct interview and telephone surveys conducted under the auspices of the National Institute on Drug Abuse and the National Institute on Alcohol Abuse and Alcoholism (NIAAA) are used to assess long-term trends in AOD use within the general population and to monitor the basic demographic correlates of AOD use and problems. Data from these surveys have provided answers to the fundamental epidemiologic questions: how many, how often, and how much. In regard to alcohol, the answers are as follows: some 65 percent of the general adult population report having consumed alcohol in the previous year (Midanik and Clark 1994 [National Alcohol Survey]; Substance Abuse and Mental Health Services Administration [SAMHSA] 1995 [National Household Survey on Drug Abuse]); some 40 to 44 percent of the population consumes alcohol 12 or more times per year (SAMHSA 1995; NIAAA 1998); and some 30 percent report consuming five or more drinks 12 or more times in the past year (NIAAA 1998). Approximately 4 percent of drinkers consume five or more drinks at least weekly (Midanik and Clark 1994). In regard to marijuana,

P.J. Gruenewald, Ph.D., is a senior research scientist at the Prevention Research Center, 2150 Shattuck Ave., Suite 900, Berkeley, CA 94704.

some 8 percent report having used this drug at least once in the previous year, and approximately 3 percent report using it weekly (SAMHSA 1995).

The many virtues of these national surveys are accompanied by one significant drawback. In the last two decades of the 20th century it has become increasingly clear that national statistics on AOD use and abuse do not represent the extent of local use observed by researchers. As greater interest has turned toward the elucidation of AOD use and problems in smaller and smaller geographic areas, the pertinence of national statistics to local prevention efforts has become increasingly unclear. Thus, the average national rate of alcohol use (65 percent) is realized in variations between neighborhoods within communities ranging from 39 percent to 97 percent (Gruenewald et al. 1996). The average rate of marijuana use (8 percent) is realized in local rates ranging from 1 percent to 41 percent within urban areas (LaScala et al. unpublished manuscript). Understandably, community-based prevention efforts sometimes labor against the dominance of national statistics. While statistically representative of the national rate of marijuana use, the global 8 percent national figure is biased relative to the locally unbiased estimate of 41 percent observed in some urban areas. The global 65 percent national figure for alcohol use is biased relative to the locally unbiased estimate of 97 percent observed in some community neighborhoods. Within some small geographic areas, the global estimates provided by national surveys will be, at best, irrelevant and, at worst, misleading.

ESTIMATES IN SMALL AREAS

The judgment as to what constitutes a "small area," of course, is relative to the statistic at hand. A national rate of marijuana use represents a national average suitable for setting national agendas with respect to this illicit substance. The national rate does not provide any additional information regarding use in other demographic strata (e.g., adults and youth) or among similar respondents in other geographic areas (e.g., States). State estimates are not representative of county rates, county estimates are not representative of community rates (depending on community size), and community estimates are not representative of neighborhood rates. In general, global estimates are not representative of local population values, particularly if local populations are heterogeneous with respect to characteristics relevant to AOD use. In broadly heterogeneous populations, rates of alcohol use may be very high (e.g., in areas where wealthy single white males reside) or quite low (e.g., in poorer areas of a community). Only in purely homogeneous populations (e.g., populations in which demographic characteristics are uniformly distributed with respect to geography) will global estimates represent local population values.

This rather obvious set of observations would be of little interest were it not for two central facts regarding the geographic distribution of AOD problems. First, large statistically stable variations in rates of AOD use and abuse are regularly observed across neighborhoods within communities. This suggests that there are strong demographic and environmental determinants of the geographic distribution of AOD problems within community settings. Second, effective interventions intended to reduce AOD use and abuse are typically local, *not* global. International interdiction efforts aside, the relevant scale of action for programs that attempt to reduce the demand for and supply of legal and illegal substances is typically the community and, in many cases, neighborhoods within communities (Tonry and Wilson 1990; Holder and Howard 1992; Davis et al. 1993; Gorman and Speer 1996). With good sense, statistical programs supportive of these community efforts should be similarly based. Ideally, data collection should take place at a geographic scale similar to that at which an intervention or treatment is applied.

The requirement that data collection take place at the same geographic scale at which a particular phenomenon takes place is, of course, at odds with the primary global goal of national surveys: the surveillance of AOD use and abuse at the national level. These instruments are *not* in place to inform local prevention and treatment efforts, but rather to help guide national priorities. Broader generalization of the results of these national surveys to local areas has, however, become a concern of the Federal agencies involved in these data collection efforts. Recognizing that States, counties, and communities are often the consumers of these data, Federal agencies involved in the collection, compilation, and distribution of statistical abstracts of the findings of national surveys have sought to generalize their results "downward" to "small areas." Thus, the development of sophisticated methods for providing local estimates within these small areas has been pursued by the National Center for Health Statistics, the Bureau of Economic Analysis, the Bureau of the Census, the Bureau of Labor Statistics, and the National Agricultural Statistics Service (Schaible 1996). These efforts, in combination with extensive work on "borrowed strength" methods developed by epidemiologists and statisticians (Purcell and Kish 1979; Elliot et al. 1992; Ghosh and Rao 1994), have provided statistical and methodological bases for estimating rates of AOD problems in small areas.

IMPUTATION IN SMALL AREAS

For all practical purposes, *small areas* can be defined as any set of demographic or geographic units logically or geographically nested within the sampling domain of a given survey. This somewhat peculiar definition reflects the two dimensions along which nesting generally takes place, demography and geography. Thus, relative to the sampling domain of a national survey, properly nested demographic subsamples of respondents—for example, ethnic groups within genders—represent a small demographic area of interest. Properly nested geographic subsamples of respondents—for example, city populations within States—represent a small geographic area of interest. Of course, the two approaches may be crossed to produce very small areas of interest—for example, ethnic groups within genders within cities within States. However, if the interest of the researcher is in obtaining national statistics, the calculation of small area statistics for these demographic and geographic subpopulations is of only secondary importance to the purposes of the survey. The sampling design for a national survey is typically oriented toward providing most efficient national estimates, not most efficient local estimates within small areas.

The point is best made clear using a hypothetical example. Imagine that a group of researchers wishes to implement a national survey of youth AOD problems. They want to use direct person-to-person interviews to assess these problems among a representative sample of youth in the United States. In order to develop a representative sample of youth, while minimizing the costs of survey implementation, they choose to apply a clustered sampling strategy. Thus, they interview clustered samples of youth obtained within randomly selected households within randomly selected counties within randomly selected States, with a view to correcting for cluster effects later in the analyses of these data. This complex sampling design is established to provide a representative sampling of youth which could be feasibly interviewed using direct survey research methods. Inferentially, the goal of the survey is to provide estimates of rates of AOD use among youthful residents of the United States. There is no intent to represent adult use (a group not logically nested within the target population), use among specific age groups (e.g., 12- to 14-year-olds, a logical demographic subgroup of the sample), or use among youthful populations within States (e.g., young people living in Montana). Although the results of the survey may provide some information on some of these demographic or geographic subgroups, it will not guarantee unbiased and efficient inference to these "small areas." Thus, for example, the 12- to 14-year-old subsample may or may not be representative of 12- to 14-year-olds in the United States, and the Montana sample of youth may or may not be representative of Montana youthful residents. Intended to support inferences to the U.S. youthful population, sampling errors in clustered sampling designs operate against attempts to generalize inferences to small areas.

The basic and quite familiar problem here is that the error variances of local estimates rise dramatically as smaller and smaller subgroups are examined. So, while the national estimates obtained from the hypothetical survey become less pertinent as the demographics of the local area depart from the demographics of the United States, the error variance increases in local estimates as smaller and smaller subgroups are defined. The sampling statistician's cure for this problem, sample stratification, will improve the efficiencies of statistics within cells (12- to 14-year-olds or youth from Montana) in proportion to the increase in sample sizes required by this quite different sampling design. Unfortunately, for any given sample size, sample stratification will increase the efficiency of local statistics (i.e., within small areas) at the expense of global statistics (i.e., across small areas). So one comes full circle. To obtain adequate sample within subgroups one must either stratify the sample to obtain the desired subgroup information (and reduce the efficiencies of national estimators) or increase sample size sufficiently to develop subgroups statistics and maintain the efficiencies of national estimators. The latter approach can be, for obvious reasons, a very expensive enterprise.

With these problems in mind, three solutions to the problem of generalizing the results from large U.S. surveys downward to smaller areas are generally given. The first, and most expensive, is to expand national surveys to cover major regions and States. In this case, sample sizes (and costs) will have to grow enormously to include even a majority of States. The second is to assume that the major compositional features of the survey (e.g., information on gender, ethnic group composition, and age) are adequate to provide indirect estimates for each State. Thus, estimates within States are corrected by accounting for differences in local demographic compositions. The third solution is to use a variety of social indicators (e.g., demographic and economic characteristics of areas) to impute local estimates from statistical models (usually regression models of one sort or another). As Schaible (1996) has pointed out, one is left contemplating either very expensive *direct* means or much less expensive *indirect* means for obtaining local estimates. Although direct estimators are, ultimately, the only statistically efficient means of obtaining estimates within States, the necessary expansion of national surveys is generally considered beyond economic reason.[1] This leaves researchers interested in developing small area estimates using statistically less efficient, but also substantially less expensive, methods for imputing estimates within small areas (so-called indirect estimators).

Figure 1 (p. 267) provides a conceptual outline of one formulation of the basic problem confronting imputation methods for small area statistics. On the left the figure shows that within any small area of interest (e.g., Montana youth) a direct estimator of any statistic (e.g., incidence of alcohol use) is available based on the direct local sample *n*. This statistic is defined to have an error variance of σ_d^2. On the right the figure shows that within the same small area of interest an indirect estimator may be constructed which uses additional information that may increase the efficiency of the local estimate. This information could include measures of the same variable in previous periods of time (temporal data), measures of the same variable in nearby geographic units (e.g., nearby similar States, spatial data), and auxiliary variables within the area which are known to be related to the incidence of alcohol use (e.g., area income). This new statistic is defined to have an error variance of σ_i^2. As the figure suggests, if $\sigma_i^2 < \sigma_d^2$, then the indirect estimator will be more efficient than the direct estimator and the goals of small area imputation will have been achieved.

In the jargon of the field, synthetic estimation procedures and social indicator models are the two methods of choice for the construction of more efficient local estimates from survey and archival data.[2] While not entirely distinct, and both subject to combination with direct survey data to provide more efficient small area statistics, the two procedures do rely on somewhat complementary data sources and estimation methods. Synthetic estimators rely upon a combination of available survey and archival data to provide small area estimates through imputations based on observed rates and proportions within demographic and geographic subgroups. Using the example from above, a U.S. survey of youth alcohol use could provide estimates of the incidence of alcohol use by gender and ethnic groups. Considering a small geographic area with its own unique gender and ethnic distribution (e.g., a predominantly white locale), local archival population figures could be used to weight and then sum separate survey-based gender and ethnic group incidences to obtain a locally unbiased estimate of the local incidence of alcohol use. So, if alcohol use was predominant among white populations, an area with a predominantly black population would have a lower incidence estimate. Referring to the schematic outline in figure 1, synthetic estimators rely upon auxiliary variables (usually demographics) to improve small area estimates.

Social indicator models may also rely upon a combination of survey and archival data to provide more efficient local estimates, but do so through the use of statistical models of the relationship of these data to the small area statistic of interest. The term "social indicators" comes from an extensive literature in the social sciences seeking to investigate the relationships between important population characteristics using commonly available archival data (see Gruenewald et al. 1997 for a brief review). For example, rates of unemployment within census tracts might be related to rates of housing starts (a macroeconomic measure of economic growth), State sales of alcohol might be related to religious affiliations (a macrosociological indicator of social integration), and so on. Theoretical considerations aside, the social indicators movement has provided a basis upon which to consider the value of archival indicators in the development of more precise local estimates for a variety of problems such as AOD abuse. Should survey estimates be available for an outcome of interest, and appropriate archival measures obtained from local, State, and national sources, a statistical model of the relationships between archival indicators and the problem outcome may be constructed and tested. The results of this modeling step may then be used to predict local levels of the outcome for areas in which little or no data are available, providing an imputation from available social indicators. Referring to the schematic outline in figure 1, social indicator models also rely upon auxiliary variables (again usually demographics) to improve small area estimates.

Within the contexts of these two basic techniques, available temporal and spatial data may be added to further increase the efficiencies of small area estimates. For example, the Bureau of Labor Statistics combines information on counties' histories of unemployment claims with data from the Census Bureau's Current Population Surveys using a "structural time series model" (Harvey 1989). The model helps determine the current rate of unemployment using prior census and unemployment data (Tiller et al. 1996). The National Agricultural Statistics Service uses a Battese-Fuller method to estimate crop acreage under cultivation within counties by combining information from farms within counties with satellite data available for analysis districts (unique geographic units smaller than counties but not necessarily concurrent with county boundaries) (Bellow et al. 1996). This procedure provides an "empirical best linear unbiased prediction" (Ghosh and Rao 1994) of local crop acreage under cultivation (equivalent to hierarchical Bayesian approaches), introducing spatial information in the form of geographically combined estimates within county areas. While the conceptual distinctions between these various statistical models are, at least to an outsider, technically arcane, the primary points to be made here are two: First, when additional temporal and spatial data are available, they may be used to increase the efficiencies of small area estimators. Second, the forms in which spatial data are integrated into these imputation methods presuppose, at best, a primitive hierarchical structure (nested geographic units). The strong possibility that information from adjacent spatial units may be used to inform local estimates has not been explicitly introduced or considered (see also Marshall 1991).

SPATIAL RELATIONSHIPS, ECOLOGICAL MODELS, AND SMALL AREA IMPUTATIONS

Social statistics are maintained by government bureaucracies for the purposes of social bookkeeping. Government agencies track particular social measures because of political exigencies (e.g., a population census for the allocation of Congressional seats), economic concerns (e.g., unemployment as an index of productivity), or public health interests (e.g., AIDS deaths as an index of progress in the combat of a fatal disease). They do not track these measures for the benefit of scientific interests. Thus, statistical programs in the United States have typically developed imputation techniques in the absence of the best current scientific knowledge regarding the social and economic processes underlying their subjects of interest. Unemployment rates are indexed to prior rates of unemployment and current population statistics, estimates of crops under cultivation are indexed to local farm surveys and satellite readings, and health characteristics are typically indexed to simple population demographics. Thus, as a comment to the development of imputation methods for the National Center for Health Statistics, Gonzalez and colleagues (1996) remarked that "the underlying rationale for synthetic estimation is that the distribution of a health characteristic is highly related to the demographic composition of the population" (p. 19). Simply put, it is assumed that the relationships of health outcomes to demographics are invariant over time and space and independent of ecological conditions. Considering the very long history of geographic epidemiology in public health models, this is a little like assuming that the incidence of cholera is independent of the temporal and spatial arrangements of sources of clean drinking water (English 1992). Fortunately, at least for residents of 19th century London, John Snow (1854) did not believe this to be the case.

As will be demonstrated in this chapter, unexplored spatial relationships among social indicators, survey estimates, population characteristics, and environmental conditions may be both a source of considerable bias in the statistical analysis of data from small areas and a source of considerable power to the imputation of small area estimates. Frequently unrecognized as a source of bias in the statistical analysis of small area rates, the spatial structure of geographic units and the spatial autocorrelation of data elements between geographic units are a substantive source of estimation bias. Unrecognized as a source of additional spatial information to contribute to the statistical imputation of small area rates, the spatial structure of geographic units and spatial autocorrelation of data between geographic units may be a further substantial source of information for improved estimation of statistics within small areas.

AN EXAMPLE FROM THE LITERATURE

Ciarlo and colleagues (1992) provided what is perhaps the most comprehensive study of synthetic estimation and social indicator models available in the literature on AOD problems. Applied to the imputation of alcohol, other drug abuse, and mental health (ADM) services in small areas, their models span the range of those typically applied by researchers to the problems of small area analysis. Their results also exhibit the most frequent outcomes of such analyses: improvements in the precision of small area estimators, the reduction of imputation methods to relatively simple empirical models, and the neglect of the ecological characteristics of the problems under study. Although the faults of these studies are common to all those in the field, their virtues are singular. It is very rare that any attempt is made to validate the multitude of synthetic and social indicator methods against one another using common data sources.

The primary sources for this discussion are Ciarlo and Tweed (1992), Ciarlo et al. (1992), Tweed and Ciarlo (1992), and Tweed et al. (1992); see these references for more detailed descriptions of the procedures discussed here. The primary goal of these studies, as noted above, was to validate indirect methods to estimate the need for ADM services within small areas. In this case the small areas were census tracts within States. A direct comparison of the performance of a suite of synthetic estimation and social indicator models was enabled by the simultaneous collection of both archival and survey data from 48 census tracts in the State of Colorado. These sources consisted of a large household probability sample of 4,800 adults age 18 and over (the direct survey measure), census data available from the tracts during a comparable period of time, and aggregate survey data from National Institute of Mental Health [NIMH] national household surveys (both the census data and the NIMH survey data were used to construct indirect estimators). Geocoded to the tract level, the survey data were used to estimate numbers of probable cases in need of ADM services by tracts. These numbers were then used to construct population rates for "diagnosable disorders" within tracts.[3] The study then compared the ability of the different imputation methods to predict these rates. It is important to note that the study provided an *internal* validation of the performance of the indirect estimation models against observed rates from the household survey. No external cross-validation of any imputation method was attempted.

Seven models were compared. These are summarized here to provide an overview of modeling strategies and allow the reader to see how each model relies upon available data sources to construct imputations:

1. *Flat rate model*: A natural point of departure for comparing estimators was the average rate of ADM disorders across all tracts. In principle, no estimator could perform worse than this, and comparisons to these baseline rates are essential to establish the worth of any imputation model.
2. *Synthetic estimation from NIMH rank-by-race model*: This synthetic estimator relies upon national household survey data to predict local rates of ADM disorders using combined census and survey information. Survey information provides rate estimates for aggregate demographic groups. Census information provides information on the distribution of demographic groups within census tracts. Combining the two sources of information provides an adjusted imputed rate for any area. This imputation relies upon a variety of measures, including percent males in low occupational statuses, percent population in poverty, and so on.
3. *Synthetic age-adjusted rates with social indicator modifications (A)*: This estimator starts by estimating local area rates from age distributions within areas (the synthetic step from national data) and then adjusts this estimate based upon standardized scores for six social indicators from census data (e.g., percent population in poverty).
4. *Synthetic age-adjusted rates with social indicator modifications (B)*: This estimator is, in essence, the same as the third model, but with an additional adjustment incorporated to reflect variances in measures across areas (e.g., "up-weighting" some estimates to reduce shrinkage to the mean, a common statistical problem in all imputation procedures).[4]

5. *Pure social indicator model (A)*: Five social indicators are used to estimate the local rates of ADM disorders using a ranking procedure (with probabilities of ADM disorders assigned to indicators based on previous research).
6. *Pure social indicator model (B)*: Survey rates of ADM disorders are regressed over two social indicators (percent households with only one person, percent separated or divorced males), with the obtained model coefficients used to estimate local rates.
7. *Synthetic estimation from individual-level predictors*: Distinct from the first model, an individual-level regression model is constructed estimating likelihood of ADM disorders from individual demographic characteristics (72 degrees of freedom worth). These individual expectations are summed over demographic groups within census tracts.

To cut to the chase here, three observations were made based on validation tests of these models. First, all the models that included additional information about each census tract (2 through 7) performed better than the flat rate model. Second, models 2 through 5 performed rather poorly, providing relatively "flat" rate estimates of ADM rates over census tract areas. Third, models 6 and 7 performed best, particularly when model 6 was "optimized" with respect to the local data (i.e., reestimated for the census tracts at hand) or when purely local estimates were used in the first place (model 7).

There is a degree to which these findings are not terribly surprising. The best performing models were those that relied on the most local information (6 and 7). The worst models were those that relied on imputation techniques based on data collected outside the areas of study. Although the synthetic estimates from models 2 and 3 reflected local rates better than the flat rate model, their reliance on national data to synthesize local rates inadvertently weighted the estimates toward characteristics exhibited by populations largely outside of the target area (e.g., urban populations living in New York and California). Generalization of synthetic estimators across disparate geographic units is difficult when the units depart so widely in environmental and population characteristics. As shown by the studies of Ciarlo and colleagues, the same point is true for social indicator models. The best social indicator model, by their criterion, was that "optimized" with respect to local data. Clearly, reliance on local information is best, when it is available. The question for the current chapter is whether these estimation procedures, even under the best of conditions, are obtaining "best" imputations of local area ADM disorder rates. The answer is "no."

WEAK AND STRONG ECOLOGIES AND THE NEGLECT OF SPACE

The reasons why these estimation procedures are not obtaining best imputations are, first, that they are only weakly ecological and, second, that they do not take into account the spatial characteristics of ecological processes. Considering these matters brings us to the heart of the problem with current studies of imputation techniques for small areas. It also takes us to the frontiers of the next wave of ecological and geostatistical models for small area analysis.

The first consideration is not a trivial one. The history of "ecological" studies in alcohol research, for instance, is replete with confusions of the merely "environmental" with the truly ecological. At best, these studies include occasional measures of environmental characteristics (e.g., outlet densities) which are exogenous to the persons under study (e.g., populations of communities) and reasonably affect some of the conditions of alcohol use. At worst, they represent a recycling of individual-level characteristics in aggregate disguise. This would be the case, for example, when census tract measures of unemployment are related to individual measures of alcohol use in community settings. In the former case, a first step is taken toward the ecological (the theory, measurement, and description of organism-environment interactions) with the inclusion of environmental measures in the analysis of individual data. In the latter case, unless there is an explicit ecological theory of how the unemployment of others affects an individual's alcohol use, any statistical relationship between the two variables may as well represent individual-level effects (with the attendant statistical problems which arise from using aggregate-level data as a surrogate for individual measures, aggregation bias).[5] It is an unfortunate observation for the field that the vast majority of so-called ecological studies are of the latter type.[6] In this sense, then, the data and theory underlying the imputation methods of Ciarlo and colleagues are only weakly ecological. Strongly ecological models require theoretical definition of relevant organism-environment interactions and some consideration of "space," the geographic distribution of individuals and environments.

The second consideration, which bears upon the first and expands upon it, addresses what is "spatial" about ecological studies. Noting that the truly ecological is the study of organism-environment interactions, the first data element researchers need is some measure of an environmental characteristic that is theoretically related to the outcome of interest. It is an important observation that whatever environmental characteristic comes under consideration by the researcher will be a "spatial" one: a characteristic of the environment exogenous to individuals in the environment and having some location in space and time. Thus, the spatial enters the ecological and is central to ecological theorizing of all sorts. From a statistician's point of view, organism-environment interactions take place in spatial fields, places where the geography of relationships between measured variables matters and the independence of locally measured variables is suspect.

A somewhat naive, but effective, example of how ecological models invariably imply spatial relationships is given in a study of the relationships between the physical availability of alcohol (from bars, restaurants, and other outlets) and alcohol-related motor vehicle crashes (Gruenewald et al. 1996). In this study it was assumed that alcohol-related crash rates would be related to use of alcohol at bars and restaurants: individual drinkers would drive to a bar or restaurant, consume some alcohol, get back into a car, and drive home. Greater availability of alcohol through more bars and restaurants would imply greater use of these outlets by drinkers, greater numbers of drinkers on the road originating from these outlets, and greater likelihood of alcohol-related crashes in and around the areas of bars and restaurants. Thus, the underlying ecological theory for alcohol-related crashes was expected to produce a specific geographic signature: crashes were expected to appear in a geographic pattern around outlets, with more crashes near and fewer crashes further away from the outlets. Similar geographic signatures are characteristic of all strong ecological theories, and, in fact, theoretical prediction and empirical testing of these geographic signatures are central activities of ecological research.

Be that as it may, there is still a very great distance between the formulation and testing of such theories in AOD studies and their application to small area imputation. Since in the current state of affairs most theoretical enterprises in these fields bear little upon ecological issues, it is not surprising that the work of Ciarlo and colleagues is uninformed by any ecological point of view. This is also likely the primary reason for the lack of theoretical underpinnings to statisticians' efforts to develop small area imputations. Ecological theory in AOD studies is insufficiently developed, and this insufficiency leads to the neglect of spatial issues.

The Problem and the Solutions

The basic theoretical problem for studies of small areas of any size is the construction of feasible ecological models of variable interactions within and between areas of study. In the example presented above, the variable of interest was alcohol-related traffic crashes and the relevant questions to be asked were as follows:

1. What are the social, economic and physical processes that lead to these events?
2. How are these processes bound to the spatial arrangements of relevant social activities, economic factors, and physical conditions that enable these events?
3. How do the spatial arrangements of the factors producing the outcome act to focus the distribution of the events in time and space?
4. Given any arbitrary distribution of the factors producing the event, what is the expected distribution of events in time and space?

Each of these questions could be answered relatively easily for alcohol-related crashes:

1. The social, economic, and physical processes underlying crashes are well known. Drinking takes place alone or in social groups whose activities are concentrated about the locations of bars and restaurants, at home, or

at the homes of friends or relatives. Economic sources of alcohol are on- and off-premise outlets. The former provides a venue for social drinking. The physical constraints on driving are obvious. The roadway system enables vehicular use.

2. Each of these processes is geographically bound in obvious ways. Locations of drinking are distributed in either residential areas (e.g., own or other's homes) or in commercial areas near residences (e.g., downtown areas with retail outlets). Economic factors provide distribution networks for alcohol that minimize geographic distances between outlets and residential locations while at the same time preserving competitive advantage. Therefore, outlets will be near, but not in, residential areas. The geographic structure of the roadway system enables travel to and from alcohol outlets.
3. The temporal characteristics of alcohol-related crashes are well known. Alcohol is most involved in crashes involving a single vehicle late in the evening hours. The spatial characteristics of these crashes can easily be inferred from answers 1 and 2. Crashes will appear on the roadway system near places where consumers drink, such as on-premise outlets and own and other's homes. The geographic distribution of these crashes will radiate away from places where people drink.
4. Given a map of the roadway system, locations of on-premise drinking places, and locations of single-vehicle crashes that take place late in the evening hours, crashes will be predictably distributed along the roadway system.

The answers to these questions naturally lead to tests of the relationships between the event of interest (e.g., alcohol-related crashes) and the ecological structure of the factors that go into producing the event (e.g., locations of on-premise outlets). Answers to these questions also lead to the explicit delimitation of the geographic distribution of variables relevant to the maximization of the performance of any imputation model. Again referring to the example, it was expected that crash rates would be high near on-premise outlets, but also high in adjacent areas away from outlets, effecting a positive relationship between crash rates across adjacent geographic areas. If one were to correlate crash rates between areas, one should find that high and low rate areas cluster together.

The basic empirical problem for studies of small areas of any size is that these theoretical considerations lead us to suspect that observations in adjacent or nearby units are not independent of one another. This is the problem of spatial autocorrelation, the tendency of data from one area to be systematically related to that from adjacent areas. The failure of an observation in one place to be independent of that in another undermines the application of classical statistical models to data from geographic areas. As we shall see, these autocorrelations are also a source of information to be capitalized upon in making small area imputations; if adjacent units are not independent, then knowledge of the value of a variable in one area can be used to impute something about the value in another.

To provide a feel for the nature of the problem, figure 2 (p. 268) presents an example of positive and negative spatially autocorrelated observations. To the left side of the figure are two contour plots of Gaussian random data generated over a 25 x 25 cell matrix (A and C). The plots are identical representations of a map of 625 rectangularly arrayed geographic units. The average value of the random variable across these units is scaled at 100, with a standard deviation of 10. Since each variable value for each unit is drawn independently (at random), the spatial autocorrelation between units is, on average, zero. In plot B of figure 2, these data have been transformed under the assumption that each area is positively spatially autocorrelated with each adjacent area (spatial autocorrelation of 0.4). Note that the map has achieved a somewhat smooth appearance, with adjacent areas tending to have similar values for the otherwise random measure. In plot D of figure 2, the same random data have been transformed under the assumption that each area is negatively spatially autocorrelated with each adjacent area (spatial autocorrelation of –0.4). Note that the map has achieved a somewhat spiked appearance, with adjacent areas tending to have dissimilar values. These are the typical visual characteristics of the geographic distributions of positively and negatively autocorrelated spatial variables.

Considering the maps in figure 2 from the perspective of one interested in small area imputations, the importance of spatial autocorrelation should be clear. If one knows that data are positively spatially autocorrelated across a map, then one knows that the value of a variable in one area will resemble that in adjacent areas (implying a sort of spatial average). If one knows that data are negatively spatially autocorrelated across a map, then one knows that the value of a variable in one area will resemble the inverse of that in adjacent areas (implying a sort of spatial difference). Regardless of the form of spatial autocorrelation, knowing the value of a variable in one area will help to ascertain the value of the variable in an adjacent area, and this information can contribute substantively to the imputation of the value of a variable in small areas.

When using a social indicator model to form the basis for imputation, substantive biases will arise in the regression model used to initially analyze spatially autocorrelated data. Regression models applied to the analysis of positively autocorrelated data will produce Type I errors (i.e., smaller apparent p values). Regression models applied to the analysis of negatively autocorrelated data will produce Type II errors (i.e., greater apparent p values). In each case, greater or lesser numbers of indicators may be included in the ultimate social indicator model used to form imputations. Premised upon the independence of spatial units, imputations from these models will themselves suffer from some degree of misspecification bias: the failure to include appropriate variables in the indicator model, or the inclusion of inappropriate variables in the indicator model.[7]

The geostatistical estimation of spatial autocorrelation and the construction of regression models that take this feature of small area analysis into account are not the province of this chapter. For current purposes it suffices to recognize the theoretical underpinnings of the problem and the empirical ramifications of spatial autocorrelation. The reader will find an excellent introduction to this issue in Griffith (1987), advanced discussions in Griffith (1988) and Anselin (1988), and additional content-oriented introductions in biological ecology from Sokol and Oden (1978) and in epidemiology from Marshall (1991) and Richardson (1992).

WHEN A "CORRELATION" IS NOT A TRUE CORRELATION

The province of this chapter is the illumination, with examples, of how small area imputation methods go awry. Noting the ambiguity in the term "small area" discussed above, these areas may be States (a unit economists are fond of because alcohol taxes are generally levied at this level), counties (a unit popular with State alcohol and drug control and problem prevention agencies), communities (the region at which most prevention activities take place), and neighborhoods (the areas in which most of us live). All regression analyses of these units are subject to the same problem, and all analyses of data from these units require the same diagnostic assessments. The risk of Type I or Type II errors in these analyses is far too great to go without a diagnostic assessment of spatial autocorrelation. The example I would like to put forward here is that of a simple spatial correlation and regression. One measures a dependent measure, such as rates of abstention from alcohol, over a set of geographic units and wishes to relate this measure statistically to exogenous measures presumed to affect these rates. Although weakly ecological (in the sense defined above), the example will demonstrate the degree to which researchers may get into trouble by assuming that the observed units are independent.

Table 1 (p. 270) presents a set of spatial autocorrelations exhibited by 13 measures taken from 144 geographic units arrayed across six communities in the United States. These data were collected as part of a large-scale community alcohol prevention project (Holder et al. 1997). The name of each measure is followed by a statistic representing the form and degree of spatial autocorrelation (the Moran coefficient [MC]), followed by this statistic's z-test and p value. The MC generally runs between –1 and +1, like the Pearson product-moment correlation coefficient, and indicates the degree to which data from any given target unit resembles data from its surrounding units. Thus, percent income ≥ 60K is strongly positively correlated, with MC = 0.429, $z = 3.716$, and $p < 0.001$. High-income residences tend to cluster together geographically. Another measure, percent male, exhibits virtually no spatial autocorrelation (MC = 0.006, $z = 0.113$, $p = 0.455$). Number of children per household less than 18 exhibits some slight negative autocorrelation (MC = –0.068, $z = -0.523$, $p = 0.301$). We wish to relate these measures to the measure of percent abstainers estimated in each geographic unit. This measure itself is spatially autocorrelated, with MC = 0.254, $z = 2.222$, and $p = 0.013$.

Figure 3 (p. 269) presents a plot of observed Pearson product-moment correlations between the variables in table 1 with the percent abstainers from alcohol, a simple spatial correlation. Each correlation is plotted over each measure's estimated level of spatial autocorrelation (represented by the MC from table 1). As the graph makes clear, the observed bivariate Pearson product-moment correlation coefficient generally increases as a function of the degree of spatial autocorrelation in the independent measures. In this case, assuming independence (an almost nonsensical assumption at this point), the correlation of correlations is "significant." Regardless of one's interpretation of the rise in observed spatial correlations as a function of the spatial autocorrelation of component measures, this observation can be repeated with both empirically obtained and randomly generated measures (Haining 1991). As Haining's work makes clear, spatial autocorrelation will strongly bias simple spatial correlations and, without correction, will seriously mislead the unwary researcher. To leave spatial autocorrelations undiagnosed and unaccounted for is to leave one's research without a window onto a central problem in analysis of data from small areas.

SPATIAL REGRESSION AND IMPUTATION: AN EXAMPLE

Problems similar to this also occur, of course, in the context of regression models using spatially autocorrelated dependent and independent measures. There is no classical linear regression model that will overcome these problems. Rather, what is required is a spatial regression model in which spatial autocorrelation is taken into account. By statistically controlling for spatial autocorrelation in the dependent measure, and effectively making it numerically zero, biases due to spatial autocorrelations in the independent measures are also removed (see Haining 1991). Spatial regression models of this sort are discussed by Griffith (1988) and Anselin (1988).

Not only do spatial regression models take into account statistical biases arising through spatial autocorrelations, they also allow the user to consider the spatial effects of independent measures on dependent measures—effects that sometimes account for much of the spatial autocorrelation in dependent measures. For example, as Gruenewald and colleagues (1996) were able to show, there is a lagged effect of outlet densities on alcohol-related crashes. That is, high-outlet-density areas are associated with locally high alcohol-related crash rates *and* with elevated crash rates in surrounding areas (the spatially lagged effect). In their data, the spatial lag effect of outlet densities on crash rates largely accounts for the positive spatial autocorrelations observed in alcohol-related crash rates across neighborhood areas.[8] Thus, examining the effects of independent measures taken in surrounding areas is often very informative to the evaluation of an outcome in a given target area. In this way, well-formulated spatial regression models enable the user to separate unit intrinsic effects, those relating independent to dependent measures within units, from extrinsic spatial lag effects, those relating independent measures outside each target unit to dependent measures within units, and to statistically control for sources of spatial autocorrelated error. These analytic techniques thus form a powerful adjunct to small area analysis and imputation.

Table 2 (p. 270) outlines the results of a spatial regression model applied to estimating rates of abstention over neighborhood areas using the same data shown in table 1. This time the model is a standard linear regression model corrected for the observed level of spatial autocorrelation (spatial autocorrelated error equal to 0.300). The model is the second of two steps of analysis, the first using all the independent measures from table 1. Here only the significant ($p < 0.05$) variables from the initial model are retained. Importantly, a large number of weakly environmental measures are significantly related to rates of abstention. These include neighborhood incomes, average age of the local population, education, marital status, and ethnic composition of the neighborhoods.

Going a bit further, table 2 also presents the first-order spatial lagged effects of independent measures upon the percent of abstainers observed in each geographic unit. Here we see that the percent unemployment of surrounding areas depresses the rate of abstention in target areas. The number of children per household less than 18 in surrounding areas increases the rate of abstention in target areas. Note that both of these effects were obtained controlling for the direct local effects of unemployment and household composition. These results suggest some normative effects of surrounding area influences on drinking on local abstention rates. Regardless of interpretation, the analysis also shows that it is possible to obtain significant spatial lagged effects in the context of a model with significant residual spatial autocorrelated error.

The implications of the results of a model such as this should be obvious. Presume that we had as our suite of social indicator variables the measures presented in table 2 and that we wished to impute the level of abstention from alcohol for all areas in the United States. The regression model we would use for evaluating the relationships between the social indicators and our measure of abstention (where available) should include explicit controls for spatial autocorrelated error *and* include spatially lagged independent measures (in the best case where theoretically appropriate). The results of the modeling step would, at the least, provide unbiased tests of effects. It would also, however, provide a locally efficient model with which one could impute local area estimates for rates of abstention.

As the analysis presented in table 2 suggests, there are both significant unit intrinsic and spatial lag effects relating the exogenous measure to rates of abstention within geographic units. In addition, the analysis demonstrates that errors in these estimates are positively spatial autocorrelated. That is, an underestimate of a value in area A will be accompanied by an underestimate (by an estimable amount) of the value for adjacent area B. Thus, the full imputation model should include both unit intrinsic and spatially lagged independent measures and some adjustment for spatial autocorrelated errors. For example, if an estimate for area A was low, the estimate for imputed adjacent area B should be raised. If an estimate for area A was high, the estimate for imputed adjacent area B should be lowered. The most efficient geographically local estimation procedure will take into account (1) unit intrinsic effects, (2) spatially lagged effects, and (3) corrections for spatial autocorrelated errors.

FUTURE PROSPECTS: AREAL ANALYSIS AND POINT PROCESSES

The efficiency potentially gained by application of these procedures to social indicator data remains to be demonstrated. These procedures will constitute much of the next wave of studies as the geostatistical analysis of small area data grows in sophistication. Looking to the future, three areas of growth seem quite likely from the current perspective: advances in geostatistical sampling theory applied to small area analysis, the introduction of point process models into the analysis of data from small areas, and the application of advanced techniques for the efficient evaluation of spatial autocorrelation. Each of these deserves some final comment.

This chapter, and virtually every social indicator and synthetic estimation model, has assumed that the data on which analyses and imputations are based are fixed to particular geographic units. Indeed, given the retrospective nature of much social indicator and survey data, measuring behavior and demographic characteristics at some time in the past, the data are fixed. Data elements are sampled from fixed entities (e.g., stratified geographic units within States), demographic characteristics characterize populations in fixed census tracts, and measures taken are fixed by the empirical agendas of parent agencies (e.g., drug usage by youth or adults, population counts). It is, however, possible to take a prospective view of these matters and consider issues regarding efficient geographic sampling of data up front. That is, before a round of surveying is conducted, ask the questions, Do we wish to have efficient global estimates of effects? and Do we wish to have efficient local estimates of effects? An affirmative answer to the former question would lead one to the standard survey designs currently in the field. An affirmative answer to the latter question would lead one to locally efficient geostatistical sampling strategies. These nonstandard approaches to geographic sampling provide means for maximizing the efficiency of local estimates of unit intrinsic effects (e.g., levels of effluent observed in soil samples) and provide methods for efficient sampling in the context of autocorrelated measures (e.g., examining the downstream effects of effluents). Extensively studied in the context of soil sampling (Webster and Oliver 1990), these more efficient local sampling methods could also enable researchers to efficiently assess the local characteristics of neighborhoods in the presence of known degrees of spatial autocorrelated error (Thompson 1992). For example, one could determine the most efficient sampling design for a community survey that determines the level of illegal drug sales in community areas and their effects upon the spread of use across community areas. The statistical bases for these designs are thoroughly developed by Thompson (1992).

One of the other assumptions of this chapter, and again virtually all social indicator and synthetic estimation models, is that available data come from areas. The emphasis upon areal analysis is justified by the exclusive concerns with this sort of data from the perspective of both small area researchers and public institutions (Schaible 1996). This concern, of course, is more institutional than scientific. Considering that many of the interesting events related to AOD use (e.g., drug sales and alcohol-related crashes) occur at specific locations rather than over broad geographic areas, areal aggregates of these data may not provide the most efficient geographic representation of these outcomes. Rather, when related to either other point location data or areal characteristics, the point locations of these outcomes may be far more informative than areal rates alone. For example, the point locations of alcohol-related crashes may be far more efficiently related to the point locations of alcohol outlets than rates of crashes related to densities of outlets within geographic areas. Indeed, these so-called point process models are far more efficient than their aggregate cousins in discerning local statistical relationships between variables (Bailey and Gatrell 1995). So, for example, one would expect point locations of crashes to cluster in meaningful ways about point locations of outlets, with reductions in associated relationships with increased distances between outlets and crashes. In essence, the spatial locations of outlets would be correlated with the spatial location of crashes to more efficiently assess the relationships between these spatial events.

This last observation, of course, once again calls up the specter of spatial autocorrelation, the central unavoidable concern of any analysis of data from small areas. In correspondence to the areal analysis techniques discussed in this chapter, there are techniques for the evaluation of spatial autocorrelations using point location data. These techniques have been developed over the past 50 years and constitute much of the central concern of geostatistical analysis (Isaaks and Srivastava 1989; Bailey and Gatrell 1995). The question asked with regard to spatial autocorrelation in this case is whether the clustering of point locations in space is correlated over spatial locations. Positive spatial autocorrelation leads to the strong clustering of point data. Negative spatial autocorrelation leads to the regular spacing of point data. If such correlations exist, they bias the results of point process models in the same way that spatial autocorrelations bias the results of the areal analysis models presented here. Without assessing the spatial autocorrelation of point events, point process models are as bereft of validity as spatial regression models conducted without similar assessments.

The rapidity with which the fields of AOD studies move into these emerging areas will be a function of the ability of researchers to both absorb these new technologies and develop sound ecological approaches to the study of AOD problems. No doubt the second constraint will be the most important of the two. Without an adequate scientific base, no amount of geostatistical massaging will bring forth an adequate understanding of small area data. However, with careful scientific thought and the suitable application of geostatistical methods, there is much to look forward to in the emerging areas of ecological theories of AOD use, imputation and assessment of community AOD problems, and the development of efficient local evaluations of community-based interventions. Small area analysts have much to do.

ACKNOWLEDGMENTS

Research for and preparation of this manuscript were supported by National Institute on Alcohol Abuse and Alcoholism grants AA09146 and AA06282.

NOTES

1. The asserted efficiency of direct surveys is made notwithstanding alternative procedures for improving direct survey estimators. Ratio adjustments and capture-recapture methods provide alternative means of reducing bias and increasing the efficiencies of survey estimates using alternative sources of data. These techniques rely on (a) the existence of an in-place survey at the appropriate level of analysis, (b) calibration of other sources with respect to the survey source, and (c) an assumption of source independence which may or may not obtain in the current circumstances. An excellent treatment of these issues with regard to the U.S. census appears in Wright (1998).
2. A third approach related to these two methods is not discussed here. Component flow models directly estimate the level of a local statistic based upon purely theoretical considerations. For example, population change can be deterministically modeled in terms of local birth, death, immigration, and emigration rates. Estimated for different small areas (i.e., demographic groups and geographic locations), these rates can be combined to provide direct estimates of population change and integrated to provide direct estimates of population levels. The theoretical bases of component flow models for AOD use are not sufficiently well developed to justify further discussion of this approach here.
3. Ciarlo and colleagues (1992) outlined the data collection procedures in some detail. For current purposes it is sufficient to note that the household survey evaluated "diagnosable disorders" in terms of the Diagnostic Interview Schedule, a standardized direct interview protocol that may be used to assess ADM problems.
4. Shrinkage to the mean occurs as an artifact of the imperfect performance of regression models used to fit social indicator data. Unless the

data are perfectly fit (i.e., $R^2 = 1$), predicted values from any model used to construct imputations will exhibit less variation than the raw data themselves.

5. The related problems of aggregation bias and errors in variables bias, which arise in multilevel studies, are considered in depth by Geronimus and colleagues (1996). Aggregation bias arises when aggregate-level measures are used as surrogates for individual-level variables; the effect of truncated range in the aggregate measure is to downward bias (toward zero) estimates of effects. Errors in variables bias, due to errors in estimation of aggregate-level and/or individual-level effects, either downward or upward bias estimates of effects.

6. This is not to say that theoretical models of this sort cannot be constructed. Social disorganization theory, for example, argues that aggregate measures of social disorganization (which include unemployment) affect individual behaviors by disrupting the otherwise stable course of social relationships. In this case, aggregate measures represent sources of disruption in personal social networks (see, e.g., Sampson et al. 1997).

7. A statistical fine point for the current discussion is that some sources of spatial autocorrelation also bias effects estimates from regression models (b coefficients). Fixed endogenous autoregressive processes, cases in which an endogenous measure affects its own values across spatial units, are the source of such biases (Griffith 1988).

8. Note that this test was motivated by the naive, but necessary, theory relating drinking at on-premise establishments to the geographic patterning of crashes.

REFERENCES

Anselin, L. *Spatial Econometrics: Methods and Models.* Dordrecht, The Netherlands: Kluwer Academic Publishers, 1988.

Bailey, T.C., and Gatrell, A.C. *Interactive Spatial Data Analysis.* Essex, England: Longman Group, 1995.

Bellow, M.; Graham, M.; and Iwig, W.C. County estimation of crop acreage using satellite data. In: Schaible, W.L., ed. *Indirect Estimators in U.S. Federal Programs.* New York: Springer-Verlag, 1996. pp. 104–128.

Ciarlo, J.A., and Tweed, D.L. VI. Implementing indirect needs-assessment models for planning state mental health and substance abuse services. *Evaluation and Program Planning* 15:191–210, 1992.

Ciarlo, J.A.; Tweed, D.L.; Shern, D.L.; Kirkpatrick, L.A.; and Sachs-Ericsson, N. Validation of indirect methods to estimate need for mental health services: Concepts, strategy, and general conclusions. *Evaluation and Program Planning* 15:115–131, 1992.

Davis, R.C.; Lurigio, A.J.; and Rosenbaum, D.P. *Drugs and the Community.* Springfield, IL: Thomas, 1993.

Elliot, P.; Cuzick, J.; English, D.; and Stern, R. *Geographical and Environmental Epidemiology: Methods for Small-Area Studies.* New York: Oxford University Press, 1992.

English, D. Geographical epidemiology and ecological studies. In: Elliot, P.; Cuzick, J.; English, D.; and Stern, R., eds. *Geographical and Environmental Epidemiology: Methods for Small-Area Studies.* New York: Oxford University Press, 1992. pp. 3–13.

Geronimus, A.T.; Bound, J.; and Neidert, L.J. On the validity of using census geocode characteristics to proxy individual socioeconomic characteristics. *Journal of the American Statistical Association* 91:529–537, 1996.

Ghosh, M., and Rao, J.N.K. Small area estimation: An appraisal. *Statistical Science* 9:55–93, 1994.

Gonzalez, J.F., Jr.; Placek, P.J.; and Scott, C. Synthetic estimation in followback surveys at the National Center for Health Statistics. In: Schaible, W.L., ed. *Indirect Estimators in U.S. Federal Programs.* New York: Springer-Verlag, 1996. pp. 16–27.

Gorman, D.M., and Speer, P.W. Preventing alcohol abuse and alcohol-related problems through community interventions: A review of evaluation studies. *Psychology and Health* 11:95–131, 1996.

Griffith, D.A. *Spatial Autocorrelation.* Washington, DC: Association of American Geographers, 1987.

Griffith, D.A. *Advanced Spatial Statistics.* Dordrecht, The Netherlands: Kluwer Academic Publishers, 1988.

Gruenewald, P.J.; Millar, A.B.; Treno, A.J.; Ponicki, W.R.; Yang, Z.; and Roeper, P. The geography of availability and driving after drinking. *Addiction* 91:967–983, 1996.

Gruenewald, P.J.; Treno, A.J.; Taff, G.; and Klitzner, M. *Measuring Community Indicators: A Systems Approach to Drug and Alcohol Problems.* Thousand Oaks, CA: Sage Publications, 1997.

Haining, R. Bivariate correlation with spatial data. *Geographical Analysis* 23:210–227, 1991.

Harvey, A.C. *Forecasting Structural Time Series Models and the Kalman Filter.* New York: Cambridge University Press, 1989.

Holder, H.D., and Howard, J.M. *Community Prevention Trials for Alcohol Problems.* Westport, CT: Praeger, 1992.

Holder, H.D.; Saltz, R.F.; Grube, J.W.; Voas, R.B.; Gruenewald, P.J.; and Treno, A.J. A community prevention trial to reduce alcohol-involved accidental injury and death: Overview. *Addiction* 92 (Suppl 2):155–171, 1997.

Isaaks, E.H., and Srivastava, R.M. *An Introduction to Applied Geostatistics.* Oxford, England: Oxford University Press, 1989.

Marshall, R.J. A review of methods for the statistical analysis of spatial patterns of disease. *Journal of the Royal Statistical Society* 154:421–441, 1991.

Midanik, L.T., and Clark, W.B. Demographic distribution of US drinking patterns in 1990: Description and trends from 1984. *Am J Public Health* 84:1218–1222, 1994.

National Institute on Alcohol Abuse and Alcoholism (NIAAA). *Drinking in the United States: Main Findings From the 1992 National Longitudinal Alcohol Epidemiologic Survey (NLAES).* U.S. Alcohol Epidemiologic Data Reference Manual, Vol. 6, First Edition. Bethesda, MD: NIAAA, 1998.

Purcell, N.J., and Kish, L. Estimation for small domains. *Biometrics* 35:365–384, 1979.

Richardson, S. Statistical methods for geographical correlation studies. In: Elliot, P.; Cuzick, J.; English, D.; and Stern, R., eds. *Geographical and Environmental Epidemiology: Methods for Small-Area Studies.* New York: Oxford University Press, 1992. pp. 181–204.

Sampson, R.J.; Raudenbush, S.W.; and Earls, F. Neighborhoods and violent crime: A multilevel study of collective efficacy. *Science* 277:918–924, 1997.

Schaible, W.L. *Indirect Estimators in U.S. Federal Programs.* New York: Springer-Verlag, 1996.

Snow, J. *On the Mode of Communication of Cholera.* 2d ed. London: Churchill Livingstone, 1854.

Sokol, R.R., and Oden, N.L. Spatial autocorrelation in biology 1. Methodology. *Biological Journal of the Linnean Society* 10:199–228, 1978.

Substance Abuse and Mental Health Services Administration. *National Household Survey on Drug Abuse: Population Estimates 1995.* Rockville, MD: U.S. Department of Health and Human Services, 1995.

Thompson, S.K. *Sampling.* New York: John Wiley, 1992.

Tiller, R.; Brown, S.; and Tupek, A. Bureau of Labor Statistics' state and local area estimates of employment and unemployment. In: Schaible, W.L., ed. *Indirect Estimators in U.S. Federal Programs.* New York: Springer-Verlag, 1996. pp. 83–103.

Tonry, M., and Wilson, J.Q. *Drugs and Crime.* Chicago: University of Chicago Press, 1990.

Tweed, D.L., and Ciarlo, J.A. IV. Social-indicator models for indirectly assessing mental health service needs: Epidemiologic and statistical properties. *Evaluation and Program Planning* 15:165–179, 1992.

Tweed, D.L.; Ciarlo, J.A.; Kirkpatrick, L.A.; and Shern, D.L. V. Empirical validity of indirect mental health needs-assessment models in Colorado. *Evaluation and Program Planning* 15:181–194, 1992.

Webster, R., and Oliver, M.A. *Statistical Methods in Soil and Land Resource Survey.* Oxford, England: Oxford University Press, 1990.

Wright, T. Sampling and Census 2000: The concepts. *American Scientist* 86: 245–253, 1998.

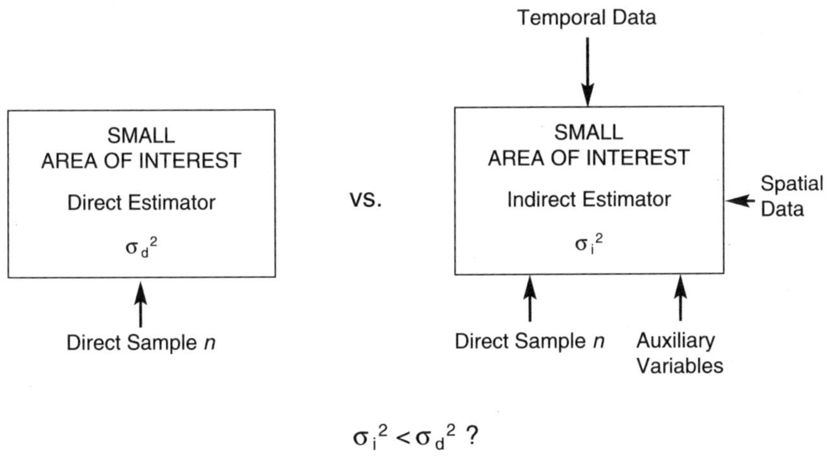

Figure 1. Schematic outline of statistical goals of small area imputation strategies.

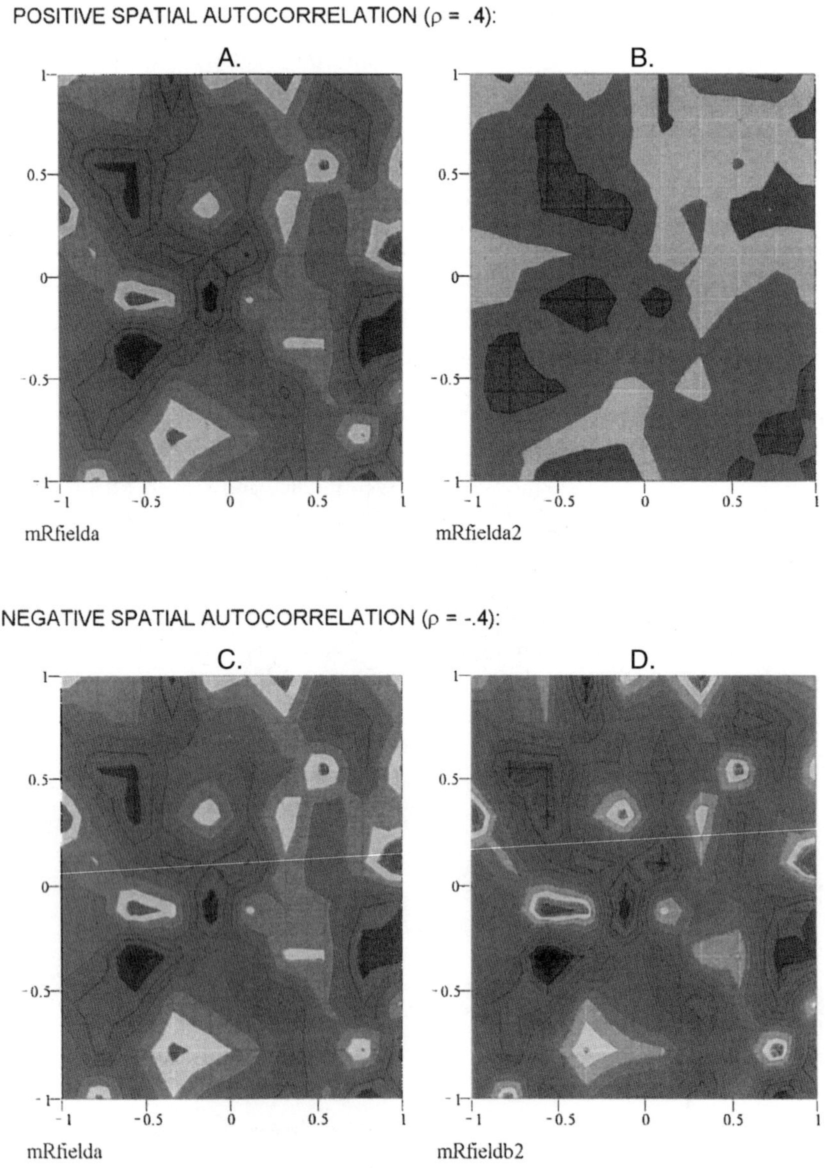

Figure 2. Positive and negative spatial autocorrelation among elements of a random valued rectangular field.

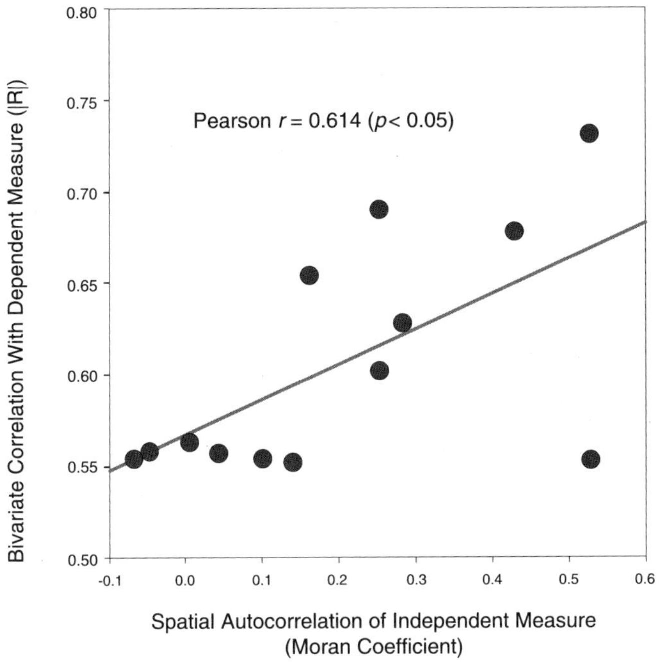

Figure 3. Effects of spatial autocorrelation upon observed bivariate correlations.

Table 1. Spatial Autocorrelations of Demographic and Drinking Measures.

Variable	Moran Coefficient	*z*	*p*
% Income < 20K	0.162	1.430	0.076
% Income ≥ 60K	0.429	3.716	< 0.001*
% Unemployment	0.044	0.432	0.333
Mean age	0.101	0.921	0.180
% Education < high school	0.283	2.468	0.007*
% Education ≥ college	0.253	2.217	0.013*
% Married adults	–0.047	–0.342	0.366
% Single adults	0.140	1.255	0.105
% Male	0.006	0.113	0.455
% Black	0.527	4.458	< 0.001*
% Hispanic	0.528	4.556	< 0.001*
% Other ethnic	0.253	2.217	0.013*
Number of children < 18	–0.068	–0.523	0.301

*$p < 0.05$.

Table 2. Spatial Regression Model of Rates of Abstention Over Demographic Measures (Reduced Model With Spatial Lags).

Variable*	*b*	*z*	*p*
Constant	10.104	0.887	0.188
% Income < 20K	0.137	2.092	0.018
% Income ≥ 60K	–0.160	–2.071	0.019
% Unemployment	0.309	1.640	0.051
Mean age	0.448	2.414	0.008
% Education ≥ college	–0.192	–2.583	0.005
% Married adults	0.125	1.803	0.036
% Black	0.177	2.198	0.014
Number of children < 18	0.821	0.320	0.374
Spatial lags (first order)			
% Unemployment	–0.758	–1.674	0.047
Number of children < 18	6.951	2.475	0.007
Spatial autocorrelated error (ρ)	0.300	2.575	0.005

*Community effects not presented in table.